Rick Steves

# GREAT
# BRITAIN
# 2002

AVALON
TRAVEL

**Other ATP travel guidebooks by Rick Steves**
*Rick Steves' Best of Europe*
*Rick Steves' Europe 101: History and Art for the Traveler* (with Gene Openshaw)
*Rick Steves' Europe Through the Back Door*
*Rick Steves' Mona Winks: Self-Guided Tours of Europe's Top Museums*
   (with Gene Openshaw)
*Rick Steves' Postcards from Europe*
*Rick Steves' France, Belgium & the Netherlands* (with Steve Smith)
*Rick Steves' Germany, Austria & Switzerland*
*Rick Steves' Ireland* (with Pat O'Connor)
*Rick Steves' Italy*
*Rick Steves' Scandinavia*
*Rick Steves' Spain & Portugal*
*Rick Steves' Florence* (with Gene Openshaw)
*Rick Steves' London* (with Gene Openshaw)
*Rick Steves' Paris* (with Steve Smith and Gene Openshaw)
*Rick Steves' Rome* (with Gene Openshaw)
*Rick Steves' Venice* (with Gene Openshaw)
Rick Steves' Phrase Books for: French, German, Italian, Spanish/Portuguese,
   and French/Italian/German

Thanks to my wife, Anne, for making "home" my favorite travel destination.
Thanks also to Roy and Jodi Nicholls for their research help, to our readers for
their input, and to local friends listed in this book who put the "Great" in Britain.

Avalon Travel Publishing, 5855 Beaudry Street, Emeryville, CA 94608

Printed in the United States of America by R. R. Donnelley
First printing January 2002
Distributed to the book trade by Publishers Group West, Berkeley, California

For the latest on Rick's lectures, guidebooks, tours, and public television
series, contact Europe Through the Back Door, Box 2009, Edmonds,
WA 98020, tel. 425/771-8303, fax 425/771-0833, www.ricksteves.com,
or e-mail: rick@ricksteves.com.

ISSN 1090-6843
ISBN 1-56691-362-4

**Europe Through the Back Door Editors:** Risa Laib, Jacquie Maupin
**Avalon Travel Publishing Editor:** Kate Willis
**Research Assistance:** Jacquie Maupin
**Copy Editor:** Chris Hayhurst
**Production & Typesetting:** Kathleen Sparkes, White Hart Design
**Design:** Linda Braun
**Cover Design:** Janine Lehmann
**Maps:** David C. Hoerlein
**Cover Photo:** Tower Bridge, London, England; Leo de Wys Inc./
   Steve Vidler

# CONTENTS

## Top Destinations in Great Britain

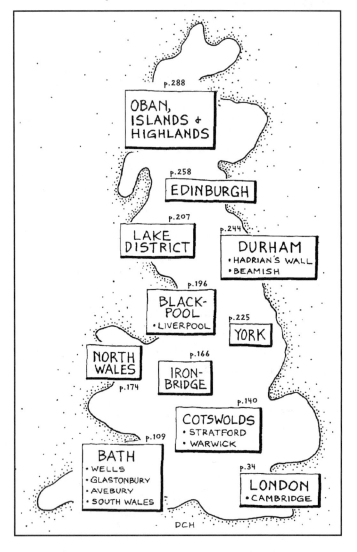

# INTRODUCTION

This book breaks Britain into its top big-city, small-town, and rural destinations. It gives you all the information and opinions necessary to wring the maximum value out of your limited time and money in each of these destinations. If you plan a month or less for Britain and have a normal appetite for information, this lean and mean little book is all you need. If you're a travel-info fiend, this book sorts through all the superlatives and provides a handy rack upon which to hang your supplemental information.

Experiencing British culture, people, and natural wonders economically and hassle-free has been my goal for more than 25 years of traveling, tour guiding, and travel writing. With this new edition I pass on to you the lessons I've learned, updated for your trip in 2002. Note that Northern Ireland—part of Britain—is covered in my latest book, *Rick Steves' Ireland*.

*Rick Steves' Great Britain* is a personal tour guide in your pocket. The places I cover are balanced to include a comfortable mix of exciting big cities and great-to-be-alive-in small towns. While including the predictable biggies (such as Big Ben, Stratford, and Stonehenge), the book also mixes in a healthy dose of Back Door intimacy (windswept Roman lookouts, angelic boys' choirs, and nearly edible Cotswold villages). I've been selective. On a short trip, visiting both Oxford and Cambridge is redundant; I cover just the best (Cambridge). There are plenty of great countryside palaces; again, I recommend just the best (Blenheim).

The best is, of course, only my opinion. But after more than two busy decades of travel writing, lecturing, and tour guiding, I've developed a sixth sense for what tickles the traveler's fancy. The places featured in this book will knock your spots off.

## This Information Is Accurate and Up-to-Date

Most publishers of guidebooks that cover a country from top to bottom can afford an update only every two or three years, and then it's often just by letter. Since this book is selective, covering only the top month of sightseeing, I'm able to update it each year. Even with annual updates, prices, and key information change. Travel with the current edition of this book; I guarantee it's the most up-to-date information available (for the latest, see www.ricksteves.com/update). If you're packing an old book, you'll learn the seriousness of your mistake ...in Britain. Your trip costs about $10 per waking hour. Your time is valuable. This guidebook saves you lots of time.

## Planning Your Trip

This book is organized by destinations, each one a mini-vacation on its own, filled with exciting sights and homey, affordable places to stay. In each chapter, you'll find the following:

**Planning Your Time**, a suggested schedule with thoughts on how to best use your limited time.

**Orientation**, including tourist information, city transportation, and an easy-to-read map designed to make the text clear and your arrival smooth.

**Sights**, with ratings: ▲▲▲—Don't miss; ▲▲—Try hard to see; ▲—Worthwhile if you can make it; No rating—Worth knowing about.

**Sleeping** and **Eating**, with addresses and phone numbers of my favorite good-value hotels and restaurants.

**Transportation Connections** to nearby destinations by train or bus and route tips for drivers.

The **appendix** is a traveler's tool kit, with information on history, architecture, TV, climate, telephoning, and a British-Yankee vocabulary list.

Browse through this book, choose your favorite destinations, and link them up. Then have a great trip! You'll travel like a temporary local, getting the absolute most out of every mile, minute, and dollar. You won't waste time on mediocre sights because, unlike others, this guidebook covers only the best. Since your major financial pitfall is lousy, expensive hotels, I've worked hard to assemble the best accommodation values for each stop. And as you travel the route I know and love, I'm happy you'll be meeting some of my favorite British people.

## Trip Costs

Five components make up your trip costs: airfare, surface transportation, room and board, sightseeing/entertainment, and shopping/miscellany.

**Airfare:** Don't try to sort through the mess. Find a good travel agent. A round-trip U.S.A.-to-London flight costs $500 to $1,000 (even cheaper in winter), depending on where you fly from and when. Consider saving time and money by flying "open-jaw" (into one city and out of another; for instance, into London and out of Edinburgh).

**Surface Transportation:** For a three-week whirlwind trip of all my recommended British destinations, allow $450 per person for public transportation (train pass and key buses), or $500 per person (based on 2 people sharing) for three weeks of car rental, gas, and insurance. Car rental is cheapest if arranged from the United States. Train passes are normally available only outside of Europe. You may save money by simply buying tickets as you go (see "Transportation" below).

**Room and Board:** You can thrive in Britain on $70 per day per person for room and board (allow $90 per day for London). A $70-per-day budget allows $10 for lunch, $15 for dinner, and $45 for lodging (based on 2 people splitting a $90 double room that includes breakfast). That's doable, particularly outside London. Students and tightwads can do it on $40 ($20 for a bed, $20 per day for meals and snacks). But budget sleeping and eating require the skills and information covered below (and in greater detail in my book, *Rick Steves' Europe Through the Back Door*).

**Sightseeing and Entertainment:** In big cities, figure $5 to $10 per major sight (Imperial War Museum—$7.50, Edinburgh Castle—$9), $2 for minor ones (climbing church towers), $10 for guided walks, and $25 for bus tours and splurge experiences (Welsh and Scottish folk evenings). An overall average of $15 a day works for most. Don't skimp here. After all, this category directly powers most of the experiences all the other expenses are designed to make possible.

You will be tempted to buy the British Heritage Pass, which gets you into more than 500 British Heritage and National Trust properties: £35 for seven days, £46 for 15 days, £60 for 30 days (sold at Heathrow Airport TI and the Britain Visitors Centre on Regent Street in London; if you're bringing children, don't buy passes for them since kids get in free or cheap at most sights).

Of the 580 sights included (a list comes with the pass), here are the sights I describe and recommend for a three-week tour of Britain, along with their adult admission prices. A typical sightseer with three weeks will probably pay to see nearly all of these: Tower of London-£11.50 (London); Shakespeare's Birthplace-£5.50 (Stratford); Anne Hathaway's Cottage-£5 (Stratford); Warwick Castle-£9.75 (near Stratford); Blenheim Palace-£9.50 (near the Cotswolds and Oxford); Roman and Medieval Baths-£7.50 (Bath); Stonehenge-£4.70 (near Bath); Caerphilly Castle-£2.50 and Tintern Abbey-£2.50 (South Wales); Caernarfon Castle-£4.20 (North Wales); Wordsworth's Dove Cottage-£5.50 (Lake District); House-steads Roman Fort-£3 (Hadrian's Wall); Edinburgh Castle-£7.50, Georgian House-£5, Gladstone's Land-£3.50, and Holyrood Palace-£6.50 (Edinburgh); Culloden Battlefield-£4 (near Inverness); and Urquhart Castle-£5 (near Loch Ness). This totals about £102; a pass takes the pain out of all these admissions with one big pill. People traveling by car—easily able to get to the more remote sights—are more likely to get their money's worth out of the pass if traveling in peak season (Easter–Oct). The British Heritage pass is a lesser value off-season (Nov–Easter) when many of the smaller, out-of-the-way sights are closed.

**Shopping and Miscellany:** Figure $1 per postcard, tea, or ice-cream cone and $2 per beer. Shopping can vary in cost from nearly nothing to a small fortune. Good budget travelers find that this category has little to do with assembling a trip full of lifelong and wonderful memories.

## Exchange Rates

I list prices in pounds (£) throughout this book.

> One British pound (£1) = about $1.50

While the euro is now the currency of most of Europe, Britain is sticking with its pound sterling. The British pound (£), also called a "quid," is broken into 100 pence (p). Pence means "cents." You'll find coins ranging from 1p to £2 and bills from £5 to £50. To roughly convert pounds to dollars, add about 50 percent to British prices: £6 is about $9, £3 is about $4.50, and 80p is about $1.20. Scotland and Northern Ireland issue their own currency in pounds, worth the same as an English pound. English, Scottish, and Northern Ireland's Ulster pounds are technically interchangeable in each region, although Scottish and Ulster pounds are "undesirable" in England. Banks in any of the three regions will convert your Scottish or Ulster pounds into English pounds at no charge. Don't worry about the coins, which are accepted throughout Britain.

## Prices, Times, and Discounts

The prices in this book, as well as the hours and telephone numbers, are accurate as of mid-2001. Britain is always changing, and I know you'll understand that this guidebook, like any other, starts to yellow even before it's printed.

In Britain you'll be using the 24-hour clock. After 12:00 noon, keep going—13:00, 14:00 .... For anything over 12, subtract 12 and add p.m. (14:00 is 2 p.m.).

While discounts (called "concessions" in Britain) are not listed in this book, nearly all British sights are discounted for seniors (loosely defined as anyone retired or willing to call themselves a "senior"), youths (ages 8–18), students, groups of 10 or more, and families (2 full-price parents take kids in for about half price).

## When to Go

July and August are peak season—my favorite time—with very long days, the best weather, and the busiest schedule of tourist fun. Prices and crowds don't go up as dramatically in Britain as they do in much of Europe. Still, travel during "shoulder season" (May, early June, Sept, and early Oct) is easier and a bit less expensive. Shoulder-season travelers get minimal crowds, decent weather, the full range of sights and tourist fun spots, and the joy of being able to just grab a room almost whenever and wherever they like—often at a flexible price.

Winter travelers find absolutely no crowds and soft room prices, but shorter sightseeing hours and fewer activities. Some attractions are open only on weekends or are closed entirely in the winter (Nov–Feb). Confirm your sightseeing plans locally, especially when traveling outside of peak season. The weather can be cold and dreary, and nightfall draws the shades on sightseeing well before dinnertime. While England's rural charm falls with the leaves, city sightseeing is fine in the winter.

Plan for rain no matter when you go. Just keep going and take full advantage of "bright spells." Conditions can change several times in a day, but rarely is the weather extreme. Daily averages throughout the year range between 42 and 70 degrees Fahrenheit. Temperatures below 32 or over 80 degrees are cause for headlines (see the climate chart in the appendix). July and August are not much better than shoulder months, though May and June can be lovely. While sunshine may be rare, summer days are very long. The summer sun is up from 06:30 until 22:30. It's not uncommon to have a gray day, eat dinner, and enjoy hours of sunshine afterward.

## Sightseeing Priorities

Depending on the length of your trip, here are my recommended priorities:

|  |  |
|---|---|
| 3 days: | London |
| 5 days, add: | Bath, Cotswolds, Blenheim |
| 7 days, add: | York |
| 9 days, add: | Edinburgh |
| 11 days, add: | Stratford, Warwick, Cambridge |
| 14 days, add: | North Wales, Wells/Glastonbury/Avebury |
| 17 days, add: | Lake District, Hadrian's Wall, Durham |
| 21 days, add: | Ironbridge Gorge, Blackpool, Scottish Highlands |
| 24 days, add: | South Wales |

(The Whirlwind Tour map and 3-week itinerary on the following pages include everything in the above 24 days.)

## Itinerary Tips

Most people fly into London and remain there for a few days. Instead, consider a gentler small-town start in Bath, and visit London at the end of your trip. You'll be more rested and ready to tackle Britain's greatest city. Heathrow Airport has direct connections to Bath and other cities.

To give yourself a little rootedness, minimize one-night stands. It's worth a long drive after dinner to be settled into a town for two nights. B&Bs are also more likely to give a good price to someone staying more than one night.

Many people save a couple of days and a lot of miles by going directly from the Lake District to Edinburgh and skipping the long joyride through Scotland. If it's Celtic Britain you're after, visit Wales rather than Scotland.

## Best Three-Week Trip in Britain by Car

| Day | Plan | Sleep in |
|-----|------|----------|
| 1 | Arrive in London, bus to Bath | Bath |
| 2 | Bath | Bath |
| 3 | Pick up car, Avebury, Wells, Glastonbury | Bath |
| 4 | South Wales, St. Fagans, Tintern | Chipping Camden |
| 5 | Explore the Cotswolds, Blenheim | Chipping Camden |
| 6 | Stratford, Warwick, Coventry | Ironbridge Gorge |
| 7 | Ironbridge Gorge, Ruthin banquet | Ruthin (if banquet) or Conwy |
| 8 | Highlights of North Wales | Ruthin or Conwy |
| 9 | Liverpool, Blackpool | Blackpool |
| 10 | Southern Lake District | Keswick area |
| 11 | Northern Lake District | Keswick area |
| 12 | Drive up west coast of Scotland | Oban |
| 13 | Highlands, Loch Ness, Scenic Highlands Drive | Edinburgh |
| 14 | More Highlands or Edinburgh | Edinburgh |
| 15 | Edinburgh | Edinburgh |
| 16 | Hadrian's Wall, Beamish, Durham evensong | Durham |
| 17 | York Moors, York, turn in car | York |
| 18 | York | York |
| 19 | Early train to London | London |
| 20 | London | London |
| 21 | London | London |
| 22 | Side trip to Cambridge or Greenwich, London | Whew! |

While this three-week itinerary is designed to be done by car, it can be done by train and bus or, better yet, with a rail 'n' drive pass (best car days: Cotswolds, North Wales, Lake District, Scottish Highlands, Hadrian's Wall). For three weeks without a car, I'd probably cut back on the recommended sights with the most frustrating public transportation (South and North Wales, Ironbridge Gorge, the Highlands). Lacing together the cities by train is very slick. With more time, everything is workable without a car.

## Whirlwind Three-Week Tour of Great Britain

## Red Tape and Taxes

You need a passport, but no visa or shots, to travel in Britain.

**Sales Tax:** Britain's sales tax—the "value added tax," or VAT (15 percent)—is built into the price of nearly everything you buy. Tourists can get this VAT refunded on souvenirs they take out of the country. But unless you buy something worth at least $100, your refund won't be worth the trouble. Before you make a substantial purchase of merchandise, ask the store clerk if you will be able to get a VAT refund. You'll likely get a "Tax-Free Shopping Cheque," which is redeemable for cash or credit-card credit at the airport before you fly home.

## Banking

Throughout Britain, cash machines are the way to go. Bring an ATM or debit card (with a 4-digit PIN) to withdraw funds from cash machines as you travel, and carry traveler's checks only as a backup. Since fees are charged per exchange and most ATM screens top out at £200, save money by pushing the "other amount" button and asking for a higher amount.

Bring a credit card, handy for booking rooms and theater and transportation tickets over the phone—and necessary for renting a car. For cash advances you'll find that Barclays, National West-minster, and places displaying an Access or Eurocard sign accept MasterCard. Visa is accepted at Barclays and Midland banks. In general, Visa is far more widely accepted than American Express.

Traveler's checks work fine in Britain, but banks commonly charge a commission fee of £2 to £4 or even more.

Even in jolly olde England you should use a money belt (for our free newsletter/catalog, call 425/771-8303 or visit www.ricksteves.com). Thieves target tourists. A money belt provides peace of mind. You can carry lots of cash safely in a money belt—and, given the high bank fees, you should.

Bank holidays bring most businesses to a grinding halt on Christmas, December 26, New Year's Day, Good Friday, Easter Monday, the first Monday in May, and in 2002, the first Monday and Tuesday in June (in honor of the Queen's 50-year reign), and the last Monday in August.

## Travel Smart

Upon arrival in a new town, lay the groundwork for a smooth departure. Reread this book as you travel and visit local tourist information offices. Buy a phone card and use it for reservations and confirmations. You speak the language—use it! Enjoy the friendliness of the local people. Ask questions. Most locals are eager to point you in their idea of the right direction. Those who expect to travel smart do. Bring along a pocket-size notebook to organize your thoughts. Plan ahead for banking, laundry, post office chores, and picnics. Mix intense and relaxed periods. Every trip (and every traveler) needs at least a few slack days. Pace your-self. Assume you will return.

As you read this book, make note of festivals, colorful market days, and days when sights are closed. Sundays have pros and cons, as they do for travelers in the United States (special events, limited hours, closed shops and banks, limited public transportation, no rush hours). Saturdays are virtually weekdays. Popular places are even more popular on weekends—especially sunny weekends, which are sufficient cause for an impromptu holiday in this soggy corner of Europe.

Consider making the travel arrangements and reservations listed below before your trip or within a few days of arrival.

## Before You Go

- Reserve a room for your first night.
- If you'll be traveling in late June, July, or August and want to sleep in my lead listings, book your B&Bs (and the Ruthin Medieval Banquet) as soon as you're ready to commit to a date.
- Confirm car rental and pick-up plans with your rental agency (picking up a car on Saturday afternoon or Sunday may be difficult).
- If you'll be attending the Edinburgh Festival (Aug 11–31 in 2002), you can book tickets in advance (from mid-April on) by calling the festival office at 0131/473-2000 or ordering online (www.eif.co.uk). And while you're at it, book your Edinburgh room.
- If you want to attend the pageantry-filled Ceremony of the Keys at the Tower of London, write for tickets (see details in the London chapter under "Sights—East London").

## Within a Day or Two of Arrival

- If you'll be in London the last night of your trip, reserve a room and book tickets for a London play or concert. You can book a play from home (see details in the London chapter under "Entertainment and Theater in London"), but for simplicity, I book plays while in London.
- If the Royal Shakespeare Company will be performing at the Stratford Theater when you're in or near Stratford, consider booking a ticket (tel. 01789/403-403, www.rsc.org.uk).

## Tourist Information

Virtually every town in Britain has a tourist information center (abbreviated "TI" in this book). Take full advantage of this service. Arrive (or telephone) with a list of questions and a proposed sightseeing plan. Pick up maps, brochures, and walking-tour information. In London you can pick up everything you'll need for Britain in one stop at the Britain Visitors Centre.

While TIs can be good resources, remember they are money-making enterprises. Each year they become more of a shop and ticket-and-advertising agency than a true information service. If a hotel or activity doesn't pay its dues and follow tourist-board dictates, it disappears from their material. This is a particular problem with room-finding services offered by TIs. Getting a room through the TI can be handy in a jam, but it comes with bloated prices and fees—and the TI takes a cut from your host. Many of my best listings are blacklisted by the tourist boards for their independence.

Britain's national tourist office in the United States has a wealth of information. Before your trip request any information you may want (such as city maps and schedules of upcoming festivals).

**British Tourist Authority (BTA):** 551 Fifth Avenue, seventh floor, New York, NY 10176, tel. 800/462-2748, fax 212/986-1188, www.travelbritain.org, e-mail: travelinfo@bta.org.uk. Ask for the Britain Vacation Planner and free maps of London and Britain (the same maps are sold for £1.40 each at TIs in Britain). You can get regional information, an updated garden-tour map, and an urban cultural activities brochure.

## Recommended Guidebooks

You may want some supplemental travel guidebooks, especially if you're traveling beyond my recommended destinations. I know it hurts to spend $25 or $35 on extra books and maps, but when you consider the money they'll save you and the improvements they'll make in your $3,000 vacation, not buying them would be penny-wise and pound-foolish.

While this book offers everything you'll need for the structure of your trip, each place you will visit has plenty of great little guidebooks to fill you in on local history. For cultural and sight-seeing background in bigger chunks, Michelin and Cadogan guides to London, England, and Britain are good. The best budget travel guides to Britain are the Lonely Planet and Let's Go guidebooks. Lonely Planet's guidebook is more thorough and informative (but it's not annually updated). Let's Go is youth oriented, with good coverage of nightlife, hostels, and cheap transportation deals (updated annually).

## Rick Steves' Books and Videos

*Rick Steves' Europe Through the Back Door 2002* gives you budget-travel skills, such as minimizing jet lag, packing light, planning your itinerary, traveling by car or train, finding beds without reservations, changing money, avoiding rip-offs, outsmarting thieves, staying healthy, taking great photographs, and much more. The book also includes chapters on 35 of my favorite "Back Doors," six of which are in Britain.

**Rick Steves' Country Guides** are a series of eight guidebooks—including this book—covering my favorite continent: Best of Europe; Ireland; France/Belgium/Netherlands; Italy; Spain/Portugal; Scandinavia; and Germany/Austria/Switzerland. All are updated annually and come out in December and January.

My **City Guides** cover London, Paris, and Rome (available

in January), and—new for 2002—Venice and Florence (available in March). These practical guides offer in-depth coverage of the sights, hotels, restaurants, and nightlife in these grand cities along with illustrated tours of their great museums.

*Rick Steves' Europe 101: History and Art for the Traveler* (co-written with Gene Openshaw, 2000) gives you the story of Europe's people, history, and art. Written for smart people who were sleeping in their history and art classes before they knew they were going to Europe, *101* helps Europe's sights come alive. However, this book has far more coverage of the Continent than of Britain.

*Rick Steves' Mona Winks* (cowritten with Gene Openshaw, 2001), provides fun, easy-to-follow, self-guided tours of Europe's top 25 museums and cultural sites. In London, *Mona* leads the way through the British Museum, British Library, National Gallery, Tate Britain, Westminster Abbey, and the historic Westminster neighborhood.

My new PBS-TV series, *Rick Steves' Europe*, began airing 16 new shows in 2001; four are on Britain. Fifty-two episodes of my first series, *Travels in Europe with Rick Steves* (with 6 shows on Britain) still air nationally on public television and the Travel Channel. These are also available in information-packed home videos, along with my two-hour slide-show lecture on Britain (for our free newsletter/catalog, call us at 425/771-8303 or visit www.ricksteves.com).

*Rick Steves' Postcards from Europe* (1999), my autobiographical book, packs more than 25 years of travel anecdotes and insights into the ultimate 3,000-mile European adventure. Through my guidebooks, I share my favorite European discoveries with you. *Postcards* introduces you to my favorite European friends.

All of my books are published by Avalon Travel Publishing (www.travelmatters.com).

## Maps

The maps in this book, designed and drawn by Dave Hoerlein, are concise and simple. Dave, who is well traveled in Britain, has designed the maps to help you locate recommended places and get to the tourist information office, where you'll find more in-depth, cheap (or free) maps of the city or region.

**Maps to buy in England:** Train travelers can do fine with a simple rail map (such as the one that comes with your train pass) and city maps from TIs. (Get a free map of London and Britain from the BTA before you go; see "Tourist Information," above.) If you're driving, get a road atlas (1 inch equals 3 miles) covering all of Britain. Ordnance Survey, AA, and Bartholomew editions are available for about £7 in TIs, gas stations, and bookstores. Drivers, hikers, and bikers may want more detailed maps for the Cotswolds, North Wales, and Lake District (easy to buy locally).

## Tours of London and Britain

Travel agents can tell you about all the normal tours, but they won't tell you about ours. At Europe Through the Back Door (ETBD) we offer 20-day tours of Britain (departures May–Sept, 24 people max) featuring the all-stars covered in this book, two great guides, and a big roomy bus. Our newest tour in the region is a 14-day look at the best of pastoral and historic South England (departures May–Sept). And consider our seven-day getaways to London (call us at 425/771-8303, www.ricksteves.com). ETBD tour guides Roy and Jodi Nicholls also lead a variety of their own tours in their spare time (visit www.brittours.com).

## Transportation in Britain

### By Car or Train?

Cars are best for three or more traveling together (especially families with small kids), those packing heavy, and those scouring the countryside. Trains and buses are best for solo travelers, blitz tourists, and city-to-city travelers.

Britain has a great train-and-bus system, and travelers who don't want (or can't afford) to drive a rental car can enjoy an excellent tour using public transportation. Britain's 100-mph train system is one of Europe's best. Buses pick you up when the trains let you down.

In Britain, my choice is to connect big cities by train and to explore rural areas (the Cotswolds, North Wales, Lake District, and the Highlands) footloose and fancy-free by rental car. The mix works quite efficiently (e.g., London, Bath, Edinburgh, and York by train with a rental car for the rest). You might consider a BritRail Pass 'n Drive, which gives you various combinations of rail days and car days to use within a month's time.

### Deals on Rails, Wheels, and Wings in Britain

Regular tickets on Britain's great train system (15,000 departures from 2,400 stations daily) are the most expensive per mile in all of Europe. Those who go round-trip (leaving after 9:30 in the morning), buy in advance, or ride the bus, and save big.

**Buying Train Tickets in Advance:** Either go direct to any station or call and book your ticket with a credit card. To book ahead, call 08457-484-950 (from the States call 011/44/8457-484-950, phone answered 24 hours) to find out the schedule and best fare for your journey; then you'll be referred to the appropriate number to call—depending on the particular rail company—to book your ticket (or book online, see below). Here are a few of the many deals:

## Sample Train Journey

Here is a typical example of a personalized train schedule printed out by Britain's train stations. At the Llandudno Junction station in North Wales, I told the clerk I wanted to leave after 16:30 for Moreton-in-Marsh, in the Cotswolds.

| Stations | Arrive | Depart | Accom. |
| --- | --- | --- | --- |
| Llandudno Junction | —— | 16:41 | Standard |
| Crewe | 17:56 | 18:11 | Standard |
| Smethwick | 19:20 | 19:33 | Standard |
| Worcester | 20:20 | 20:58 | 1st/Std |
| Moreton-in-Marsh | 21:37 | —— | |

Even though the trip involved three transfers, this schedule allowed me to easily navigate the rails. It's helpful to ask at the info desk (or any conductor) for the final destination of your next train so you'll be able to quickly figure out the platform it's departing from (e.g., upon arrival at Worcester, look for "Oxford" on the station's overhead train schedule to determine where to catch your train to Moreton-in-Marsh; often the conductor on your previous train can even tell you the platform your next train will depart from, but it's wise to confirm). Note that on the smaller runs, only standard (2nd) class is available. If you're exploring Britain's backcountry with a BritRail pass, rather than invest the extra money in first class, buy standard class—because that's how you'll travel.

**Bargain Return** fares offer the greatest savings but must be booked at least seven days in advance and usually apply to journeys of about 250 miles (i.e., London-Edinburgh) or longer, but sometimes shorter journeys qualify—ask. Note that a Bargain Return is a round-trip ticket, but you can use it only one-way if you want. **Apex** fares, which must be booked at least seven days in advance, apply to journeys of about 100 miles (i.e., London-York) or longer. (You can book Apex and Bargain Return tickets as early as six to eight weeks before your journey; be warned that cheap fares go fast in summer, tickets have refund restrictions, and you'll need to pin down dates and times—for schedules, visit www.reiseauskunft.bahn.de/bin/query.exe/en or www.railtrack.co.uk).

To save a few pounds, get a **Super Advance** ticket (for any journey on any day) by buying your ticket before 18:00 the day before your journey. To save a little less, purchase a **Super Saver** ticket the day you want to travel, leave after 09:30, and avoid traveling on Friday or summer Saturdays. A **Saver** ticket is a bit pricier, also purchasable on the same day of travel, and good for any day

**Prices listed are for 2001. My free *Rick Steves' Guide to European Railpasses* has the latest on 2002 prices. To get the railpass guide, call us at 425/771-8303 or visit www.ricksteves.com/rail.**

# BRITRAIL CLASSIC PASS

| | Adult first class | Adult standard | Senior (60+) first class | 16-25 youth standard |
|---|---|---|---|---|
| 8 consecutive days | $ 399 | $ 265 | $ 339 | $ 215 |
| 15 consecutive days | 599 | 399 | 509 | 279 |
| 22 consecutive days | 759 | 499 | 639 | 355 |
| 1 month | 899 | 599 | 759 | 419 |

"Standard" is the polite British term for "second" class. No senior discounts for standard class. For each adult pass you buy, one child (5-15) gets a free pass of the same type (ask for the "Family Pass"). Additional kids pay the normal half-adult rate. Kids under 5: free. These rules also apply to the Flexipasses listed below.

# BRITRAIL FLEXIPASS

| | Adult first class | Adult standard | Senior (60+) first class | 16-25 youth standard |
|---|---|---|---|---|
| 4 days in 2 months | $ 349 | $ 235 | $ 299 | $ 185 |
| 8 days in 2 months | 509 | 339 | 435 | 239 |
| 15 days in 2 months | 769 | 515 | 655 | 359 |

# BRITRAIL PASS 'N DRIVE

Any 3 rail days and 2 car days in 2 months.

| | 1st class | 2nd class | extra car day |
|---|---|---|---|
| Mini car | $355 | $257 | $47 |
| Compact car | 362 | 265 | 60 |
| Intermediate car | 375 | 275 | 71 |

Prices are approximate per person for 2 traveling together. 3rd and 4th person sharing car pay $295 in 1st or $199 in 2nd class. Senior, child, and single adult rates also available. To order Britrail Pass 'N Drive, call your travel agent or Rail Europe at 800/438-7245.

**Britain & Ireland:**

The map shows approximate point-to-point one-way 2nd-class fares in $US by rail (solid line) and bus (dashed line). Add up fares for your itinerary to see whether a railpass will save you money.

# BRITRAIL SOUTHEAST PASS

| | First class | Standard class |
|---|---|---|
| 3 out of 8 days | $106 | $73 |
| 4 out of 8 days | 142 | 106 |
| 7 out of 15 days | 189 | 142 |

Covers trips from London to much of southeast England including Oxford, Cambridge, Salisbury, and Exeter. Not valid for Bath, on service via Reading, on Great Western trains, Heathrow Express, or for discounts on the Chunnel. The pass is valid on the Gatwick Express. Kids 5-15 pay $31 (1st cl) or $21 (2nd cl) flat fare per pass.

# FREEDOM OF WALES FLEXIPASS

| | |
|---|---|
| Any 4 rail days within 8 consecutive bus days | $85 |
| Any 8 rail days within 15 consecutive bus days | $159 |

Standard class on rail and major bus routes. Kids 5-15 half fare.

# FREEDOM OF SCOTLAND TRAVELPASS

| | |
|---|---|
| 4 days out of 8 flexi | $134 |
| 8 days out of 15 flexi | 168 |
| 12 days out of 20 flexi | 219 |

Good on all trains, standard class only, and covers Caledonian MacBrayne and Strathclyde ferry service to Scotland's most popular islands, some Citylink busses & more. Children 5-15 half fare. Children under 5 free. Also available in Scotland.

# BRITRAIL PLUS IRELAND PASS

| | First class | Standard class |
|---|---|---|
| 5 days out of 1 month | $529 | $399 |
| 10 days out of 1 month | 749 | 569 |

This pass covers the entire British Isles (England, Wales, Scotland, Northern Ireland and the Republic of Ireland) including a round-trip Stena Line ferry crossing between Wales or Scotland and the Emerald Isle during the pass's validity (okay to leave via one port and return via another). Reserve boat crossings a day or so in advance—sooner for holidays. One child (5-15) travels along free with each pass. Extra kiddies pay half fare; under 5 free. For cheaper deals in Ireland see our railpass guide or *Rick Steves' Ireland*.

of the week, but you can't start your trip before 08:32 Monday through Friday.

There can be up to 30 different prices for the same journey. A clerk at any station (or the helpful folks at tel. 08457-484-950, 24 hours daily) can figure out the cheapest fare for your trip. Savings can be significant. For a London-Edinburgh round-trip (standard class), the regular fare is £119, Saver is £83, (no Super Saver option exists for this trip), Super Advance is £65, Apex is

# BritRail Routes

**KEY:**                    ✳ MAP NOT TO SCALE

**London Stations:**

1  **Victoria** - S + SE Eng, conn. to Paris + Brussels
2  **Charing Cross** - S.E. Eng
3  **Waterloo** - S. England, Paris + Bruss. (Chunnel)
4  **Liverpool St.** - East Anglia, Amsterdam
5  **King's Cross** - Midlands, N.E. Eng., E. Scotland
6  **St. Pancras** - E. Midlands
7  **Euston** - Midlands, N Wales, N.W. Eng., W. Scot.
8  **Paddington** - W. Eng, S Wales

→ **RAIL**   --- **BUS**
⋯⋯ **FERRY** with
(6H)   Crossing time
**NOTE:** Faster English
Channel crossings with
Hovercraft + Hydrofoil
on some runs. Check!
The Chunnel is
faster still...

**London Airports:** ✈
A - HEATHROW   B - GATWICK
C - LUTON   D - STANSTED

£51, and Bargain Return is £36. For a York-London round-trip, the regular fare is £122, Saver is £63, Super Saver is £61, Super Advance is £45, Apex is £38, and Bargain Return is £30.

You can book rail tickets online at www.thetrainline.com, but ordering by phone is more foolproof. If you order online, be sure you know what you want; it's tough to reach a person when you want to change a ticket later. You pick up your ticket at the station (unless your order was lost—this service still has some glitches). If you want your ticket mailed to you in the United States, you need to allow a couple weeks and cover the shipping costs. Note that BritRail passholders cannot use this Web site to make reservations.

**Railpasses:** Consider getting a railpass. The BritRail pass comes in "consecutive day" and "flexi" versions, with price breaks for youths, seniors, and second class ("standard" class, available to anyone). Standard class is a good choice since many of the smaller train lines don't even offer first-class cars. BritRail passes cover England, Scotland, and Wales. There are now Scotland passes, England/Ireland passes, Southeast Britain passes, and BritRail Plus Car passes (which offer you some rail days and some car-rental days). BritRail Classic, Flexi, and Plus Ireland passes, as well as Eurailpasses, get you a discount on the Eurostar train that zips you to continental Europe under the English Channel. These passes are sold outside of Europe only. For specifics, contact your travel agent or Europe Through the Back Door (tel. 425/771-8303).

**Senior, Youth, and Family Deals:** To get a third off the price of most point-to-point rail tickets, seniors can buy a Senior Railcard (for age 60 and over, www.senior-railcard.co.uk), and young people can buy a Young Persons Railcard (for ages 16–25, or full-time students 26 and over with a valid ISIC card). Each card costs £18. A Family Railcard allows adults to travel cheaper (about 33 percent) while their kids age 5 to 15 receive an 80 percent discount for most trips (£20, maximum of 4 adults and 4 kids). Any of these cards are valid for a year on virtually all trains except special runs like the Heathrow Express and Eurostar (fill out application at station, brochures on racks in info center, need to show passport). Youth also need to submit a passport-type photo for the Young Persons Card and have to pay a minimal fare for journeys starting before 10:00 on weekdays.

**Buses:** Although buses are about 33 percent slower than trains, they're also a lot cheaper. Round-trip bus tickets usually cost less than two one-way fares (e.g., London-York one-way costs £19; round-trip costs £28). And buses go many places that trains don't. Budget travelers can save a wad with a bus pass. The National Express sells Tourist Trail bus passes (over the counter, tel. 08705-808-080, www.gobycoach.com); passes cost £49 (any 2 days out of 3 consecutive days), £85 (any 5 days within 30), £135 (any 8 days within 30), £190 (any 15 days within 30), and

£205 (any 15 days within 60). If you want to take a bus from your last destination to Heathrow or Gatwick, ask about the many National Express Flight Link and Jet Link buses. In Britain, bus stations are normally at or near train stations (in London, the bus station is a block southwest of Victoria Station). The British distinguish between "buses" (for local runs with lots of stops) and "coaches" (long-distance express runs).

A couple of companies offer **backpacker's bus circuits**. These hop-on hop-off bus circuits take mostly youth hostelers around the country super cheap and easy with the assumption that they'll be sleeping in the hostels along the way. For instance, **Stray Travel** network does a six-day-or-more "tour," making a 1,000-mile circle connecting London, Bath, Stratford, the lakes, Edinburgh, York, Cambridge, and London hostels (£139 for 6 days, pass good for 4 months, 3 buses weekly, driver provides commentary and books passengers' rooms at hostels; also offers loop trips of Ireland and Europe; tel. 020/7373-7737, www .straytravel.com). **Haggis Backpacker** offers a similar deal, with buses circling Scotland (£69, 600 miles: Edinburgh, Oban, Glencoe, Fort William, Skye, Inverness, Edinburgh; 4 buses weekly, ticket good for 3 months, tel. 0131/557-9393, www .radicaltravel.com, e-mail: haggis@radicaltravel.com).

**Flights:** If you've got more money than time, don't buy a ticket for a long train trip without considering a flight offered by one of the discount airlines. BMI British Midland, which has been around the longest, offers reasonable flights such as Heathrow-Dublin (8/day, 75 min, about £137 one-way, as little as £103 round-trip with a stay over Sat) and Heathrow-Edinburgh (8/day, 75 min, as little as £75 round-trip with a stay over Sat). British Midland also offers decent fares to Paris (£153 one-way, £75 round-trip with a stay over Sat), Brussels (£79/£161), and Amsterdam (£58/£141). To get the lowest fares, book months in advance and go round-trip, leaving and returning on a weekday (Mon–Thu), and staying over a Saturday. For reservations and information, call British tel. 0870-607-0555. The U.S. office of BMI British Midland sells Discover Europe air passes: flights out of London that are less than 500 miles—say, to Paris or Amsterdam—cost $109 plus tax; flights over 500 miles cost $159 plus tax (U.S. tel. 800/788-0555). For more information, visit www.flybmi.com.

Other cut-rate airlines include Ryanair (British tel. 0870-333-1231, www.ryanair.com), Virgin Express (British tel. 020/7744-0004, www.virgin-express.com), and Easy Jet (British tel. 0870-600-0000, www.easyjet.com). Also consider www .cheapflights.co.uk. Returns can be cheaper than one-way—ask. To get the best prices, book far in advance, as soon as you have a date set. Each flight has an allotment of cheap seats; these sell fast, leaving the higher-priced seats for latecomers.

## Car Rental

To save money, arrange your car rental from the States (either on your own or through your travel agent) rather than in Britain. The best rates are weekly with unlimited mileage or leasing (possible for rentals of over 3 weeks). You can pick up and drop off just about anywhere, anytime. For a trip covering both Britain and Ireland you're better off with two separate car rentals. If you pick up the car in a smaller city, such as Bath, you'll more likely survive your first day on the British roads. If you drop the car off early or keep it longer, you'll be credited or charged at a fair, prorated price. Big companies have offices in most cities. (Ask to be picked up at your hotel.) Small local rental companies can be cheaper but aren't as flexible.

The Ford 1.3-liter Escort-category car costs about $50 more per week more than the smallest cars but feels better on the motorways and safer on the small roads. Remember, mini-buses are a great budget way to go for five to nine people.

For peace of mind, spring for the CDW insurance (Collision Damage Waiver, about $15 per day), which gives a zero (or low) deductible rather than the standard value-of-the-car "deductible." A few "gold" credit cards cover CDW insurance; quiz your credit-card company on the worst-case scenario.

## Driving

Your U.S. license is all you need to drive in Britain. Driving in Britain is basically wonderful—once you remember to stay on the left and after you've mastered the "roundabouts." Traffic in roundabouts has the right of way, entering traffic yields (look to your right as you merge). It helps to remember that the driver is always in the center of the road. But be warned: Every year I get a few cards from traveling readers advising me that, for them, trying to drive Britain was a nerve-racking and regrettable mistake. If you want to get a little slack on the roads, drop by a gas station or auto shop and buy a green "L" (new driver with license) sign to put in your window (don't get the red "L" sign, which means you're a student driver without a license, prohibited from driving on motorways).

A British Automobile Association membership comes with most rentals. Understand its towing and emergency-road-service benefits. Gas (petrol) costs over $4 per gallon and is self-serve. Green pumps are unleaded. Seat belts are required by law. Speed limits are 30 mph in town, 70 mph on the motorways, and 50 or 60 mph elsewhere. The national sign for 60 mph is a white circle with a black slash. Note that road-surveillance cameras strictly enforce speed limits. Any driver (including foreigners renting cars) photographed speeding will get a nasty bill in the mail. (Cameras—you'll see the foreboding gray boxes—flash on your rear license

## Standard European Road Signs

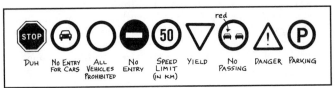

plate in order not to invade the privacy of anyone sharing the front seat with someone who they shouldn't be with.) Avoid driving in big cities whenever possible. Most have modern ring roads to skirt the congestion. The shortest distance between any two points is usually the motorway. Road signs can be confusing, too few, and too late. Study your map before taking off. Know the cities you'll be lacing together since road numbers are inconsistent. Miss a motorway exit and you can lose 30 minutes. A Britain road atlas (sold at gas stations and bookstores) is $10 well spent.

Parking is confusing. One yellow line marked on the pavement means no parking Monday through Saturday during work hours. Double yellow lines mean no parking at any time. Broken yellow lines mean short stops are OK, but you should always look for explicit signs or ask a passerby. White lines mean you're free to park.

Even in small towns, rather than fight it, I just pull into the most central and handy "pay and display" car park I can find. Rates are reasonable by U.S. standards. Locals love to share "pay and display" stickers. If you stand by the machine, invariably someone on their way out with time left on their sticker will give it to you. Keep a bag of coins in the ashtray for parking meters.

Set your car up for a fun road trip. Establish a cardboard-box munchies pantry. Buy a rack of liter boxes of juice for the trunk. Buy some Windex and a roll of paper towels for cleaner sightseeing.

## Telephones, Mail, and E-mail

Use the telephone routinely. You can make long-distance calls directly, cheaply, and easily, and there's no language barrier. Call ahead to reserve or reconfirm rooms, check opening hours, confirm tour times, and reserve theater tickets.

To call long distance you'll need the correct area code. For long distance you'll find area codes listed throughout this book, or you can get them from directory assistance (free and happy to help, dial 192 in Britain). Phone numbers and area codes rarely have a standard number of digits. For information on telephoning throughout Europe, see the appendix.

Easy-to-find public phone booths are either coin- or card-operated. Phones clearly list which coins they'll take (usually from 10p to £1), and a display shows how your money supply's doing.

Only completely unused coins will be returned, so put in biggies with caution. (If money's left over, rather than hanging up, push the "make another call" button.)

**Phone Cards:** The phone-card booths are common only in cities. You can purchase British Telecom (BT) phone cards for £3, £10, or £20 at newsstands, hotels, tourist offices, and post offices. (Some "credit-card phones" have a slot that will take—but not accept—a BT phone card.)

BT phone cards are being replaced by BT Phonecard Plus. You can make a call with a Plus card by either inserting it in a phone in a phone booth, or by dialing the PIN (a scratch-off Personal Identification Number) from any phone, even from your hotel room. You can recharge a Plus card using your credit or debit card by calling the operator's number listed on the phone card.

Many different brands of PIN cards—which allow you to call home at about 20 cents per minute—are flooding the market (sold for £5, £10, and £20 at most newsstands, exchange bureaus, and mini-marts; unless you specifically want a BT Phone Card Plus, simply ask for an "international calling card"). Because PIN cards are occasionally duds, avoid the high denominations.

To use a PIN card, dial the toll-free access number listed on the card; then, at the prompt, enter your PIN (also listed on card), dial the number you want to call (for calls to the U.S., dial 00-1-area code-local number; for calls within Britain, dial area code-local number; when using a PIN card, the area code must be dialed even if you're calling across the street). PIN cards work only within the country of purchase (e.g., a PIN card bought in Britain won't work in France).

To make numerous calls with a PIN card without having to redial the long access number each time, press the keys (see instructions on card) that allow you to launch directly into your next call.

The only tricky British phones you'll use are the expensive Mickey Mouse coin-op ones in bars and B&Bs. Some require money before you dial, while others wait until after you've connected. Many have a button you must push before you begin talking. But all have clear instructions. Long distance in Britain is most expensive from 08:00 to 13:00 and cheapest from 17:00 to 08:00 and on weekends. A short call is quite inexpensive; don't hesitate to call long distance. Remember that Northern Ireland is part of Britain and just a long-distance call away (simply dial the area code and the local number).

**Dialing Direct:** You'll save money by dialing direct rather than going through an operator. You just need to learn to break the codes. For a listing of **international access codes and country codes**, see the appendix.

When making an international call to Britain, first dial the international access code (00 if you're calling from Europe,

011 from the U.S. or Canada), then Britain's country code (44), then the area code (without its initial zero) and the local number. For example, London's area code is 020. To call one of my listed London B&Bs from New York, I dial 011 (U.S. international access code), 44 (Britain's country code), 20 (London's area code without its initial zero), then 7730-8191 (the B&B's number).

When calling long distance within Britain, first dial the area code (which starts with zero), then the local number. To call the London B&B from Britain's old York, dial 020/7730-8191.

To call my office from Britain, I dial 00 (Britain's international access code), 1 (U.S. country code), 425 (Edmonds' area code), then 771-8303.

**Calling Cards**: USA Direct Services (with an AT&T, MCI, or Sprint calling card) are popular for calling the United States from any kind of phone. While these used to be a fine deal, direct-dial rates have since plummeted, and now you can call home much more cheaply by using coins or locally-bought phone cards. For a list of calling-card operators, see the appendix. It's a rip-off to use USA Direct for making calls between European countries—instead, call direct.

**Cell Phones**: Affluent travelers like to buy cell phones (about $60 on up) in Europe to use for making local and international calls. The cheaper phones generally work only if you're making calls from the country where you purchased it (e.g., a phone bought in Britain won't work in Ireland). Pricier phones allow you to call from any country but it'll cost you about $40 per country to outfit the phone with the necessary chip and prepaid phone time. If you're interested, stop by any European shop that sells cell phones (you'll see an array of phones prominently displayed in the store window). Depending on your trip and budget, ask for a phone that works only in that country or one that can be used throughout Europe. And if you're really on a budget, skip cell phones and use PIN cards instead.

**Mail:** Get stamps at the neighborhood post office, newsstands within fancy hotels, and some mini-marts and card shops. To arrange for mail delivery, reserve a few hotels along your route in advance and give their addresses to friends or use American Express mail services (available to anyone who has at least one AmEx traveler's check). Allow 10 days for a letter to arrive. Phoning is so easy that I've dispensed with mail stops altogether.

**E-mail:** More and more hoteliers have e-mail addresses and Web sites; I've listed these whenever available. Note that mom-and-pop pensions, which can get deluged by e-mail, are not always able to respond immediately to an e-mail you've sent.

Internet access points are available in most cities. Look for the places listed in this book, or ask the local TI, computer store, or your B&B host.

## Sleeping

In the interest of smart use of your time, I favor accommodations (and restaurants) handy to your sightseeing activities. Rather than list hotels scattered throughout a city, I choose two or three favorite neighborhoods and recommend the best accommodations values in each, from $15 bunk beds to fancy-for-my-book $200 doubles. Outside of London you can expect to find good doubles for $60 to $100, including cooked breakfasts and tax.

I've described my recommended hotels and B&Bs with a standard code. Prices listed are for one-night stays in peak season, include a hearty breakfast (unless otherwise noted), and assume you're booking direct and not through a TI. Prices can soften off-season, for stays of two nights or longer, or for payment in cash (rather than credit card). Particularly at nicer hotels, ask about deals (usually offered for 2-night stays, sometimes midweek or weekends, often called Leisure Breaks); the room price doesn't drop dramatically, but the pricey breakfasts are usually included. Booking a big hotel in advance usually gets you the highest-priced "rack rate." Calling the same day often gets you a deeply discounted rate.

When establishing prices with a hotelier or B&B owner, confirm if the charge is per person or per room (if a price is too good to be true, it's probably per person). Because many places in Britain charge per person, small groups often pay the same for a single and a double as they would for a triple. Note: In this book, room prices are listed per room, not per person.

Most places I list have three floors of rooms, steep stairs, and no elevator. If you're concerned about stairs, call and ask about ground-floor rooms.

Virtually all rooms have sinks. Rooms with a private bath-room (toilet plus shower and/or tub) are called "en suite"; rooms that lack private plumbing are "standard." As more rooms go en suite, the hallway bathroom is shared with fewer standard rooms. If money's tight, ask for standard rooms.

Britain has a rating system for hotels and B&Bs. These dia-monds and stars are supposed to imply quality, but I find that they mean only that the place sporting symbols is paying dues to the tourist board. Rating systems often have little to do with value.

### Bed-and-Breakfasts (B&Bs)

Compared to hotels, bed-and-breakfast places give you double the cultural intimacy for half the price. In 2002, you'll pay £20 to £35 ($30–53) per person for a B&B. Prices include a big cooked breakfast. How much coziness, tea, and biscuits are tossed in varies tremendously.

If you have a reasonable but limited budget, skip hotels. Go the B&B way. If you can use a telephone and speak English, you'll

## Sleep Code

To give maximum information with a minimum of space, I use this code to describe accommodations listed in this book. Prices are listed per room, not per person. Breakfast is included.

**S** = Single room, or price for one person in a double.

**D** = Double or twin room. (I specify double- and twin-bed rooms only if they are priced differently, or if a place has only one or the other. When reserving, you should specify.)

**T** = Three-person room (often a double bed with a single).

**Q** = Four-person room (adding an extra child's bed to a T is usually cheaper).

**b** = Private bathroom with toilet and shower or tub.

**s** = Private shower or tub only. (The toilet is down the hall.)

**CC** = Accepts credit cards (Visa and MasterCard, rarely American Express).

**no CC** = Does not accept credit cards; pay in local cash.

**No smoking**—With this edition, about 80 percent of my recommended B&Bs prohibit smoking. While some places allow smoking in the sleeping rooms, breakfast rooms are nearly always smoke free.

**Family deal**—Indicates that parents with young children can easily get a room with an extra child's bed or a discount for larger rooms. Call to negotiate the price. Teenage kids are generally charged as adults. Little kids sleep almost free.

According to this code, a couple staying at a "Db-£60, CC" hotel would pay a total of £60 (about $90) per night for a room with a private toilet and shower (or tub). The hotel accepts credit cards or cash.

enjoy homey, friendly, clean rooms at a great price by sticking to my listings. Always call first.

If you're traveling beyond my recommended destinations, you'll find B&Bs where you need them. Any town with tourists has a TI that books rooms or can give you a list and point you in the right direction. In the absence of a TI, ask people on the street for help.

"Twin" means two single beds, and "double" means one double bed. If you'll take either one, let them know or you might be needlessly turned away. "Standard" rooms come with just a sink (many better places have standard rooms that they don't even advertise). If you want a room that contains a private bathroom, specify "en suite"; B&B owners sometimes use the term "private bathroom" for a bathroom down the hall that only your room has the key for.

B&Bs range from large guest houses with 15 to 20 rooms to small homes renting out a spare bedroom. The philosophy of the management determines the character of a place more than its size and facilities offered. Avoid places run as a business by absentee owners. My top listings are run by couples who enjoy welcoming the world to their breakfast table.

The B&Bs I've recommended are nearly all stocking-feet comfortable and "homely," as they say in England. I look for a place that is friendly (i.e., enjoys Americans); located in a central, safe, quiet neighborhood; clean, with firm beds; a good value; and not mentioned in other guidebooks (and therefore filled mostly by English travelers). In certain cases my recommendations don't meet all of these prerequisites. I'm more impressed by a handy location and a fun-loving philosophy than hair driers and shoeshine machines.

A few tips: B&B proprietors are selective as to whom they invite in for the night. At some B&Bs, children are not welcome. Risky-looking people (2 or more single men are often assumed to be troublemakers) find many places suddenly full. If you'll be staying for more than one night you are a "desirable." Sometimes staying several nights earns you a better price—ask about it. If you book through a TI, it takes a 10 percent commission. If you book direct, the B&B gets it all (and you'll have a better chance of getting a discount). I have negotiated special prices with this book (often for cash). You should find prices quoted here good through 2002 (except for major holidays and festivals). In popular weekend-getaway spots you're unlikely to find a place to take you for Saturday night only. If my listings are full, ask for guidance. (Mentioning this book can help.) Owners usually work together and can call up an ally to land you a bed.

B&Bs are not hotels; if you want to ruin your relationship with your hostess, treat her like a hotel clerk. Americans often assume they'll get new towels each day. The British don't, and neither will you. Hang them up to dry and reuse.

B&Bs have plenty of stairs. Expect good exercise and be happy you packed light. Some B&Bs stock rooms with a hot-water pot, cups, tea bags, and coffee packets (if you prefer decaf, buy a jar at a grocery, and dump into a baggie for easy packing). Electrical outlets sometimes come with switches on the outlet to turn the current on or off; if your electrical appliance isn't working, flip the switch.

In B&Bs, no two showers are alike. Sometimes you'll encounter "telephone" showers—a hand-held nozzle in a bathtub. Many

B&Bs have been retrofitted with plumbing, and water is heated individually for each shower rather than by one central heating system. While the switch is generally left on, in some rooms you'll have a hot-water switch to consider. Any cord hanging from the ceiling is for lights (not emergencies). Once in the shower you'll find a multitude of overly clever mechanisms designed to somehow get the right amount and temperature of water. Good luck.

## Cheap Modern Hotels

Hotel chains, offering predictably comfortable accommodations at reasonable prices, are popping up in the center of big cities in Britain. The biggies are Travelodge (reservations tel. 0870-905-6343, also has freeway locations for tired drivers, www.travelodge.co.uk), Travel Inn (reservations tel. 0870-242-8000, www.travelinn.co.uk), and Premier Lodge (their older ones are a little scruffy but OK, reservations tel. 0870-201-0203, www.premierlodge.co.uk). The Irish chain, Jurys Inn, also has some hotels in Britain (reserve at Irish tel. 01/607-0000, call their hotels directly, or book online at www.jurys.com).

These super-convenient hotels offer simple, clean, and modern rooms for up to four people (2 adults/2 children) for £50 to £90, depending on the location. Most rooms have a double bed, single bed, five-foot trundle bed, private shower, WC, and TV. Hotels usually have an attached restaurant, good security, and a 24-hour staffed reception desk. Of course they are as cozy as a Motel 6, but they're great for families, and many travelers love them. You can book over the phone (or online) with a credit card, then pay when you check in. When you check out, just drop off the key, Lee.

Couples could also consider Holiday Inn Express, spreading throughout Britain. These are like a Holiday Inn Lite, with cheaper prices and no restaurant. Some of their hotels allow only two per room, other take up to four (Db-about £60–100, make sure Express is part of the name or you'll pay more for a regular Holiday Inn, reservations tel. 0800-897-121, www.hiexpress.com).

## Making Reservations

It's possible to travel at any time of year without reservations, but given the high stakes, erratic accommodations values, number of people traveling with this book, and the quality of the gems I've listed, I highly recommend calling ahead for rooms at least a few days in advance as you travel. When tourist crowds are down, you might make a habit of calling your hotel between 9:00 and 10:00 on the day you plan to arrive, when the hotel knows who'll be checking out and just which rooms will be available. I've taken great pains to list telephone numbers with long-distance instructions (see "Telephones, Mail, and E-mail" above; also see the appendix). Get a phone card and use it to confirm and reconfirm as you travel. A hotel receptionist will trust you and hold a room until 16:00 without a deposit, though some will ask for a credit-card number.

*Honor your reservations or cancel by phone: Trusting travelers to show up is a huge, stressful issue and a financial risk for small B&B owners.* I promised the owners of the places I list that you will be reliable when you make a telephone reservation; please don't let them (or me) down. If you'll be delayed or won't make it, simply call in. Americans are notorious for reserving B&Bs long in advance and never showing up (causing B&B owners to lose money—and respect for Americans). Being late is no problem if you are in telephone contact. Long distance is cheap and easy from public phone booths.

While it's generally easy to find a room, a few national holidays jam things up (especially "bank holiday" Mondays) and merit reservations long in advance. Mark these dates in red on your travel calendar for 2002: Good Friday, Easter plus Easter Monday, the first Monday in May, the first Monday and Tuesday in June, the last Monday in August, Christmas, December 26, and New Year's Day. Monday bank holidays are preceded by busy weekends; book the entire weekend in advance.

If you know exactly which dates you need and really want a particular place, reserve a room before you leave home. To reserve from home, call, e-mail, fax, or write the hotel. To fax or e-mail, use the form in the appendix (online at www.ricksteves.com/reservation). If you're writing, add the postal code and confirm the need and method for a deposit. A two-night stay in August would be "two nights, 16/8/02 to 18/8/02"—Europeans write the date day/month/year, and hotel jargon uses your day of departure. You'll often receive a letter back requesting one night's deposit. Your credit-card number and expiration date will usually be accepted as a deposit, though you may need to send a signed traveler's check or a bank draft in the local currency. If your credit card is the deposit, you can pay with your card or cash when you arrive. If you don't show up (or if you cancel with short notice), you'll be billed for one night.

Hotels in larger cities sometimes have strict cancellation policies (you might lose, say, a deposit if you cancel within 2 weeks of your reserved stay, or you might be billed for the entire visit if you leave early); ask about cancellation policies before you book.

On the road, reconfirm your reservations a day in advance for safety (or you may be bumped—really). Also, don't just assume you can extend. Take the time to consider in advance how long you'll stay.

## Hostels

If you're traveling alone, hosteling is the best way to conquer hotel loneliness. Hostels are also a tremendous source of local

and budget travel information. You'll pay an average of £11 for
a bed and £3 for breakfast. Anyone of any age can hostel in
Britain. While there are no membership concerns for private
hostels, IYHF hostels require membership. Those without cards
simply buy one-night guest memberships for £1.50.

Britain has hundreds of hostels of all shapes and sizes. Hostel
selectively. Hostels can be historic castles or depressing huts, serene
and comfy or overrun by noisy children. Unfortunately, many of
the international youth hostels have become overpriced, and, in
general, I no longer recommend them. The only time I do is if
you're on a very tight budget, want to cook your own meals, or
are traveling with a group that likes to sleep on bunk beds in big
rooms. The informal private hostels are often more fun, easygoing,
and cheaper. These alternatives to the International Youth Hostel
Federation (IYHF) hostels are more common than ever. Hostels
of Europe (U.S. tel. 519/251-8821, www.hostelseurope.com) and
the Internet Guide to Hostelling (www.hostels.com) have good
listings. You can book online for many hostels (London: www
.hostellondon.com, for England and Wales: www.yha.org.uk,
and for Scotland: www.hostel-scotland.co.uk).

## Eating

I don't mind English food. But then, I liked dorm food. True, England isn't famous for its cuisine and probably never will be, but we
tourists have to eat. If there's any good place to cut corners to stretch
your budget, it's in eating. Here are a few tips on budget eating.

The traditional "fry" is famous as a hearty way to start the
day. Also known as a "heart attack on a plate," the breakfast is
especially feasty if you've just come from the land of the skimpy
continental breakfast across the Channel. Your standard fry gets
off to a healthy start with juice and cereal or porridge. (Try Weet-
abix, a soggy English cousin of shredded wheat. Scotland serves
great porridge.) Next, with tea or coffee, you get a heated plate
with a fried egg, lean Canadian-style bacon, a bad sausage, a
grilled tomato, and often a slice of delightfully greasy pan toast
and sautéed mushrooms. Many B&B hosts are evangelical about
their black pudding (beware). Toast comes on a rack (to cool
quickly and crisply) with butter and marmalade. Order kippers
(herring filets smoked in an oak fire). This meal tides many travelers over until dinner. Order only what you'll eat. A B&B hostess,
your temporary local mother, doesn't like to see food wasted. And
there's nothing wrong with skipping the "fry"—few locals actually
start their day with this heavy traditional breakfast.

These days, the best coffee is served in a *cafetiére* (also called
a French press). When your coffee has steeped as long as you like,
plunge down the filter and pour. To revitalize your brew, pump
the plunger again.

Many B&Bs don't serve breakfast until 08:00. If you need an early start, ask politely if it's possible. While they may not make you a cooked breakfast, they can usually put out cereal, toast, juice, and coffee.

Picnicking saves time and money. Try boxes of orange juice (pure, by the liter), fresh bread, tasty English cheese, meat, a tube of Colman's English mustard, local eatin' apples, bananas, small tomatoes, a small tub of yogurt (they're drinkable), gorp or nuts, plain or chocolate-covered "Digestive Biscuits," and any local specialties. At open-air markets and supermarkets you can get produce in small quantities (3 tomatoes and 2 bananas cost me 50p). Supermarkets often have good deli sections (even offering Indian dishes) and sometimes salad bars. Decent, packaged sandwiches (£2–3) are sold everywhere. I often munch a relaxed "meal on wheels" in a car, train, or open-top bus tour or river cruise to save 30 precious minutes for sightseeing.

At classier restaurants, look for "early bird specials," allowing you to eat well and affordably, but early (around 17:30–19:00, last order by 19:00). A top-end £25-for-dinner-type restaurant often serves the same quality two-course lunch deals for £10. Some restaurants can be pricey, but cheap alternatives abound: fish-and-chips joints, Chinese and Indian take-outs, cafeterias, pubs (see below), and your typical good old greasy-spoon cafés. At a sit-down place with table service, tip around 10 percent—unless the service charge is already listed on the bill.

For fresh, fast, and cheap lunches, bakeries have meat pies (and microwaves), pastries, yogurt, and cartons of "semi-skimmed" milk. Pasties are "savory" (not sweet) meat pies that originated in the mining country. They had big crust handles so miners with filthy hands could eat them and toss the crust.

People of leisure punctuate their afternoon with a "cream tea" at a tearoom. You'll get a pot of tea, two homemade scones, jam, and thick, creamy-as-honey clotted cream. For maximum pinkie-waving taste per calorie, slice your scone thin like a miniature loaf of bread. Tearooms, which often serve appealing light meals, are usually open for lunch and close around 17:00, just before dinner.

## English Chocolate

My chocoholic readers are enthusiastic about English chocolate. Their favorites include: Cadbury Wispa Gold bars (filled with liquid caramel), Cadbury Crunchie bars, Nestle's Lion Bars, Cadbury's Boost bar (a shortcake biscuit with caramel in milk chocolate), and Galaxy chocolate bars (especially the ones with hazelnuts). British M&Ms (Smarties) are better than American ones. Thornton shops (often in larger train stations) sell a box of sweets called Continental Assortment, which comes with a tasting guide. The highlight is the mocha white chocolate truffle. For a few extra pence, adorn your ice-cream cone with a "flake"—a chocolate bar stuck right into the middle.

## Pub Grub and Beer

Pubs are a basic part of the British social scene, and whether you're a teetotaler or a beer guzzler they should be a part of your travel here. Pub is short for "public house." It's an extended living room where, if you don't mind the stickiness, you can feel the pulse of Britain. Most traditional atmospheric pubs are in the countryside and smaller towns. Unfortunately, many city pubs have been afflicted with an excess of brass, ferns, and video games. Many others have found selling beer is more profitable than selling meals and only cook at lunchtime. In any case, smart travelers use the pubs to eat, drink, get out of the rain, watch the latest sporting event, and make new friends.

Pub grub gets better each year. It's Britain's best eating value. For £5 you'll get a basic budget hot lunch or dinner in friendly surroundings. The *Good Pub Guide*, published annually by the British Consumers Union, is excellent. Pubs attached to restaurants often have fresher food and a chef who knows how to cook.

I recommend many specific pubs, but good places can go bad, and your B&B host is usually up-to-date on the best neighborhood pub grub. Ask for advice (but adjust for nepotism and cronyism, which run rampant). Locals will rarely recommend a rough pub that's a local hangout. If you want this experience (the food will be cheaper but not very good), ask for a "spit-and-sawdust" place. Big-city spit-and-sawdust places may not welcome tourists. Rural and village ones will. They are the most interesting.

Pubs generally serve assorted meat pies, such as steak and kidney pie or shepherd's pie, curried dishes, fish, quiche, vegetables, and (invariably) chips and peas. Better pubs let you substitute a "jacket potato" (baked potato) or fresh vegetables for your fries. Meals are usually served from 12:00 to 14:00 and 18:00 to 20:00, not throughout the day. There's no table service in British pubs. Order drinks and meals at the bar. Pay as you order and don't tip. Servings are hearty, service is quick, and you'll rarely spend more than £5 to £7 ($8–11). Your beer or cider adds another pound or two. Free tap water is always available. In Britain a "ploughman's lunch" is a modern "traditional English meal" that nearly every tourist tries...once. Pubs that advertise their food and are crowded with locals are less likely to be the kind that serve only lousy microwaved snacks.

In a pub you order your beer at the bar. Part of the experience is standing before a line of "hand pulls" and wondering which on-tap beer you want. The British take great pride in their beer. They think that drinking beer cold and carbonated, as Americans do, ruins the taste. At pubs, long hand pulls are used to pull the traditional rich-flavored "real ales" up from the cellar. These are the connoisseur's favorites: Ales are fermented naturally, vary from sweet to bitter, and often include a hoppy or nutty flavor. Notice the fun names. England had microbrews before that word was invented. Experiment. Short hand pulls at the bar mean colder, fizzier, mass-produced, and less interesting keg beers. Mild beers are sweeter, with a creamy malt flavor. Stout is dark and bitter, like Guinness (imported from Ireland and almost always available). For a cold, refreshing, basic American-style beer, ask for a lager. Try the draft cider (sweet or dry)...carefully. Proper English ladies like a half-beer and half-lemonade "shandy." Teetotalers can order a soft drink. Drinks are served by the pint or the half pint. (It's almost feminine for a man to order just a half; I order mine with quiche.)

Pub hours vary. The strictly limited wartime hours (designed to keep the wartime working force sober and productive) finally ended a few years ago, and now pubs can serve beer from 11:00 to 23:00, and Sunday from noon to 22:30. Children are served food and soft drinks in pubs (sometimes in a courtyard or the restaurant section), and you must be 18 to order a beer. A cup of darts is free for the asking. People go to a "public house" to be social. They want to talk. Get vocal with a local. Sitting or standing at the bar indicates you're interested in a conversation (while sitting at a table, you're likely to be left alone). Pubs are the next best thing to relatives in every town.

## Stranger in a Strange Land

We travel all the way to Europe to enjoy differences—to become temporary locals. You'll experience frustrations. There are certain truths that we find God-given and self-evident, such as cold beer, ice in drinks, bottomless cups of coffee, easy shower faucets, and driving on the right side of the road. One of the benefits of travel is the eye-opening realization that there are logical, civil, and even better alternatives. A willingness to go local ensures that you'll enjoy a full dose of hospitality.

## Back Door Manners

While updating this book, I heard over and over again that my readers are considerate and fun to have as guests. Thank you for traveling as temporary locals who are sensitive to the culture. It's a joy to follow you in my travels.

## Send Me a Postcard, Drop Me a Line

If you enjoy a successful trip with the help of this book and would like to share your discoveries, please fill out and send the survey at the end of this book to me at Europe Through the Back Door, Box 2009, Edmonds, WA 98020. I personally read and value all feedback. Thanks in advance—it helps a lot.

For our latest travel information, tap into www.ricksteves.com. To check on any updates for this book, visit www.ricksteves.com /update. My e-mail address is rick@ricksteves.com. Anyone can request a free issue of our newsletter.

Judging from the happy postcards I receive from travelers, it's safe to assume you're on your way to a great, affordable vacation— with the finesse of an independent, experienced traveler. Thanks, and happy travels!

# BACK DOOR TRAVEL PHILOSOPHY
## As Taught in *Rick Steves' Europe Through the Back Door*

*Travel is intensified living—maximum thrills per minute and one of the last great sources of legal adventure. Travel is freedom. It's recess, and we need it.*

*Experiencing the real Europe requires catching it by surprise, going casual . . . "Through the Back Door."*

*Affording travel is a matter of priorities. (Make do with the old car.) You can travel—simply, safely, and comfortably—anywhere in Europe for $80 a day plus transportation costs. In many ways, spending more money only builds a thicker wall between you and what you came to see. Europe is a cultural carnival and, time after time, you'll find that its best acts are free and the best seats are the cheap ones.*

*A tight budget forces you to travel close to the ground, meeting and communicating with the people, not relying on service with a purchased smile. Never sacrifice sleep, nutrition, safety, or cleanliness in the name of budget. Simply enjoy the local-style alternatives to expensive hotels and restaurants.*

*Extroverts have more fun. If your trip is low on magic moments, kick yourself and make things happen. If you don't enjoy a place, maybe you don't know enough about it. Seek the truth. Recognize tourist traps. Give a culture the benefit of your open mind. See things as different but not better or worse. Any culture has much to share.*

*Of course, travel, like the world, is a series of hills and valleys. Be fanatically positive and militantly optimistic. If something's not to your liking, change your liking. Travel is addictive. It can make you a happier American as well as a citizen of the world. Our earth is home to 6 billion equally important people. It's humbling to travel and find that people don't envy Americans. They like us, but, with all due respect, they wouldn't trade passports.*

*Globetrotting destroys ethnocentricity. It helps you understand and appreciate different cultures. Travel changes people. It broadens perspectives and teaches new ways to measure quality of life. Many travelers toss aside their hometown blinders. Their prized souvenirs are the strands of different cultures they decide to knit into their own character. The world is a cultural yarn shop. And Back Door Travelers are weaving the ultimate tapestry. Come on, join in!*

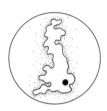

# LONDON

London is more than 600 square miles of urban jungle. With 9 million struggling people—many of whom speak English— it's a world in itself and a barrage on all the senses. On my first visit I felt very, very small. London is much more than its museums and famous landmarks. It's a living, breathing, thriving organism.

London has changed dramatically in recent years, and many visitors are surprised to find how "un-English" it is. Whites are now a minority in major parts of the city that once symbolized white imperialism. Arabs have nearly bought out the area north of Hyde Park. Chinese take-outs outnumber fish-and-chips shops. Many hotels are run by people with foreign accents (who hire English chambermaids), while outlying suburbs are home to huge communities of Indians and Pakistanis. London is learning— sometimes fitfully—to live as a microcosm of its formerly vast empire. Many see the English Channel Tunnel as another foreign threat to the Britishness of Britain.

With just a few days here, you'll get no more than a quick splash in this teeming human tidal pool. But, with a quick orientation, you'll get a good look at its top sights, history, and cultural entertainment, as well as its ever-changing human face.

Have fun in London. Blow through the city on the open deck of a double-decker orientation tour bus, and take a pinch-me-I'm-in-Britain walk through downtown. Ogle the crown jewels at the Tower of London, hear the chimes of Big Ben, and see the Houses of Parliament in action. Hobnob with the tomb-stones in Westminster Abbey, duck WWII bombs in Churchill's underground Cabinet War Rooms, and brave the earthshaking

Imperial War Museum. Overfeed the pigeons at Trafalgar Square. Visit with Leonardo, Botticelli, and Rembrandt in the National Gallery. Whisper across the dome of St. Paul's Cathedral and rummage through our civilization's attic at the British Museum. Cruise down the Thames River. You'll enjoy some of Europe's best people-watching at Covent Garden and snap to at Buckingham Palace's Changing of the Guard. Just sit in Victoria Station, at a major tube station, at Piccadilly Circus, or in Trafalgar Square, and observe. Spend one evening at a theater and the others catching your breath.

## Planning Your Time

The sights of London alone could easily fill a trip to Britain. It's a great one-week getaway. On a three-week tour of Britain I'd give it three busy days. If you're flying in, consider starting your trip in Bath and make London your British finale. Especially if you hope to enjoy a play or concert, a night or two of jet lag is bad news.

Here's a suggested schedule:

**Day 1**: 09:00–Tower of London (Beefeater tour, crown jewels), 12:00–Munch a sandwich on the Thames while cruising from the Tower to Westminster Bridge, 13:00–Follow the self-guided Westminster Walk (see below) with a quick visit to the Cabinet War Rooms, 15:30–Trafalgar Square and National Gallery, 17:30–Visit the Britain Visitors Centre near Piccadilly, planning ahead for your trip, 18:30–Dinner in Soho. Take in a play or 19:30 concert at St. Martin-in-the-Fields.

**Day 2**: 08:30–If traveling around Britain, spend 30 minutes in a phone booth getting all essential elements of your trip nailed down. If you know where you'll be and when, call those B&Bs now. 09:00–Take the Round London bus tour (consider hopping off near the end for the 11:30 Changing of the Guard at Buckingham Palace), 12:30–Covent Gardens for lunch and people watching, 14:00–Tour the British Museum. Have a pub dinner before a play, concert, or evening walking tour.

**Days 3 and 4**: Choose among these remaining London highlights: Tour Westminster Abbey, British Library, Imperial War Museum, the two Tates (Tate Modern on the south bank for modern art, Tate Britain on the north bank for British art), St. Paul's Cathedral, Museum of London, or London Eye Ferris wheel; cruise to Kew or Greenwich; do some serious shopping at one of London's elegant department stores or open-air markets; or consider another historic walking tour.

After considering nearly all of London's tourist sights, I have pruned them down to just the most important (or fun) for a first visit of up to seven days. You won't be able to see all of these, so don't try. You'll keep coming back to London. After 25 visits myself, I still enjoy a healthy list of excuses to return.

## Orientation (area code: 020)

To grasp London comfortably, see it as the old town without
the modern, congested sprawl. Most of the visitor's London lies
between the Tower of London and Hyde Park—about a three-
mile walk. Mentally—maybe even physically—scissor down your
map to include only the area between the Tower, King's Cross
Station, Paddington Station, the Victoria and Albert Museum,
and Victoria Station. With this focus and a good orientation,
you'll find London manageable and even fun.

## Tourist Information

The **Britain Visitors Centre** is the best information service in
town (Mon–Fri 9:00–18:30, Sat–Sun 10:00–16:00, phone not
answered after 17:00 Mon–Fri and not at all Sat–Sun, booking
service, just off Piccadilly Circus at 1 Lower Regent Street, tel.
020/8846-9000, www.visitbritain.com). It's great for London
information; buy your city map here (Bensons £2 Mapguide is
best, also sold at newsstands). If you're traveling beyond London,
take advantage of its well-equipped London/England desk, Wales
desk (tel. 020/7808-3838), Ireland desk (tel. 020/7808-3841),
and Scotland desk. At the center's extensive bookshop, gather
whatever guidebooks, hostel directories, maps, and information
you'll need. For trips through Britain, consider the *Michelin Green
Guide to Britain* (£9.25; Green Guide just for London also available), the Britain road atlas (£10), and Ordnance Survey maps
for areas you'll be exploring by car. The tourist office has a
travel agency upstairs plus computers displaying only their
Web site: www.visitbritain.com.

Nearby you'll find the **Scottish Tourist Centre** (mid-June–
mid-Sept Mon–Fri 9:00–18:00, Sat 10:00–17:00, off-season Mon–
Fri 9:30–17:30, Sat 12:00–16:00, Cockspur Street, tel. 0131/472-
2035, www.visitscotland.com) and the slick **French National
Tourist Office** (Mon–Fri 10:00–18:00, Sat until 17:00, closed
Sun, 178 Piccadilly Street).

Unfortunately, **London's Tourist Information Centres**
are now owned by the big hotels' exchange bureaus and are simply
businesses selling advertising space to companies with fliers to dis-
tribute. They are reasonably helpful but biased. Locations include
Heathrow Airport's tube station, which serves Terminals 1, 2, and
3 (daily 8:00–18:00, most convenient and least crowded); Victoria
Station (daily 8:00–20:00, crowded and commercial); and Waterloo International Terminal Arrivals Hall (daily 8:30–22:30, serving
trains from Paris; if you arrive by train when the TI is mobbed,
skip it, buy city map at newsstand upstairs in station lobby, then
return downstairs to catch the tube or a taxi to your hotel).

Bring your itinerary and a checklist of questions to any of
the TIs and pick up these publications: *London Planner* (a great

## It's Party Time Again

It's been two years since the big millennium bash, so it's about time for another party.

In 2002 Britain hosts a Golden Jubilee Celebration to commemorate the 50-year reign of Queen Elizabeth. You can expect festivities throughout the U.K. as the queen makes her rounds from May through July. The biggest party is in London from June 1 through 4, with concerts at Buckingham Palace (classical on June 1, pop on June 3—when the queen rocks), bell-ringing across the U.K. (June 2), fireworks (June 3), and a Procession to St. Paul's plus a Carnival Pageant (June 4). In honor of the queen's reign, a new covered Jubilee Bridge will cross the Thames, to the delight of pedestrians frustrated by the wobbly Millennium Bridge. This new bridge (attached to the Cannon Railway Bridge between Southwark and London Bridges) does what the Millennium Bridge was supposed to do—it provides a pedestrian-friendly way to connect North and South Bank sights. As part of the Jubilee celebration, a London String of Pearls festival (www.stringofpearls.org.uk) showcases sights all along the Thames, with exhibitions, tours, and performances through-out the summer. Britain knows how to throw a royal party. For your invitation, see www.goldenjubilee.gov.uk.

free monthly that lists all the sights, events, and hours), walking-tour schedule fliers, a theater guide, Central London bus guide, and the Thames River Services brochure.

TIs sell BT phone cards, long-distance bus tickets and passes, British Heritage Passes, and tickets to plays (20 percent booking fee). And they book rooms (avoid their £5 booking fee by calling hotels directy).

The **London Pass** gives free entrance to most of the city's sights, but—especially with many museums lowering or eliminating their entrance fees in 2002 and with the cluttery decisions a pass adds to your trip (should I go here, there, or everywhere...?)—it's worthwhile only for torrid sightseers (£18/1 day, £27/2 days, £32/3 days, £43/6 days). London does have many mildly interesting sights worth a quick look but perhaps not their steep £6 admission fee. With the pass, you can just go crazy.

TIs also sell **"Fast Track" tickets** to some of London's attractions (at no extra cost), allowing you to skip the queue at the sights. They're worthwhile for places notorious for long ticket lines such as the Tower of London, London Eye Ferris wheel, and Madame Tussaud's Wax Museum.

## Helpful Hints

**U.S. Embassy:** 24 Grosvenor Square (for passport concerns, open Mon–Fri 08:30–11:30 plus Mon, Wed, Fri 14:00–16:00, tube: Bond Street, tel. 020/7499-9000).

**Theft Alert:** The Artful Dodger is alive and well in London. Be on guard, particularly when using public transportation and in places crowded with tourists. Tourists, considered naive and rich, are targeted. Over 7,500 handbags are stolen annually at Covent Garden alone. Thieves paw you so you don't feel the pickpocketing.

**Changing Money:** ATMs are the way to go. For changing traveler's checks, standard transaction fees at banks are £2 to £4. American Express offices offer a fair rate and change any brand of traveler's checks for no fee. Handy AmEx offices are at Heathrow's Terminal 4 tube station (daily 7:00–19:00) and near Piccadilly (June–Sept Mon–Fri 8:30–19:00, Sat 9:00–18:30, Sun 10:00–17:00; Oct–May Mon–Sat 9:00–17:30, Sun 10:00–17:00; 30 Haymarket, tel. 020/7484-9600). Marks & Spencer Department stores offer good rates with no fees.

Avoid changing money at exchange bureaus. Their latest scam: They advertise very good rates with a same-as-the-banks fee of 2 percent. But the fine print explains that the fee of 2 percent is for buying pounds. The fee for *selling* pounds is 9.5 percent. Ouch!

**What's Up:** For the best listing of what's happening (plays, movies, restaurants, concerts, exhibitions, protests, walking tours, shopping, and children's activities) and a look at the trendy London scene, pick up a current copy of *Time Out* (£2, www .timeout.co.uk) or *What's On* at any newsstand. The TI's free monthly *London Planner* lists sights, plays, and events at least as well. For a chatty, *People Magazine*–type Web site on London's entertainment, theater, restaurants, and news, visit www .thisislondon.com. For plays, try www.officiallondontheatre.co.uk.

**Sights:** There's talk of making most sights free of charge in 2002. Currently the British Museum, British Library, National Gallery, National Portrait Gallery, Tate Britain (British art), and Tate Modern (modern art), along with many other top London museums, are free—though special exhibitions cost extra.

Telephoning first to check hours and confirm plans, especially off-season when hours can shrink, is always smart.

**Internet Access:** The astonishing easyEverything offers up to 500 computers per store, 24 hours daily. Depending on demand, a mere £2 ticket buys anywhere from 80 minutes to six hours of computer time. The ticket is valid for four weeks and multiple visits at any of their five branches: Victoria Station (across from front of station, near taxis and buses, long lines), Trafalgar Square, Tottenham Court Road, Oxford Street, and Kensington High Street (www.easyEverything.com).

**Travel Bookstores:** Stanfords Travel Bookstore is good

and stocks current editions of my books at Covent Garden (12 Long Acre, tel. 020/7836-1321) and 156 Regent Street (tel. 020/7434-4744). There are two impressive Waterstones Bookstores: the biggest in Europe on Piccadilly and one on the corner of Trafalgar Square (next to Coffee Republic café, tel. 020/7839-4411).

**Travel Agency:** The student travel agency, USIT, across from Victoria Station, has great deals on flights for people of all ages (Mon–Fri 9:00–18:00, Sat 10:00–17:00, Sun 11:00–15:00, Buckingham Palace Road, tel. 020/7823-5363, www.usitcampus .co.uk). Also, take a look in the Sunday *Times* travel section for cheap flights.

**Beatles:** Fans of the still-Fabulous Four can take one of the Beatles walks (5/week, offered by Original London Walks, under "Tours of London," below), visit the Beatles Shop (231 Baker Street, next to Sherlock Holmes Museum, tube: Baker Street), or go to Abbey Road and walk the famous crosswalk (at intersection with Grove End, tube: St. John's Wood).

**Luggage Lockers:** Victoria Station has a huge room full of lockers (3 sizes: £4, £5, and £8/24 hrs, daily 7:00–22:15, up ramp behind platform 8). The airports also have places to check bags. If leaving London and returning later, it may be possible to leave a box or bag at your hotel for free—assuming you'll be staying there again.

## Arrival in London

**By Train:** London has eight train stations, all connected by the tube (subway) and all with exchange offices and luggage storage. From any station, ride the tube or taxi to your hotel.

**By Bus:** The bus station is one block southwest of Victoria Station, which has a TI and tube entrance.

**By Plane:** For detailed information on getting from London's airports to downtown London, see "Transportation Connections" at the end of this chapter.

## Getting Around London

London's taxis, buses, and subway system make a private car unnecessary. To travel smart in a city this size, you must get comfortable with public transportation. For tube and bus information 24 hours a day, call 020/7222-1234 (www.transportforlondon.gov.uk).

**By Taxi:** London is the best taxi town in Europe. Big, black, carefully-regulated cabs are everywhere. I never met a crabby cabbie in London. They love to talk and know every nook and cranny in town. I ride in one a day just to get my London questions answered. Rides start at £1.50 and cost about £1.50 per tube stop. Connecting downtown sights is quick and easy and will cost you about £4 (e.g., St. Paul's to the Tower of London). For a short ride, three people in a cab travel at tube prices. Groups of four or five should taxi everywhere (though families save money, if not

# London

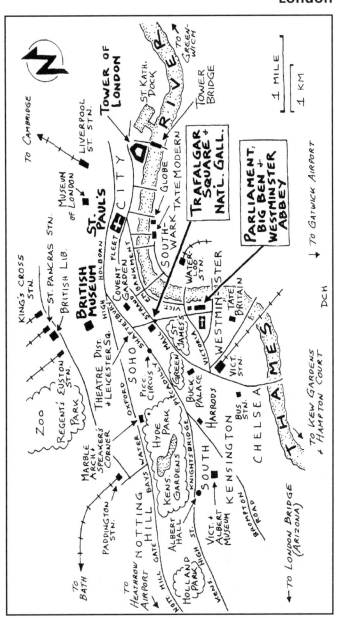

time, with the "One Day Family Travel Card" sold at tube stops). If a cab's top light is on, just wave it down. (Drivers flash lights when they see you.) They have a tiny turning radius, so you can wave at cabs going in either direction. If waving doesn't work, ask someone where you can find a taxi stand. While telephoning a cab gets one in minutes, it's generally not necessary and adds to the cost. London is such a great wave-'em-down taxi town that most cabs don't even have a radio phone. Don't worry about meter cheating. British cab meters come with a sealed computer chip and clock that ensures you'll get the regular tariff #1 most of the time, tariff #2 during "unsociable hours" (18:00–06:00 and Sat–Sun), and tariff #3 only on holidays. All extra charges are explained in writing on the cab wall. The only way a cabbie can cheat you is by taking a needlessly long route. There are alternative cab companies driving normal-looking, non-metered cars that charge fixed rates based on postal codes of your start and end points. These are generally honest and can actually be cheaper when snarled traffic drives up the cost of a metered cab.

**By Bus:** London's extensive bus system is easy to follow. Just pick up a free "Central London Bus Guide" map from a TI or tube station. Signs at stops list routes clearly. There are two kinds of buses. Those without a conductor (pay the driver as you enter) and those with a conductor (just hop on, take a seat, relax, and sooner or later the conductor will come by and collect £1). Any ride in downtown London costs £1. (The best views are upstairs.) If you have a Travel Card (see below), get in the habit of hopping buses for quick little straight shots, even just to get to a metro stop. During bump-and-grind rush hours (8:00–10:00 and 16:00–19:00), you'll go faster by tube. Consider two special bus deals: all day for £2 and a ticket six-pack for £4.

**By Tube:** London's subway is one of this planet's great people movers and the fastest—and cheapest—long-distance transport in town (runs daily about 05:00–24:00). Any ride in the Central Zone (on or within the Circle Line, including virtually all my recommended sights and hotels) costs £1.50. You can avoid ticket-window lines in tube stations by buying tickets from coin-op machines; practice on the punchboard to see how the system works (hit "adult single" and your destination). Again, nearly every ride will be £1.50. (These tickets are valid only on the day of purchase.) Beware: Overshooting your zone nets you a £10 fine.

Most city maps include a tube map with color-coded lines and names (free at any station window). Each line has a name (such as Circle, Northern, or Bakerloo) and two directions (indicated by end stop). In stations you'll have a choice of two platforms per line. Navigate by signs leading to the platforms (usually labeled north, south, east, or west) that clearly list the stops served by each line, or ask a local or a blue-vested staff person for help.

All city maps have north on top. If you know which general direction you're heading, tube navigation suddenly becomes easier. Some tracks are shared by several lines, and electronic signboards announce which train is next and the minutes remaining until various arrivals. Each train has its final destination or line name above its windshield. Depending on the particular line, trains run roughly every 3 to 10 minutes. Bring something to do to make your wait productive. The system is fraught with construction delays and breakdowns (pay attention to signs and announcements explaining necessary detours, etc). The Circle Line is notorious for problems. And always...mind the gap.

You can't leave the system without feeding your ticket to the turnstile. Save time by choosing the best street exit (look at the maps on the walls or ask any station personnel). "Subway" means pedestrian underpass in "English."

**London Tube and Bus Passes:** Consider using these passes, valid on both the tube and buses (all passes are available for more zones and are purchased as easily as a normal ticket at any station):

One-Day passes: If you figure you'll take three rides in a day, a day pass is a good deal. The "One Day Travel Card," covering Zones 1 and 2, gives you unlimited travel for a day, starting after 9:30 and anytime on weekends, for £4. The all-zone version of this card costs £4.90 (and includes Heathrow Airport). The "One Day LT Card," covering Zones 1 and 2 with no time restriction, costs £5.10. Families save with the "One Day Family Travel Card" (price varies depending on number in family).

Weekend pass: The "Weekend Travel Card," which covers Saturday, Sunday, and Zones 1 and 2 for £6, costs 25 percent less than two one-day cards.

Seven-day pass: The "7-Day Travel Card" costs £19, covers Zones 1 and 2, and requires a passport-type photo (cut one out of any snapshot and bring it from home). If you have no photo, the TI at Heathrow Airport sells a similar "Visitor's Card" for about the same price without requiring a photo.

Ten rides: If you want to travel a little each day or if you're part of a group, an £11.50 "carnet" is a great deal: You get 10 separate tickets for tube travel in Zone 1 (£1.15 per ride rather than £1.50). Wait for the machine to lay all 10 tickets. Groups of 10 or more can travel all day on the tube for £3 each (not on buses).

## Tours of London

▲▲▲**Hop-on Hop-off Double-Decker Bus Tours**—Two competitive companies ("Original" and "Big Bus") offer essentially the same tours with buses that have live (English-only) guides as well as some marked buses with a tape-recorded, dial-a-language narration. This two-hour, once-over-lightly bus tour drives by all the famous sights, providing a stressless way to get your bearings and at least see the biggies. You can sit back and enjoy the entire two-hour orientation tour (a good idea if you like the guide and the weather) or "hop-on and hop-off" at any of the nearly 30 stops and catch a later bus. Buses run about every 10 to 15 minutes in summer, every 20 minutes in winter. It's an inexpensive form of transport as well as an informative tour. Grab one of the maps from a TI and study it. Buses run daily (from about 9:00 until early evening in summer, until late afternoon in winter) and stop at Victoria Street (1 block north of Victoria Station), Marble Arch, Piccadilly Circus, Trafalgar Square, and elsewhere.

Each company offers a core two-hour overview tour, two other routes, and a narrated Thames boat tour covered by the same ticket (buy ticket from driver, credit cards are accepted at major stops such as Victoria Station, ticket good for 24 hrs, bring a sweater and extra film). Note: If you start at Victoria at 9:00, you'll finish near Buckingham Palace in time to see the Changing of the Guard (at 11:30); ask your driver for the best place to hop off. Sunday morning—when the traffic is light and many museums are closed—is a fine time for a tour. The last full loop leaves Victoria at 18:00. Both companies have entertaining and boring guides. The narration is important. If you don't like your guide, jump off and find another. If you like your guide, settle in for the entire loop.

**Original London Sightseeing Bus Tour:** Live guided buses have a Union Jack flag and a yellow triangle on the front of the bus. If the front has many flags or a green triangle, it's a tape-recorded multilingual tour—avoid it, unless you have kids who'd enjoy the entertaining recorded kids' tour (£14, £2.50 discount with this book—limit 2 discounts per book, they'll rip off the corner of this page—raise bloody hell if they don't honor this discount, ticket good for 24 hrs, tel. 020/8877-1722). Your ticket includes a 50-minute-long circular boat tour from the London Eye (2/hr until 22:00, tape-recorded narration).

**Big Bus Hop-on Hop-off London Tours:** These are also good. For £15 you get the same basic tour plus coupons for four different one-hour London walks and the scenic and usually entertainingly guided Thames boat ride (normally £5) between Westminster Pier and the Tower of London. The pass and extras are valid for 24 hours. Buses with live guides are marked in front with a picture of a blue bus; buses with tape-recorded spiels display a picture of a yellow bus and headphones. While the price is steeper, Big Bus guides seem more dynamic than the Original guides (office a block from Victoria Station at 48 Buckingham Palace Road, daily 8:30–17:30, tel. 020/7233-9533, www.bigbus.co.uk).

**At Night:** The London by Night Sightseeing Tour runs basically the same circuit as the other companies after hours. While the narration is pretty lame (the driver does little more than call out the names of famous places as you roll by), the views at twilight are grand (£9, pay driver or buy tickets at Victoria Station TI, April–Oct, 2-hr tour with live guide, can hop on and off, departs at 20:00, 21:00, and 22:00 from Victoria Station, Taxi Road, at front of station near end of Wilton Road, tel. 020/8646-1747).

▲▲**Walking Tours**—Many times a day top-notch local guides lead (often big) groups through specific slices of London's past. Schedule fliers litter the desks of TIs, hotels, and pubs. *Time Out* lists many but not all scheduled walks. Simply show up at the announced location, pay £5, and enjoy two chatty hours of Dickens, the Plague, Shakespeare, Legal London, the Beatles, Jack the Ripper, or whatever is on the agenda. Original London Walks, the dominant company, lists their extensive daily schedule in a beefy, plain black-and-white *The Original London Walks* brochure. They also run Explorer daytrips, a good option for those with limited time and transportation (different trip daily: Stonehenge/Salisbury, Oxford/Cotswolds, York, Bath, and so on; walks offered year-round—even Christmas, get schedule at hotel or TI, private tours for £80, tel. 020/7624-3978, www.walks.com).

Standard rates for London's registered guides are £85 for four hours, £136 for eight hours (tel. 020/7403-2962, www.touristguides.org.uk). Robina Brown leads tours with small groups in her Toyota Previa (£185/3 hrs, £270–400/day, tel. 020/7228-2238, e-mail: robina.brown@which.net). Brit Lonsdale, an energetic mother of twins, is another registered London guide (tel. 020/7386-9907). Chris Salaman is a clearinghouse for guides who do specialty tours (just dream up a topic: industrial, famous London women, you name it) and tours of London's characteristic boroughs for a low rate (£40/group for a private 2-hr tour, tel. 020/8672-1270).

▲▲**Cruise the Thames**—Boat tours with entertaining commentaries sail regularly from **Westminster Pier** (at the base of Westminster Bridge under Big Ben). You can cruise to the **Tower of London** (£5—included with Big Bus London tour, £6 round-trip, daily 9:00–21:00, until 15:45 Nov–March, 2/hr, 30 min, tel. 020/7930-9033); **Greenwich** (£6.30, £7.60 round-trip, 10:00–17:00, 2/hr, 1 hr, likely narrated only downstream, tel. 020/7930-4097); and **Kew Gardens** (£7, £11 round-trip, 5/day, generally departing 10:00–14:00, 90 min, 30 min narrated, some boats continue on to **Hampton Court** for extra £3, tel. 020/7930-2062). For pleasure and efficiency, consider combining a one-way cruise with a tube ride back. Fifty minute round-trip cruises leave regularly from the London Eye (included with Original London Bus tickets—see above).

**Frog Tours**—A bright-yellow amphibious vehicle takes you streetside past some famous sights (Big Ben, Buckingham Palace, Piccadilly Circus), then splashes into the Thames for a 30-minute cruise (£15, daily 10:00–18:00, 80 min, live commentary, these book up in advance, departs from County Hall near London Eye Ferris Wheel, tube: Waterloo or Westminster, tel. 020/7928-3132, www.frogtours.com).

## Sights—From Westminster Abbey to Trafalgar Square

▲▲**Westminster Walk**—Just about every visitor to London strolls the historic Whitehall boulevard from Big Ben to Trafalgar Square. Beneath London's modern traffic and big-city bustle lies 2,000 fascinating years of history. This three-quarter-mile, self-guided orientation walk (see map on page 46) gives you a whirl-wind tour and connects the sights listed in this section.

Start halfway across **Westminster Bridge** (#1 on map) for that "Wow, I'm really in London!" feeling. Get a close-up view of the **Houses of Parliament** and **Big Ben** (floodlit at night). Downstream you'll see the **London Eye Ferris wheel**. Down the stairs are boats to the Tower of London and Greenwich.

En route to Parliament Square, you'll pass a statue of **Boadicea** (#2), the Celtic queen defeated by Roman invaders in A.D. 60.

To thrill your loved ones (or bug the envious), call home from a pay phone near Big Ben at about three minutes before the hour. You'll find a phone on Great George Street, across from Parliament Square. As Big Ben chimes, stick the receiver outside the booth and prove you're in London: Ding dong ding dong... dong ding ding dong.

Wave hello to Churchill in Parliament Square (#3). To his right is **Westminster Abbey** with its two stubby, elegant towers.

Walk north up Parliament Street (which turns into White-hall) toward Trafalgar Square. You'll see the thought-provoking **Cenotaph** (#5) in the middle of the street, reminding passersby of Britain's many war dead. To visit the Cabinet War Rooms (see "Sights," below) take a left before the Cenotaph, on King Charles Street (#4).

Continuing on Whitehall, stop at the barricaded and guarded little **10 Downing Street** to see the British "White House" (#6), home of the prime minister. Break the bobby's boredom and ask him a question.

Nearing Trafalgar Square, look for the **Horse Guards** behind the gated fence (11:00 inspection Mon–Sat, 10:00 on Sun; dismounting ceremony daily at 16:00) and the 17th-century **Banqueting House** across the street (#7; see "Sights," below).

The column topped by Lord Nelson marks **Trafalgar Square** (#8). The stately domed building on the far side of the square is the **National Gallery** (free), which has a classy café (upstairs in the Sainsbury wing). To the right of the National Gallery is **St. Martin-in-the-Fields Church** and its Café in the Crypt.

To get to Piccadilly from Trafalgar Square, walk up

## Westminster Walk

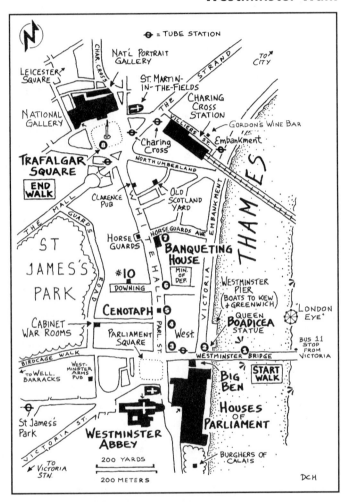

⊖ = TUBE STATION

N

LEICESTER SQUARE

NAT'L PORTRAIT GALLERY

CHAR. CROSS

ST. MARTIN-IN-THE-FIELDS

THE STRAND

TO CITY

NATIONAL GALLERY

CHARING CROSS STATION

VILLIERS ST.

GORDON'S WINE BAR

Charing Cross

Embankment

TRAFALGAR SQUARE

NORTHUMBERLAND

THAMES

END WALK

CLARENCE PUB

OLD SCOTLAND YARD

EMBANKMENT

THE MALL

GUARDS ROAD

HORSE GUARDS AVE

ST JAMES'S PARK

HORSE GUARDS

BANQUETING HOUSE

MIN. OF DEF.

#10 DOWNING

THE MALL

WESTMINSTER PIER (BOATS TO KEW & GREENWICH)

LONDON EYE

CABINET WAR ROOMS

CENOTAPH

PARL. ST.

VICTORIA

QUEEN BOADICEA STATUE

BIRDCAGE WALK

TO WELL. BARRACKS

PARLIAMENT SQUARE

WEST.

BUS 11 STOP FROM VICTORIA

WESTMINSTER BRIDGE

WEST-MINSTER ARMS PUB

START WALK

St James's Park

VICTORIA ST.

BIG BEN

HOUSES OF PARLIAMENT

TO VICTORIA STN.

WESTMINSTER ABBEY

200 YARDS

200 METERS

BURGHERS OF CALAIS

DCH

Cockspur Street to Haymarket, then take a short left on Coventry
Street to colorful **Piccadilly Circus**.

Near Piccadilly you'll find the **Britain Visitors Centre** and
piles of theaters. **Leicester Square** (with its half-price ticket
booth for plays) thrives just a few blocks away. Walk through
seedy **Soho** (north of Shaftesbury Avenue) for its fun pubs
(see "Eating," below, for "Food is Fun" Dinner Crawl). From
Piccadilly or Oxford Circus, you can taxi, bus, or tube home.

▲▲▲**Westminster Abbey**—As the greatest church in the English-speaking world, Westminster Abbey has been the place where England's kings and queens have been crowned and buried since 1066. A thousand years of English history—3,000 tombs, the remains of 29 kings and queens, and hundreds of memorials—lie within its walls and under its stone slabs. Like a stony refugee camp huddled outside St. Peter's gates, this place has a story to tell and the best way to enjoy it is with a **tour** (audioguide-£2, live-£3; many prefer the audioguide because it's self-paced, both tours include entry to cloister museums). Experience an **evensong** service—awesome in a nearly-empty church (weekdays except Wed at 17:00, Sat–Sun at 15:00). The free **organ recital** on Sunday is another highlight (17:45, 40 min). Organ concerts here are great and inexpensive; look for signs with schedule details.

Enter on the Big Ben side (often with a sizable line, visit early to avoid crowds) and then follow a one-way route through this English hall of fame around the church and cloisters (with the 3 small museums), back through the nave, and out (£6 for abbey entry, Mon–Fri 9:15-16:45, Wed also 18:00–19:45, Sat 9:30–14:45, last admission 1 hr before closing, photography prohibited, closed on Sun except for worship, coffee in cloister, tube: Westminster or St. James' Park, call for tour schedule, tel. 020/7222-7110). Since the church is often closed to the public for special services, it's wise to call first.

Three tiny **museums** ring the cloister (£1 covers all, on top of your abbey ticket; or free with either the audioguide or live tour): the Chapter House (where the monks held their daily meetings, notable for its fine architecture and well-described but faded medieval art), the Pyx Chamber (containing an exhibit on the king's treasury), and the Abbey Museum (which tells of the abbey's history, royal coronations, and burials). Look into the impressively realistic eyes of Henry VII's funeral effigy (one of a fascinating series of wax-and-wood statues that, for three centuries, graced royal coffins during funeral processions).

For a free peek inside and a quiet sit in the nave, you can tell a guard at the west end (where the tourists exit) that you'd like to pay your respects to Britain's Unknown Soldier.

▲▲**Houses of Parliament (Palace of Westminster)**—This neo-Gothic icon of London, the royal residence from 1042 to 1547, is now the meeting place of the legislative branch of government. Tourists are welcome to view debates in either the bickering House of Commons or the genteel House of Lords (when in session—indicated by a flag flying atop the Victoria Tower). While the actual action is generally extremely dull, it is a thrill to be inside and see the British government inaction (House of Commons: Mon–Wed 14:30–22:30, Thu 11:30–19:30, Fri 9:30–15:00, generally less action and no lines after 18:00, use

St. Stephen's entrance, tube: Westminster, tel. 020/7219-4272 for schedule, www.parliament.uk). The House of Lords has more pageantry, shorter lines, and less-interesting debates (Mon–Wed 14:30 until they finish, Thu from 15:00 on, sometimes Fri from 11:00 on, tel. 020/7219-3107 for schedule). If confronted with a too-long House of Commons line, see the House of Lords first. Once you've seen the Lords (hide your HOL flier), you can often slip directly to the House of Commons and join the gang waiting in the lobby. If there's only one line outside, it's for the House of Commons. Go to the gate and tell the guard you want the Lords. You may pop right in.

After passing security, slip to the left and study the big dark **Westminster Hall**, which survived the 1834 fire. The hall is from the 11th century, and its famous self-supporting hammer-beam roof was added in 1397. The Houses of Parliament are located in what was once the Palace of Westminster, long the palace of England's medieval kings, until it was largely destroyed by fire in 1834. The palace was rebuilt in Victorian Gothic style (a move away from neoclassicism back to England's Christian and medieval heritage, true to the Romantic Age). It was completed in 1860.

**Houses of Parliament tours** are given in August and September (£3.50, Mon, Fri, Sat 9:15–16:30, Tue–Thu 13:15–16:30, 75 min). Meet your Blue Badge guide (at the Sovereign's Entrance—far south end) for a behind-the-scenes peek at the royal chambers and both the House of Commons and House of Lords. Tickets are sold at the Westminster Hall ticket booth (Mon–Sat 8:45-13:00, closed Sun, or tel. 020/7344-9966).

The **Jewel Tower** is (along with Westminster Hall) all that survives of the old Palace of Westminster. It contains a fine little exhibit on Parliament: first floor—history; second floor—Parliament today, with a 25-minute video and lonely picnic-friendly benches (£1.60, daily April–Sept 10:00–18:00, Oct 10:00–17:00, Nov–March 10:00–16:00, across street from St. Stephens Gate, tel. 020/7222-2219).

**Big Ben**, the clock tower (315 feet high), is named for its 13-ton bell, Ben. The light above the clock is lit when the House of Commons is sitting. The face of the clock is huge—you can actually see the minute hand moving. For a hip HOP view, walk halfway over Westminster Bridge.

▲▲**Cabinet War Rooms**—This is a fascinating walk through the underground headquarters of the British government's fight against the Nazis in the darkest days of the Battle for Britain. The 21-room nerve center of the British war effort was used from 1939 to 1945. Churchill's room, the map room, and other rooms are just as they were in 1945. For all the blood, sweat, toil, and tears details, pick up an audioguide at the entry and follow the included and excellent 45-minute tour; be patient—it's worth it (£5, daily

April–Oct 9:30–18:00, Nov–March 10:00–18:00, last entry 45 min before closing, on King Charles Street 200 yards off Whitehall, follow the signs, tube: Westminster, tel. 020/7930-6961). For a nearby pub lunch, try Westminster Arms (food served downstairs, on Storey's Gate, a couple blocks south of War Rooms).

**Horse Guards**—The Horse Guards are inspected daily at 11:00 (10:00 on Sun), and there's a colorful dismounting ceremony daily at 16:00. The rest of the day they just stand there—terrible for camcorders (on Whitehall, between Trafalgar Square and #10 Downing Street, tube: Westminster). While Buckingham Palace pageantry is canceled when it rains, the horse guards change regardless of the weather.

▲**Banqueting House**—England's first Renaissance building was designed by Inigo Jones around 1620. It's one of the few London landmarks spared by the 1666 fire and the only surviving part of the original Palace of Whitehall. Don't miss its Rubens ceiling, which, at Charles I's request, drove home the doctrine of the legitimacy of the divine right of kings. In 1649—divine right ignored—Charles I was beheaded on the balcony of this building by a Cromwellian parliament. Admission includes a restful 20-minute audiovisual history, which shows the place in banqueting action; a 30-minute tape-recorded tour—interesting only to history buffs; and a look at an exquisite banqueting hall (£3.90, Mon–Sat 10:00–17:00, closed Sun, last entry at 16:30, subject to closure for government functions, aristocratic WC, immediately across Whitehall from the Horse Guards, tube: Westminster, tel. 020/7930-4179). Just up the street is Trafalgar Square.

## Sights—Trafalgar Square

▲▲**Trafalgar Square**—London's central square is a thrilling place to just hang out. Lord Nelson stands atop his 185-foot-tall fluted granite column, gazing out to Trafalgar (off Spain's southern coast), where he lost his life but defeated the French fleet. Part of this 1842 memorial is made from the melted-down cannons of his victims at Trafalgar. He's surrounded by giant lions, hordes of people, and—until recently—even more pigeons. London's new mayor, nicknamed "Red Ken" for his passion for an activist government, decided that London's "flying rats" were a public nuisance and evicted the venerable seed salesmen. This high-profile square is the climax of most marches and demonstrations (tube: Charing Cross).

▲▲▲**National Gallery**—Displaying Britain's top collection of European paintings from 1250 to 1900 (works by Leonardo, Botticelli, Velázquez, Rembrandt, Turner, van Gogh, and the Impressionists), this is one of Europe's great galleries. While the collection is huge, following the 30-stop route suggested on the map on page 50 will give you my best quick visit.

# National Gallery Highlights

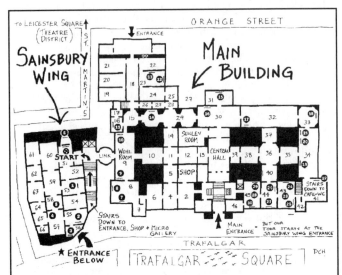

**Medieval and Early Renaissance**
1. Wilton Diptych
2. UCCELLO—Battle of San Romano
3. VAN EYCK—Arnolfini Marriage
4. CRIVELLI—Annunciation with St. Emidius
5. BOTTICELLI—Venus and Mars

**High Renaissance**
6. LEONARDO DA VINCI— Virgin and Child (painting and cartoon)
7. MICHELANGELO—Entombment
8. RAPHAEL—Pope Julius II

**Venetian Renaissance**
9. TITIAN—Bacchus and Ariadne
10. TINTORETTO —Origin of the Milky Way

**Northern Protestant Art**
11. VERMEER—Young Woman
12. REMBRANDT—Belshazzar's Feast
13. REMBRANDT—Self-Portrait

**Baroque and Rococo**
14. RUBENS—The Judgment of Paris
15. VAN DYCK—Charles I on Horseback

16. VELÁZQUEZ—The Rokeby Venus
17. CARAVAGGIO—Supper at Emmaus
18. BOUCHER—Pan and Syrinx

**British**
19. CONSTABLE—The Hay Wain
20. TURNER—The Fighting Téméraire
21. TURNER—Rain, Steam, Speed
22. DELAROCHE—The Execution of Lady Jane Grey

**Impressionism and Beyond**
23. MONET—Gare St. Lazare
24. MONET—The Water Lily Pond
25. MANET—The Waitress (La Servante de Bocks)
26. RENOIR— Boating on the Seine
27. SEURAT—Bathers at Asnières
28. DEGAS—Miss La La at the Cirque Fernando
29. VAN GOGH—Sunflowers
30. CÉZANNE—Bathers

The audioguide tours are the best I've used in Europe (entirely voluntary £4 donation requested). Don't miss the "Micro Gallery," a computer room even your dad could have fun in (closes 30 min earlier than museum); you can study any artist, style, or topic in the museum and even print out a tailor-made tour map (free, daily 10:00–18:00, likely Thu–Sat until 21:00 in 2002, free 1-hr overview tours daily at 11:30 and 14:30 plus Wed at 18:30, photography prohibited, on Trafalgar Square, tube: Charing Cross or Leicester Square, tel. 020/7747-2885).

▲▲**National Portrait Gallery**—Put off by halls of 19th-century characters who meant nothing to me, I used to call this "as interesting as someone else's yearbook." But a selective walk through this 500-year-long Who's Who of British history is quick and free and puts faces on the story of England. A bonus is the chance to admire some great art by painters such as Holbein, Van Dyck, Hogarth, Reynolds, and Gainsborough. The collection is well described, not huge, and in historical sequence, from the 16th century on the second floor to today's royal family on the ground floor.

Some **highlights**: Henry VIII and wives; several fascinating portraits of the "Virgin Queen" Elizabeth I, Sir Francis Drake, and Sir Walter Raleigh; the only real-life portrait of Shakespeare; Oliver Cromwell and Charles I with his head on; self-portraits and other portraits by Gainsborough and Reynolds; the Romantics (Blake, Byron, Wordsworth, and company); Queen Victoria and her era; and the present royal family, including the late Princess Diana.

The excellent audioguide tours (£3 donation requested) describe each room (or era in British history) and more than 300 paintings. You'll learn more about British history than art and actually hear interviews with 20th-century subjects as you stare at their faces (free, daily 10:00–18:00, Thu–Fri until 21:00, entry 100 yards off Trafalgar Square, around corner from National Gallery, opposite Church of St. Martin-in-the-Fields, tel. 020/7306-0055, www.npg.org.uk). The elegant Portrait Restaurant on the top floor comes with views and high prices (cheaper Potrait café in basement).

▲**St. Martin-in-the-Fields**—This church, built in the 1720s, with a Gothic spire placed upon a Greek-type temple, is an oasis of peace on the wild and noisy Trafalgar Square. St. Martin cared for the poor. "In the fields" was where the first church stood on this spot (in the 13th century), between Westminster and the city. Stepping inside, you still feel a compassion for the needs of the people in this community. A free flier provides a brief yet worthwhile self-guided tour. The church is famous for its concerts. Consider a free lunchtime concert (Mon, Tue, and Fri at 13:05) or an evening concert (£6–16, Thu–Sat at 19:30, CC, box office tel. 020/7839-8362, church tel. 020/7766-1100). Downstairs you'll find a ticket office for concerts, a good shop, a brass-rubbing center, and a fine support-the-church cafeteria (see "Eating," below).

## London's Top Squares

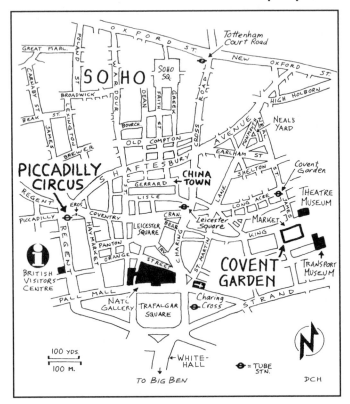

## More Top Squares: Piccadilly, Soho, and Covent Garden

▲▲**Piccadilly Circus**—London's most touristy square got its name from the fancy ruffled shirts—*picadils*—made in the neighborhood long ago. Today the square is surrounded by fascinating streets and is swimming with youth on the rampage. The **Rock Circus** offers a gimmicky history of rock music with Madame Tussaud wax stars. While overpriced, it's an entertaining hour for wealthy rock 'n' roll romantics (£8.25, daily 10:00–17:30, plenty of photo ops, tube: Piccadilly Circus, tel. 020/7734-7203). For overstimulation, drop by the extremely trashy **Pepsi Trocadero Center**'s "theme park of the future" for its Segaworld virtual-reality games, nine-screen cinema, and thundering IMAX theater (admission to Trocadero is free; individual attractions cost £2–8; find a discount ticket at brochure racks at TI or hotels before paying full price for IMAX; between Coventry and Shaftesbury, just off Piccadilly). Chinatown, to the east, has swollen since Hong Kong lost its independence. Nearby Shaftesbury Avenue and Leicester Square teem with fun seekers, theaters, Chinese restaurants, and street singers.

**Soho**—North of Piccadilly, seedy Soho is becoming trendy and is well worth a gawk. Soho is London's red-light district, where "friendly models" wait in tiny rooms up dreary stairways and voluptuous con artists sell strip shows. While venturing up a stairway to check out a model is interesting, anyone who goes into any one of the shows will be ripped off. Every time. Even a £5 show in a "licensed bar" comes with a £100 cover or minimum (as it's printed on the drink menu) and a "security man." You may accidentally buy a £200 bottle of bubbly. And suddenly, the door has no handle. By the way, telephone sex is hard to avoid these days in London. Phone booths are littered with racy fliers of busty ladies "new in town." Some travelers gather six or eight phone booths' worth of fliers and take them home for kinky wallpaper.

▲▲**Covent Garden**—This boutique-ish shopping district is a people watcher's delight with cigarette eaters, Punch-and-Judy acts, food that's good for you (but not your wallet), trendy crafts, sweet whiffs of marijuana, two-tone hair (neither natural), and faces that could set off a metal detector (tube: Covent Garden). For better Covent Garden lunch deals, walk a block or two away from the eye of this touristic hurricane (check out the places a block or two north of the tube station along Endell and Neal Streets).

## Museums near Covent Garden

▲▲**Somerset House**—Just opened to the public, this grand 18th-century civic palace provides Londoners with a marvelous new public space and riverside terrace (between the Strand and the Thames). The palace, which once housed the national registry that records Britain's births, marriages, and deaths ("where they hatched 'em, latched 'em, and dispatched 'em"), now houses three collections of fine art. Step into the courtyard to enjoy the fountain. Go ahead...walk through it; the 55 jets get playful twice an hour. Surrounding you are three small and sumptuous sights: the Courtauld Gallery (paintings), Gilbert Collection (fine arts), and Hermitage Rooms (finest art of czarist Russia). All have the same hours (Mon–Sat 10:00–18:00, Sun 12:00–18:00, easy bus #6, #9, #11, #13, #15, or #23 from Trafalgar Square, tube: Temple or Covent Garden, tel. 020/7848-2526, www.somerset-house.org.uk). The Web site lists a busy schedule of tours, kids' events, and concerts. The riverside terrace is picnic-friendly (deli inside lobby).

**Courtauld Gallery**—While far less impressive than the National Gallery, this wonderful collection of paintings is a joy. The gallery is part of the Courtauld Institute of Art, and the thoughtful

## Central London

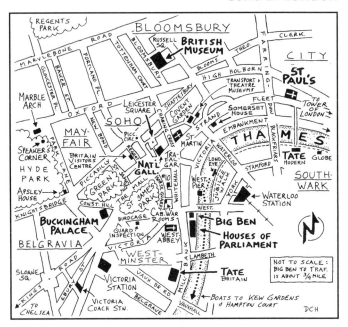

descriptions of each piece of art remind visitors that the gallery is still used for teaching. You'll see medieval European paintings, works by Rubens, Impressionists (Manet, Monet, Degas, Seurat), Post-Impressionists (such as Cézanne), and more (£4, free Mon 10:00–14:00).

The **Hermitage Rooms** offer a taste of Romanov imperial splendor. Since tourists are staying away from Russia because of its struggles, someone had the bright idea to send the best Russian art to London to raise some hard cash. These five rooms host a different collection each six months with a standard intro to the czar's winter palace in St. Petersburg (£6, includes great live video of the square, tel. 020/7420-9410). The excellent audioguide costs £3 . . . consider it charity for Russia.

The **Gilbert Collection** displays 800 pieces of the finest in European decorative arts, from gold, diamond-studded snuff boxes to intricate Italian mosaics. Maybe you've seen Raphael paintings and Botticelli frescoes, but this lush collection is refreshingly different (£4, includes free audioguide with a highlights tour and a kid-friendly family tour, free Mon 10:00–14:00).

▲**London Transport Museum**—This wonderful museum is a delight for kids. Whether you're cursing or marveling at the buses and tube, the growth of Europe's biggest city has been made possible by its public transit system. Watch the growth of the tube, then sit in the simulator to "drive" a train (£6, kids under 16 free, Sat–Thu 10:00–18:00, Fri 11:00–18:00, 30 yards southeast of Covent Garden's marketplace, tel. 020/7379-6344).

**Theatre Museum**—This earnest museum, probably worthwhile only for theater buffs, traces the development of British theater from Shakespeare to today (£4.50, kids under 16 free, Tue–Sun 10:00–18:00, closed Mon, call about guided tours, makeup demos, and costume workshops, a block east of Covent Garden's market-place down Russell Street, tel. 020/7943-4700).

## Sights—North London
**▲▲▲British Museum, Great Court, and Reading Room**— Simply put, this is the greatest chronicle of civilization... anywhere. A visit here is like taking a long hike through Encyclo-pedia Britannica National Park. Enjoy the museum's recent facelift: Entering on Great Russell Street, you'll step into the Great Court, the new glass-domed hub of a two-acre cultural complex, containing restaurants, shops, and lecture halls plus the just-reopened Round Reading Room.

The most popular sections of the museum fill the ground floor: Egyptian, Mesopotamian, and ancient Greek—with the famous Elgin Marbles from the Pantheon. Huge winged lions (which guarded Assyrian palaces 800 years before Christ) guard these great ancient galleries. For a brief tour, connect these ancient dots:

Start with the **Egyptian**. Wander from the Rosetta Stone past the many statues. At the end of the hall, climb the stairs to mummy land.

Back at the winged lions, wander through the dark, violent, and mysterious **Assyrian** rooms. The Nimrud Gallery is lined with royal propaganda reliefs and wounded lions.

The most modern of the ancient art fills the **Greek** section. Find room 11 behind the winged lions and start your walk through Greek art history with the simple and primitive Cycladic fertility figures. Later, painted vases show a culture really into partying. The finale is the Elgin Marbles. The much-wrangled-over bits of the Athenian Parthenon (from 450 B.C.) are even more impressive than they look. To best appreciate these ancient carvings, take the free audioguide tour (available in this gallery).

Be sure to venture upstairs to see artifacts from Roman Britain (room 50) that surpass anything you'll see at Hadrian's Wall or else-where in Britain. Nearby, the Dark Age Britain exhibits (especially the Sutton Hoo Ship Burial artifacts from a 7th-century royal burial on the east coast of England—room 41) offer a worthwhile peek at that bleak era. Room 90 contains a rare Michelangelo cartoon.

The British Museum is revving up for its 250th birthday in 2003. The immense yet empty King's Library (once the home of the treasures of the British Library—now housed elsewhere) lines the east side of the Great Court. The plan: restore it to its Regency splendor (1827), restock the shelves with the leather-bound volumes from the House of Commons Library, and fill the hall with a special exhibit featuring museums of the Enlightenment.

The newly opened **Queen Elizabeth II Great Court** is Europe's largest covered square—bigger than a football field. This people-friendly court—delightfully out of the London rain—was for 150 years one of London's great lost spaces...closed off and gathering dust. While the vast British Museum wraps around the court, its centerpiece is the stately **Reading Room**—famous as the place Karl Marx hung out while formulating his ideas on communism and writing *Das Kapital*. The Reading Room—one of the fine cast-iron buildings of the 19th century—is free to wander, but there's little to see that you can't see from the doorway.

The British Museum and the Reading Room are both free (£2 donation requested, daily 10:00–17:30, Thu–Fri until 20:30, least crowded weekday late afternoons, Great Russell Street, tube: Tottenham Court Road, tel. 020/7323-8000 or 020/7388-2227, www.thebritishmuseum.ac.uk). The museum offers three kinds of **tours** of its immense collection: Highlights (£7, 90 min), Focus (£5, 1 hr), and Eye Openers (free, nearly hrly, 50 min). For tour times, call ahead or check schedule and brochures at entry.

▲▲▲**British Library**—The British Empire built its greatest monuments out of paper. And it's in literature that England made her lasting contribution to civilization and the arts. Opened in 1998, Britain's national archives has more than 12 million books, 180 miles of shelving, and the deepest basement in London. But everything that matters for your visit is in one delightful room labeled "The Treasures." This room is filled with literary and historical documents that changed the course of history. You'll trace the evolution of European maps over 800 years. Follow the course of the Bible—from the earliest known gospels (written on scraps of papyrus) to the first complete Bible to the original King James version and the Gutenberg Bible. You'll see Leonardo's doodles, the Magna Carta, Shakespeare's First Folio, the original *Alice in Wonderland* in Lewis Carroll's handwriting, and manuscripts by Beethoven, Mozart, Lennon, and McCartney. Finish in the fascinating *Turning the Pages* exhibit, which lets you actually browse through virtual manuscripts of a few of these treasures on a computer (free, Mon–Fri 9:30–18:00, Tue until 20:00, Sat until 17:00, Sun 11:00–17:00; 1-hr tours for £5 usually offered Mon, Wed, and Fri–Sun at 15:00, also Tue 18:30, Sat 10:30, and Sun 11:30, tel. 020/7412-7332 to confirm schedule and reserve, tube: King's Cross, turn right out of station and walk a block to 96 Euston

Road, library tel. 020/7412-7000, www.bl.uk). The ground-floor café is next to a vast and fun pull-out stamp collection, and the cafeteria upstairs serves good hot meals.

▲**Madame Tussaud's Waxworks**—This is expensive but dang good. The original Madame Tussaud did wax casts of heads lopped off during the French Revolution (e.g., Marie Antoinette). She took her show on the road and ended up in London. And now it's much easier to be featured. The gallery is one big Who's Who photo-op—a huge hit with the kind of travelers who skip the British Museum. Don't miss the "make a model" exhibit (showing Jerry Hall getting waxed) or the gallery of has-been heads that no longer merit a body (such as Sammy Davis Jr. and Nikita Khruschev). After looking a hundred famous people in their glassy eyes and surviving a silly hall of horror, you'll board a Disney-type ride and cruise through a kid-pleasing "Spirit of London" time trip (£11.50, children-£8, under 5 free, Jan–Sept daily 9:00–17:30, Oct–Dec Mon–Fri 10:00–17:30, Sat–Sun 9:30–17:30, last entry 30 min before closing, Marylebone Road, tube: Baker Street; combined ticket for Tussaud's and Planetarium is £14 for adults, £9.50 for kids). The waxworks are popular. Avoid a wait by either booking ahead to get a ticket with an entry time (tel. 0870-400-3000, online at www.madame-tussaud.com, or any London TI) or arriving late in the day—90 minutes is plenty of time for the exhibit.

**Sir John Soane's Museum**—Architects and fans of eclectic knick-knacks love this quirky place (free, Tue–Sat 10:00–17:00, closed Sun–Mon, 5 blocks east of British Museum, tube: Holborn, 13 Lincoln's Inn Fields, tel. 020/7405-2107).

## Sights—Buckingham Palace

▲**Buckingham Palace**—This lavish home has been Britain's royal residence since 1837. When the queen's at home, the royal standard flies; otherwise the Union Jack flaps in the wind (£11 for state apartments and throne room, open early Aug–Sept only, daily 9:30–16:30, only 8,000 visitors a day—come early to get an appointed visit time or call 020/7321-2233 and reserve a ticket with CC, tube: Victoria).

**The Royal Mews**—Actually the queen's working stables, visitors can wander among stalls, talk to the horse-keeper, and see the well-groomed horses. Marvel at the gilded coaches paraded during royal festivals, see fancy horse gear—all well-described—and learn how skeptical the attendants were when the royals first parked a car in the stables (£5, Aug–Sept daily 10:30–16:30, Oct–July Mon–Thu 12:00–16:00, on Buckingham Palace Road, tel. 020/7839-1377).

▲▲**Changing of the Guard at Buckingham Palace**—The guards change with much fanfare at 11:30 daily April through August and generally every even-numbered day September through March (no band when wet; worth a 50p phone call any day to confirm that they'll change, tel. 090-505-452). Join the mob behind the palace (the front faces a huge and extremely private park). You'll need to be early or tall to see much of the actual changing of the guard, but for the pageantry in the street you can pop by at 11:30. Stake out the high ground on the circular Victoria Monument for the best general views. The marching troops and bands are colorful and even stirring, but the actual changing of the guard is a nonevent. It is interesting, however, to see nearly every tourist in London gathered in one place at the same time. Hop into a big black taxi and say, "Buck House, please." The show lasts about 30 minutes: Three troops parade by, the guard changes with much shouting, the band plays a happy little concert, and then they march out. On a balmy day, it's a fun happening.

For all the color with none of the crowds, see the **Inspection of the Guard Ceremony** at 11:00 in front of the **Wellington Barracks**, 500 yards east of the palace on Birdcage Walk. Afterward, stroll through nearby St. James' Park (tube: Victoria, St. James' Park, or Green Park).

## Sights—West London
▲**Hyde Park and Speakers' Corner**—London's "Central Park"—originally Henry VIII's hunting grounds—has more than 600 acres of lush greenery, a huge man-made lake, the royal Kensington Palace (not worth touring), and the ornate neo-Gothic Albert Memorial across from the Royal Albert Hall. Early afternoons on Sunday, Speakers' Corner offers soapbox oratory at its best (tube: Marble Arch). "The grass roots of democracy" is actually a holdover from when the gallows stood here, and the criminal was allowed to say just about anything he wanted to before he swung. I dare you to raise your voice and gather a crowd—it's easy to do.

▲**Apsley House (Wellington Museum)**—Having beaten Napoleon at Waterloo, the Duke of Wellington was the most famous man in Europe. He was given London's ultimate address, #1 London. His newly refurbished mansion offers one of London's best palace experiences. An 11-foot-tall marble statue (by Canova) of Napoleon clad only in a fig leaf greets you. Downstairs is a small gallery of Wellington memorabilia (including a pair of Wellington boots). The lavish upstairs shows off the duke's fine collection of paintings, including works by Velázquez and Steen (£4.50, Tue–Sun 11:00–17:00, closed Mon, well-described by included audioguide, 20 yards from Hyde Park Corner tube station, tel. 020/7499-5676). Hyde Park's pleasant and picnic-wonderful rose garden is nearby.

▲▲**Victoria and Albert Museum**—The world's top collection of decorative arts is a gangly (150 rooms over 12 miles of corridors) but surprisingly interesting assortment of artistic stuff from the West as well as Asian and Islamic cultures. The V & A, which

## West London

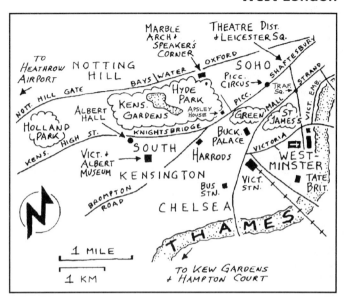

grew out of the Great Exhibition of 1851—that ultimate festival celebrating the Industrial Revolution and the greatness of Britain—was originally for manufactured art. But after much support from Queen Victoria and Prince Albert, it was renamed after the royal couple, and its present building was opened in 1909. The idealistic Victorian notion that anyone can be continually improved by education and example remains the driving force behind this museum.

While just wandering works well here, consider catching one of the free 60-minute orientation tours (daily, at :30 past each hr from 10:30–15:30) or buying the fine £5 *Hundred Highlights* guidebook or the handy 80p *What to See at the V & A* brochure (outlines 5 speedy self-guided tours). Experts give free tours on various topics daily at 13:00. Or walk through these ground-floor **highlights**: Medieval Treasury (room 43, well-described treasury of Middle Age European art), the finest collection of Indian decorative art outside India (room 41), the Dress Gallery (room 40, 400 years of English fashion corseted into 40 display cases), the Raphael Gallery (room 48a, 7 huge watercolor cartoons painted as designs for tapestries to hang in the Sistine Chapel, among the greatest art treasures in Britain and the best works of the High Renaissance), reliefs by the Renaissance sculptor Donatello (room 16), a close-up look at medieval stained glass (room 28, much more upstairs), the fascinating Cast Courts (rooms 46a and 46b, filled with plaster

copies of the greatest art of our civilization—such as Trajan's
*Column* and Michelangelo's *David*—made for the benefit of 19th-
century art students who couldn't afford a railpass), and the hall
of "great" fakes and forgeries (room 46). Upstairs you can walk
through the newly-renovated British Galleries for centuries of
British furniture, clothing, glass, jewelry, and sculpture (free,
possible fee for special exhibits, daily 10:00–17:45, open Wed
and last Fri of month until 22:00 except mid-Dec–mid-Jan; tube:
South Kensington, a long tunnel leads directly from tube station
to museum, tel. 020/7942-2000, www.vam.ac.uk).

▲**Natural History Museum**—Across the street from the Victoria
and Albert Museum, this mammoth museum is housed in a giant
and wonderful Victorian neo-Romanesque building. Built in the
1870s specifically to house the huge collection (50 million speci-
mens), it presents itself in two halves: the Life Galleries (creepy-
crawlies, human biology, the origin of species, "our place in
evolution," and awesome dinosaurs) and the Earth Galleries (mete-
ors, volcanoes, earthquakes, and so on). Exhibits are wonderfully
explained with lots of creative interactive displays. Free 45-minute
tours occur daily about every hour from 11:00–16:00 (free, possible
fee for special exhibits, Mon–Sat 10:00–17:50, Sun 11:00–17:50, a
long tunnel leads directly from South Kensington tube station to
museum, tel. 020/7942-5000, www.nhm.ac.uk). Pop in if only for
the wild collection of dinosaurs and the roaring *T. Rex.*

## Sights—East London: "The City"

▲▲**The City of London**—When Londoners say "The City,"
they mean the one-square-mile business, banking, and journalism
center that 2,000 years ago was Roman Londinium. The outline
of the Roman city walls can still be seen in the arc of roads from
Blackfriars Bridge to Tower Bridge. Within the City are 24
churches designed by Christopher Wren, mostly just ornamentation
around St. Paul's Cathedral. Today, while home to only 5,000 residents, the City thrives with more than 500,000 office workers coming and going daily. It's a fascinating district to wander, but since
almost nobody actually lives there, it's dull on Saturday and Sunday.

▲**Old Bailey**—To see the British legal system in action—lawyers
in little blond wigs speaking legalese with a British accent—
spend a few minutes in the visitors' gallery at "Old Bailey" (free,
Mon–Fri 10:00–13:00 and 14:00–14:30 most weeks, no kids under
14, no bags or cameras, purses OK, you can check your bag at the
SPAR grocery across the street for £1, tube: St. Paul's, 2 blocks
northwest of St. Paul's on Old Bailey Street, follow signs to public
entrance, tel. 020/7248-3277).

▲▲▲**St. Paul's Cathedral**—Wren's most famous church is the
great St. Paul's, its elaborate interior capped by a 365-foot dome.
The crypt (included with admission) is a world of historic bones

## East London: "The City"

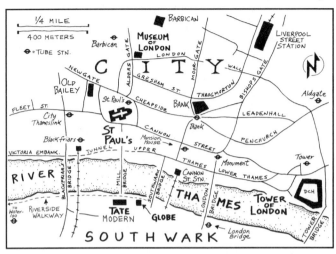

and memorials, including Admiral Nelson's tomb and interesting cathedral models. The great West Door is opened only for great occasions, such as the wedding of Prince Charles and the late Princess Diana in 1981. Stand in the back of the church and imagine how Diana felt before making the hike to the altar with the world watching. Sit under the second-largest dome in the world and eavesdrop on guided tours.

Since World War II, St. Paul's has been Britain's symbol of resistance. Despite 57 nights of bombing, the Nazis failed to destroy the cathedral, thanks to the St. Paul's volunteer fire watch who stayed on the dome. Climb the dome for a great city view and some fun in the whispering gallery—where the precisely designed barrel of the dome lets sweet nothings circle audibly around to the opposite side (£5 entry; Mon–Sat 8:30–16:30, last entry 16:00, closed Sun except for worship; allow 1 hr to climb up and down dome—closed Sun; no photography allowed within church; £2.50 for guided 90-min "super tours" of cathedral and crypt offered at 11:00, 11:30, 13:30, and 14:00; £3.50 for an audioguide tour anytime; Sun services at 8:00, 10:15, 11:30, 15:15, and 18:00; inexpensive and cheery café in crypt; tube: St. Paul's; tel. 020/7236-4128). The **evensong** services are free, but nonpaying visitors are not allowed to linger afterward (Mon–Sat at 17:00, Sun at 15:15, 40 min).

▲**Museum of London**—London, a 2,000-year-old city, is so littered with Roman ruins that when a London builder finds Roman antiquities he doesn't stop work. He simply documents the finds, moves the artifacts to a museum, and builds on. If you're asking,

## In the Wake of the Millennium

London had been hell-bent on hosting the world's grandest
millennium celebrations in a thousand years. The year 2000
brought London revamped museums, a huge Ferris wheel,
and a giant dome at Greenwich. Now that the stardust of
the millennium has long since settled, what's left?

Greenwich's Millennium Dome was a disappointment.
It needed to draw 35,000 people a day to recoup its huge
costs—and didn't come close. Today, it's a big white elephant, looking for an owner (who never heard about "location, location, location") and a society wondering why on
earth they spent a billion pounds on something like that.

The new pedestrian Millennium Bridge opened for a
few days. But, loaded with people, it wiggled and has been
closed since—an embarrassing monument to a design that
didn't work. Someday (maybe in 2002) it will be open to the
public—linking the old, sedate St. Paul's Cathedral with the
new great Tate.

The striking Tate Modern, which opened in 2000, is as
modern as its art. And around it, a revitalized South Bank is
springing to life in thoroughly 21st-century style.

The London Eye Ferris wheel, for the silly thrill of it, is
a delightful way to see London from a 450-foot-high perch.
The towering wheel adds a carnival whirl to London's
stodgy skyline.

The British Museum opened the glass-domed Great
Court, lined with shops, cafés, and lecture halls, to create a
formal entry and offer visitors a classy place to hang out
after the museum closes. Karl Marx enjoyed the museum's
Round Reading Room, which is now freshly restored and
once again ready for someone to give utopia a chance.

"Why did the Romans build their cities underground?" a trip to
the creative and entertaining London Museum is a must. Stroll
through London history from pre-Roman times through the Blitz
up to today. This regular stop for the local school kids gives the
best overview of London history in town (£5, free after 16:30,
Mon–Sat 10:00–18:00, Sun 12:00–18:00, tube: Barbican or St.
Paul's, tel. 020/7600-3699).

**Geffrye Decorative Arts Museum**—Walk through English
front rooms from 1600 to 1990 (free, Tue–Sat 10:00–17:00, Sun
12:00–17:00, closed Mon, tube: Liverpool Street, then bus #149
or #242 north, tel. 020/7739-9893).

▲▲▲**Tower of London**—The Tower has served as a castle in

wartime, a king's residence in peace, and, most notoriously, as the prison and execution site of rebels. This historic fortress is host to more than 3 million visitors a year. Enjoy the free and entertaining 50-minute Beefeater tour (leaves regularly from inside the gate, last one is usually at 15:30). The crown jewels, dating from the Restoration, are the best on Earth—and come with hour-long lines for most of the day. To avoid the crowds, arrive at 9:00 and go straight for the jewels, doing the Beefeater tour and White Tower later—or do the jewels after 16:30 (£11.50, 1-day combo ticket with Hampton Court Palace-£19, March–Oct Mon–Sat 9:00–18:00, Sun 10:00–18:00, Nov–Feb Tue–Sat 9:00–17:00, Sun–Mon 10:00–17:00, last entry 1 hr before closing, the long but fast-moving ticket line is worst on Sun, no photography allowed of jewels or in chapels, tube: Tower Hill, tel. 020/7709-0765, recorded info: tel. 020/7680-9004). You can avoid the long lines by picking up your ticket at any London TI or the Tower Hill tube station ticket office.

**Ceremony of the Keys:** Every night at 21:30, with pageantry-filled ceremony, the Tower of London is locked up (as it has been for the last 700 years). To attend this free 30-minute event, you need to request an invitation at least two to three months before your visit. Write to: Ceremony of the Keys, H.M. Tower of London, London EC3N 4AB. Include your name; the addresses, names, and ages of all people attending (up to 7 people, nontransferable, no kids under 8 allowed); requested date; alternative dates; and an international reply coupon (buy at U.S. post office).

**Sights next to the Tower**—The best remaining bit of London's **Roman Wall** is just north of the tower (at Tower Hill tube station). Freshly painted and restored, **Tower Bridge Experience**—the neo-Gothic maritime gateway to London—has an 1894-to-1994 history exhibit (£6.25, daily 10:00–18:30, last entry at 17:15, good view, poor value, tel. 020/7403-3761). The chic **St. Katherine Yacht Harbor**, just east of the Tower Bridge, has mod shops and the classic old Dickens Inn, fun for a drink or pub lunch. Across the bridge is the South Bank, with the upscale Butlers Wharf area, museums, and promenade.

## Sights—South London, on the South Bank

The South Bank is a thriving arts and cultural center tied together by a riverside path. This trendy, pub-crawling walk—called the Jubilee Promenade—stretches from the Tower of London bridge past Westminster Bridge, where it offers grand views of the Houses of Parliament. (The promenade hugs the river except just east of London Bridge, where it cuts inland for a couple of blocks.)

▲▲▲**London Eye Ferris Wheel**—Built by British Air, the wheel towers above London opposite Big Ben. At 450 feet, this is the world's highest observational wheel, giving you a chance to fly British Air without leaving London. Built like a giant bicycle wheel, it's a pan-European undertaking: British steel and Dutch engineering, with Czech, German, French, and Italian mechanical parts. It's also very "green," running extremely efficiently and virtually silently. Twenty-five people ride in each of its 32 air-conditioned capsules for the 30-minute rotation (each capsule has a bench, but most people stand). From the top of the wheel—the highest public viewpoint in the city—Big Ben looks small. You only go around once; save a shot on top for the glass capsule of people next to yours.

A big hit with Londoners and tourists alike, the ride gets booked up fast, especially on weekends. To save time and guarantee a spot, book a time slot a day ahead—at a London TI, in person at the office near the base of the wheel, at the Big Bus Information Centre (daily 8:30–17:30, 48 Buckingham Palace Road, a block from Victoria Station), possibly through your hotel (ask), or online at www.ba-londoneye.com. You can also book by phone, but allow at least five days before your ticket is available (pick up ticket at wheel office, 50p charge, automated booking tel. 0870-500-0600). Whether you book ahead or just stand in line, you'll be assigned—or you can request—a half-hour time slot. You must arrive at the wheel during this time (earlier is better) to ensure getting on. Advance booking, which costs nothing extra, allows you to skip the queue to buy tickets. No one escapes the second queue, the ticket-holders' line to get on the wheel (line starts forming 10 min before your 30-min time slot begins; listen for announcement).

Freewheeling types who don't care for lines or prebooking can usually avoid the line by riding at night. It's open until 22:00 in peak season (last boarding 21:30). If you're lucky, you can waltz right on (£9, daily 9:30–22:00, mid-Sept–March 10:00–20:00, at County Hall, shop with binoculars for rent, tube: Waterloo or Westminster, www.ba-londoneye.com).

**The Dalí Universe**—Cleverly located next to the hugely popular London Eye Ferris wheel, this exhibit features 500 works of mind-bending art by Salvador Dalí. While pricey, it's entertaining if you like surrealism and want to learn about Dalí (£7, daily 10:00–17:30, generally summer eves until 20:00, tel. 020/7620-2720).

▲▲**Imperial War Museum**—This impressive museum covers the wars of the last century, from heavy weaponry to love notes and Varga Girls, from Monty's Africa campaign tank to Schwartzkopf's Desert Storm uniform. You can trace the development of the machine gun; watch footage of the first tank battles; see one of over a thousand V2 rockets (each with over a ton of explosives) Hitler rained on Britain in 1944; hold your breath through the gruesome WWI trench experience; and buy WWII-era toys in the fun museum shop. The "Secret War" section gives a fascinating peek into the intrigues of espionage in World War I and

World War II. The new Holocaust Exhibit is one of the best on the subject anywhere. Rather than glorify war, the museum does its best to shine a light on the powerful human side of one of mankind's most persistent traits (£6.50, free for kids under 16 and over 60, free for anyone after 16:30, daily 10:00–18:00, 90 min is enough time for most visitors, tube: Lambeth North or bus #12 from Westminster, tel. 020/7416-5000). The museum is housed in what was the Royal Bethlam Hospital. Also known as "the Bedlam asylum," the place was so wild it gave the world a new word for chaos: "bedlam." Back in Victorian times, locals—without trash-talk shows and cable TV—came here for their entertainment. The asylum actually opened the place to the paying public on weekends to view the "bedlam."

**Bramah Tea and Coffee Museum**—Aficionados of tea or coffee will find this small museum fascinating. It tells the story of each drink almost passionately. The owner, Mr. Bramah, comes from a big tea family and wants the world to know how the advent of commercial television, with breaks not long enough to brew a proper pot of tea, required a faster hot drink. In came the horrible English instant coffee. Tea countered with finely chopped leaves in tea bags, and it's gone downhill ever since (£4, daily 10:00–18:00, in the Butlers Wharf complex just across the bridge from the tower, behind Design Museum, tel. 020/7378-0222). Its café, which serves more kinds of coffees and teas than cakes, is open to the public (same hrs as museum).

**▲▲Globe Theater**—The original Globe Theater has been rebuilt—half-timbered and thatched—exactly as it was in Shakespeare's time. (This is the first thatch in London since they were outlawed after the great fire of 1666.) The Globe originally accommodated 2,000 seated and another 1,000 standing. (Today, leaving space for reasonable aisles, the theater holds 900 seated and 600 groundlings.) Its promoters brag that the theater forges "the three A's": actors, audience, and architecture, with each contributing to the play. Open as a museum and working theater, it hosts authentic old-time performances of Shakespeare's plays. The theater can be toured when there are no plays. The Globe's exhibition on Shakespeare is the world's largest, with interactive displays and film presentations, a sound lab, a script factory, and costumes (£7.50, mid-May–Sept daily 9:00–12:00, Oct–mid-May 10:00–17:00, includes guided 30-min tour offered on the half hr, on South Bank directly across the Thames over Southwark Bridge from St. Paul's, tube: Mansion House or London Bridge, tel. 020/7902-1500, www.shakespeares-globe.org, for details on seeing a play see "Entertainment," below).

**▲▲Tate Modern**—Dedicated in the spring of 2000, this striking new museum across the river from St. Paul's opened the new century with art from the old one (remember the 20th century?).

Its powerhouse collection of Monet, Matisse, Dalí, Picasso, Warhol, and much more is displayed in a converted power house (museum free, fee for special exhibitions, daily 10:00–18:00, Fri–Sat until 22:00—a good time to visit, various audioguide tours-£1, free guided tours, call for schedule, view café on top floor, walk the Millennium Bridge—if it's open—from St. Paul's, or get off at the Southwark tube stop for a 7-min walk, tel. 020/7887-8008, www.tate.org.uk).

A river-bus service connects Tate Modern with Tate Britain (either free or minimal charge, runs May–Sept—maybe longer; ask for schedule at information desk at either Tate).

▲**Millennium Bridge**—This new pedestrian bridge should link St. Paul's Cathedral and Tate Modern across the Thames. Nick-named "a blade of light" for its sleek minimalist design—370 yards long, 4 yards wide, stainless steel with teak planks—it includes clever aerodynamic handrails to deflect wind over the heads of pedestrians. This is London's only pedestrian bridge and its first new bridge in a century (free). Since it wiggles with people on it, it was closed days after it opened. The $25 million bridge will cost $7 million to stabilize, and skeptics doubt it will reopen in 2002.

▲▲**The Old Operating Theatre Museum and Herb Garret**— Climb a tight and creaky wooden spiral staircase to a church attic where you'll find: a garret used to dry medicinal herbs, a fascinating exhibit on Victorian surgery, cases of well-described 19th-century medical paraphernalia, and a special look at "anes-thesia, the defeat of pain." Then you stumble upon Britain's oldest operating theater, where limbs were sawed off way back in 1821 (£3.50, daily 10:30–17:00, tube: London Bridge, 9a St. Thomas Street, tel. 020/8806-4325).

▲▲**Vinopolis: City of Wine**—While it seems illogical to have a huge wine museum in London, Vinopolis makes a good case. It's built over a Roman wine store and fills the massive vaults of an old wine warehouse. Visitors follow an excellent audioguide through a light yet earnest history of wine. Sipping your various wines, ports, and champagnes—immersed in your headset as you stroll—you learn about wine from its Georgian origins to Chile to a Vespa ride through Chianti country in Tuscany. Allow yourself some time, as the tour takes 90 minutes (the sipping can slow things down wonderfully, £11.50 with 5 tastes, £14 for 10, don't worry…for £2.50 you can buy 5 more tastes inside, daily 11:00–18:00, last entry 16:00, tube: London Bridge, between the Glove and Southwark Cathedral at 1 Bank End, tel. 0870-241-4040).

## More South Bank Sights, in Southwark

These sights are mediocre but worth knowing about. The area stretching from Tate Modern to London Bridge, known as Southwark (suth-uck), was for centuries the place Londoners

## The South Bank

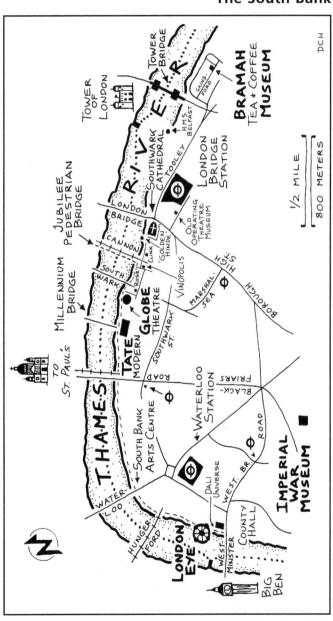

would go to escape the rules and decency of the city and let their medieval hair down. Bear-baiting, brothels, rollicking pubs and theater—you name it, your dreams could be fulfilled just across the Thames. Through the 20th century a run-down warehouse district, in the last decade it's been gentrified with classy restaurants, office parks, pedestrian promenades, major new sights (such as the Tate Modern and the Globe Theatre), and this colorful collection of lesser sights. The area is easy on foot and a scenic—though circuitous—way to connect St. Paul's and the Tower of London.

**Southwark Cathedral**—While made a cathedral only in 1905, this has been the neighborhood church since the 13th century and comes with some interesting history (Mon–Sat 10:00–18:00, Sun 11:00–17:00, evensong services weekdays at 17:30, tel. 020/7367-6711). The adjacent church-run **Long View of London Exhibition** tells the story of Southwark (£3, same hrs as church).

**The Clink Prison**—Proudly the "original clink," this was where law-abiding citizens threw Southwark troublemakers until 1780. Today it's a low-tech torture museum filling grotty old rooms with papier-mâché gore. Unfortunately, there's little to seriously deal with the fascinating problem of law and order in Southwark, where 18th-century Londoners went for a good time (overpriced at £4, daily 10:00–18:00, 1 Clink Street, tel. 020/7378-1558).

**Rose Theatre**—Here, in the basement of an 11-story office building, you can see the scant remains of the 16th-century theater that once stood here. The Rose Theatre was built in 1587, 12 years before the original Globe, and excavated in 1989. In this barren site, you view a 25-minute video on the history of theater in the days of Shakespeare (£4, daily 11:00–17:00).

*Golden Hinde*—This is a full-size replica of the 16th-century warship in which Sir Francis Drake circumcised the globe from 1577 to 1580. Commanding this boat, Drake earned the reputation as history's most successful pirate. The original is long gone but this boat has logged over 100,000 miles, including its own voyage around the world. While fun to see, the interior is not worth touring (£2.50, daily 9:30–17:30).

**HMS** *Belfast*—"The last big gun–armored warship of World War II" clogs the Thames just upstream from the Tower Bridge. This huge vessel—now manned with wax sailors—thrills kids who always dreamed of sitting in a turret shooting off their imaginary guns. If you're into WWII warships, this is the ultimate... otherwise it's just lots of exercise with a nice view of the Tower Bridge (£5.40, daily 10:00–18:00).

## Sights—South London, on the North Bank
▲▲**Tate Britain**—One of Europe's great art houses, Tate Britain specializes in British painting: 16th century through the 20th, including Pre-Raphaelites. Commune with the mystical Blake and

romantic Turner (free, daily 10:00–17:50, fine £3 audioguide, free tours: 11:30—Turner, 14:30 and 15:30—British Highlights, call to confirm schedule, no photography allowed, tube: Pimlico, then 7-min walk, or arrive directly at museum by taking bus #88 from Oxford Circus or #77A from National Gallery, tel. 020/7887-8000, recorded info tel. 020/7887-8008, www.tate.org.uk). A river-bus service connects Tate Britain with Tate Modern (either free or minimal charge, runs May–Sept—maybe longer; ask for schedule at information desk at either Tate).

## Sights—Greater London

▲Kew Gardens—For a fine riverside park and a palatial greenhouse jungle to swing through, take the tube or the boat to every botanist's favorite escape, Kew Gardens. While to most visitors the Royal Botanic Gardens of Kew is simply a delightful opportunity to wander among 33,000 different types of plants, it's also notable because it's run by a hardworking organization committed to understanding and preserving the botanical diversity of our planet. The Kew tube station drops you in a little business community a two-block walk from Victoria Gate (the main garden entry). Pick up a map brochure and check at the gate for a monthly listing of best blooms.

Garden lovers could spend days exploring Kew's 300 acres. For a quick visit, spend a fragrant hour wandering through three buildings: the Palm House, a humid Victorian world of iron, glass, and tropical plants built in 1844; a Waterlily House that Monet would swim for; and the Princess of Wales Conservatory, a modern greenhouse with many different climate zones growing countless cacti, bug-munching carnivorous plants, and more (£6.50, £4.50 at 16:45, Mon–Fri 9:30–18:30, Sat–Sun 9:30–19:30, until 16:30 or sunset off-season, galleries and conservatories close at 17:30, consider £2.50 narrated floral joyride on little train departing from 11:00–15:30 from Victoria Gate, tube: Kew Gardens, tel. 020/8332-5000). For a sun–dappled lunch, walk 10 minutes from the Palm House to the Orangery (£6 hot meals, daily 10:00–17:30).

▲Hampton Court Palace—Fifteen miles up the Thames from downtown (£15 taxi ride from Kew Gardens) is the 500-year-old palace of Henry VIII. Actually, it was the palace of his minister, Cardinal Wolsey. When Wolsey, a clever man, realized Henry VIII was experiencing a little palace envy, he gave it to his king. The Tudor palace was also home to Elizabeth I and Charles I. Parts were updated by Christopher Wren for William and Mary. The palace stands stately overlooking the Thames and includes some impressive Tudor rooms, including a Great Hall, with its magnificent hammer-beam ceiling. The industrial-strength Tudor kitchen was capable of keeping 600 schmoozing courtesans thoroughly—if not well—fed. The sculpted garden features a rare Tudor tennis court and a popular maze.

## Greater London

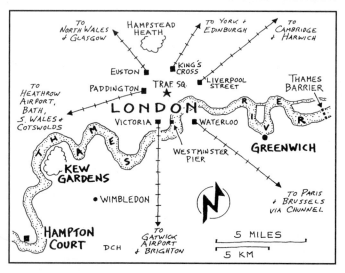

The palace, fully restored after a 1986 fire, tries hard to please, but it doesn't quite sparkle. From the information center in the main courtyard, visitors book times for tours with tired costumed guides or pick up audioguides for self-guided tours of various wings of the palace (all free). The Tudor Kitchens, Henry VIII's Apartments, and the King's Apartments are most interesting. The Georgian Rooms are pretty dull. The maze in the nearby garden is a curiosity some find fun (maze free with palace ticket, otherwise £2.50). The train (2/hr, 30 min) from London's Waterloo station drops you just across the river from the palace (£10.80, 1-day combo ticket with Tower of London-£19, Mon 10:15–18:00, Tue–Sun 9:30–18:00, Nov–March until 16:30, tel. 020/8781-9500).

**Royal Air Force Museum**—A hit with aviation enthusiasts, this huge aerodrome and airfield contain planes from World War II through the Battle of Britain up to the Gulf War. You can climb inside some of the planes, try your luck in a cockpit, and fly with the Red Arrows in a flight simulator (£7.50, daily 10:00–18:00, café, shop, parking, tube: Colindale—on the Northern Line, Grahame Park Way, tel. 020/8205-2266, www.rafmuseum.org.uk).

## Disappointments of London

The venerable BBC broadcasts from Broadcasting House. Of all its productions, its "BBC Experience" tour for visitors is among the worst. On the South Bank, the London Dungeon, a much-visited but amateurish attraction, is just a highly advertised, overpriced haunted house—certainly not worth the £10 admission, much less your valuable London time. It comes with long and rude lines. Wait for Halloween and see one in your hometown to support a better cause. The Design Museum (next to the Bramah Tea and Coffee Museum) and "Winston Churchill's Britain at War Experience" (next to London Dungeon) waste your time. The Kensington Palace State Apartments are lifeless and not worth a visit.

## Shopping in London

**Harrods**—Filled with wonderful displays, Harrods is London's most famous and touristy department store. Big yet classy, Harrods has everything from elephants to toothbrushes. The food halls are sights to savor. If anything, ride the ornate Egyptian escalator (Mon–Sat 10:00–19:00, closed Sun, on Brompton Road, tube: Knightsbridge, tel. 020/7730-1234). Many readers report that Harrods is now overpriced (its £1 toilets are the most expensive in Europe), snooty, and teeming with American and Japanese tourists. Still, it's the palace of department stores. The nearby Beauchamp Place is lined with classy and fascinating shops.

**Harvey Nichols**—Princess Diana's favorite, this remains the department store *du jour* (Mon, Tue, Sat 10:00–19:00, Wed–Fri until 20:00, Sun 12:00–18:00, near Harrods, tube: Knightsbridge, 109 Knightsbridge, www.harveynichols.com). Its fifth floor is a veritable food fest with a gourmet grocery store, a fancy (smoky) restaurant, a Yo! Sushi bar, and a lively café. Consider a take-away tray of sushi to eat on a bench in the Hyde Park rose garden two blocks away. On Friday nights, the café hosts a popular "Film on Five" event: a three-course dinner followed by recently-released films shown on big-screen televisions (£35, 20:00–24:00, for reservations tel. 020/7201-8562).

**Toys**—The biggest toy store in Britain is **Hamleys**, with seven floors buzzing with 28,000 toys managed by a staff of 200. At the "Bear Factory," kids can get a made-to-order teddy bear by picking out a "bear skin" and watch while it's stuffed and sewn (Mon–Sat 10:00–20:00, Sun 12:00–18:00, tube: Oxford Circus, 188 Regent Street, tel. 020/7494-2000).

**Street Markets**—Antique buffs, people watchers, and folks who brake for garage sales love London's street markets. There's good early-morning market activity somewhere any day of the week. The best are **Portobello Road** (roughly Mon–Sat 9:00–17:00, go on Sat for antiques until 17:30—plus the regular junk, clothes, and produce; tube: Notting Hill Gate, tel. 020/7229-8354) and **Camden Market** (daily 10:00–18:00, trendy arts and crafts, tube: Camden Town, tel. 020/7284-2084). The TI has a complete, up-to-date list. If you like to haggle, there are no holds barred in London's street markets. Warning: Markets attract two kinds of people—tourists and pickpockets.

**Famous Auctions**—London's famous auctioneers welcome the curious public for viewing and bidding. For schedules, call **Sotheby's** (Mon–Fri 9:00–16:30, 34-35 New Bond Street, tube: Oxford Circus, tel. 020/7293-5000, www.sothebys.com) or **Christie's** (Mon–Fri 9:00–16:30, Tue 9:00–20:00, 8 King Street, tube: Green Park, tel. 020/7839-9060, www.christies.com).

## Entertainment and Theater in London

London bubbles with top-notch entertainment seven days a week. Everything's listed in the weekly entertainment magazines, available at newsstands. Choose from classical, jazz, rock, and far-out music, Gilbert and Sullivan, dance, comedy, Baha'i meetings, poetry readings, spectator sports, film, and theater.

London's **theater** rivals Broadway's in quality and beats it in price. Choose from the Royal Shakespeare Company, top musicals, comedy, thrillers, sex farces, and more. Performances are nightly except Sunday, usually with one matinee a week. Matinees, held on Wednesday, Thursday, or Saturday, are cheaper and rarely sell out. Tickets range from about £8 to £35.

Most theaters, marked on tourist maps, are in the Piccadilly/Trafalgar area. Box offices, hotels, and TIs offer a handy "Theater Guide." To book a seat, simply call the theater box office directly, ask about seats and dates available, and buy a ticket with your credit card. You can call from the United States as easily as from England (photocopy your hometown library's London newspaper theater section or check out www.officiallondontheatre.co.uk). Pick up your ticket 15 minutes before the show. You can also book through www.ticketmaster.co.uk (fee).

Ticket agencies are scalpers with an address. Booking through an agency (at most TIs or scattered throughout London) is quick and easy, but prices are inflated by a standard 25 percent fee. If buying from an agency, look at the ticket carefully (your price should be no more than 30 percent over the printed face value; the 17.5 percent VAT tax is already included in the face value) and understand where you're sitting according to the floor plan (if your view is restricted it will state this on ticket). Agencies are worthwhile only if a show you've got to see is sold out at the box office. They scarf up hot tickets, planning to make a killing after the show is sold out. U.S. booking agencies get their tickets from another agency, adding even more to your expense by involving yet another middleman. Many tickets sold on the streets are forgeries. With cheap international phone calls and credit cards, there's no reason not to book direct.

**Theater lingo:** stalls (ground floor), dress circle (1st balcony), upper circle (2nd balcony), balcony (sky-high 3rd balcony).

**Cheap theater tricks:** Most theaters offer returned-ticket, standing-room, matinee, and senior or student stand-by deals.

These "concessions" are indicated with a "conc" or "s" in the listings. Picking up a late return can get you a great seat at a cheap-seat price. If a show is "sold out," there's usually a way to get a seat. Call the theater box office and ask how. I buy the second-cheapest tickets directly from the theater box office.

The famous "half-price booth" in Leicester (LES-ter) Square sells discounted tickets for good seats to shows on the push list the day of the show only (Mon–Sat 12:00–18:30, matinee tickets Tue–Sun from noon, cash only). The real half-price booth is a freestanding kiosk at the edge of the garden in Leicester Square. Several dishonest outfits advertise "official half-price tickets" at agencies closer to the tube station. Avoid these.

Many theaters are so small that there's hardly a bad seat. After the lights go down, "scooting up" is less than a capital offense. Shakespeare did it.

**Royal Shakespeare Company**—If you'll ever enjoy Shakespeare, it'll be in Britain. The RSC performs at London's Barbican Centre from December through May (office open daily 9:00–20:00, box office tel. 020/7638-8891, recorded information tel. 020/7628-9760) and in Stratford year-round (tel. 01789/403-403). To get a schedule, you can call (numbers listed above), write (Royal Shakespeare Theatre, Stratford-upon-Avon, CV37 6BB Warwickshire), or visit www.rsc.org.uk.

Tickets range in price from £10 to £30 (discounts for young and old). Book direct by telephone and credit card and pick up your ticket at the door (Barbican Centre, Silk Street, tube: Barbican).

**Shakespeare at the Globe Theater**—To see Shakespeare in a replica of the theater for which he wrote his plays, attend a play at the Globe. This thatch-roofed, open-air round theater does the plays much as Shakespeare intended (with no amplification). The play's the thing from mid-May through September (usually Tue–Sat 14:00 and 19:30, Sun at either 13:00 and 18:30 or 16:00 only, no plays Mon). You'll pay £5 to stand and £10 to £26 to sit (usually on a backless bench; only a few rows and the pricier Gentlemen's Rooms have seats with backs). The £5 "groundling" tickets—while the only ones open to rain—are most fun. Scurry in early to stake out a spot on the stage's edge leaning rail—where the most interaction with the actors occurs. You're a crude peasant. You lean your elbows on the stage, munch a picnic dinner, or walk around. I've never enjoyed Shakespeare as much as here, performed as it was meant to be in the "wooden O." Plays can be long. Many groundlings leave before the end. If you like, hang out an hour before the finish and beg or buy a ticket from someone leaving early (groundlings are allowed to come and go).

The theater is on the South Bank directly across the Thames over Southwark Bridge from St. Paul's (tube: Mansion House, or walk across the Millennium Bridge—if it's open—

from St. Paul's, tel. 020/7902-1500, box office tel. 020/7401-9919, www.shakespeares-globe.org). The Globe is inconvenient for public transport, but the courtesy phone in the lobby gets a minicab in minutes. (These have set fees—e.g., £8 to South Kensington—but generally cost less than a metered cab and provide fine and honest service.)

**Music**—For easy, cheap, or free concerts in historic churches, check the TI's listings for lunch concerts (especially Wren's St. Bride's Church; St. James at Piccadilly—free lunch concerts on Mon, Wed, and Fri at 13:00, info tel. 020/7381-0441; and St. Martin-in-the-Fields—free lunch concerts on Mon, Tue, and Fri at 13:05, church tel. 020/7766-1100). St. Martin-in-the-Fields also hosts fine evening concerts by candlelight (£6–16, Thu–Sat at 19:30, CC, box office tel. 020/7839-8362). For a fun classical event (mid-June–early Sept), attend a "Prom Concert." This is an annual music festival with nightly concerts in the Royal Albert Hall at give-a-peasant-some-culture prices (£3 standing-room spots sold at the door, £5 restricted view seats, most £21.50, CC, tube: South Kensington, tel. 020/7589-8212, www.royalalberthall.com).

**Cruises**—Of the Thames River evening cruises that offer four-course meals and dancing, London Showboat offers the best value (£48, April–Oct Wed–Sun, departs 19:00 from Westminster Pier, Thu–Sat evening cruises through the winter, 3.5 hrs, tel. 020/7237-5134, www.citycruises.com). For more on cruising, get the Thames River Services brochure from a London TI.

## Daytrips from London

Greenwich, Windsor, and Cambridge are three good daytrip pos-sibilities near London (covered under "Near London," below).

You could fill a book with the many easy and exciting daytrips from London (Earl Steinbicker did: *Daytrips London: Fifty-One Day Adventures by Rail or Car, in and around London and Southern England*). **Original London Walks** offers a variety of Explorer day-trips using the train for about £10 plus transportation costs (see their walking-tour brochure, tel. 020/7624-3978, www.walks.com).

Several **bus-tour companies** take London-based travelers out and back every day. If you're going to Bath and want to stay overnight, consider taking a day tour to Bath and skipping the trip back to London. Depending on the type and availability of tour, you'll pay about £48, which also includes a visit to Stone-henge (compare to a £31 one-way 2nd-class train ticket from London to Bath). Evan Evans' tour leaves from the Victoria Coach station daily every morning at 9:00 (you can stow your bag under the bus), stops in Stonehenge (45 min), and then stops in Bath for lunch and a city tour before returning to London (£48, offered year-round, fully-guided, admissions included). You can book the tour at the Victoria Coach station; the Evan Evans'

## London Daytrips

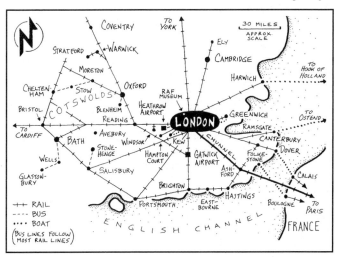

office (258 Vauxhall Bridge Road, near Victoria Coach station, tel. 020/7950-1777, www.evanevans.co.uk); or the Green Line Travel Office (4a Fountain Square, across from Victoria Coach station, tel. 020/7950-1777). Golden Tours offers a similar daily and fully-guided tour of Stonehenge and Bath for comparable prices (departs from Fountain Square, across from Victoria Coach station, tel. 020/7233-6668, www.goldentours.co.uk).

The British rail system uses London as a hub and normally offers round-trip fares (after 9:30) that cost virtually the same as one-way fares. For daytrips, "day return" tickets are best (and cheapest). You can save a little money if you purchase Super Advance tickets before 18:00 on the day before your trip. But given the high cost of big-city living and the charm of small-town England, rather than side tripping, I'd see London and get out.

## Sleeping in London
**(£1 = about $1.50, country code: 44, area code: 020)**
Sleep Code: **S** = Single, **D** = Double/Twin, **T** = Triple, **Q** = Quad, **b** = bathroom, **s** = shower only, **CC** = Credit Cards accepted, **no CC** = Credit Cards not accepted. Unless otherwise noted, prices include a generous breakfast and all taxes.

London is expensive. For £50 ($75) you'll get a double with breakfast in a safe, cramped, and dreary place with minimal service. For £60 ($90) you'll get a basic, clean, reasonably cheery double in a usually cramped, cracked-plaster building or a soulless but comfortable room without breakfast in a huge Motel 6–type place. My London splurges, at £100 to £150 ($150–230), are spacious, thoughtfully-appointed places you'd be happy to entertain or make love in. Hearty English or generous buffet breakfasts are included unless otherwise noted, and TVs are standard in rooms.

Reserve your London room with a phone call or e-mail as soon as you can commit to a date. To call a London hotel from the United States or Canada, dial 011-44-20 (London's area code without the initial zero), then the local eight-digit number. A few places will hold a room with no deposit if you promise to arrive by midday. Most take your credit-card number as security. Many inexpensive places don't take credit cards and require a cash deposit (generally a personal check if 6 weeks in advance, otherwise a bank draft in pounds). The pricier ones have expensive cancellation policies (such as no refund if you cancel with less than 2 weeks' notice). Some fancy £120 rooms rent for a third off if you arrive late on a slow day and ask for a deal.

### Sleeping in Victoria Station Neighborhood, Belgravia

The streets behind Victoria Station teem with budget B&Bs. It's a safe, surprisingly tidy, and decent area without a hint of the trashy touristy glitz of the streets in front of the station. Here in Belgravia, your neighbors include Andrew Lloyd Webber and Margaret Thatcher (her policeman stands outside 73 Chester Square). Decent eateries abound (see "Eating," below). Cheaper rooms are relatively dumpy. Don't expect £90 cheeriness in a £50 room. Off-season it's possible to save money by arriving late without a reservation and looking around. Fierce competition softens prices, especially for multinight stays. Particularly on hot summer nights, request a quiet back room. All are within a five-minute walk of the Victoria tube, bus, and train stations. There's a £15-per-day (with a hotel voucher) garage, a nearby **launderette** (daily 8:00–20:30, self-service or full-service, past Warwick Square at 3 Westmoreland Terrace, tel. 020/7821-8692), and an easygoing little dance club (Club D'Jan, £5 includes drink, Wed–Sat, 63 Wilton Road).

**Winchester Hotel** is family run and perhaps the best value, with 18 fine rooms, no claustrophobia, and a wise and caring management (Db-£85, Tb-£110, Qb-£140, no CC, no groups, no infants, 17 Belgrave Road, London SW1V 1RB, tel. 020/7828-2972, fax 020/7828-5191, run by Jimmy).

In **Woodville House** the quarters are dollhouse tight, showers are down the hall, and several of its 12 rooms are on the noisy street (doubles on quiet backside, twins and singles on street). Still, this well-run, well-worn place is a good value, with lots of travel tips and friendly chat—especially about the local rich and famous—from Rachel Joplin (S-£42, D-£62, bunky family deals-£80–110 for 3–5 people, CC, 107 Ebury Street, SW1W 9QU,

tel. 020/7730-1048, fax 020/7730-2574, www.woodvillehouse
.co.uk, e-mail: woodville.house@cwcom.net).

**Lime Tree Hotel**, enthusiastically run by David and Marilyn Davies, comes with spacious and thoughtfully-decorated rooms and a fun-loving breakfast room. While priced a bit steep, the place has character (Sb-£75, Db-£105–115, Tb-£145, family room-£160, CC but possible discount with cash, David deals in slow times and is creative at helping travelers in a bind, 135 Ebury Street, SW1W 9RA, tel. 020/7730-8191, fax 020/7730-7865, www.limetreehotel.co.uk).

**James House** and **Cartref House** are two nearly-identical, well-run, smoke-free, 10-room places on either side of Ebury Street (S-£50, Sb-£60, D-£68, Db-£82, T-£90, Tb-£105, family bunkbed quad-£130, CC, 5 percent discount with cash, all rooms with fans; James House at 108 Ebury Street, tel. 020/7730-2511; Cartref House at 129 Ebury Street, tel. 020/7730-6176, fax for both: 020/7730-7338, www.jamesandcartref.co.uk, e-mail: jandchouse@cs.com).

**Elizabeth Hotel** is a stately old place overlooking Eccleston Square with fine public spaces and 37 spacious and decent rooms (D-£68, small Db-£83, big Db-£95, Tb-£108, Qb-£120, Quint with b-£125, CC, 37 Eccleston Square, tel. 020/7828-6812, fax 020/7828-6814, www.elizabeth-hotel.com, e-mail: info@elizabeth-hotel.com). Be careful not to confuse this hotel with the Elizabeth House. This one is big and comfy, the other small and dumpy.

**Elizabeth House** feels institutional and bland—as you might expect from a former YMCA—and it's run-down and none too clean. But the price is right (S-£30, D-£40, Db-£50, T-£60, Q-£70, plus extra £10/room for D or Db in July–Aug, CC, 118 Warwick Way, SW1 4JB, tel. 020/7630-0741, fax 020/7630-0740, e-mail: elizabethhouse@ehlondon.fsnet.co.uk).

**Quality Hotel Eccleston** is big, modern, well-located, and a fine value for no-nonsense comfort (Db-£125, on slow days drop-ins can ask for "saver prices"—33 percent off on first night, breakfast extra, CC, nonsmoking floor, elevator, 82 Eccleston Square, SW1V 1PS, tel. 020/7834-8042, fax 020/7630-8942, e-mail: admin@gb614.u-net.com).

**Georgian House Hotel** has 50 rooms and a cheaper annex that works well for backpackers (tiny D on 4th floor-£42, Db-£66, annex Db-£56, Tb-£82, Qb-£90, CC, Internet access, 35 St. George's Drive, SW1V 4DG, tel. 020/7834-1438, fax 020/7976-6085, www.georgianhousehotel.co.uk, e-mail: georgian @wildnet.co.uk).

**Enrico Hotel**, with 26 simple rooms, is basic, well-worn, and affordable (S-£45, D-£55, Ds-£60, CC, nonsmoking, 77 Warwick Way, SW1V 1QP, tel. 020/7834-9538, fax 020/7233-9995, www.enricohotel.fsnet.co.uk).

# London, Victoria Station Neighborhood

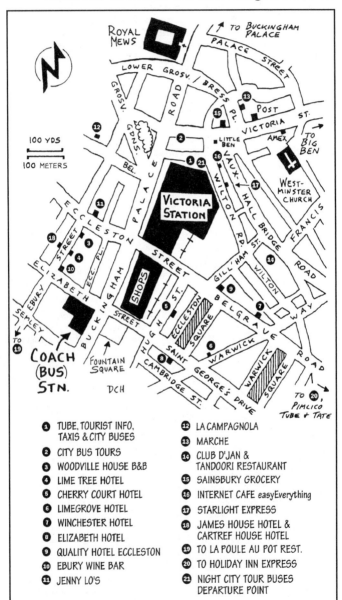

**1** TUBE, TOURIST INFO, TAXIS & CITY BUSES
**2** CITY BUS TOURS
**3** WOODVILLE HOUSE B&B
**4** LIME TREE HOTEL
**5** CHERRY COURT HOTEL
**6** LIMEGROVE HOTEL
**7** WINCHESTER HOTEL
**8** ELIZABETH HOTEL
**9** QUALITY HOTEL ECCLESTON
**10** EBURY WINE BAR
**11** JENNY LO'S

**12** LA CAMPAGNOLA
**13** MARCHE
**14** CLUB D'JAN & TANDOORI RESTAURANT
**15** SAINSBURY GROCERY
**16** INTERNET CAFE easyEverything
**17** STARLIGHT EXPRESS
**18** JAMES HOUSE HOTEL & CARTREF HOUSE HOTEL
**19** TO LA POULE AU POT REST.
**20** TO HOLIDAY INN EXPRESS
**21** NIGHT CITY TOUR BUSES DEPARTURE POINT

✳ **Cherry Court Hotel**, run by the friendly and industrious Patel family, offers tight, basic rooms for good value in a central location (Sb-£42, Db-£48, Tb-£70, Qb-£90, Quint/b-£100, prices promised with this book through 2002, CC, using CC adds 5 percent extra, fruit-basket breakfast in room, nonsmoking, Internet access, 23 Hugh Street, SW1V 1QJ, tel. 020/7828-2840, fax 020/7828-0393, www.cherrycourthotel.co.uk, e-mail: info @cherrycourthotel.co.uk).

**Holiday Inn Express** fills an old building with 52 fresh, modern, and efficient rooms (Db-£97, Tb-£107, CC, up to 2 kids free, some discounts on Web site, nonsmoking floor, elevator, tube: Pimlico, 106 Belgrave Road, Victoria, tel. 020/7630-8888 or 0800-897-121, fax 020/7828-0441, www.hiexpress.com, e-mail: expressvictoria@hotmail.com).

## Big, Cheap, Modern Hotels

These places—popular with budget tour groups—are well-run and offer elevators and all the modern comforts in a no-frills practical package. The doubles for £60 to £75 are a great value for London.

**London County Hall Travel Inn**, literally down the hall from a $400-a-night Marriott Hotel, fills one end of London's massive former City Hall. This place is wonderfully located near the base of the London Eye Ferris wheel and across the Thames from Big Ben. Its 300 slick and no-frills rooms come with all the necessary comforts (Db-£75 for 2 adults and up to 2 kids under age 15, couples can request a bigger family room—same price, CC, breakfast extra, book in advance, no-show rooms are released at 16:00, elevator, some smoke-free and easy-access rooms, 500 yards from Westminster tube stop and Waterloo Station where the Chunnel train leaves for Paris, Belvedere Road, SE1 7PB, you can call 0870-242-8000 or 020/7902-1600 but you'll be put on hold, you can fax at 020/7902-1619 but you might not get a response, it's easiest to book online at www.travelinn.co.uk).

**Other London Travel Inns** charging about £65 per room include **London Euston** (a big, blue Lego-type building on a handy but noisy street packed with Benny Hill families on vacation, 141 Euston Road, NW1 2AU, tube: Euston, tel. 020/7554-3400), **Tower Bridge** (tube: London Bridge, tel. 020/7940-3700), and **London Putney Bridge** (farther out, tube: Putney Bridge, tel. 020/7471-8300). For any of these, call 0870-242-8000, fax 0870-241-9000, or best, book online at www.travelinn.co.uk.

**Hotel Ibis London Euston**, which feels classier than a Travel Inn, is located on a quiet street a block behind Euston Station (380 rooms, Db-£70, CC, no family rooms, breakfast extra, nonsmoking floor, 3 Cardington Street, NW1 2LW, tel. 020/7388-7777, fax 020/7388-0001, e-mail: h0921@accor-hotels.com).

**Jurys Inn** rents 200 mod, compact, and comfy rooms near King's Cross Station (Db/Tb-£89, 2 adults and 2 kids—under age 12—can share 1 room, breakfast extra, CC, nonsmoking floors, 60 Pentonville Road, Islington, N1 9LA, tube: Angel, tel. 020/7282-5500, fax 020/7282-5511, www.jurys.com).

**Premier Lodge** opens in the spring of 2002 near Shakespeare's Globe Theatre on the South Bank (55 rooms, Db for up to 2 adults and 2 kids-£70, Bankside, 34 Park Street, London SE1, tel. 0870-700-1456, www.premierlodge.com).

## "South Kensington," She Said, Loosening His Cummerbund

To live on a quiet street so classy it doesn't allow hotel signs, surrounded by trendy shops and colorful restaurants, call "South Ken" your London home. Shoppers like being a short walk from Harrods and the designer shops of King's Road and Chelsea. When I splurge, I splurge here. Sumner Place is just off Old Brompton Road, 200 yards from the handy South Kensington tube station (on Circle Line, 2 stops from Victoria Station, direct Heathrow connection). There's a taxi rank in the median strip at the end of Harrington Road. The handy "Wash & Dry" **Laundromat** is on the corner of Queensberry Place and Harrington Road (daily 8:00–21:00, bring 20p and £1 coins).

**Aster House Hotel**—run by friendly and accommodating Simon and Leona Tan—has a sumptuous lobby, lounge, and breakfast room. Its newly renovated rooms are comfy and quiet, with TVs, phones, air-conditioning, and refrigerators. Enjoy breakfast or just lounging in the whisper-elegant Orangery, a Victorian greenhouse (Sb-£75–99, Db-£135, bigger Db-£150, deluxe 4-poster Db-£180, CC, entirely nonsmoking, 3 Sumner Place, SW7 3EE, tel. 020/7581-5888, fax 020/7584-4925, www.asterhouse.com).

**Five Sumner Place Hotel** was recently voted "the best small hotel in London." The rooms in this 150-year-old building are tastefully decorated and the breakfast room is a Victorian-style conservatory/greenhouse (13 rooms, Sb-£100, Db-£153, third bed-£22, CC; TV, phones, and fridge in rooms by request; non-smoking rooms, elevator, 5 Sumner Place, South Kensington, SW7 3EE, tel. 020/7584-7586, fax 020/7823-9962, www.sumnerplace .com, e-mail: reservations@sumnerplace.com, Tom).

**Sixteen Sumner Place**, a lesser value for classier travelers, has over-the-top formality and class packed into its 37 un-numbered but pretentiously-named rooms, plush lounges, and quiet garden (Db-£170 with shower, £200 with bath, CC, breakfast in your room, elevator, 16 Sumner Place, SW7 3EG, tel. 020/7589-5232, fax 020/7584-8615, U.S. tel. 800/592-5387, e-mail: reservations@numbersixteenhotel.co.uk).

## London, South Kensington Neighborhood

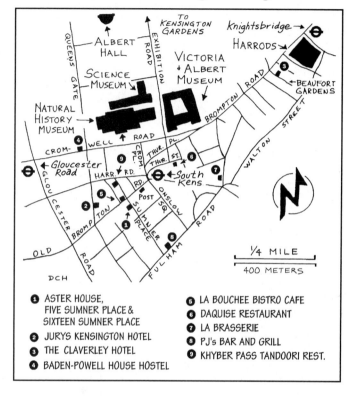

**●1** ASTER HOUSE,
     FIVE SUMNER PLACE &
     SIXTEEN SUMNER PLACE
**●2** JURYS KENSINGTON HOTEL
**●3** THE CLAVERLEY HOTEL
**●4** BADEN-POWELL HOUSE HOSTEL

**●5** LA BOUCHEE BISTRO CAFE
**●6** DAQUISE RESTAURANT
**●7** LA BRASSERIE
**●8** PJ's BAR AND GRILL
**●9** KHYBER PASS TANDOORI REST.

**Jurys Kensington Hotel** is big and stately with a greedy pricing scheme (Sb/Db/Tb-£100–220 depending upon "availability," ask for a deal, breakfast extra, CC, piano lounge, nonsmoking floor, elevator, Queen's Gate, South Kensington, SW7 5LR, tel. 020/7589-6300, fax 020/7581-1492).

**The Claverley**, two blocks from Harrods, is on a quiet street similar to Sumner Place. The 30 fancy dark-wood and marble rooms come with all the comforts (S-£70, Sb-£85–120, Db-£120–150, sofa bed Tb-£190–215, prices may be flexible Dec–March, CC, plush lounge, nonsmoking rooms, elevator, may renovate in 2002, 13-14 Beaufort Gardens, SW3 1PS, tube: Knightsbridge, tel. 020/7589-8541, fax 020/7584-3410, U.S. tel. 800/747-0398, www.claverleyhotel.co.uk).

**Baden-Powell House Hostel** is a huge, modern, institutional place built to inexpensively house Boy and Girl Scouts and their families in central London. Those with a relative in a scouting organization get about a 30 percent discount. It's a big, bright, smoke-free place that feels safe and is well-run (180 single beds, Sb-£65, Scout rate Sb-£44, Db-£88, Scout rate Db-£66, Tb-£114, Scout rate Tb-£90, extra bed-£12, dorm beds-£27, Scout rate dorm beds-£22, CC, air-con, cheap meals served, rooms are spacious with yacht-type bathrooms, receive discount with a letter from your Boy or Girl Scout troop saying you're "family," across from Natural History Museum on corner of Cromwell Road and Queen's Gate at 65 Queen's Gate, tube: South Kensington, tel. 020/7584-7031, fax 020/7590-6902, www.scoutbase.org.uk, e-mail: bph.hostel@scout.org.uk).

### Sleeping in Notting Hill Gate Neighborhood

Residential Notting Hill Gate has quick bus and tube access to downtown, is on the A2 Airbus line from Heathrow, and, for London, is very "homely." It has a self-serve launderette, an artsy theater, a late-hours supermarket, and lots of fun budget eateries (see "Eating," below).

**Westland Hotel** is comfortable, convenient, and hotelesque, with a fine lounge and spacious 1970s-style rooms (Sb-£88, Db-£105, cavernous deluxe Db-£121, sprawling Tb-£122, gargantuan Qb-£149, 10 percent discount with this book through 2002, CC, elevator, free garage with 7 spaces, between Notting Hill Gate and Queensway tube stations, 154 Bayswater Road, W2 4HP, tel. 020/7229-9191, fax 020/7727-1054, www.westlandhotel.co.uk, e-mail: reservations@westlandhotel.co.uk).

**Vicarage Private Hotel**, understandably popular, is family-run and elegantly British in a quiet, classy neighborhood. It has 18 rooms furnished with taste and quality, a TV lounge, and facilities on each floor. Mandy, Richard, and Tere maintain a homey and caring atmosphere (S-£45, D-£74, Db-£98, T-£90, Q-£98, no CC, 6-min walk from the Notting Hill Gate and High Street Kensington tube stations, near Kensington Palace at 10 Vicarage Gate, Kensington, W8 4AG, tel. 020/7229-4030, fax 020/7792-5989, www.londonvicaragehotel.com, e-mail: reception@londonvicaragehotel.com).

**Abbey House Hotel**, next door, is similar but has no lounge and is not as cozy (16 rooms, S-£45, D-£74, T-£90, Q-£100, Quint-£110, no CC, 11 Vicarage Gate, Kensington, W8 4AG, tel. 020/7727-2594, fax 020/7727-1873, www.abbeyhousekensington .com, Rodrigo).

**Norwegian YWCA (Norsk K.F.U.K.)** is for women under 30 only (and men with Norwegian passports). Located on a quiet, stately street, it offers nonsmoking rooms, a study, TV room, piano lounge, and an open-face Norwegian ambience. They have mostly quads, so those willing to share with strangers are most likely to get a place (July–Aug: Ss-£29, shared double-£27.50/bed,

## London, Notting Hill Gate Neighborhood

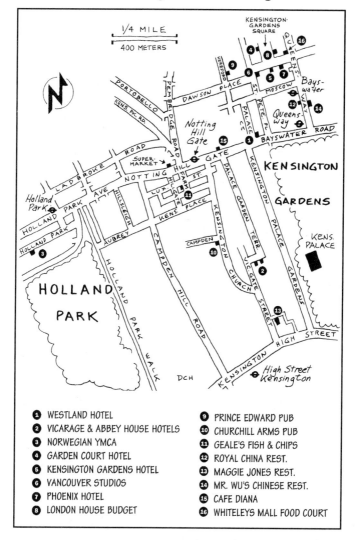

1/4 MILE
400 METERS

1. WESTLAND HOTEL
2. VICARAGE & ABBEY HOUSE HOTELS
3. NORWEGIAN YMCA
4. GARDEN COURT HOTEL
5. KENSINGTON GARDENS HOTEL
6. VANCOUVER STUDIOS
7. PHOENIX HOTEL
8. LONDON HOUSE BUDGET
9. PRINCE EDWARD PUB
10. CHURCHILL ARMS PUB
11. GEALE'S FISH & CHIPS
12. ROYAL CHINA REST.
13. MAGGIE JONES REST.
14. MR. WU'S CHINESE REST.
15. CAFE DIANA
16. WHITELEYS MALL FOOD COURT

shared triple-£23/bed, shared quad-£20/bed, with breakfast;
Sept–June: same prices include dinner; CC, 52 Holland Park,
W11 3RS, tel. & fax 020/7727-9897, www.kfuk.dial.pipex.com).
With each visit I wonder which is easier to get—a sex change
or a Norwegian passport?

## Sleeping on Kensington Gardens

Several big old hotels line the quiet Victorian Kensington Gardens, a block off the bustling Queensway shopping street near the Bayswater tube station. Popular with young international travelers, Queensway is a multicultural festival of commerce and eateries (such as Mr. Wu's Chinese Buffet and the Whiteleys Mall Food Court—see "Eating," below). These hotels come with the least traffic noise of all my downtown recommendations. **Brookford Wash & Dry**, at Queensway and Bishop's Bridge Road (daily 7:00–19:30, service from 9:00–17:30, computerized pay point takes all coins), is one of several Laundromats in the area.

**Garden Court** rents 34 comfortable rooms and is one of London's best values. It's friendly and has a garden (S-£40, Sb-£59, D-£59, Db-£89, T-£73, Tb-£99, Q-£83, Qb-£120, 10 percent discount with this book, CC, 30 Kensington Gardens Square, W2 4BG, tel. 020/7229-2553, fax 020/7727-2749, www.gardencourthotel.co.uk, e-mail: info@gardencourthotel.co.uk, Edward Connolly).

**Kensington Gardens Hotel** laces 16 decent rooms together in a tall, skinny place with lots of stairs (Ss-£55, Sb-£62, Db-£85, Tb-£105, CC, 9 Kensington Gardens Square, W2 4BH, tel. 020/7221-7790, fax 020/7792-8612, www.kensingtongardenshotel.co.uk).

**Vancouver Studios** offers 45 modern rooms with all the amenities, and gives you a fully-equipped kitchenette (utensils, stove, microwave, and fridge) rather than breakfast (small Sb-£56, big Sb-£77, small Db-£97, big Db-£112, Tb-£130, extra bed-£10, CC, homey lounge and private garden, 30 Prince's Square, W2 4NJ, tel. 020/7243-1270, fax 020/7221-8678, www.vienna-group.co.uk, e-mail: vancouverstudios@vienna-group.co.uk).

**Phoenix Hotel**, a Best Western modernization of a 125-room hotel, offers American business-class comforts; spacious and plush public spaces; and big, fresh, modern-feeling rooms (Sb-£94, Db-£120, Tb-£165, CC, elevator, 1-8 Kensington Gardens Square, W2 4BH, tel. 020/7229-2494, fax 020/7727-1419, U.S. tel. 800/528-1234, www.phoenixhotel.co.uk).

**London House Budget Hotel** is a threadbare, nose-ringed slumber-mill renting 240 beds in 93 stark rooms (S-£40, Sb-£50, twin-£54, Db-£68, dorm bed-£17, includes continental breakfast, CC, lots of school groups, 81 Kensington Gardens Square, W2 4DJ, tel. 020/7243-1810, fax 020/7243-1723, e-mail: londonhousehotel@aol.com).

## Sleeping in Other Neighborhoods

**Paddington Station: The Royal Norfolk Hotel** is a 60-room place on a busy corner just one short block from the Paddington Station terminus of the Heathrow Express train (Db-£100, superior Db-£111, Tb-£130, 25 percent discount for 3-night stay, CC, elevator, 25 London Street, tel. 020/7723-3386, fax 020/7724-8442, www.royalnorfolk.co.uk, e-mail: 106165.1413 @compuserve.com).

**Euston Station:** The **Methodist International Centre**, a modern, youthful Christian residence, fills its lower floors with international students and its top floor with travelers. Rooms are modern and simple yet comfortable, with fine bathrooms, phones, and desks. The atmosphere is friendly, safe, clean, and controlled, with a spacious lounge and game room (Sb-£48, Db-£69, 2-course buffet dinner-£8, CC, nonsmoking rooms, elevator, on a quiet street a block southwest of Euston Square, 81-103 Euston Street, not Euston Road, W1 2EZ, tube: Euston Station, tel. 020/7380-0001, fax 020/7387-5300, e-mail: sales@micentre.com). In June, July, and August, when the students are gone, they rent simple £38 singles.

**Cottage Hotel** is tucked away a block off the west exit of Euston Station. Established in 1950, it's a bit tired, cramped, and smoky. But it's cheap and quiet (40 rooms, D-£50, Db-£60, T-£65, Tb-£75, Qb-£85, CC, 10 percent discount for 2-night cash-only stays, 67 Euston Street, tel. 020/7387-6785, fax 020/7383-0859, managed by Ali).

**Downtown near Baker Street:** For a less-hotelesque alternative in the center, consider renting one of the 18 stark, hardwood, comfortable rooms in **22 York Street B&B** (Db-£100, Tb-£141, CC, strictly smoke-free, inviting lounge, social breakfast, from Baker Street tube station walk 2 blocks down Baker Street and take a right, 22 York Street, tel. 020/7224-3990, fax 020/7224-1990, www.myrtle-cottage.co.uk/callis.htm, energetically run by Liz and Michael).

**Near Buckingham Palace: Vandon House Hotel**, formerly run by the Salvation Army, is now run by the Central University of Iowa. While filled by students most of the year, they rent their 33 rooms to travelers from late May through August at great prices. The rooms, while institutional, are comfy, and the location is excellent (S-£40, D-£62, Db-£79, Tb-£115, Qb-£145, prices promised with this book through 2002, CC, only single beds, nonsmoking, elevator, on a tiny road 2 blocks west of St. James Park tube station, near east end of Petty France Street at 1 Vandon Street, tel. 020/7799-6780, fax 020/7799-1464, www.vandonhouse.com, e-mail: info@vandonhouse.com).

**Near St. Paul's:** The **City of London Youth Hostel** is clean, modern, friendly, and well-run. You'll pay about £25 for a bed in their three- to eight-bed rooms, £28 for a single (hostel membership required, 200 beds, CC, cheap meals, tube: St. Paul's, 36 Carter Lane, EC4V 5AD, tel. 020/7236-4965, fax 020/7236-7681, e-mail: city@yha.org.uk).

## Sleeping near Gatwick and Heathrow Airports

**Near Gatwick Airport:** The **Gatwick Travelodge** is a budget hotel two miles from the airport (Db-£50, CC, breakfast extra, free shuttle from south terminal, Church Road, Lowfield Heath, Crawley, tel. 0870-905-6343, www.travelodge.co.uk). The **London Gatwick Airport Travel Inn** also rents cheap rooms (Db-£50, CC, located at airport, tel. 01293/568-158, www .travelinn.co.uk).

**Barn Cottage**, a converted 17th-century barn, sits in the peaceful countryside with a tennis court, small swimming pool, and a good pub within walking distance. It has two wood-beamed rooms, antique furniture, and a large garden that makes you forget Gatwick is 10 minutes away (S-£35–40, D-£55, no CC, can drive you to airport or train station for £6, Leigh, Reigate, Surrey, RH2 8RF, tel. 01306/611-347, warmly run by Pat and Mike Comer).

The **Wayside Manor Farm** is another rural alternative to a bland airport hotel. This four-bedroom countryside place is a 10-minute drive from the airport (Db-£60, Norwood Hill, near Charlwood, tel. 01293/862-692, www.waysidefm.freeserve.co.uk).

**Near Heathrow Airport:** It's so easy to get to Heathrow from central London, I see no reason to sleep there. But for budget beds near the airport, consider **Heathrow Ibis** (Db-£60, Db-£40 on Fri–Sun nights, breakfast extra, CC, £2.50 shuttle bus to/from terminals except T-4, 112 Bath Road, tel. 020/8759-4888, fax 020/8564-7894, www.ibishotel.com, e-mail: h0794@accor-hotels.com). **Heathrow Airport Travelodge** is another option (300 rooms, Db-£70, Db-£50 Fri–Sun, 2 kids sleep free, CC, free shuttle to/from all terminals, Bath Road, off A4, behind Le Meridien Excelsior Hotel, half-mile from airport, tel. 0870-905-6343, www.travelodge.co.uk).

## Eating in London

If you want to dine (as opposed to eat), check out the extensive listings in the weekly entertainment guides sold at London newsstands (or catch a train for Paris). The thought of a £30 meal in Britain generally ruins my appetite, so my London dining is limited mostly to easygoing, fun, but inexpensive alternatives. I've listed places by neighborhood—handy to your sightseeing or hotel.

Your £7 budget choices are pub grub, a café, fish and chips, pizza, ethnic, or picnic. Pub grub is the most atmospheric bud get option. Many of London's 7,000 pubs serve fresh, tasty buffets under ancient timbers, with hearty lunches and dinners priced from £6 to £8. (While pubs are going strong, the new phenomenon is coffee shops: Starbucks and its competitors have sprouted up all over town, providing cushy and social watering holes with comfy chairs, easy WCs, £2 lattes, and a nice break between sights.)

Ethnic restaurants from all over the world add spice to England's lackluster cuisine scene. Eating Indian or Chinese is "going local" in London. It's also going cheap (cheaper if you take it out). Most large museums (and many churches) have inexpensive, cheery cafeterias. Sandwich shops (try "tikka chicken"—curry flavored) are a hit with local workers eating on the run. Of course, picnicking is the fastest and cheapest way to go. Good grocery stores and sandwich shops, fine park benches, and polite pigeons abound in Britain's most expensive city.

### Eating near Trafalgar Square

For a tasty meal on a monk's budget sitting on somebody's tomb in an ancient crypt, descend into the **St. Martin-in-the-Fields Café in the Crypt** (£5–7 cafeteria plates, cheaper sandwich bar, Mon–Sat 10:00–20:00, Sun 12:00–20:30, profits go to the church; underneath St. Martin-in-the-Fields on Trafalgar Square, tel. 020/7839-4342).

**Chandos Bar's Opera Room** floats amazingly apart from the tacky crush of tourism around Trafalgar Square. Look for the pub opposite the National Portrait Gallery (corner of William Street and St. Martin's Lane) and climb the stairs to the Opera Room. They serve £6 pub lunches and dinners (kitchen open daily 11:00–19:00, tel. 020/7836-1401). This is a fine Trafalgar rendezvous point—smoky, but wonderfully local.

✳ **Gordon's Wine Bar** is ripe with atmosphere. A simple steep staircase leads into a 14th-century cellar filled with dusty old wine bottles, faded British memorabilia, local nine-to-fivers, and candle-light (hot meals only for lunch, fine plate of cheeses or various cold cuts with salad buffet all day until 21:00—1 plate of each feeds 2 for £7). While it's crowded, you can normally corral two chairs and grab the corner of a table (Mon–Sat 12:00–22:00, closed Sun, arrive before 18:00 to get a seat, 2 blocks from Trafalgar Square, bottom of Villiars Street at #47, near Embankment tube station, tel. 020/7930-1408).

Down Whitehall (toward Big Ben), a block south of Trafalgar Square, you'll find the touristy but atmospheric **Clarence Pub** (lunch only, decent grub) and several cheaper cafeterias and pizza joints.

For a classy lunch in the National Gallery, treat your palate to the moderately-priced light Mediterranean cuisine at **Crivelli's Garden** (daily 10:00–17:00, 1st floor of Sainsbury Wing).

**Simpson's on the Strand** serves a stuffy, aristocratic, old-time carvery dinner—where the chef slices your favorite red meat from a fancy trolley at your table—in their elegant, smoky old dining room (£20, Mon–Sat 12:15–14:30, 17:30–22:45, no tennis shoes or T-shirts, at #100 the Strand, tel. 020/7836-9112).

## Eating near Piccadilly

Hungry and broke in the theater district? Head for Panton Street (off Haymarket, 2 blocks southeast of Piccadilly Circus) for cheap Thai, Chinese, and two famous London eateries. **Stockpot** is a mushy-peas kind of place, famous and rightly popular for its edible, cheap meals (daily 7:00–22:00, 38 Panton Street). The **West End Kitchen** (across the street at #5, same hrs and menu) is a direct competitor that's just as good.

The palatial **Criterion Brasserie** serves a special £15 two-course "Anglo-French" *menu* (or £18 for 3 courses) under gilded tiles and chandeliers in a dreamy Byzantine-church setting from 1880. It's right on Piccadilly Circus but a world away from the punk junk. The house wine is great and so is the food (specials available Mon–Sat 12:00–14:30 and 17:30–18:30, dinner served until 23:00, CC, closed Sun lunch, tel. 020/7930-0488). Anyone can drop in for coffee or a drink.

## The "Food Is Fun" Dinner Crawl: From Covent Garden to Soho

London has a trendy generation X scene that most Beefeater seekers miss entirely. For a multicultural movable feast and a chance to sample some of London's most popular eateries, consider sampling these. Start around 18:00 to avoid lines, get in on early specials, and find waiters willing to let you split a meal. Prices, while reasonable by London standards, add up. Servings are large enough to share. All are open nightly.

**Suggested nibbler's dinner crawl for two:** Arrive before 18:00 at **Belgo** and split the early-bird dinner special: a kilo of mussels, fries, and dark Belgian beer. At **Yo! Sushi**, have beer or sake and a few dishes. Slurp your last course at **Wagamama**. Then, for dessert, people watch at Leicester Square, where the serf's always up.

**Belgo Centraal** is a space-station world overrun with Trappist monks serving hearty Belgian specialties. The classy restaurant section requires reservations, but just grabbing a bench in the boisterous beer hall (no reservations possible) is more fun. The same menu and specials work on both sides. Belgians claim they eat as well as the French and as heartily as the Germans. Specialties include mussels, great fries, and a stunning array of dark, blond, and fruity Belgian beers. Belgo actually makes things Belgian trendy—a formidable feat (£14 meals; open daily till very late; Mon–Fri 17:00–18:30 "beat the clock" meal specials cost only the time ... £5-6.30, and you get mussels, fries, and beer; no meal splitting after 18:30 and they are not licensed to serve anyone just a beer; daily £5 lunch special 12:00–17:00; 1 block north of Covent Garden tube station at intersection of Neal and Shelton Streets, 50 Earlham Street, tel. 020/7813-2233).

# From Covent Garden to Soho, "Food is Fun"

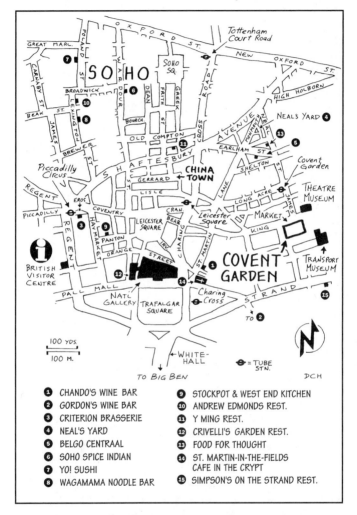

- **1** CHANDO'S WINE BAR
- **2** GORDON'S WINE BAR
- **3** CRITERION BRASSERIE
- **4** NEAL'S YARD
- **5** BELGO CENTRAAL
- **6** SOHO SPICE INDIAN
- **7** YO! SUSHI
- **8** WAGAMAMA NOODLE BAR
- **9** STOCKPOT & WEST END KITCHEN
- **10** ANDREW EDMONDS REST.
- **11** Y MING REST.
- **12** CRIVELLI'S GARDEN REST.
- **13** FOOD FOR THOUGHT
- **14** ST. MARTIN-IN-THE-FIELDS CAFE IN THE CRYPT
- **15** SIMPSON'S ON THE STRAND REST.

**Yo! Sushi** is a futuristic Japanese-food-extravaganza experience. With thumping rock, Japanese cable TV, a 60-meter-long conveyor-belt, the world's longest sushi bar, a robotic drink trolley, and automated sushi machines, just sipping a sake on a bar stool here is a trip. For £1 you get *miso* soup, unlimited tea (on request), or water (from spigot at bar, with or without gas). Grab dishes as they rattle by (priced by color of dish; check the chart) and a drink off the trash-talking robot. Weekdays from 15:00–19:00 they serve a "rainbow special"—five different colored plates for £10 (daily 12:00–24:00, 2 blocks south of Oxford Street, where Lexington Street becomes Poland Street, 52 Poland Street, tel. 020/7287-0443). For more-serious drinking on tatami mats, go downstairs into "Yo Below."

⌇ **Wagamama Noodle Bar** is a noisy, pan-Asian organic slurp-athon. As you enter, check out the kitchen and listen to the roar of the basement, where benches rock with happy eaters. Every-body sucks. Stand against the wall to feel the energy of all this "positive eating" (daily 12:00–23:00, crowded after 20:00, non-smoking, 10A Lexington Street, tel. 020/7292-0990). If you like this place, there are now branches all over town (including a handy one near the British Museum on Streatham Street).

**Soho Spice Indian** is where modern Britain meets Indian tradition—fine Indian cuisine in a trendy jewel-tone ambience. The £15 "Tandoori selections" meal is the best "variety" dish and big enough for two (daily 11:30–24:00, nonsmoking section available Sun–Tue, CC, 5 blocks north of Piccadilly Circus at 124 Wardour Street, tel. 020/7434-0808).

**Y Ming Chinese Restaurant**, across Shaftesbury Avenue from the ornate gates, clatter, and dim sum of Chinatown, has clean European décor, serious but helpful service, and authentic Northern Chinese cooking (good £10 meal deal offered 12:00–18:00, Mon–Sat 12:00–23:30, closed Sun, 35 Greek Street, tel. 020/7734-2721).

**Andrew Edmunds Restaurant** is a tiny candlelit place where you'll want to hide your camera and guidebook and act as local as possible. The modern-European cooking is worth the splurge (3 courses for £25, daily 12:30–15:00, 18:00–22:45, 46 Lexington Street in Soho, reservations are generally necessary, tel. 020/7437-5708).

For cheap, hip, and healthy near Covent Garden, the area around Neal's Yard is busy with fun, hippie-type cafés. One of the best is **Food for Thought** (good £5 vegetarian meals, Mon–Sat 12:00–20:30, Sun 12:00–17:00, nonsmoking, 2 blocks north of tube: Covent Garden, 31 Neal Street, tel. 020/7836-0239). Neal's Yard itself is a food circus of trendy, healthy eateries.

## Eating near Recommended Victoria Station Accommodations

Here are places a couple of blocks southwest of Victoria Station where I've enjoyed eating (see map on page 78).

**Jenny Lo's Tea House** is a simple, for-the-joy-of-good-food kind of place serving up eclectic Chinese-style meals to locals in the know (£5–7, Mon–Fri 11:30–15:00, 18:00–22:00, Sat 12:00–15:00, 18:00–22:00, closed Sun, no CC, 14 Eccleston Street, tel. 020/7259-0399 or 020/7823-6331).

The small but classy **La Campagnola** is Belgravia's favorite budget Italian restaurant (£12–15, Mon–Sat 12:00–15:00, 18:00–23:30, closed Sun, CC, 10 Lower Belgrave Street, tel. 020/7730-2057).

The **Ebury Wine Bar**, filled with young professionals, provides a classy atmosphere and pricey but delicious meals (£15–18, daily 12:00–15:00, 18:00–22:30, CC, 139 Ebury Street, at intersection with Elizabeth Street, near bus station, tel. 020/7730-5447). Several cheap places are around the corner on Elizabeth Street (#23 for take-out or eat-in super-absorbent fish and chips).

The **Duke of Wellington** pub is a good, if smoky, neighborhoody place for dinner (£6 meals, Mon–Sat 11:00–23:00, Sun 12:00–22:30, 63 Eaton Terrace, at intersection with Chester Row, tel. 020/7730-1782).

**La Poule au Pot**, ideal for a romantic splurge, offers a classy candlelit ambience with well-dressed patrons and expensive but fine Mediterranean and Provencal-style French food (£20–25 dinners, daily 12:30–14:30, 19:00–23:00, Sun until 22:00, leafy patio dining, reservations smart, end of Ebury, at intersection with Pimlico, 231 Ebury Street, tel. 020/7730-7763).

**Jomuna Tandoori** serves quality Indian cuisine (daily 12:00–15:00, 18:00–23:30, 74 Wilton Road, near Eccleston Hotel, tel. 020/7828-7509).

The **Marche** is an easy but pricey cafeteria a couple of blocks north of Victoria Station at Bressenden Place (Mon–Sat 7:30–23:00, Sun 11:00–21:00, CC, tel. 020/7630-1733). If you miss America, there's a mall-type food circus at Victoria Place, upstairs in Victoria Station. **Café Rouge** offers the best food there (£8–11 dinners, daily 9:30–22:30).

**Groceries:** The late-hours **Whistle Stop** at the station has decent sandwiches, fresh fruit, snacks, and beverages (daily, 24 hrs). A larger grocery, **Sainsbury Local**, is on Victoria Street in front of the station, just past the buses (Mon–Fri 7:00–22:00, Sat 7:00–21:00, Sun 10:00–16:00).

### Eating near Recommended Notting Hill Gate B&Bs and Bayswater Hotels

Queensway is lined with lively and inexpensive eateries. See map on page 83.

The exuberantly rustic and very English **Maggie Jones** serves my favorite £20 London dinner. You'll get solid English cuisine, including huge plates of crunchy vegetables—by candlelight (daily 12:30–14:30, 18:30–23:00, much-less-expensive lunch menu, CC, 6 Old Court Place, just east of Kensington Church Street, near High Street Kensington tube stop, reservations recommended—request upstairs for noisy but less-cramped section, tel. 020/7937-6462). If you eat well once in London, eat here (and do it soon, before it burns down).

The **Churchill Arms** pub is a local hangout, with good beer and old-English ambience in front and hearty £6 Thai plates in an enclosed patio in the back. You can bring the Thai food into the smoky but wonderfully atmospheric pub section. Arrive by 18:00 to avoid a line (Mon–Sat 12:00–14:30, 18:00–21:30, Sun 12:00–14:30, 119 Kensington Church Street, tel. 020/7792-1246).

**Prince Edward Pub** serves good traditional pub grub with great pub ambience (£8 meals, daily 12:00–15:00, 18:00–22:00, CC, indoor/outdoor seating, 2 blocks north of Bayswater Road at the corner of Dawson Place and Hereford Road, 73 Prince's Square, tel. 020/7727-2221).

**Cafe Diana** is a healthy little eatery serving sandwiches and Middle Eastern food. It's decorated with photos of Princess Diana because she used to drop by for pita sandwiches (daily 8:00–22:30, 5 Wellington Terrace, on Bayswater Road, opposite Kensington Palace Garden Gates—where Diana once lived, tel. 020/7792-9606).

**The Royal China Restaurant** is filled with London's Chinese who consider this one of the city's best eateries. It's black, white, chrome, and candles with brisk waiters and fine food (£7–9 dishes, dim sum, daily 12:00–17:00, CC, 13 Queens-way, tel. 020/7221-2535).

**Mr. Wu's Chinese Restaurant** serves a 10-course buffet in a bright and cheery little place. Just grab a plate and help yourself (£4.50, daily 12:00–23:00, check quality of buffet—right inside entrance—before committing, pickings can get slim, across from Bayswater tube station, 54 Queensway, tel. 020/7243-1017).

**Whiteleys Mall Food Court** offers a fun selection of ethnic and fast-food eateries in a delightful mall (good salads at Café Rouge, 2nd floor, corner of Porchester Gardens and Queensway).

**Supermarket: Europa** is a half block from the Notting Hill Gate tube stop (Mon–Fri 8:00–23:00, Sun 12:00–18:00, 112 Notting Hill Gate, near intersection with Pembridge Road).

## Eating near Recommended Accommodations in South Kensington

Popular eateries line Old Brompton Road and Thurloe Street (tube: South Kensington). See map on page 81.

**La Bouchee Bistro Café** is a classy hole-in-the-wall touch of France serving early-bird three-course meals for £11 before 19:00 and *plats du jour* for £8 all *jour* (daily 12:00–23:00, CC, 56 Old Brompton Road, tel. 020/7589-1929).

**Daquise**, an authentic-feeling Polish place, is ideal if you're in the mood for kielbasa and kraut. It's fast, cheap, family-run, and a part of the neighborhood (£10 meals, daily until 23:00, CC, nonsmoking, 20 Thurloe Street, tel. 020/7589-6117).

The **Khyber Pass Tandoori Restaurant** is a nondescript but handy place serving great Punjabi-style Indian cuisine. Locals in-the-know eat here (£10 dinners, daily 12:00–14:30, 18:00–23:30, CC, 21 Bute Street, tel. 020/7589-7311).

**La Brasserie** fills a big "nicotine yellow" room with ceiling fans, a Parisian ambience, and good traditional French cooking at reasonable prices (2-course £16 "regional *menu*," £13 bottle of house wine, CC, nightly until 23:30, 272 Brompton Road, tel. 020/7581-3089).

**PJ's Bar and Grill** is lively with the yuppie Chelsea crowd for a good reason. Traditional "New York Brasserie"–style yet trendy, it's dressy tables surround a centerpiece bar. It serves pricey, cosmopolitan cuisine from a menu that changes with the seasons (£20 meals, CC, nightly until 24:00, 52 Fulham Road, at intersection with Sydney Street, tel. 020/7581-0025).

### Eating Elsewhere in London
**Near St. Paul's, in the City:** The **Counting House**, formerly an elegant old bank, offers great £7 meals, nice homemade meat pies, fish, and fresh vegetables (Mon–Fri 12:00–20:00, closed Sat–Sun, gets really busy with the buttoned-down 9-to-5 crowd after 12:15, near Mansion House in the City, 50 Cornhill, tel. 020/7283-7123).

**Near the British Library:** Drummond Street (running just east of Euston Station) is famous in London for very cheap and good Indian and vegetarian food. Consider **Chutneys** and **Ravi Shankar** for a good *thali*.

## Transportation Connections—London

### Flying into London's Heathrow Airport
Heathrow Airport is the world's fourth busiest. Think about it: 60 million passengers a year on 425,000 flights from 200 destinations riding 90 airlines...some kind of global Maypole dance. While many complain about it, I like it. It's user-friendly. Read signs, ask questions. For Heathrow's airport, flight, and transfers information, call the switchboard at 0870-000-0123. It has four terminals: T-1 (mostly domestic flights with some European), T-2 (mostly European flights), T-3 (mostly flights from the United States), and T-4 (British Air transatlantic flights and BA flights to Paris, Amsterdam, and Athens). Taxis know which terminal you'll need.

Each terminal has an airport information desk, car-rental agencies, exchange bureaus and ATMs, a pharmacy, a VAT refund desk (VAT info tel. 020/8910-3682; you must present the VAT claim form from the retailer here to get your 15 percent tax rebate on items purchased in Britain), and a £3.50/day baggage-check desk (open 05:30–23:00). There are post offices in T-2 and T-4. Each terminal has cheap eateries (such as the cheery Food Village self-service cafeteria in T-3). The American Express desk, in the tube station at Terminal 4 (daily 7:00–19:00), has rates similar to the exchange bureaus upstairs, but they don't charge a commission (typically 1.5 percent) for cashing any type of traveler's check.

Heathrow's small TI gives you all the help that London's Victoria Station does, but with none of the crowds (daily 8:30–18:00, 5-min walk from Terminal 3 in the tube station, follow signs to "underground"; bypass the queue for transit info to reach the window for London questions). If you're riding the Airbus into London, have your partner stay with the bags at the terminal. At the TI, get a free map and brochures, and if you're taking the tube into London, buy a Travel Card day pass to cover the ride (see below). Heathrow's "Internet Exchange" provides Internet access 24 hours a day (Terminal 3).

### Transportation to London from Heathrow Airport

**By Tube (Subway):** For £3.50, the tube takes you 14 miles to downtown London in 50 minutes (6/hr, depending on your destination, may require a change). Even better, buy a £4.90 Travel Card that covers your trip into London and all your tube travel for the day (starting at 9:30). Buy it at the ticket window at the tube. You can hop on the tube at any terminal.

**By Airport Bus:** The Airbus, running between the airport and London's King's Cross Station, serves the Notting Hill Gate and Bayswater neighborhoods (£7, £10-round-trip, 2/hr, 1 hr, 06:30–21:15, departs from each terminal, buy ticket from driver). The tube works fine, but with baggage I prefer the Airbus (assuming it serves my hotel neighborhood) because there are no connections underground and there's a lovely view from the top of the double-decker bus. Ask the driver to remind you when to get off. For people heading to the airport, exact pick-up times are clearly posted at each bus stop.

If you're staying in London's Victoria Station neighborhood, consider the National Express bus that runs between Heathrow's central bus station and the Victoria Coach Station, which is one block from Victoria Station (£6, kids go free, 2/hr, 40 min, 05:40–21:45 from Heathrow, 7:45–24:00 from Victoria, tel. 08705-808-080).

**By Taxi:** Taxis from the airport cost about £40. For four people traveling together this can be a deal. Hotels can often line up a cab back to the airport for £30. For the cheapest taxi to the airport don't order one from your hotel. Simply flag down a few and ask them for their best "off-meter" rate (I managed a ride for £25).

**By Heathrow Express Train:** This slick train service zips you between Heathrow Airport and London's Paddington Station. At Paddington Station you're in the thick of the tube system, with easy access to any of my recommended neighborhoods—Notting Hill Gate is just two stops away (£12, but ask about discount promos at Heathrow ticket desk, children under 16 ride free if you buy tickets before boarding, £2 surcharge for tickets purchased on train, CC, covered by Britrail pass; 4/hr, daily 05:10–23:30, 15 min to downtown from Terminals 1, 2, 3; 20 min from T-4; works as a free transfer between terminals, tel. 0845-600-1515, www.heathrowexpress.co.uk); a "Go Further" ticket (£13.50) includes one tube ride from Paddington to get you to your hotel (valid only on same day and in Zone 1, saves time). For one person, combining the Heathrow Express with either a tube or taxi ride (between your hotel and Paddington) is as fast as and half the cost of taking a cab directly to (or from) the airport.

**If you're flying out of Heathrow, check in at London's Paddington station.** Take advantage of the calm, easy airline check-in at Paddington. If you're using any of the 26 represented airlines (including British Airways, British Midland, American, Lufthansa, SAS, Swiss Air, United Airlines, Air Canada, and Canadian Airlines), you can get a boarding pass and check your luggage (daily 05:00–21:00, last check-in 1 hour before departure with a carry-on, 2 hrs with bags to check). You'll avoid the crowded chaos of check-in at Heathrow and, even better, you'll have a little more time to sightsee before heading out to the airport. (On the morning of my most recent departure, I checked my luggage at Paddington—6 hrs before my flight—then went on the London Eye Ferris wheel, which I'd booked the day before.) You can also check bags here and then ride the cheaper tube out to Heathrow.

## Buses from Heathrow to Destinations beyond London

The **National Express Central Bus Station** offers direct bus connections to **Gatwick Airport** (2/hr, 75 min). There are two services: Speedlink for £17 and Jetlink for £12 (from central bus station, a 5-min walk to terminals 1, 2, or 3). Several direct buses run daily to **Bath** (11/day, 2.5 hrs, £12.50, direct, tel. 08705-757-747). Britrail passholders may prefer the 2.5-hour Heathrow-Bath bus/train connection via Reading (free with pass, otherwise £29.20, payable at desk in terminal, CC); catch the twice-hourly RailAir Link shuttle bus to Reading (RED-ding), then hop on the hourly express train to Bath. Most Heathrow buses depart from the common area serving terminals 1, 2, and 3, although some depart from T-4 (bus tel. 08705-747-777).

## Flying into London's Gatwick Airport

More and more flights, especially charters, land at Gatwick Airport, halfway between London and the southern coast (airport recorded info tel. 0870-000-2468). Trains—clearly the best way into London from here—shuttle conveniently between Gatwick and London's Victoria Station (£10.20, £19.50 round-trip, 4/hr during day, 1–2/hr at night, 40 min, runs 24 hrs daily, can purchase tickets on train at no extra charge, tel. 08705-301-530, www.gatwickexpress.co.uk). To get to Bath from Gatwick, catch the Flight Link bus to Heathrow and the bus to Bath from there.

## London's Other Airports

If you're flying into or out of **Stansted** (airport tel. 0870-0000-303), you can take the Airbus between the airport and downtown London's Victoria Coach Station (£8, 2/hr, 90 min, runs 04:00–24:00, picks up and stops throughout London, tel. 08705-747-777) or take the Stansted Airport Rail Link (departs London's Liverpool Station, 40 min, 2–4/hr, 05:00–23:00).

For **Luton** (airport tel. 01582/405-100, www.london-luton .com), try Green Line's bus #757, which runs between the airport and London's Victoria Station at Buckingham Palace Road—stop 6 (£7.50, 2/hr, 1–1.25 hrs depending on time of day, runs 04:30–24:00, tel. 0870-608-7261, www.greenline.co.uk).

## Discounted Flights from London

BMI British Midland has been around the longest, but Virgin Express and Ryanair generally offer cheaper flights.

**BMI British Midland**, the local discount airline, can be cheaper than the train. You can fly inexpensively to Edinburgh (as little as £75 round-trip if you stay over Sat); to Dublin, Ireland (as little as £103 round-trip over Sat); to Paris (as little as £75 round-trip over Sat); and elsewhere. For the latest, call British tel. 0870-607-0555 or U.S. tel. 800/788-0555 (www.flybmi.com). The further you book in advance (up to about 9–12 months or as few as 3 weeks), the cheaper the fares. You can book right up until the flight departs, but the cheap seats will have sold out long before, leaving the expensive seats for latecomers.

**Virgin Express** is a British-owned company with good rates (book by phone and pick up ticket at airport 1 hour before your flight, tel. 020/7744-0004, www.virgin-express.com). Virgin Express flies from London Heathrow and Brussels. From its hub in Brussels you can connect cheaply to Barcelona, Madrid, Nice, Malaga, Copenhagen, Rome, or Milan (round-trip from Brussels to Rome for as little as £105). Their prices stay the same whether or not you book in advance.

**Ryanair** is a creative Irish airline that prides itself on offering the lowest fares. They fly from London (mostly Stansted airport) to obscure airports in Dublin, Glasgow, Frankfurt, Stockholm, Oslo, Venice, Turin, and elsewhere. Sample fares: London-Dublin—£78 round-trip, London-Frankfurt—£67 round-trip (Irish tel. 01/609-7881, British tel. 0870-333-1231, www.ryanair.com). Because they offer promotional deals any time of year, it's not essential that you book long in advance to get the best deals.

## Trains and Buses

London has a different train station for each region. Waterloo handles the Eurostar to Paris. King's Cross covers northeast England and Scotland (tel. 08457-225-225). Paddington covers west and southwest England (Bath) and South Wales (tel. 08457-000-125). For the others, call 08457-484-950. Also see the BritRail Routes map in the Introduction.

National Express' excellent bus service is considerably cheaper than taking the train. (For a busy signal, call 08705-808-080, or visit www.nationalexpress.co.uk or the bus station a block southwest of Victoria Station.)

**To Bath:** Trains leave London's Paddington Station every hour (at a quarter after) for the 75-minute ride to Bath (costs roughly £31 if you leave after 9:30). As an alternative, consider taking a guided bus tour from London to Stonehenge and Bath and abandoning the tour in Bath. Evan Evans' tour comes fully guided, with admissions, for £48 (for details, see "Daytrips from London," on page 74). Golden Tours also runs a fully-guided Stonehenge-Bath tour for a similar price (departs from Fountain Square, across from Victoria Coach Station, tel. 020/7233-6668, www.goldentours.co.uk).

**To points north:** Trains run hourly from London's King's Cross Station, stopping in York (2 hrs), Durham (3 hrs), and Edinburgh (5 hrs).

**To Dublin, Ireland:** The boat/rail journey takes between 10 and 11 hours and goes all day or all night (£24–35, 7/day, tel. 08705-143-219, www.eurolines.co.uk). Consider a cheap 70-minute Ryanair flight instead (see above).

## Crossing the English Channel

**By Eurostar Train:** The fastest and most convenient way to get from Big Ben to the Eiffel Tower is by rail. In London, advertisements claim "more businessmen travel from London to Paris on the Eurostar than on all airlines combined." Eurostar is the speedy passenger train that zips you (and up to 800 others in 18 sleek cars) from downtown London to downtown Paris (15/day, 3 hrs) or Brussels (9/day, 3 hrs) faster and more easily than flying. The train goes 80 miles per hour in England and 190 miles per hour on the Continent. (When the English segment gets up to speed the journey time will shrink to 2 hrs.) The actual tunnel crossing is a 20-minute, black, silent, 100-mile-per-hour nonevent. Your ears won't even pop. You can go direct to Disneyland Paris (1/day, more frequent with transfer at Lille) or change at Lille to catch a TGV to Paris' Charles de Gaulle Airport.

Channel fares (essentially the same to Paris or Brussels) are reasonable but complicated. For the latest, call 800/EUROSTAR in the United States. These are prices from 2001: The "Leisure

Ticket" is cheap ($139 second class, $219 first class, 50 percent refundable up to 3 days before departure). "Full Fare" first class costs $279 and includes a meal (a dinner departure nets you more grub than breakfast); second class (or "standard") costs $199 (fully refundable even after departure date). Discounts are available to travelers holding railpasses that include France, Belgium, or Britain ($155 for first class, $75 for second); seniors over 60 ($189 for first class); youths under 26 ($79 in second class); and children under 12 (about half the fare of your ticket).

Cheaper seats can sell out. Book from home if you're ready to commit to a date and time. Compare fares sold by U.S. rail agents (www.raileurope.com) and British agents (www.eurostar .co.uk). If you're ready to commit to a date, time, and U.S. prices, you can book by calling 800/EUROSTAR, visiting www .raileurope.com, or having your travel agent do it all for you (prices do not include FedEx ticket delivery). For the British fares, book by calling 08705-186-186 or visiting www.eurostar .co.uk (pick up ticket at station).

Buying a Eurostar ticket in London is easy. Here are some sample London-Paris standard—that's second-class—fares from 2001 (London-Brussels fares are about the same). Avoid the "standard flexi" fare: one-way for £165, round-trip for £300. Those with a railpass pay £50 one-way, any day. Without a rail-pass, a same-day round-trip on a Saturday or Sunday costs £70. The various second-class round-trip Leisure Tickets (for stays over a Sat) are affordable: Leisure Flexi—£160 (partially refundable if not used), Leisure—£120 (not refundable), Leisure Apex 7— £95 (not refundable, purchase at least 7 days in advance), Leisure Apex 14—£70 (not refundable, purchase at least 14 days in advance, stay 2 nights or over a Sat). Many cheaper fares sell out in advance. One-way tickets for departures after 14:00 Friday or anytime Sat-urday or Sunday cost £105. Youth tickets (for those under 26) are £45 one-way to either Paris or Brussels (£75 round-trip, exchange-able but not refundable). First-class and business-class fares are much higher. Remember, round-trip tickets over a Saturday are much cheaper than the basic one-way fare . . . you know the trick.

In Europe you can get your Eurostar ticket at any major train station (in any country) or at any travel agency that handles train tickets (expect a booking fee). In Britain you can book and pay for tickets over the phone with a credit card by calling 08705-186-186 and pick up your tickets at London's Waterloo station an hour before the Eurostar departure. Note: Britain's time zone is one hour earlier than the Continent's. Times listed on tickets are local times.

**By Bus and Boat or Train and Boat:** The old-fashioned way of crossing the channel is cheaper than crossing via Eurostar. It's also twice as romantic, complicated, and time-consuming.

You'll get better prices arranging your trip in London than you would in the United States. Taking the bus is cheapest, and round-trips are a bargain.

By **bus** to Paris, Brussels, or Amsterdam from Victoria Coach Station (via boat or chunnel): £32 one-way, £52 round-trip; 7 hrs to Paris—7/day; 7 hrs to Brussels—10/day; 11.25 hrs to Amsterdam—6/day; day or overnight, on Eurolines (tel. 08705-143-219, www.eurolines.co.uk).

The **Hoverspeed ferry** runs between Dover, England, and Calais, France (tel. 08705-240-241, www.hoverspeed.com). Hoverspeed sells rail and ferry packages for trips between London and Paris: £39 one-way; £49 round-trip with five-day return; and £58 round-trip over more than five days. You can buy this package deal in person at Waterloo or Charing Cross stations. If you book by phone (number listed above), you must book at least two weeks in advance and the ticket will be mailed to you (no ticket pick-up at station for bookings by phone).

By **P&O Stena Line ferry** from Dover to Calais: £26 one-way; £48 round-trip with five-day return; £52 round-trip over more than five days (tel. 0870-600-0613, www.posl.com). Prices are for the ferry only; you need to book your own train tickets.

**By Plane:** Typical fares are £110 regular, less for student standby. Call in London for the latest fares. Consider BMI British Midland (see "Discounted Flights," above) for its cheap round-trip fares to Paris.

# NEAR LONDON: WINDSOR, GREENWICH, AND CAMBRIDGE

## WINDSOR

The pleasant pedestrians-only shopping zone of Windsor litters the approach to its famous palace with fun temptations. You'll find the **TI** on 24 High Street (daily 10:00-17:00, tel. 01753/743-900, www.windsor.gov.uk).

▲▲**Windsor Palace**—Windsor claims to be the largest and oldest occupied castle in the world. The official residence of England's royal family for 900 years, the queen considers this sprawling and fortified palace her primary residence. Thankfully, touring it is simple: you'll see immense grounds, lavish staterooms, a crowd-pleasing dollhouse, an art gallery, and the chapel.

Immediately upon entering you pass through a simple modern building housing an historical overview of the castle. This excellent intro is worth a close look since you're basically on your own after this. Inside you'll find the motte (artificial mound) and bailey (fortified stockade around it) of William the Conqueror's castle still visible. Dating from 1080, this was his first castle in England.

Follow the signs to the staterooms/gallery/dollhouse.

Queen Mary's Dollhouse—a palace in miniature (1/12 scale from 1923) and "the most famous dollhouse in the world"—comes with the longest wait. You can skip that line and go immediately into the lavish staterooms. Strewn with history and the art of a long line of kings and queens, it's the best I've seen in Britain—and well-restored after the devastating 1992 fire. The adjacent gallery is a changing exhibit featuring the royal art collection (and some big names such as Michelangelo and Leonardo). Signs direct you (downhill) to St. George's Chapel. Housing ten royal tombs, it's a fine example of Perpendicular Gothic with classic fan vaulting spreading out from each pillar (about 1500). Next door is the sumptuous 13th-century Albert Memorial Chapel redecorated after the death of Queen Victoria's beloved Prince Albert in 1861 and dedicated to his memory. (Admission: £11, £28/family, £3 audioguide is better than official guidebook for help throughout, daily 9:45-17:15, last entry 16:00, Nov-Feb closes at 16:15, changing of the guard most days at 11:00, evensong in the chapel at 17:15, recorded info tel. 01753/831-118, live info at tel. 01753/869-898, www.windsor-tourism.co.uk).

**Legoland Windsor**—This huge kid-pleasing park next to Windsor Palace has dozens of tame but fun rides (often with very long lines) scattered throughout its 150 acres. An impressive Mini-Land has 28 million Lego pieces glued together to create 800 tiny buildings and a virtual mini-tour of Europe. The place is fun for Legomaniacs under 12 (£19, kids-£16, under 3 free, £8 if you enter during last 2 hrs, daily 10:00-17:00, 18:00, or 19:00 depending upon season and day, shuttle bus runs from Windsor's Parish Church twice hrly except 14:00-15:15 "while the driver has his lunch," clearly sign-posted, easy free parking, tel. 08705-040-404, www.legoland.co.uk).

## Transportation Connections—Windsor

**By train**: Windsor has two train stations: Windsor Central (5-min walk to palace and TI) and Windsor & Eton Riverside (10-min walk to palace and TI). Thames Trains run between London's Paddington Station and Windsor Central (2/hr, 40 min, change at Slough, www.thamestrains.co.uk). South West Trains run between London's Waterloo Station and the Windsor & Eton Riverside station (2/hr, 50 min, www.swtrains.co.uk).

   **By bus:** Buses #700 and #702 run hourly between London's Victoria Station and Windsor, where the bus stops in front of Legoland and near the palace—the stop is "Parish Church" (1.5 hrs).

   **By car**: Windsor, 20 miles from London and just off Heathrow airport's landing path, is well sign-posted from the M4 motorway. It's a convenient stop for anyone arriving at Heathrow, picking up a car, and not going into London.

# GREENWICH

The palace at Greenwich was favored by the Tudor kings. Henry VIII was born here. Later kings commissioned Inigo Jones and Chris Wren to beautify the town and palace. In spite of Greenwich's architectural and royal treats, this is England's maritime capital, and visitors go for things salty. Greenwich hosts historic ships, nautical shops, and hordes of tourists.

See the two ships—*Cutty Sark* and *Gipsy Moth IV*—upon arrival. Then walk the shoreline promenade with a possible lunch or drink in the venerable Trafalgar Tavern before heading up to the National Maritime Museum and Old Royal Observatory.

The TI, facing the riverside square a few paces from the *Cutty Sark*, has a café, WC, and displays that provide a brief history of the town (daily 10:00–17:00, 2 Cutty Sark Gardens, Pepys House, tel. 0870-608-2000, www.greenwich.gov.uk). Guided walks cover the big sights (£4, daily 12:15 and 14:15). A shuttle bus runs from Greenwich Pier to the observatory on top of the hill (£1.50, ticket good all day, daily 11:00–17:00, every 15 min). Greenwich throbs with daytrippers on weekends because of its arts-and-crafts and antique markets; to avoid crowds, visit on a weekday.

## Sights—Greenwich

▲▲*Cutty Sark*—The Scottish-built *Cutty Sark* was the last of the great China tea clippers. Handsomely restored, she was the queen of the seas when first launched in 1869. With 32,000 square feet of sail, she could blow with the wind 300 miles in a day. Below deck you'll see the best collection of merchant-ship figureheads in Britain and exhibits giving a vivid peek into the lives of Victorian sailors back when Britain ruled the waves. Stand at the big wheel and look up at the still-rigged main mast towering 150 feet above. You may meet costumed storytellers telling tales of the high seas and local old salts giving knot-tying demonstrations (£3.50; discounts for kids under 16, seniors, and students; daily 10:00–17:00, tel. 020/8858-3445, www.cuttysark.org.uk).

▲*Gipsy Moth IV*—Tiny next to the *Cutty Sark*, the 53-foot *Gipsy Moth IV* is the boat Sir Francis Chichester used for the first solo circumnavigation of the world in 1966 and 1967. Upon Chichester's return, Queen Elizabeth II knighted him in Greenwich, using the same sword Elizabeth I had used to knight Francis Drake in 1581 (free; viewable anytime, but interior not open to public).

**Stroll the Thames to Trafalgar Tavern**—From the *Cutty Sark* and *Gipsy Moth*, pass the pier and wander east along the Thames on Five Foot Walk (the width of the path) for grand views in front of the Old Royal Naval College (see below). Founded by William III as a naval hospital and designed by Wren, the college was split in two because Queen Mary didn't want the view from Queen's House blocked. The riverside view is good, too, with the twin-domed towers of the college (one giving the time, the other the direction of the wind) framing Queen's House and the Royal Observatory Greenwich crowning the hill beyond.

Continuing downstream, just past the college, you'll see the Trafalgar Tavern. Dickens knew the pub well and even used it as the setting for the wedding breakfast in *Our Mutual Friend*. Built in 1837 in the Regency style to attract Londoners downriver, the tavern is still popular with Londoners (and tourists) for its fine lunches. The upstairs Nelson Room is still used for weddings. Its formal moldings and elegant windows with balconies over the Thames are a step back in time (Mon–Sat 11:30–23:00, Sun from 12:00, lunch 12:00–15:00, £6–10 dinners Tue–Sat 17:00–22:00, no dinner Sun–Mon, CC, Park Row, tel. 020/8858-2437). From the pub, enjoy views of the Millennium Dome a mile downstream.

From the Trafalgar Tavern, you can walk the two long blocks up Park Row and turn right onto the park leading up to the Royal Observatory Greenwich.

**Old Royal Naval College**—Now that the Royal Navy has moved out, the public is invited in to see the elaborate Painted Hall and Chapel, grandly designed by Wren and completed by other architects in the 1700s (£3, free on Sun, Mon–Sat 10:00–17:00, Sun 12:30–17:00, in the 2 college buildings farthest from river, choral service Sun at 11:00 in chapel—all are welcome).

**Queen's House**—The building, the first Palladian-style villa in Britain, was designed in 1616 by Inigo Jones for James I's wife, Anne of Denmark. All traces of the queen are now gone and the Great Hall and Royal Apartments serve as an art gallery for rotating exhibits (free, daily 10:00–17:00, tel. 020/8858-4422).

**▲▲National Maritime Museum**—Great for anyone remotely interested in the sea, you'll see everything from *Titanic* tickets to Captain Scott's reindeer-hide sleeping bag (from his 1910 Antarctic expedition) to the uniform Admiral Nelson wore when he was killed at Trafalgar. Under a big glass roof to the sound of creaking wooden ships and crashing waves, slick, modern displays depict lighthouse technology, a whaling cannon, and a Greenpeace "survival pod." The Nelson Gallery, while taking up just a fraction of the floor space, deserves at least half your time here. It offers an intimate look at his life, the Napoleonic threat, Nelson's rise to power, and his victory and death at Trafalgar. Don't miss Turner's *Battle of Trafalgar*—his largest painting and only royal commission. Kids love the All Hands Gallery where they can send secret messages by Morse code and operate a mini dockside crane (free, daily 10:00–17:00, look for the events board at entrance: singing, treasure hunts, storytelling, particularly on weekends, tel. 020/8312-6565, www.nmm.ac.uk).

**▲▲The Royal Observatory Greenwich**—Located on the prime meridian line—at longitude zero degrees—the observatory is the

## Greenwich

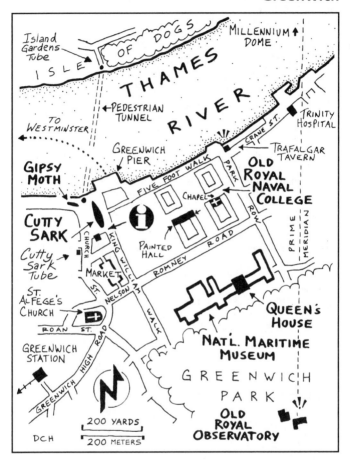

point from which all time is measured. However, the observatory's early work had nothing to do with coordinating the world's clocks to GMT, Greenwich mean time. The observatory was founded in 1675 by Charles II to find a way to determine longitude at sea. Today the Greenwich time signal is linked with the BBC (which broadcasts the "pips" worldwide at the top of the hour). In the courtyard, set your wristwatch to the digital clock showing GMT to a tenth of a second and straddle the prime meridian (called the Times meridian at the observatory, in deference to the *London Times*, which paid for the courtyard sculpture and the inset meridian line that runs banner headlines of today's *Times*—I wish I were

kidding). It's less commercial—and cheaper—to straddle the
meridian marked on the path outside the museum's courtyard.
Nearby (also outside the courtyard), see how your foot measures
up to the foot where the public standards of length are cast in
bronze. Look up to see the orange Time Ball, also visible from the
Thames, which drops daily at 13:00. Inside, check out the historic
astronomical instruments and camera *obscura*. Listen to costumed
actors tell stories about astronomers and historical observatory
events (may require small fee, daily July–Sept, Easter, and bank
holidays). Finally, enjoy the view: the symmetrical royal buildings;
the Thames; the square-mile "City" of London, with its skyscrapers and the dome of St. Paul's; the Docklands, with its busy cranes;
and the huge Millennium Dome. At night (17:00–24:00), look for
the green laser beam the observatory shines in the sky (best viewed
in winter), extending along the prime meridian for 15 miles (free,
daily 10:00–17:00, tel. 020/8858-4422, www.rog.nmm.ac.uk).
Planetarium shows twinkle on weekdays at 14:30 and on Saturday
and Sunday at 14:00 and 15:00 (£2; buy tickets at observatory, a 2-
min walk from planetarium).

**Greenwich Town**—Save time to browse the town. Covered markets and outdoor stalls make weekends lively. The arts-and-crafts
market is an entertaining mini-Covent Garden between College
Approach and Nelson Road (Thu–Sun 10:00–17:00, biggest on
Sun), and the antique market sells old ends and odds at high prices
on Greenwich High Road near the post office. Wander beyond
the touristy Church Street and Greenwich High Road to where
flower stands spill into the side streets and antique shops sell brass
nautical knickknacks. King William Walk, College Approach,
Nelson Road, and Turnpin Lane are all worth a look.

## Sights—Near Greenwich

**Thames Barrier**—East of Greenwich, the world's largest movable
flood barrier welcomes visitors. You'll get a good video and exhibition on the river they claim is the cleanest urban waterway in
the world, its floods, and how it was tamed (£3.40, Mon–Fri
10:00–17:00, Sat–Sun 10:30–17:30, tel. 020/8305-4188). To get to
the Thames Barrier from London, catch a boat from Westminster
Pier (70 min, first boat leaves about 10:15 in peak season, tel.
020/7930-3373) or take the train (a 20-min ride from Charing
Cross station to Charlton, then a 15-min walk). To reach the
Barrier from Greenwich, take a 30-minute cruise (3/day, first
boat leaves at 11:15 from Greenwich, tel. 020/8305-0300).

## Transportation Connections—Greenwich

Getting to the town of Greenwich is a joy by boat or a snap by
tube. From London, you can cruise down the Thames from central
London's piers at Westminster, Charing Cross, or Tower of

London; or take the tube to *Cutty Sark* in Zone 2 (free with tube pass). Trains also go from London several times each hour.

# CAMBRIDGE

Cambridge, 60 miles north of London, is world famous for its prestigious university. Wordsworth, Isaac Newton, Tennyson, Darwin, and Prince Charles are a few of its illustrious alumni. This historic town of 100,000 people is more pleasant than its rival, Oxford. Cambridge is the epitome of a university town, with busy bikers, stately residence halls, plenty of bookshops, and proud locals who can point out where electrons and DNA were discovered and where the first atom was split.

In medieval Europe, higher education was the domain of the Church and was limited to ecclesiastical schools. Scholars lived in "halls" on campus. This scholarly community of residential halls, chapels, and lecture halls connected by peaceful garden courtyards survives today in the colleges that make the universities at Cambridge and Oxford. By 1350 Cambridge had eight colleges (Oxford is roughly 100 years older), each with a monastic-type courtyard and lodgings. Today Cambridge has 31 colleges. While a student's life revolves around his or her independent college, the university organizes lectures, presents degrees, and promotes research.

The university dominates—and owns—most of Cambridge. The approximate term schedule is late January to late March (called Lent term), mid-April to mid-June (Easter term), and early October to early December (Michaelmas term). The colleges are closed to visitors during exams, from mid-April until late June, but King's College Chapel and the Trinity Library stay open, and the town is never sleepy.

## Planning Your Time

Cambridge is worth most of a day but not an overnight. The cheap day-return train plan makes Cambridge easy and economical as a side trip from London (from London's King's Cross Station, £14.60, 2/hr, 1 hr, fast trains depart at :15 and :45 past each hr each way; the budget ticket requires a departure after 9:30 except Sat–Sun). You can arrive in time for the 11:30 walking tour—an essential part of any visit—and spend the afternoon touring King's College and Fitzwilliam Museum (closed Mon) and simply enjoying the ambience of this stately old college town.

## Orientation (area code: 01223)

Cambridge is small but congested. There are two main streets separated from the river by the most interesting colleges. The town center, brimming with tearooms, has a TI and a colorful open-air market (daily 9:00–16:00 on Market Hill Square; arts and crafts on Sun, clothes and produce rest of week). Also on the main square is a Marks & Spencer grocery (Mon–Sat 8:30–19:00, Sun 11:00–17:00). A J. Sainsbury supermarket, with longer hours and a better deli, is three blocks away on Sidney Street, just north of Green Street. A good picnic spot is Laundress Green, a grassy park on the river, at the end of Mill Lane near the Silver Street punts. Everything is within a pleasant walk.

**Tourist Information:** At the station, a Guide Friday office dispenses free city maps and sells fancier ones. The official TI, well signed and just off Market Hill Square, is more harried than helpful (40p maps, Easter-Oct Mon–Fri 10:00–17:30, Sat 11:00–17:00, Sun 11:00–16:00; Nov–Easter Mon–Sat 10:00–17:00, Sun 11:00–16:00; closed Sun in Jan; tel. 01223/322-640).

**Arrival in Cambridge:** To get to downtown Cambridge from the train station, take a 20-minute walk (the Guide Friday map is fine for this), a £4 taxi ride, or bus #5 (90p, every 10 min). Drivers can follow signs to any of the handy and central Short Stay Parking Lots.

## Tours of Cambridge

▲▲**Walking Tour of the Colleges**—A walking tour is the best way to understand Cambridge's mix of "town and gown." Walks give a good rundown on the historic and scenic highlights of the university as well as some fun local gossip. Walks are run by and leave from the TI. From mid-June through August, tours start at 10:30, 11:30, 13:30, and 14:30. In September they start at 10:30, 11:30, and 13:30. The rest of the year they often leave at 11:30 and always at 13:30. Tours cost £7 and include admission to King's College Chapel. Drop by the TI one hour early to snare a spot. Particularly if you're coming from London, call the TI (tel. 01223/322-640) at least to confirm that a tour is scheduled and not full. Private guides are also available.

**Bus Tours**—Guide Friday hop-on hop-off bus tours are informative and cover the outskirts (£8.50, departing every 15 min, can use CC to buy tickets in their office in the train station), but walking tours go where the buses can't—right into the center.

## Sights—Cambridge

▲▲**King's College Chapel**—Built from 1446 to 1515 by Henrys VI through VIII, England's best example of Perpendicular Gothic is the single most impressive building in town. Stand inside, look up, and marvel, as Christopher Wren did, at what was the largest single span of vaulted roof anywhere—2,000 tons of incredible fan vaulting. Wander through the Old Testament via the 25 16th-century stained-glass windows (the most Renaissance stained glass anywhere in one spot; it was taken out for safety during World War II then painstakingly replaced). Walk to the altar and admire

# Cambridge

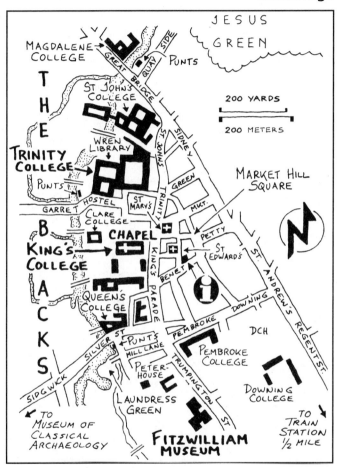

Rubens' masterful *Adoration of the Magi* (£3.50, erratic hours depending on school and events, but usually daily 10:00–16:30). During term you're welcome to enjoy an evensong service (Mon–Sat at 17:30, Sun at 15:30, tel. 01223/331-155).

▲▲**Trinity College**—Half of Cambridge's 63 Nobel Prize winners came from this richest and biggest of the town's colleges, founded in 1546 by Henry VIII. Don't miss the Wren-designed library, with its wonderful carving and fascinating original manuscripts (£2, 10p leaflet, Mon–Fri 12:00–14:00, also Sat 10:30–12:30 during term). Just outside the library entrance, Sir Isaac Newton, who spent 30 years at Trinity, clapped his hands and timed the echo to measure the speed of sound as it raced down the side of the cloister and back. In the library's display cases (covered with brown cloth that you flip back), you'll see handwritten works by Newton, Milton, Byron, Tennyson, and Housman, alongside Milne's original *Winnie the Pooh* (the real Christopher Robin attended Trinity College).

▲▲**Fitzwilliam Museum**—Britain's best museum of antiquities and art outside of London is the Fitzwilliam. Enjoy its wonderful paintings (Old Masters and a fine English section featuring Gainsborough, Reynolds, Hogarth, and others, plus works by all the famous Impressionists), old manuscripts, and Greek, Egyptian, and Mesopotamian collections (free, £3 guided tour at 14:30 on Sun only, Tue–Sat 10:00–17:00, Sun 14:15–17:00, closed Mon, tel. 01223/332-900, www.fitzmuseum.cam.ac.uk).

**Museum of Classical Archaeology**—While this museum contains no originals, it offers a unique chance to see accurate copies (19th-century casts of the originals) of virtually every famous ancient Greek and Roman statue. More than 450 statues are on display (free, Mon–Fri 10:00–17:00, sometimes also Sat 10:00–13:00 during term, Sidgwick Avenue, tel. 01223/335-153). The museum is a five-minute walk west of Silver Street Bridge; after crossing the bridge, continue straight till you reach a sign reading "Sidgwick Site" (museum is on your right; the entrance is away from the street).

▲**Punting on the Cam**—For a little levity and probably more exercise than you really want, try hiring one of the traditional (and inexpensive) flat-bottom punts at the river and pole yourself up and down (around and around, more likely) the lazy Cam. Once you get the hang of it, it's a fine way to enjoy the scenic side of Cambridge. After 17:00 it's less crowded and less embarrassing. Three places, one at each bridge, rent punts (£60 deposit required, CC OK) and offer £10 45-minute punt tours. Trinity Punt, at Garrett Hostel Bridge near Trinity College, has the best prices (£10/hr rental, ask for short lesson, free). Scudamore's runs the other two locations: the central Silver Street (£12/hr rentals) and the less-convenient Quayside at Great Bridge, at the north end of town (£10/hr, tel. 01223/359-750, www.scudamores.com). Depending on the weather, punting season runs daily Easter through October, with Silver Street open weekends year-round.

## Transportation Connections—Cambridge

**By train to:** London's **King's Cross Station** (fast train departures at :15 and :45 past each hr, 45 min, one-way £15.60, cheap day-return for £14.60), **York** (1/hr, 2.5 hrs, transfer in Petersborough), **Heathrow** (1 bus/hr, 3.5 hrs). Train info tel. 08457-484-950.

# BATH

Any tour of Britain that skips Bath stinks. Two hundred years ago this city of 80,000 was the trendsetting Hollywood of Britain. If ever a city enjoyed looking in the mirror, Bath's the one. It has more "government-listed" or protected historic buildings per capita than any other town in England. The entire city, built of the creamy warm-tone limestone called "Bath stone," beams in its cover-girl complexion. An architectural chorus line, it's a triumph of the Georgian style. Proud locals remind visitors that the town is routinely banned from the "Britain in Bloom" contest to give other towns a chance to win. Bath's narcissism is justified. Even with its mobs of tourists (2 million a year), it's a joy to visit.

Long before the Romans arrived in the first century, Bath was known for its hot springs. What became the Roman spa town of Aquae Sulis has always been fueled by the healing allure of its 116-degree mineral hot springs. The town's importance carried through Saxon times, when it had a huge church on the site of the present-day Abbey and was considered the religious capital of Britain. Its influence peaked in 973, when England's first king, Edgar, was crowned in the Abbey. Bath prospered as a wool town.

Bath then declined until the mid-1600s, when it was just a huddle of huts around the Abbey and some hot springs, with 3,000 residents oblivious to the Roman ruins 18 feet below their dirt floors. Then, in 1687, Queen Mary, fighting infertility, bathed here. Within 10 months she gave birth to a son...and a new age of popularity for Bath.

The town boomed as a spa resort. Ninety percent of the buildings you'll see today are from the 18th century. Local architect John Wood was inspired by the Italian architect Palladio to build a "new Rome." The town bloomed in the neoclassical style, and streets were lined not with scrawny sidewalks but with wide "parades," upon which the women in their stylishly wide dresses could spread their fashionable tails.

Beau Nash (1673–1762) was Bath's "master of ceremonies." He organized both the daily regimen of the aristocratic visitors and the city, lighting and improving street security, banning swords, and opening the Pump Room. Under his fashionable baton, Bath became a city of balls, gaming, and concerts and the place to see and be seen in England. This most civilized place became even more so with the great neoclassical building spree that followed.

## Planning Your Time

Bath needs two nights even on a quick trip. On a three-week British trip, spend three nights in Bath, with one day for the city and one for a side trip to Wells, Glastonbury, and Avebury. Bath could easily fill another day. Ideally, use Bath as your jet-lag recovery pillow and do London at the end of your trip.

Consider starting a three-week British vacation this way:

**Day 1:** Land at Heathrow. Connect to Bath (either by National Express bus or train—see below). While you don't need or want a car in Bath, and most rental companies have an office there, those who pick up their cars at the airport can visit Windsor Castle (near Heathrow) and/or Stonehenge on their way to Bath on this day.

**Day 2:** 9:00–Tour the Roman Baths, 10:30–Catch the free city walking tour, 12:30–Picnic on the open deck of a Guide Friday tour bus, 14:30–Free time in the shopping center of old Bath, 15:30–Tour the Costume Museum.

**Day 3:** Pick up your rental car and tour Avebury, Glastonbury (Abbey and Tower), and Wells (17:15 evensong weekdays at the cathedral, 15:00 on Sun). Without a car, consider a one-day Avebury/Stonehenge/cute towns minibus tour from Bath ("Mad Max" tours are best; see "Near Bath," below).

**Day 4:** 9:00–Leave Bath for South Wales, 10:30–Tour Welsh Folk Museum, 15:00–Stop at Tintern Abbey, then drive to the Cotswolds, 18:00–Set up in your Cotswold home base.

## Orientation (area code: 01225)

Bath's town square, three blocks in front of the bus and train station, is a bouquet of tourist landmarks, including the Abbey, Roman and medieval baths, and the royal Pump Room.

**Tourist Information:** The TI is in the Abbey churchyard (Mon–Sat 9:30–18:00, Sun 10:00–16:00; Oct–April Mon–Sat until 17:00, tel. 01225/477-101, www.visitbath.co.uk). Pick up the 50p Bath miniguide, which includes a 50p map and the free, info-packed *This Month in Bath*. Browse through scads of fliers, books, and maps (including the Cotswolds). Skip their room-finding service (£5) and book direct. The TI sells a **Bath Pass**, giving you free entry to all the sights in town, but you have to work pretty hard to make it pay (£19/1 day, £29/2 days, £39/3 days). An American Express office is tucked into the TI (decent rates, no commission on any checks, open same hrs as TI).

**Arrival in Bath:** The Bath train station is a pleasure (small-town charm, an international tickets desk, and a Guide Friday office masquerading as a TI). The bus station is immediately in front of the train station. To get to the TI, walk two blocks up Manvers Street from either station and turn left at the triangular "square," following the small TI arrow on a signpost. My recommended B&Bs are all within a 10- or 15-minute walk or a £3.50 taxi ride from the station.

Driving within Bath is a nightmare of one-way streets. Nearly everyone gets lost. Ask for advice from your hotelier and minimize driving in town. Even consider hiring and following a taxi to your place.

## Helpful Hints

**Festivals:** The International Music Festival bursts into song from May 17 to June 2 in 2002 (classical, folk, jazz, contemporary, tel. 01225/462-231), overlapped by the eclectic Fringe Festival from late May to mid-June (theater, walks, talks, bus trips, tel. 01225/480-079, www.bathfringe.co.uk). Bath's box office sells tickets for most every event and can tell you exactly what's on tonight (2 Church Street, tel. 01225/463-362, www.bathfestivals.org.uk).

**Internet Access:** The Click Café has two branches, one across from the train station on Manvers Street and the other on 19 Broad Street, near the YMCA (£2.50/30 min, daily 10:00–22:00, tel. 01225/337-711). Other places offering Internet access are the Itchy Feet Café & Travel Store (4 Bartlett Street, near Costume Museum) and the Bath Backpackers Hostel (13 Pierrepont Street; coming from train station, you pass hostel on your way to the TI).

**Farmers' Market:** This is held on the first and third Saturday of the month at Green Park Station (9:00–15:00).

**Car Rental:** Avis (behind the station and over the river at Unit 4B Riverside Business Park, Lower Bristol Road, tel. 01225/446-680), Enterprise (Lower Bristol Road, tel. 01225/443-311), and Hertz (just outside the train station, tel. 01225/442-911) are all trying harder. Most offices are a 10-minute walk from most recommended accommodations. Consider hotel delivery (usually £5, free with Enterprise). Most offices close Saturday afternoon and all day Sunday, complicating weekend pickups. Ideally, pick up your car only on the way out and into the countryside. Take the train or bus from London to Bath and rent a car as you leave Bath rather than in London.

## Tours of Bath

▲▲**City Bus Tours**—The Guide Friday green-and-cream open-top tour bus makes a 70-minute figure-eight circuit of Bath's main sights with an exhaustingly informative running commentary. For one £8.50 ticket (buy from driver), tourists can stop and go at will for a whole day. The buses cover the city center and the surrounding hills (17 signposted pick-up points, 3/hr spring and fall—runs 9:30–17:00, 4/hr in summer—9:30–18:00, 1/hr in winter—9:30–15:30, tel. 01225/464-446). This is great in sunny weather and a feast for photographers. You can munch a sandwich, work on a tan, and sightsee at the same time. Several competing hop-on hop-off tour-bus companies offer basically the same tour, but in 45 minutes and without the swing through the countryside, for a couple pounds less. Generally, the Guide Friday guides are better. (These tour buses are technically "public service vehicles"—a loophole they use to be able to run the same routes as transit buses. Consequently, tour buses are required to take passengers across town for the normal £1 fare. Nervy tourists have the right to hop on and just ask for a "single fare" and pay £1.)

▲▲▲**Walking Tours**—These free two-hour tours, offered by "The Mayor's Corps of Honorary Guides"—volunteers who want to share their love of Bath with its many visitors—are a chatty, historical, gossip-filled joy, essential for your understanding of this town's amazing Georgian social scene. How else will you learn that the old "chair ho" call for your sedan chair evolved into today's "cheerio" greeting? Tours leave from in front of the Pump Room (year-round daily at 10:30 plus Sun–Fri at 14:00; evening walks offered May–Sept at 19:00 on Tue, Fri, and Sat). For Ghost Walks and Bizarre Bath Comedy Walks, see "Nightlife," below. For a private walking tour, call the local guide's bureau (£45/2 hrs, tel. 01225/337-111).

## Sights—Bath

▲▲▲**Roman and Medieval Baths**—In ancient Roman times, high society enjoyed the mineral springs at Bath. From Londinium, Romans traveled so often to Aquae Sulis, as the city was called, to "take a bath" that finally it became known simply as Bath. Today a fine museum surrounds the ancient bath and is, with its well-documented displays, a one-way system leading you past Roman artifacts, mosaics, a temple pediment, and the actual mouth of the spring, piled high with Roman pennies. Enjoy some quality time looking into the eyes of Minerva, goddess of the hot springs. The included self-guided tour audioguide makes the visit easy and plenty informative. For those with a big appetite for Roman history, in-depth 40-minute tours leave from the end of the museum at the edge of the actual bath (included, on the hour, a poolside clock is set for the next departure time). You can revisit

# Bath

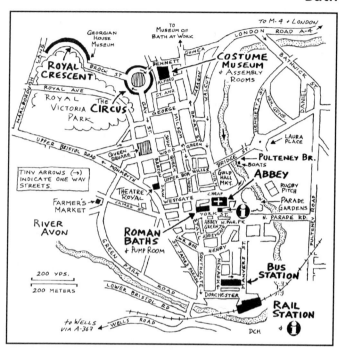

the museum after the tour (£7.50, £9.50 combo ticket includes
Costume Museum at a good savings, family combo-£25, combo
tickets good for 1 week; April–Sept daily 9:00–18:00, in July–
Aug until 22:15—last entry at 21:00, Oct–March until 17:00,
tel. 01225/477-000).

**Bath Spa**—In October of 2002, Bath's natural thermal springs
will once again be used for bathing and treatments in a complex
combining restored old buildings and a new, state-of-the-art
leisure spa (£17/2 hrs, £23/half day, £35/day).

▲**Pump Room**—For centuries, Bath was forgotten as a spa.
Then, in 1687, the previously barren Queen Mary bathed here,
became pregnant, and bore a male heir to the throne. Word of
its wonder waters spread and once again Bath was back on the
aristocratic map. High society soon turned the place into one big
pleasure palace. The Pump Room, an elegant Georgian hall just
above the Roman baths, offers the visitor's best chance to raise a
pinky in this Chippendale elegance. Drop by to sip coffee or tea
or enjoy a light meal (9:30–12:00 Morning Coffee, 12:00–14:30
lunch—£12 2-course menu, 14:30–17:30 traditional High Tea—

£8, 17:30–20:30 dinner, £7 tea/coffee and pastry available anytime except during lunch, string trio or live pianist 10:00–17:00, tel. 01225/444-477). Above the newspaper table and sedan chairs a statue of Beau Nash himself sniffles down at you. Now's your chance to have a famous (but forgettable) "Bath bun" and split (and spit) a 50p drink of the awfully curative water. Convenient public WCs are in the entry hallway that connects the Pump Room with the Baths.

▲**Abbey**—Bath town wasn't much in the Middle Ages. But an important church has stood on this spot since Anglo-Saxon times. In 973, Edgar, the first king of England, was crowned here. Dominating the town center, the present church—the last great medieval church of England—is 500 years old and a fine example of Late Perpendicular Gothic, with breezy fan vaulting and enough stained glass to earn it the nickname "Lantern of the West" (worth the £2 donation, Mon–Sat 9:00–18:00, Sun 13:00–14:30, 15:30–17:30, closes at 16:30 in winter, handy flier narrates a self-guided 19-stop tour). The schedule for concerts, services, and **evensong** (Sun at 15:30 year-round, plus most Sat in Aug at 17:00) is posted on the door. Take a moment to really appreciate the Abbey's architecture from the Abbey Green square.

The Abbey's **Heritage Vaults**, a small but interesting exhibit, tells the story of Christianity in Bath since Roman times (£2, Mon–Sat 10:00–16:00, closed Sun, entrance just outside church, south side).

▲**Pulteney Bridge, Parade Gardens, and Cruises**—Bath is inclined to compare its shop-lined Pulteney Bridge to Florence's Ponte Vecchio. That's pushing it. To best enjoy a sunny day, pay £1 to enter the Parade Gardens below the bridge (daily 10:00–19:00, until 20:00 June–Aug, free after 20:00, includes deck chairs, ask about the concerts held some Sun at 15:00 in summer).

Across the bridge at Pulteney Weir, tour boats run cruises from under the bridge (£4.50, up to 7/day if the weather's good, 50 min to Bathampton and back, WCs on board). Just take whatever boat is running. Avon Cruisers stop in Bathampton if you'd like to walk back; Pulteney Cruisers come with a sundeck ideal for picnics.

▲▲**Royal Crescent and the Circus**—If Bath is an architectural cancan, these are the kickers. These first elegant Georgian "condos" by John Wood (the Elder and the Younger) are well explained in the city walking tours. "Georgian" is British for "neoclassical," or dating from the 1770s. As you cruise the Crescent, pretend you're rich. Pretend you're poor. Notice the "ha ha fence," a drop in the front yard offering a barrier, invisible from the windows, to sheep and peasants. The round Circus is a colosseum turned inside out. Its Doric, Ionic, and Corinthian capital decorations pay homage to its Greco-Roman origin.

▲▲**Georgian House at #1 Royal Crescent**—This museum

(on the corner of Brock Street and the Royal Crescent) offers your best look into a period house. It's worth the £4 admission to get behind one of those classy exteriors. The volunteers in each room are determined to fill you in on all the fascinating details of Georgian life...like how high-class women shaved their eyebrows and pasted on carefully trimmed strips of furry mouse skin in their place (Tue–Sun 10:30–17:00, closed Mon, closes at 16:00 in Nov, closed Dec–mid-Feb, "no stiletto heels, please," tel. 01225/428-126).

▲▲▲**Costume Museum**—One of Europe's great museums, displaying 400 years of fashion—one frilly decade at a time— is housed within Bath's Assembly Rooms. Follow the included, excellent audioguide tour. On display through October 2002 are 14 dresses worn by Queen Elizabeth II—a special exhibit marking the queen's 50-year reign (£4.20, a £9.50 combo ticket covers Roman Baths, family combo-£25, daily 10:00–17:00, tel. 01225/ 477-789). The Assembly Rooms, which you'll see en route to the museum, are big, elegant, empty rooms where card games, concerts, tea, and dances were held in the 18th century before the advent of fancy hotels with grand public spaces made them obsolete.

▲▲▲**Museum of Bath at Work**—This is the official title for Mr. Bowler's Business, a 1900s engineer's shop, brass foundry, and fizzy-drink factory with a Dickensian office. It's just a pile of meaningless old gadgets until a volunteer guide lovingly resurrects Mr. Bowler's creative genius. Fascinating hour-long tours go regularly; just join the one in session upon arrival (£3.50, April–Oct daily 10:00–17:00, weekends only in winter, 2 blocks up Russell Street from Assembly Rooms, call to be sure a volunteer is available to give a tour, café upstairs, tel. 01225/318-348).

**Jane Austen Centre**—This new exhibition focuses on Jane Austen's five years in Bath (around 1800) and the influence Bath had on her writing. While the exhibit is thoughtfully done and is a hit with "Jane-ites," there is little of historic substance here. You'll walk through a Georgian townhouse that she didn't live in and see mostly enlarged reproductions of things associated with her writing. After a live intro explaining how this romantic but down-to-earth girl dealt with the silly, shallow, and arrogant aristocrat's world where "the doing of nothings all day prevents one from doing anything," you see a 13-minute video and wander through the rest of the exhibit (£4, Mon–Sat 10:00–17:30, Sun 10:30–17:30, 40 Gay Street between Queen's Square and the Circus, tel. 01225/443-000, www.janeausten.co.uk).

**The Building of Bath Museum**—This offers a fascinating look behind the scenes at how the Georgian city was actually built. It's just one large room of exhibits, but those interested in construction find it worth the £4 (Tue–Sun 10:30–17:00, closed Mon, near the Circus on a street called "the Paragon," tel. 01225/333-895).

▲**Impossible Microworld**—This dark two-room museum glows with a couple dozen illuminated glass bubbles that contain magnifying glasses, helping you focus on the smallest sculptures you've ever seen. These tiny creations by two artists are almost invisible. Ussa's work borders on hokey (flea riding a bicycle), but Wigan's work is remarkable. Wigan actually carves his minute work out of sugar grains, match heads, or bits of boxwood (look for the Statue of Liberty in the eye of a needle and Samson splitting a human hair). As a dyslexic kid, labeled "nothing" by a racist teacher, he was determined to make something out of nothing (£4, daily 10:00–18:00, Kingsmead Square, near Theatre Royal, tel. 01225/333-003).

**Views**—For the best views of Bath, try Alexander Park (south of city, 10-min walk from train station), Camden Crescent (10–15 min walk north), or Becksford Tower (steep 20-min walk north up Lansdown Road, www.bath-preservation-trust.org.uk).

▲**American Museum**—I know, you need this in Bath like you need a Big Mac. But this museum offers a fascinating look at colonial and early-American lifestyles. Each of 18 completely furnished rooms (from the 1600s to the 1800s) is hosted by an eager guide waiting to fill you in on the candles, maps, bedpans, and various religious sects that make domestic Yankee history surprisingly interesting. One room is a quilter's nirvana (£5.50, Tue–Sun 14:00–17:00, closed Mon and early Nov–late March, at Claverton Manor, tel. 01225/460-503). The museum is outside of town and a headache to reach if you don't have a car (15-min walk from the nearest Guide Friday stop or a 10-min walk from bus #18).

## Activities in Bath

**Walking, Biking, and Swimming**—The Bath Skyline Walk is a six-mile wander around the hills surrounding Bath (70p leaflet at TI). For more options, get *Country Walks around Bath*, by Tim Mowls (£4.50 at TI).

Consider the idyllic **walk** up the canal path to Bathampton: from downtown, walk over Pulteney Bridge, through Sydney Gardens, turn left on canal, and in 30 minutes you'll hit Bathampton, with its much-loved Old George Pub. Sailors enjoy the river cruise up to Bathampton; hikers like walking back (see "Pulteney Bridge and Cruises," above). From Bathampton it's two hours farther along the canal to the fine old town of Bradford-on-Avon, from which you can train back to Bath. You can **bike** this route (rent bikes at Avon Valley Cyclery behind train station, £9/4 hrs, £14/8 hrs, £18/24 hrs, no helmets, tel. 01225/442-442). Plenty of other scenic paths are described in the TI's literature.

The Bath Sports and Leisure Centre has a **swimming pool**—great for laps—and lots of slides and gadgets for kids (£2.70, towels rentable, daily 8:00–22:00, just across North Parade Bridge, call for open swim times, tel. 01225/462-565).

The Bath Boating Station, in an old Victorian boathouse, rents **boats** and punts (£4.50/first hr per person, then £1.50/hr, April–Sept 10:00–18:00, Forester Road, a mile northeast of center, tel. 01225/466-407).

**Shopping**—There's great browsing between the Abbey and the Assembly Rooms (Costume Museum). Shops close at 17:30, later on Thursday. Explore the antique shops lining Bartlett Street just below the Assembly Rooms. You'll find the most stalls open on Wednesday. Pick up the local paper (usually out on Friday) and shop with the dealers at estate sales and auctions listed in "What's On."

## Nightlife in Bath

*This Month in Bath* (free, available at TI) lists events.

**Plays**—The Theatre Royal, newly restored and one of England's loveliest, offers a busy schedule of London West End–type plays, including many "pre-London" dress-rehearsal runs (£11–25, cheaper matinees as low as £5, tel. 01225/448-844). Forty standby tickets per evening show go on sale starting at 12:00 on the day of the performance (either pay cash at box office or call and book with CC, 2 tickets maximum). Or you can buy a £10 last-minute seat 30 minutes before "curtain up."

**Evening Walks**—Take your choice: comedy, ghost, or history. For an immensely entertaining walking comedy act "with absolutely no history or culture," follow J. J. or Noel Britten on their creative and entertaining **Bizarre Bath** walk. This 90-minute "tour," which plays off local passersby as well as tour members, is a belly laugh a minute (£5, April–Sept nightly at 20:00, smaller groups Mon–Thu, heavy on magic, careful to insult all minorities and sensitivities, just racy enough but still good family fun; leave from Huntsman pub near the Abbey, confirm at TI or call 01225/335-124, www.bizarrebath.co.uk). **Ghost Walks** are another way to pass the after-dark hours (£4, 20:00, 2 hrs, unreliably Mon–Sat April–Oct; in winter Fri only; leave from Garrick's Head pub near Theatre Royal, tel. 01225/463-618). The TI offers **free evening walks** in summer (May–Sept at 19:00 on Tue, Fri, and Sat, 2 hrs, leave from Pump Room, confirm at TI); for more information, see "Tours of Bath," above.

## Sleeping in Bath
### (£1 = about $1.50, country code: 44, area code: 01225)

Sleep Code: **S** = Single, **D** = Double/Twin, **T** = Triple, **Q** = Quad, **b** = bathroom, **s** = shower only, **CC** = Credit Cards accepted, **no CC** = Credit Cards not accepted.

Bath is a busy tourist town. To get a good B&B, make a telephone reservation in advance. Competition is stiff, and it's worth asking any of these places for a weekday, three-nights-in-a-row, or off-season deal. Friday and Saturday nights are tightest, especially if you're staying only one night, since B&Bs favor those staying longer. If staying only Saturday night, you're very bad news. At B&Bs (and cheaper hotels), expect lots of stairs and no lifts.

**Launderettes**: The Spruce Goose Launderette is around the corner from Brock's Guest House on the pedestrian lane called Margaret's Buildings (£4-self-service, £7-full-service on same day if dropped off at 8:00, Sun–Fri 8:00–20:00, Sat 8:00–19:00, tel. 01225/483-309). Anywhere in town, "Speedy Wash" can pick up your laundry for same-day service (£6.50/bag, most hotels work with them, tel. 01225/427-616). East of Pulteney Bridge, the humble Lovely Wash is on Daniel Street (daily 9:00–21:00, self-service only).

## Sleeping in B&Bs near the Royal Crescent
These listings are all a 15-minute uphill walk or an easy £3.50 taxi ride from the train station. Or take the Guide Friday bus tour from the station and get off at the stop nearest your B&B (for Brock's: Assembly Rooms; for Marlborough listings: Royal Avenue; confirm with driver), check in, then finish the tour later in the day. All of these B&Bs are nonsmoking.

**Brock's Guest House** will put bubbles in your Bath experience. Marion and Geoffrey Dodd have redone their Georgian townhouse (built by John Wood in 1765) in a way that would make the famous architect proud. It's located between the prestigious Royal Crescent and the elegant Circus (Db-£64–72, 1 deluxe Db-£72–77, Tb-£85–87, Qb-£99–105, CC, reserve with CC number far in advance, little library on top floor, 32 Brock Street, BA1 2LN, tel. 01225/338-374, fax 01225/334-245, www.brocksguesthouse.co.uk, e-mail: marion@brocksguesthouse.co.uk).

**On Marlborough Lane:** The **Woodville House** is run by Anne and Tom Toalster. This grandmotherly little house has three tidy, charming rooms, one shared shower/WC, an extra WC, and a TV lounge. Breakfast is served at a big, family-style table (D-£40, minimum 2 nights, no CC, some parking, below the Royal Crescent at 4 Marlborough Lane, BA1 2NQ, tel. & fax 01225/319-335, e-mail: toalster@compuserve.com).

**Elgin Villa**, also thoughtfully run and a fine value, has five comfy, well-maintained rooms (Ss-£32, Sb-£45, Ds-£45, Db-£65, Tb-£85, no CC, more expensive for 1 night, discounted for 3 nights, continental breakfast served in room, parking, 6 Marlborough Lane, BA1 2NQ Bath, tel. & fax 01225/424-557, www.elginvilla.co.uk, Alwyn and Carol Landman).

**Athelney Guest House**, which also serves a continental breakfast in your room, has three spacious rooms with two shared bathrooms (D-£40–42, T-£60–63, no CC, parking, 5 Marlborough Lane, BA1 2NQ, tel. & fax 01225/312-031, e-mail: colin-davies@supanet.com, Sue and Colin Davies).

**Marlborough House Hotel** is both Victorian and vegetarian, with seven comfortable rooms—well furnished with antiques—and optional £15 organic-veggie dinners (Sb-£45–75, Db-£65–85, Tb-£75–95, price depending on season, CC, varied breakfast menu, room service, 1 Marlborough Lane, BA1 2NQ, tel. 01225/318-175, fax 01225/466-127, www.marlborough-house.net, Americans Laura and Charles).

**Prior House B&B**, with four well-kept rooms, is run by helpful Lynn and Keith Shearn (D-£40, Db-£45, CC, 3 Marlborough Lane, tel. 01225/313-587, fax 01225/443-543, e-mail: priorhouse@greatplaces.co.uk).

**Parkside Guest House** rents four Edwardian rooms but lacks B&B warmth (Db-£65, small breakfast, no CC, 11 Marlborough Lane, BA1 2NQ, tel. & fax 01225/429-444, e-mail: parkside@lynall.freeserve.co.uk, Erica and Inge Lynall).

### Sleeping in B&Bs East of the River

These listings are about a 10-minute walk from the city center.

**Near North Parade Road:** The **Holly Villa Guest House**, with a cheery garden, six bright rooms, and a cozy TV lounge, is enthusiastically and thoughtfully run by Jill and Keith McGarrigle (Ds-£45, Db-£50, Tb-£75, no CC, strictly nonsmoking, easy parking, 8-min walk from station and city center, 14 Pulteney Gardens, BA2 4HG, tel. 01225/310-331, e-mail: hollyvilla.bb @ukgateway.net). From the city center, walk over North Parade Bridge, take the first right, and then take the second left.

**Near Pulteney Road: Muriel Guy's B&B** is another good value, mixing Georgian elegance with homey warmth and artistic taste (5 rooms, S-£25, Db-£50, Tb-£60, no CC, nonsmoking, go over bridge on North Parade Road, left on Pulteney Road, cross to church, Raby Place is first row of houses on hill, 14 Raby Place, BA2 4EH, tel. 01225/465-120, fax 01225/465-283, e-mail: no way).

**The Ayrlington**, next door to a lawn-bowling green, has attractive rooms that hint of a more genteel time. Though this well-maintained hotel fronts a busy street, it feels tranquil inside, with double-paned windows. Rooms in the back have pleasant views of sports greens and Bath beyond. For the best value, request a standard double with a view of Bath (standard Db-£90–110, superior Db-£100–125, deluxe Db with Jacuzzi-£110–145, high prices on Fri, Sat, and Sun, no Sat night only, CC, access to garden in back, easy parking, 24/25 Pulteney Road, BA2 4EZ, tel. 01225/425-495, fax 01225/469-029, www.ayrlington.com, Simon and Mee-Ling).

**In Sydney Gardens:** The **Sydney Gardens Hotel** is a classy Casablanca-type place with six tastefully decorated rooms, an elegant breakfast room, garden views, and an entrance to Sydney Gardens park (Db-£75, Tb-£100, CC, request garden view, easy parking, located on busy road between park and canal, Sydney

## Bath Hotels

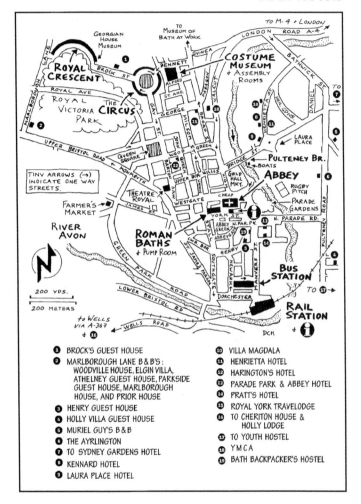

**①** BROCK'S GUEST HOUSE
**②** MARLBOROUGH LANE B&B'S:
    WOODVILLE HOUSE, ELGIN VILLA,
    ATHELNEY GUEST HOUSE, PARKSIDE
    GUEST HOUSE, MARLBOROUGH
    HOUSE, AND PRIOR HOUSE
**③** HENRY GUEST HOUSE
**④** HOLLY VILLA GUEST HOUSE
**⑤** MURIEL GUY'S B&B
**⑥** THE AYRLINGTON
**⑦** TO SYDNEY GARDENS HOTEL
**⑧** KENNARD HOTEL
**⑨** LAURA PLACE HOTEL

**⑩** VILLA MAGDALA
**⑪** HENRIETTA HOTEL
**⑫** HARINGTON'S HOTEL
**⑬** PARADE PARK & ABBEY HOTEL
**⑭** PRATT'S HOTEL
**⑮** ROYAL YORK TRAVELODGE
**⑯** TO CHERITON HOUSE &
    HOLLY LODGE
**⑰** TO YOUTH HOSTEL
**⑱** YMCA
**⑲** BATH BACKPACKER'S HOSTEL

Road, BA2 6NT, tel. 01225/464-818, fax 01225/484-347,
www.sydneygardens.co.uk, Geraldine and Peter Beaven).

### Sleeping East of Pulteney Bridge
These are just a few minutes' walk from the city center.

    Driving in from the M4 on the A4 London Road be sure to
turn left at the lights, just before the town center, onto the A36
Warminster road. (Miss this and you're toast.) Crossing the

Cleveland Bridge onto Bathwick Street, take the second right onto Henrietta Road and you're nearly there.

**Kennard Hotel** is comfortable, with 14 charming Georgian rooms and a dazzling breakfast room. Richard Ambler runs this place warmly, giving careful attention to guests (S-£48, Db-£88–98 depending upon size, CC, no kids under 12, nonsmoking, just over Pulteney Bridge, turn left at Henrietta, 11 Henrietta Street, BA2 6LL, tel. 01225/310-472, fax 01225/460-054, www.kennard.co.uk, e-mail: reception@kennard.co.uk).

**Laura Place Hotel** is another elegant Georgian place (8 rooms, 2 on the ground floor, rooftop D-£62, Db-£70–92 from small and high up to huge and palatial, CC, 2-night minimum stay, must show this book to get 10 percent discount with cash, family suite, nonsmoking, easy parking, just over Pulteney Bridge, 3 Laura Place, Great Pulteney Street, BA2 4BH, tel. 01225/463-815, fax 01225/310-222, Patricia Bull).

**Villa Magdala**, with 18 rooms in a freestanding Victorian townhouse opposite a park, is formal and hotelesque (Db-£85–105, depending on size, type of bed, and plumbing; no CC, nonsmoking, in quiet residential area, inviting lounge, parking, Henrietta Road, Bath BA2 6LX, tel. 01225/466-329, fax 01225-483-207, www.villamagdala.co.uk).

**Henrietta Hotel**, with simple basic rooms and lots of stairs, gives you a budget-hotel option in this elegant neighborhood (10 rooms, Db-£45-75, discounts for cash and 2-night stay Sun–Thu, CC, 32 Henrietta Street, tel. 01225/447-779, fax 01225/444-150, Mary).

### *Sleeping in the City Center*

**Harington's of Bath Hotel**, with 13 newly renovated rooms on a quiet street in the town center, is run by Susan and Desmond Pow (Db-£88–108, Tb-£100–130, prices decrease midweek and increase Fri–Sat, 10 percent discount with this book Sun–Thu, CC, nonsmoking, lots of stairs, attached restaurant/bar serves simple meals and pastries all day, extremely central at 10 Queen Street, BA1 1HE, tel. 01225/461-728, fax 01225/444-804, www.haringtonshotel.co.uk).

**Parade Park Hotel**, in a Georgian building, has a central location, helpful owners, and comfortable rooms decorated in a modern style (35 rooms, S-£35, D-£50, Db-£60–80, Tb-£90, Qb-£120, CC, nonsmoking, beaucoup stairs, 10 North Parade, BA2 4AL, tel. 01225/463-384, fax 01225/442-322, www.paradepark.co.uk, e-mail: info@paradepark.co.uk, Nita and David Derrick).

**Pratt's Hotel** is as proper and old English as you'll find in Bath. Its creaks and frays are aristocratic. Its public places make you want to sip a brandy, and its 46 rooms are bright, spacious, and come with all the comforts (Sb-£75, Db-£110, advanced reservations get high rack rates, drop ins often enjoy 25 percent discount, dogs-£4.95 but children free, CC, attached restaurant/bar, elevator, 2 blocks immediately in front of the station on South Parade, BA2 4AB, tel. 01225/460-441, fax 01225/448-807, e-mail: hotel@prattshotel.demon.co.uk).

The **Royal York Travelodge** offers American-style, characterless, comfortable rooms—worrying B&Bs and hotels alike with its reasonable prices (Db-£60, £70 on Fri–Sun, breakfast extra, CC, 1 York Bldg, George Street, BA1 3EB, tel. 01225/448-999, www.travelodge.co.uk).

Best Western–style **Abbey Hotel** has 60 decent rooms, some on the ground floor, a super location, and a rare elevator (standard Db-£120, deluxe Db-£130, CC, attached restaurant, nonsmoking rooms available, North Parade, BA1 1LF, tel. 01225/461-603, fax 01225/447-758, e-mail: ahres@compasshotels.co.uk).

**Henry Guest House** is a plain, simple, old, vertical, eight-room, family-run place two blocks in front of the train station on a quiet side street. Nothing matches—not the curtains, wallpaper, carpeting, throw rugs, or bedspreads—but it is the cheapest hotel in the center (S-£22.50, D-£45, T-£55, TVs in rooms, lots of narrow stairs, 3 showers and WCs for all, 6 Henry Street, BA1 1JT, tel. 01225/424-052, e-mail: cox@thehenrybath.freeserve.co.uk, Rosemary).

## Sleeping in B&Bs South of the Train Station

Up a hill a 15-minute walk south of the train station are a string of classy B&Bs in a car-friendly residential neighborhood. Here are two good ones: **Cheriton House**, with 11 well-furnished rooms (Sb-£42–60, Db-£64–85, 10 percent discount for 2 nights or more by showing this book, CC, nonsmoking, garden, 9 Upper Oldfield Park, BA2 3JX, tel. 01225/429-862, e-mail: cheriton@which.net, Iris and John Chiles); and **Holly Lodge**, with six frilly, Victorian-style rooms and a gazebo in the garden (Sb-£48–55, Db-£79–97, CC, nonsmoking, phones in rooms, tel. 01225/339-187, fax 01225/481-138, e-mail: stay@hollylodge.co.uk, Mr. George Hall).

## Sleeping in Dorms

The **YMCA**, wonderfully central on a leafy square down a tiny alley off Broad Street, has 200 beds in industrial-strength rooms and scuff-proof halls (S-£16, D-£28, T-£42, Q-£56, beds in big dorms-£11, includes meager continental breakfast, CC, families offered a day nursery for kids under 5, cheap dinners, no lockers, dorms closed from 10:00–16:00, Broad Street Place, BA1 5LH, tel. 01225/460-471, fax 01225/462-065, e-mail: info@ymcabath.u-net.com).

**White Hart Hostel** is a simple, new place offering adults and families good cheap beds in two- to six-bed dorms (£12.50/bed, D-£30, no CC, family rooms, kitchen, smoke free, no breakfast, 5-min walk behind train station at Widcombe—where Widcombe

Hill hits Claverton Street, tel. 01225/313-985, e-mail: sue
@whitehartinn.freeserve.co.uk, run by Mike and Sue).

**Bath Backpackers Hostel** bills itself as a totally fun-
packed, mad place to stay. This Aussie-run dive/hostel rents
bunk beds in 6- to 10-bed rooms (£12/bed, 2 D-£30, lockers,
Internet access for nonguests as well, bar, kitchen, a couple
of blocks toward city center from train station, 13 Pierrepont Street, tel. 01225/446-787, e-mail: stayinbath
@backpackers-uk.demon.co.uk).

The **youth hostel** is in a grand old building on Bathwick
Hill outside of town (£11/bed in 2- to 10-bed rooms, D-£31,
Db-£36, non-members pay £2 extra, breakfast not included,
bus #18 from station, tel. 01225/465-674).

# Eating in Bath

While not a great pub-grub town, Bath is bursting with quaint and
stylish eateries. There's something for every appetite and budget—
just stroll around the center of town. A picnic dinner of deli food
or take-out fish 'n' chips in the Royal Crescent Park is ideal for
aristocratic hobos.

## Eating between the Abbey and the Station

Three fine and popular places share North Parade Passage, a block
south of the Abbey: **Tilley's Bistro** serves healthy French, English, and vegetarian meals with candlelit ambience. Their fun
menu lets you build your meal choosing from an interesting array
of £6 starters (Mon–Sat 12:00–14:30, 18:30–23:00, closed Sun,
CC, reservations smart, nonsmoking, North Parade Passage, tel.
01225/484-200). **Sally Lunn's House** is a cutesy, quasi-historic
place for expensive doily meals, tea, pink pillows, and lots of lace
(£7–10, nightly, CC, smoke-free, 4 North Parade Passage, tel.
01225/461-634). It's fine for tea and buns, and customers get a
free peek at the basement Kitchen Museum (otherwise 30p). Next
door, **Demuth's Vegetarian Restaurant** serves good £15 meals
(daily 10:00–22:00, CC, vegan options available, reservations wise,
tel. 01225/446-059).

**Crystal Palace Pub**, with typical pub grub under rustic
timbers or in the sunny courtyard, is a handy standby (£6 meals,
Mon–Fri 11:00–20:30, Sat 11:00–16:30, Sun 12:00–16:00,
children welcome on patio but not indoors, 11 Abbey Green,
tel. 01225/482-666).

**Evans** is decent for fish 'n' chips (Mon–Fri 11:30–15:30,
Sat 11:30–19:00, closed Sun, on Abbeygate, near Marks & Spen-
cer). Also greasy is **Seafoods** (daily 12:00–23:00, 27 Kingsmeads
Street, just off Kingsmead Square). For more cheap meals, try
**Spike's Fish and Chips** (open very late) and the neighboring
café just behind the bus station.

## Eating between the Abbey and the Circus

George Street is lined with cheery eateries: Thai, Italian, wine bars, and so on. **Martini Restaurant** is purely Italian with class and jovial waiters (£11 entrées, £7 pizzas, daily 12:00–14:30, 18:00–22:30, CC, reservations smart, smoke-free section, 9 George Street, tel. 01225/460-818, Nunzio, Franco, and Luigi).

**Bengal Brasserie**, a Bangaladeshi place specializing in Tandoori and curries, is unpretentious with good food at good prices (lunch from 12:00, dinner from 18:00, 32 Milsom Street, tel. 01225/447-906).

**Jamuna** makes a mean curry (Mon–Sun 12:00–14:30, 18:00–24:00, Abbey views, 9-10 High Street, tel. 01225/464-631).

The **Old Green Tree Pub** on Green Street is a rare pub with good grub, locally brewed real ales, and a nonsmoking room (lunch only, served 12:00–14:30, no children, live jazz Sun–Mon 20:30 until closing, tel. 01225/448-259).

**Browns**, a popular, modern chain, offers affordable—though not great—English food throughout the day (£6 lunch special, Mon–Sat 11:00–23:30, Sun 12:00–23:30, CC, kid-friendly, half block east of the Abbey, Orange Grove, tel. 01225/461-199).

**The Moon and Sixpence,** prized by locals, offers "modern English fusion" cuisine, giving British cooking a needed international flair and flavor (£7 2-course lunch, £21 3-course dinner menu, daily 12:00–14:30, 17:30–22:30, CC, indoor/outdoor seating, 6a Broad Street, tel. 01225/460-962).

**Devon Savouries** serves greasy-but-delicious take-out pasties, sausage rolls, and vegetable pies (Mon–Sat 9:00–17:30, hours vary on Sun, on Burton Street, the main walkway between New Bond Street and Upper Borough Walls).

**Pasta Galore** serves decent (sometimes so-so) Italian food and homemade pasta outside on a patio or inside. The ground floor beats the basement (daily 12:00–14:30, 18:00–22:30, CC, 31 Barton Street, tel. 01225/463-861).

If you're missing California, try the popular **Firehouse Rotisserie** (Mon–Sat 12:00–14:30, 18:00–23:00, closed Sun, make reservations, near Queen Square on John Street, tel. 01225/482-070).

**Guildhall Market**, across from Pulteney Bridge, is fun for browsing and picnic shopping, with an inexpensive Market Café if you'd like to sip tea surrounded by stacks of used books, bananas on the push list, and honest-to-goodness old-time locals (Mon–Sat 9:00–17:00, closed Sun, a block north of the Abbey, main entrance on High Street).

The **Cornish Bakehouse**, near the Guildhall Market, has good take-away pasties (11a The Corridor, off High Street, tel. 01225/426-635).

**Supermarkets**: **Waitrose**, at the Podium shopping center, is great for groceries (Mon–Fri 8:30–20:00, Sat 8:30–19:00,

## Bath Restaurants

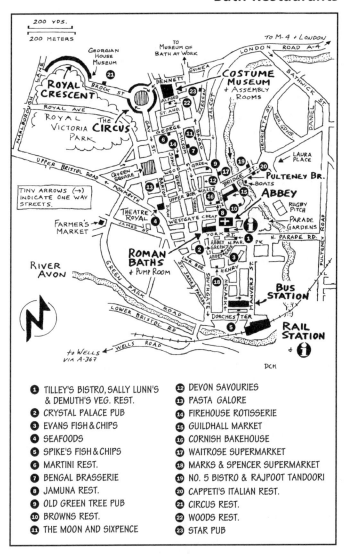

1. TILLEY'S BISTRO, SALLY LUNN'S & DEMUTH'S VEG. REST.
2. CRYSTAL PALACE PUB
3. EVANS FISH & CHIPS
4. SEAFOODS
5. SPIKE'S FISH & CHIPS
6. MARTINI REST.
7. BENGAL BRASSERIE
8. JAMUNA REST.
9. OLD GREEN TREE PUB
10. BROWNS REST.
11. THE MOON AND SIXPENCE
12. DEVON SAVOURIES
13. PASTA GALORE
14. FIREHOUSE ROTISSERIE
15. GUILDHALL MARKET
16. CORNISH BAKEHOUSE
17. WAITROSE SUPERMARKET
18. MARKS & SPENCER SUPERMARKET
19. NO. 5 BISTRO & RAJPOOT TANDOORI
20. CAPPETI'S ITALIAN REST.
21. CIRCUS REST.
22. WOODS REST.
23. STAR PUB

Sun 11:00–17:00, salad bar, just west of Pulteney Bridge and across from post office on High Street). **Marks & Spencer**, near the train station, has a good grocery at the back of its department store (Mon–Sat 9:00–17:30, Sun 11:00–17:00, Stall Street).

## Eating East of Pulteney Bridge

For a stylish, intimate setting and "new English" cuisine worth the splurge, dine at **No. 5 Bistro** (£12–15 main courses with vegetables, Mon–Sat 18:30–22:00, closed Sun, Mon–Tue are "bring your own bottle of wine" nights—no corkage fee, smart to reserve, CC, just over Pulteney Bridge at 5 Argyle Street, tel. 01225/444-499). **Rajpoot Tandoori**, next door to No. 5, serves good Indian food. You'll hike down deep into a cellar where the classy Indian atmosphere and award-winning cooking makes paying the extra pounds OK (4 Argyle Street, tel. 01225/466-833). **Cappeti's Italian Restaurant** is a checkered-tablecloth place in another deep cellar serving good Italian (Tue–Sat 12:00–14:00, 18:30–22:30, closed Sun–Mon, CC, 12 Argyle Street, tel. 01225/442-299).

## Eating near the Circus and Brock's Guest House

**Circus Restaurant** is intimate and a good value, with Mozartian ambience and candlelit prices: £17 for a three-course dinner special including great vegetables and a selection of fine desserts (daily 12:00–14:00, 18:30–22:00, reservations smart, CC, 34 Brock Street, tel. 01225/318-918, run by Felix Rosenow).

**Woods Restaurant** serves modern English cuisine to well-dressed locals in a sprawling candlelit brasserie (£8-lunches, £13–25 3-course dinners, daily 12:00–15:00, 18:00–22:30, closed Sun eve, CC, 9-13 Alfred Street, near Assembly Rooms, tel. 01225/314-812).

For real ale (but no food), try the **Star Pub** (top of Paragon Street).

# Transportation Connections—Bath

Bath's train station is called Bath Spa. The National Express bus office (Mon–Sat 8:00–17:30, closed Sun) is one block in front of the train station.

**To London's Paddington Station from Bath Spa:** By train (2/hr, 75 min, £31 one-way after 9:30), or cheaper by National Express bus to Victoria Station (nearly 1/hr, up to 3 hrs, £12.50 one-way, £20 round-trip). To get from London to Bath, consider an all-day Stonehenge-and-Bath organized bus tour from London (for details see "Daytrips from London" on page 74). Train info: tel. 08457-484-950.

**To London's airports:** By National Express bus to **Heathrow** Airport and continuing on to London (10/day, 2.5 hrs, £11.50, tel. 08705-808-080) and to **Gatwick** (2/hr, 4.5 hrs, £19.50). Trains are faster but more expensive (1/hr, 2.5 hrs, £29.20). For information on getting to Bath, see "Transportation Connections" in the London chapter.

**To the Cotswolds:** By train to **Moreton-in-Marsh** (1/hr, 2 hrs, transfer in Oxford). By National Express bus to

**Cheltenham** (1 direct bus/day, 2.5 hrs, more buses with transfer), **Stratford** (1/day, 4 hrs, transfer in Bristol or Birmingham), and **Oxford** (1 direct/day, 2 hrs, more buses with transfer). Bus info: tel. 08705/808-080.

By train to: **Oxford** (1/hr, 1 hr), **Heathrow** (1/hr, transfer at Reading to bus), **Gatwick** (1/hr, 3 hrs), **Birmingham** (1/hr, 2.5 hrs, transfer in Bristol), and **points north** (from Birmingham, a major transportation hub, trains depart for Blackpool, York, Durham, Scotland, and North Wales; use a train/bus combination to reach Ironbridge Gorge and the Lake District).

# NEAR BATH: GLASTONBURY, WELLS, AVEBURY, STONEHENGE, AND SOUTH WALES

Oooo, mystery, history. Glastonbury is the ancient home of Avalon, King Arthur, and the Holy Grail. Nearby, medieval Wells gathers around its grand cathedral, where you can enjoy an evensong service. Then get neolithic at every Druid's favorite stone circles, Avebury and Stonehenge.

An hour east of Bath, at the Museum of Welsh Life, you'll find South Wales' story vividly told in a park full of restored houses. Relish the romantic ruins and poetic wax of Tintern Abbey, the lush Wye River Valley, and the quirky Forest of Dean.

## Planning Your Time

Avebury, Glastonbury, and Wells make a wonderful day out from Bath. Splicing in Stonehenge is possible but stretching it. Everybody needs to see Stonehenge. But I'll tell you now, it looks just like it looks. You'll know what I mean when you pay to get in and rub up against the rope fence that keeps tourists at a distance. Avebury is the connoisseur's circle: more subtle and welcoming. Wells is simply a cute town, much smaller and more medieval than Bath, with a uniquely beautiful cathedral that's best experienced at the 17:15 evensong service. Glastonbury is normally done surgically, in two hours: See the abbey, climb the tower, ponder your hippie past (and where you are now), then scram.

Think of the South Wales sights as a different grouping. Ideally, they fill the day you leave Bath for the Cotswolds. Anyone interested in Welsh culture can spend four hours in the Museum of Welsh Life. Castle lovers and romantics will want to consider the Caerphilly Castle, Tintern Abbey, and Forest of Dean. See the beginning of this chapter for a day-by-day schedule.

## Getting around near Bath

Wells and Glastonbury are easily accessible by bus from Bath. **Badgerline** offers a "Day Explorer" ticket (£6, £12.50/family,

## Sights near Bath

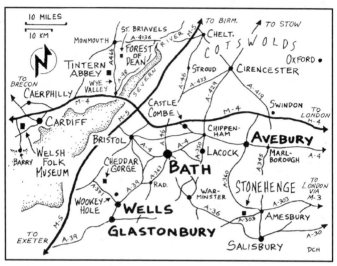

good for 1 day, CC, office located 1 block from Bath train station, Mon–Sat 8:00–17:30, closed Sun, tel. 01225/464-446); in 2002 Badgerline may also offer several day tours from Bath. You can get to South Wales by train via Bristol, connecting by bus from the Welsh train station to the various sights.

Avebury and Stonehenge are trickier. The most convenient and quickest way to see Avebury and Stonehenge if you don't have a car is to take an all-day bus tour. Of those tours leaving from Bath, "Mad Max" is the liveliest.

**"Mad Max" minibus tours** are thoughtfully organized and informative (£16, 6–14 people, daily, not Mon in winter, no CC). They last from 8:45 to 16:30 and cover 110 miles with stops in Avebury, Stonehenge, and two cute villages—Lacock and Castle Combe. Castle Combe, the southernmost Cotswold village, is as cute as they come. The Mad Max bus picks up passengers at 8:45 at the statue on Cheap Street (behind Bath Abbey). To reserve a seat, call the Bath YMCA (tel. 01225/325-900, no CC, please honor or cancel your seat reservation, e-mail: maddy@madmax.abel.co.uk).

If Mad Max is booked up, don't fret. Plenty of companies in Bath offer tours of varying lengths, prices, and destinations. The cost of admission to sites is usually not included with any tour. **Danwood Tours** offers a daily daylong City Safari tour of the southern Cotswolds, Avebury, Stonehenge, Salisbury, and Longleat for £16.50 (departs outside Abbey Hotel at 10:00, returns

Mon–Fri at 16:30, Sat–Sun at 18:00, no CC, book at Bath TI and many hotels, or tel. 07977-929-486 or 01373/461-135, e-mail: danw1@freenetname.co.uk, private car hire also available). Dan-wood also runs a round-trip tour from Bath to Wells on weekdays for the sole purpose of getting you to the Wells evensong service (£7.50, not mid-July–Aug, leave Bath's Abbey Hotel at 16:30, return at 19:00, contact info above). Another tour company, **Andrews Country Tours**, runs trips to Stonehenge, Avebury, and more (£16, Easter-Oct daily 9:00–16:00, maximum 14 people, nar-rated trip, no CC, departs from Abbey, tel. 01761/416-362, www.andrewstours.co.uk, e-mail: c.andrew@talk21.com, Chris Andrews). To tour the Cotswolds from Bath consider the **Cotswold Experience** (£21.50, April–Oct Tue, Thu, Sat, Sun 10:00–18:00, 4-person minimum, 14-seat bus, departs from Bath Abbey, book at Bath TI or call: daytime tel. 01225/477-101, evening tel. 01453/767-574, www.cotswold-tours.co.uk).

Drivers can do a loop from Bath to Avebury (25 miles) to Glastonbury (56 miles) to Wells (6 miles) and back to Bath (20 miles). A loop from Bath to South Wales is 100 miles, mostly on the 80-mph motorway. Each of the Welsh sights is just off the motorway.

## GLASTONBURY

Marked by its hill, or "tor," and located on England's most powerful line of prehistoric sights (called a "ley" line), the town of Glastonbury gurgles with history and mystery.

In A.D. 37, Joseph of Arimathea—one of Jesus' wealthy disciples—brought vessels containing the blood and sweat of Jesus to Glastonbury, and, with them, Christianity came to England. While this is "proven" by fourth-century writings and accepted by the Church, the Holy Grail legend that sprang from this in the Middle Ages isn't. Many think the grail trail ends at the bottom of the Chalice Well (described below), a natural spring at the base of the Glastonbury Tor.

In the 12th century, England needed a morale-boosting folk hero for inspiration during a war with France. The fifth-century Celtic fort at Glastonbury was considered proof enough of the greatness of the fifth-century warlord Arthur. His supposed remains (along with those of Queen Guinevere) were dug up from the abbey floor, and Glastonbury became woven into the Arthurian legends. Reburied in the abbey choir, their grave site is a shrine today.

The Glastonbury Abbey was England's most powerful in the 10th century. By the year 1500, English monasteries owned one-sixth of all English land and had four times the income of the crown. Henry VIII dissolved the abbeys in 1536. He was particu-larly harsh on Glastonbury. He not only destroyed the abbey but also hung and quartered the abbot, sending the parts of his body on four different national tours...at the same time.

But Glastonbury rebounded. In an 18th-century tourism campaign, thousands signed affidavits stating that water from the Chalice Well healed them, and once again Glastonbury was on the tourist map. Today Glastonbury and its tor are a center for searchers, too creepy for the mainstream church but just right for those looking for a place to recharge their crystals.

## Orientation (area code: 01458)

**Tourist Information**: The TI is on High Street—as are many of the dreadlocked folks who walk it (Sun–Thu 10:00–17:00, Fri–Sat 10:00–17:30, until 16:00 in winter, tel. 01458/832-954). The TI has several booklets about cycling and walking in the area. One 30p brochure outlines a good tor-to-town walk (a brisk, 10-min walk). The TI's Millennium Trail pamphlet (50p) sends visitors on a historical scavenger hunt, following 20 numbered, marble plaques embedded in the pavement throughout the town. The Lake Village Museum in the TI is nothing special (£2; stone, bone, and antler tools). Tuesday is market day—a combo crafts-, flea-, and produce-gathering behind the TI (9:00–15:00).

The **Tor Bus** shuttles visitors from the town center and abbey to the base of the tor. If you request it, the bus will stop at the Rural Life Museum and the Chalice Well (£1, 2/hr, 9:30–17:00 throughout the summer, bus does not run during lunchtime, catch bus at St. Dunstan's car park in center).

## Sights—Glastonbury

▲▲**Glastonbury Abbey**—The evocative ruins of the first Christian sanctuary in the British Isles stand mysteriously alive in a lush, 36-acre park. Start your visit in the good little museum, where a model shows the abbey in its pre-Henry VIII splendor, and exhibits tell the story of a place "grandly constructed to entice even the dullest minds to prayer." Today the abbey attracts people who find God within. Tie-dyed, starry-eyed pilgrims seem to float through the grounds naturally high. Others lie on the grave of King Arthur, whose burial site is marked off in the center of the abbey ruins. The only surviving building is the Abbot's conical kitchen, which often comes with a cheery singing monk demonstrating life in the abbey kitchen (£3.50, June–Aug daily 9:00–18:00, off-season 9:30 to dusk, last entry 30 min before closing, £1 audioguide is informative but can be long-winded, ask at entry for monk's "show" times, tel. 01458/832-267, www.glastonburyabbey.com).

**Somerset Rural Life Museum**—Exhibits include peat digging, cider making, and cheese making. The Abbey Farmhouse is now a collection of domestic and work mementos that illustrate the

# Glastonbury

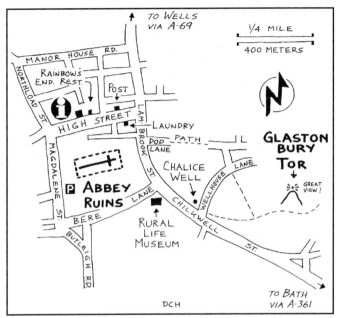

life of farmer John Hodges "from the cradle to the grave." The fine 14th-century barn, with its beautifully preserved wooden ceiling, is filled with Victorian farm tools (£2.50, Easter-Oct Tue–Fri 10:00–17:00, Sat–Sun 14:00–18:00, closed Mon and off-season, last entry 30 min before closing, free car park, 8-min walk from abbey, at intersection of Bere Lane and Chilkwell Street, tel. 01458/831-197, www.somerset.gov.uk/museums).

**Chalice Well**—The well is surrounded by a peaceful garden. According to tradition, Joseph of Arimathea brought the chalice of the Lord's Supper to Glastonbury in A.D. 37. Even if the chalice is not in the bottom of the well and the water is red from rust and not Jesus' blood, the tranquil setting is one where nature's harmony is a joy to ponder. Have a drink (£2.50) or take some of the precious water home (50–75p bottles available, daily 10:00–18:00, less off-season, 4-min walk from rural museum, on Chilkwell Street, look for red sign, tel. 01458/831-154, www.chalicewell.org.uk).

**Glastonbury Tor**—Seen by many as a Mother Goddess symbol, the tor, a natural plug of sandstone on clay, has an undeniable geological charisma. The tower is the remnant of a 14th-century church of St. Michael. A fine Somerset view rewards those who hike to its 520-foot summit.

**Shopping**—If you need spiritual guidance or just an odd rune read, wander through the **Glastonbury Experience**, a New Age mall at the bottom of High Street.

## Eating in Glastonbury

Glastonbury, quickly becoming "the windy city," has no shortage of healthy eateries. The vegetarian **Rainbow's End** (daily 10:00–16:00, a few doors up from the TI, 17 High Street, tel. 01458/833-896) is one of several fine cafés for beans, salads, and New Age people watching. If you're looking for a midwife or a male-bonding tribal meeting, check their notice board.

## Transportation Connections—Glastonbury

The nearest train station is in Bath.

**By bus to: Wells** (1/hr, 20 min) and **Bath** (5/day, 75 min).

## WELLS

This wonderfully preserved little town has a cathedral, so it can be called a city. It's England's smallest cathedral city, with one of its most interesting cathedrals and more medieval buildings still doing what they were originally built to do than in any town you'll visit. Market day fills the town square on Wednesday and Saturday.

**Tourist Information:** The TI, on the main square, has information about the town's sights and nearby cheese factories (daily, April–Oct 9:30–17:30, off-season 10:00–16:00, tel. 01749/672-552, e-mail: wells.tic@ukonline.co.uk). Edie Westmoreland is a good local guide who offers £2 town walks in the summer at 14:30 (tours start at Penniless Porch on town square, tel. 01934/832-350).

## Sights—Wells

▲▲**Wells Cathedral**—England's first completely Gothic cathedral (dating from about 1200) is the highlight of the city. The newly restored west front displays nearly 300 original 13th-century carvings (the *Last Judgment*, lots of kings, bottom row of niches empty—all too easily reached by Cromwell's men, who were hell-bent on destroying "graven images"). Stand back and imagine it as a grand Palm Sunday welcome with a cast of hundreds—all gaily painted back then, chorasters singing boldly from holes above the doors and trumpets tooting through the holes up by the 12 apostles.

Inside you're immediately struck by the general lightness and the unique "scissors" or hourglass-shaped double arch (added in 1338 to transfer weight from the west, where the foundations were sinking under the tower's weight, to the east, where they were firm). You'll be warmly greeted, reminded how expensive it is to maintain the cathedral, and given a map of its highlights.

Don't miss the fine 14th-century stained glass (the "Golden Window" on the east wall). The medieval clock does a silly but much-loved joust on the quarter hour (north transept, its face dates from 1390). The embroidery work on cushions in the choir (the central zone where the daily services are sung) is worth a close look. Walk the well-worn steps up to the grand fan-vaulted chapter house—an intimate place for the theological equivalent of a huddle among church officials. The cathedral library (14:30–16:30 only, 50p), with a few old manuscripts, offers a peek into a real 15th-century library. The requested £4 donation for the cathedral is not intended to keep you out (daily 7:30–19:00 or dusk, 45-min tours at 10:15, 11:15, 13:15, 14:15, and 15:15, pay £1 photography fee at info desk, no flash in choir, good shop and a handy restaurant, tel. 01749/ 674-483). See "Evensong," below.

Lined with perfectly pickled 14th-century houses, the oldest complete street in Europe is **Vicar's Close** (just a block north of the cathedral). It was built to house the vicar's choir, and it still houses church officials. The mediocre city museum is next door to the cathedral. For a fine cathedral-and-town view from your own leafy hilltop bench, hike 10 minutes up Tor Hill.

▲▲**Cathedral Evensong Service**—Weekdays at 17:15 and Sunday at 15:00, the cathedral choir takes full advantage of heavenly acoustics with a 45-minute evensong service (boys' and men's voices, great pipe organ, you'll sit right in the old "quire;" generally not sung when school is out in July and August unless a visiting choir is performing, tel. 01749/674-483 to check). At 17:05 the verger ushers visitors to their seats. There's usually plenty of room.

On weekdays, if you need to catch the last bus to Bath at 17:43, request a seat on the north side of the presbytry, so you can slip out the side door without disturbing the service (10-min walk to station from cathedral). Even better, take a Danwood Tour, which offers a round-trip from Bath to Wells on weekdays expressly to allow tour members to attend the entire Wells evensong service (£7.50, not mid-July–Aug, leave Bath's Abbey Hotel at 16:30, return at 19:00, tel. 07977-929-486 or 01373/461-135, e-mail: danw1@freenetname.co.uk).

**Bishop's Palace**—Next to the cathedral stands the moated Bishop's Palace. On the grounds (past the old-timers playing a proper game of croquet) is a fine garden with the idyllic springs that gave the city its name. The interior offers a look at elegant furniture and clothing (£3, Aug daily 10:30–18:00; April–Oct Tue–Fri 10:30–18:00, Sun 14:00–18:00, closed Mon and Sat, closed in winter, tel. 01749/678-691).

**Cheddar Cheese**—If you're in the mood for a picnic, drop by an aromatic cheese shop for a great selection of tasty Somerset cheeses. Real farmhouse cheddar puts "American" cheddar to Velveeta shame. The Cheese and Grain Company is a traditional cheese shop with all the local edibles (Mon–Sat 9:00–17:00, closed Sun, 14 Queen Street, tel. 01749/679-803). Ask for a pound's worth of the most interesting mix. The Cheddar Gorge (and the Cheddar Gorge Cheese Company, which welcomes and educates guests; tel. 01934/742810) is six miles down the road.

## Sleeping in Wells
### (£1 = about $1.50, country code: 44, area code: 01749)

Wells is a pleasant overnight stop. The first two guest houses and the Fountain Inn are all within a block of each other behind (east of) the cathedral. Coming in on B3139 from Bath, they're just before the cathedral. The last B&B is idyllic and in the next village.

**Furlong House B&B**, a grand old house with a huge and peaceful garden, is homey and laid-back (Db-£44–50, CC, non-smoking, easy parking, includes breakfast, behind the gate at the end of Lorne Place, a tiny and quiet lane off St. Thomas Street, Wells, BA5 2XF, tel. 01749/674-064, e-mail: johnhowardwells @cs.com, Lyn and John Howard). Guests may also stay in The Stables, an annex with wood-beamed ceilings, a communal break-fast table, and a farmhouse feel (3 Db-£44–50).

**Swan Hotel**, facing the cathedral, is a big, overpriced hotel (Sb-£75, Db-£89, often cheaper if you just show up, CC, break-fast-£9.50, nonsmoking rooms, Sadler Street, BA5 2RX, tel. 01749/836-300, fax 01749/836-301, e-mail: swan@bhere.co.uk).

**Manor Farm B&B**, in the village of Dulcote a mile or so outside Wells, rents four fine rooms in a cozy 17th-century farmhouse (D-£44, Db-£48–50, huge ground-floor easy-access Db suite-£60, no CC, includes breakfast with farm-fresh eggs and veggie options, nonsmoking, BA5 3PZ, tel. & fax 01749/672-125, www.wells-accommodation.co.uk, e-mail: rosalind.bufton @ntlworld.com). The place comes complete with friendly farm animals and the good care and cooking of Rosalind Bufton. It's a peaceful 20-minute walk through wispy farmland to the Wells Cathedral.

## Eating in Wells

**Fountain Inn** is a step above pub grub (£10–15 dinners, Mon–Sat 12:00–14:00, 18:00–22:00, Sun 12:00–14:00, 19:00–21:30, creative meals, veggie options, real ales, draft cider, reservations wise on weekends, CC, behind cathedral on St. Thomas Street, tel. 01749/672-317). Their award-winning cheese plate lets you sam-ple cheddar and its local cousins. For a good, traditional local dish, try their founders beef pie. **Anton's Bistro** on the main square is pleasant (£8–11, daily 12:00–14:00, 18:00–21:30, non-smoking section, CC, in Crown Hotel, tel. 01749/673-457). Locals like **Ritcher's**—a little pricey, but good (£17.50 2-course dinner, daily 12:00–14:00, 18:00–20:00, opposite cathedral near market square, tel. 01749/679-085). For a heavenly lunch, con-sider the **Cathedral Cloister Restaurant** (in the cathedral, a lovely stone corridor with leaded windows, £3 lunches, Mon–Sat 10:00–17:00, Sun 12:30–17:00) or the health-minded **Good Earth** for its quiche, pasta, and salad (Mon–Sat 9:00–17:30, closed Sun, 4 Priory Road at bottom of Broad Street, tel. 01749/678-600).

## Transportation Connections—Wells

The nearest train station is in Bath. The bus station in Wells is actually a bus "lot," at the intersection of Priory and Princes Roads.

**By bus to: Bath** (1/hr, 75 min), **Glastonbury** (1/hr, 20 min), **London's Victoria Coach Station** (£15.50, 1/hr, 4 hrs, change in Bristol or Bath; buses run Mon–Fri 7:25-17:45, Sat 7:00–17:55, Sun 7:55–19:15, CC, National Express, tel. 08705-808-080).

## Sights—Near Wells

▲**Wookey Hole**—This lowbrow commercial venture, possibly worthwhile as family entertainment, is a real hodgepodge. It starts with a 35-minute wookey-guided tour of some big but mediocre caves complete with history, geology lessons, and witch stories. Then you're free to wander through a traditional paper-making mill, with a demonstration, and into a 19th-century amusements room— a riot of color, funny mirrors, and old penny-arcade machines that visitors can actually play for as long as their pennies (on sale there) last. They even have old girlie shows. (£7.40 at the gate, £6.60 tickets available at the Wells TI, daily 10:00–17:00, tickets sold until 2 hrs before closing, 2 miles east of Wells, tel. 01749/672-243.) **Scrumpy Farms**—Scrumpy is the wonderfully dangerous hard cider brewed in this part of England. You don't find it served in many pubs because of the unruly crowd it attracts. (The Beehive pub in Bath still serves its scrumpy and seems to enjoy the consequences.) Scrumpy, 8 percent alcohol, will rot your socks. "Scrumpy Jack," carbonated mass-produced cider, is not real scrumpy. The real stuff is "rough farmhouse cider." This is potent stuff. It's said some farmers throw a side of beef into the vat, and when fermentation is done only the teeth remain. TIs list local cider farms open to the public, such as Mr. Wilkins Land's End Cider Farm—a great "back door" travel experience (free, Mon–Sat 10:00–20:00, Sun 10:00–13:00, near Wells in Mudgeley a quarter mile off the B3151, 2 miles south of Wedmore—tough to find, get close and ask locals, tel. 01934/712-385). Glastonbury's Somerset Rural Life Museum has a cider exhibit. Apples are pressed from August through December. Hard cider, while not quite scrumpy, is still West-country typical but more fashionable, decent, and accessible. You can have a pint drawn for you at nearly any pub.

## AVEBURY

The stone circle at Avebury is bigger (16 times the size), less touristy, and, for many, more interesting than Stonehenge.

You're free to wander among 100 stones, ditches, mounds, and curious patterns from the past, as well as the village of Avebury, which grew up in the middle of this fascinating, 1,400-foot-wide neolithic circle.

In the 14th century, in a kind of frenzy of religious paranoia, Avebury villagers buried many of these mysterious pagan stones. Their 18th-century descendants broke up the remaining stones and used them for building material. Today the buried stones have been resurrected, and concrete markers show where the broken-down stones once stood.

Take the mile walk around the circle. Visit the archaeology museum with its new interactive exhibit in a 17th-century barn (£3.50, April–Oct daily 10:00–18:00, Nov–March until 16:00, tel. 01672/539-250). Notice the pyramid-shaped Silbury Hill, a 130-foot-high, yet-to-be-explained mound of chalk just outside of Avebury. Nearly 5,000 years old, this mound is the largest man-made object in prehistoric Europe (with the surface area of London's Trafalgar Square and the height of the Nelson Memorial). It's a reminder that you've just scratched the surface of Britain's mysterious ancient and religious landscape.

The pleasant **Circle Restaurant** serves healthy vegetarian meals and unhealthy cream teas (daily, April–Oct 10:00–18:00, Nov–March until 16:00, next to National Trust store, tel. 01672/539-514). The **Red Lion Pub** has inexpensive pub grub, a creaky, well-worn, dart-throwing ambience, and a medieval well in its dining room (£6–12 meals, cooking daily 12:00–21:00, overpriced £60 rooms upstairs, CC, tel. 01672/539-266).

Sleeping in Avebury makes lots of sense since the stones are lonely and wide open all night. **Mrs. Dixon's B&B**, directly across from Silbury Hill on the main road just beyond the tourist parking lot, rents three small but tidy rooms for a fine price (S-£30, D-£38, T-£50, includes breakfast, no CC, nonsmoking, 6 Beckhampton Road, Avebury, Wiltshire, SN8 1QT, tel. 01672/539-588).

For transportation connections, see "Getting around near Bath," above.

## STONEHENGE

England's most famous stone circle, with parts older than the oldest pyramid, was built between 2800 and 1500 B.C. Many of these huge stones were rafted and then rolled on logs all the way from Wales to form a remarkably accurate celestial calendar. Even today, every summer solstice (around June 21) the sun sets in just the right slot, and Druids boogie. The monument is roped off, so even if you pay the £4.70 entry fee (which includes a worthwhile 1-hr audioguide, subject to availability), you're kept at a distance. Cheapskates see it free from the road (June–Aug daily 9:00–19:00, less off-season, live tel. 01980/625-368, lengthy info tel. 01980/624-715, www.english-heritage.org.uk). For transportation connections, see "Getting around near Bath" on page 127.

# SOUTH WALES

▲**Cardiff**—The Welsh capital (pop. 300,000) has a pleasant modern center across from its castle. A castle visit is interesting only if you catch one of the entertaining tours (every 30 min). The interior is a Victorian fantasy.

▲▲**St. Fagans' Welsh Folk Museum**—This best look at traditional Welsh folk life displays more than 30 carefully reconstructed old houses from all corners of this little country in a 100-acre park under a castle. Each is fully furnished and comes equipped with a local expert warming herself by a toasty fire and happy to tell you anything you want to know about life in this old cottage. Ask questions!

A highlight is the Rhyd-y-Car 1805 row house, which displays ironworker cottages as they might have looked in 1805, 1855, 1895, 1925, 1955, and 1985, offering a fascinating zip through Welsh domestic life. You'll see traditional crafts in action and a great gallery displaying crude washing machines, the earliest matches, elaborately carved "love spoons," an impressive costume exhibit, and even a case of memorabilia from the local man who pioneered cremation. While everything is well explained, the £2 museum guidebook is a good investment.

The museum has three sections: houses, museum, and castle/garden. If the sky's dry, see the scattering of houses first. Spend an hour in the large building's fascinating museum. The castle interior is royal enough and surrounded by a fine garden, but, if you're tired, it's not worth the hike. While the cafeteria near the entrance (Vale Restaurant) is handy, you'll eat light lunches better, cheaper, and with more atmosphere in the park at the Gwalia Tea Room. The Plymouth Arms pub just outside the museum serves the best food. (free, daily 10:00–17:00, tel. 02920/573-500.) City bus #32 runs hourly between Cardiff Castle and the Welsh Folk Museum (which is in the village of St. Fagans). Drivers leave the M4 at Junction 33 and follow the signs. Leaving the museum, jog left on the freeway, take the first exit, and circle back, following signs to the M4.

▲**Caerphilly Castle**—This impressive but gutted old castle is the second largest in Europe (after Windsor). With two concentric walls, it was considered to be a brilliant arrangement of defensive walls and moats (£2.50, daily June–Sept 9:30–18:00, May and Oct 9:30–17:00, Nov–April Mon–Sat 9:30–16:00, Sun 11:00–16:00, last entry 30 min before closing, £1 45-min audioguide, 9 miles north of Cardiff, 30 min by car from the Welsh Folk Museum, or take train from Cardiff to Caerphilly—3/hr, 20 min—and walk 5 min, tel. 02920/883-143, www.cadw.wales.gov.uk).

▲▲**Tintern Abbey**—Inspiring monks to prayer, Wordsworth to poetry, Turner to a famous painting, and rushed tourists to a thoughtful moment, this poem-worthy ruined-castle-of-an-abbey is worth a five-mile detour off the motorway. Founded in 1131 on a site chosen by Norman monks for its tranquility, it functioned as an austere Cistercian abbey until its dissolution in 1536 (£2.50, family-£7, daily 9:30–18:00 in summer, 9:30–17:00 in spring and fall, Mon–Sat 9:30–16:00, Sun 11:00–16:00 in winter, last entry 30 min before closing, £1 1-hr audioguide, tel. 01291/689-251, www.cadw.wales.gov.uk; from Cardiff catch a bus or train to Chepstow—1.5 hrs, then bus or taxi from Chepstow to abbey—20 min). Visit early or late to miss crowds. The abbey's shop sells fine Celtic jewelry and other gifts. Take an easy 15-minute walk up to St. Mary's Church for a view of England just over the River Wye.

If seduced into spending the night, you'll find plenty of B&Bs near the abbey or in the charming castle-crowned town of Chepstow just down the road. The Tintern **TI** is helpful (April–Oct 10:30–17:30, closed Nov–March, tel. 01291/689-566).

▲**Wye River Valley and Forest of Dean**—This land is lush, mellow, and historic. Local tourist brochures explain the Forest of Dean's special dialect, its strange political autonomy, and its oaken ties to Trafalgar and Admiral Nelson.

For a medieval night, check into the **St. Briavels' Castle Youth Hostel** (£11.25 beds in 4- to 12-bed dorms, nonmembers-£2 extra, 70 beds, CC, breakfast-£3.30, nonsmoking, tel. 01594/530-272, e-mail: stbriavels@yha.org.uk). The hostel hosts medieval banquets each week in August (£6.50, for hostel guests only, ask staff for schedule). An 800-year-old Norman castle used by King John in 1215 (the year he signed the Magna Carta), it's comfortable (as castles go), friendly, and in the center of the quiet village of St. Briavels just north of Tintern Abbey. For dinner, eat at the hostel or walk "just down the path and up the snyket" to the **Crown Pub** (decent food and local pub atmosphere).

## Transportation Connections—Cardiff

**By train to: Caerphilly** (3/hr, 20 min), **Bath** (2/hr, 1 hr, change in Bristol), **Birmingham** (2/hr, 2 hrs, change in Bristol), **London** (2/hr, 2 hrs), **Chepstow** (1/hr, 30 min, 6 miles to Tintern by bus). Train info: tel. 08457-484-950.

## Route Tips for Drivers

**Bath to South Wales:** Leave Bath following signs for A4, then M4, then Stroud. It's 10 miles north (on A46 past a village called Pennsylvania) to the M4 superfreeway. Zip westward, crossing a huge suspension bridge into Wales (£4.20 toll westbound only). Stay on the M4 (not M48) past Cardiff, take exit 33, and follow the brown signs south to the Welsh Folk Museum. To get to

Tintern Abbey, take the M4 to Exit 21 and get on M48. The abbey is six miles (up A466, signs to Chepstow then Tintern) off M48 at Exit 2, right where the northern bridge across the Severn hits Wales.

**Cardiff to the Cotswolds via Forest of Dean:** On the Welsh side of the big suspension bridge, take the Chepstow exit and follow signs up A466 to Tintern Abbey and the Wye River Valley. Carry on to Monmouth and, if you're running late, follow the A40 and the M50 to the Tewksebury exit, where small roads will take you into the Cotswolds.

# THE COTSWOLDS

The Cotswold Hills, a 25-by-50-mile chunk of Gloucestershire, are dotted with villages and graced with England's greatest countryside palace, Blenheim.

As with many fairy-tale regions of Europe, the present-day beauty of the Cotswolds was the result of an economic disaster. Wool was a huge industry in medieval England, and Cotswold sheep grew the best wool. The region prospered. Wool money built fine towns and houses. Local "wool" churches are called "cathedrals" for their scale and wealth. Stained-glass slogans say things like "I thank my God and ever shall, it is the sheep hath paid for all."

With the rise of cotton and the Industrial Revolution, the woolen industry collapsed. Ba-a-a-ad news. The wealthy Cotswold towns fell into a depressed time warp; the homes of an impoverished nobility became gracefully dilapidated. Today visitors enjoy a harmonious blend of man and nature—the most pristine of English countrysides decorated with time-passed villages, rich wool churches, tell-me-a-story stone fences, and kissing gates you wouldn't want to experience alone. Appreciated by hordes of 21st-century romantics, the Cotswolds are enjoying new prosperity.

## Planning Your Time

The Cotswolds are an absolute delight by car and, with patience, enjoyable even without a car. On a three-week British trip, I'd spend two nights and a day in the Cotswolds. The Cotswolds' charm has a softening effect on many tight itineraries. You could spend days of enjoyable walking from a home base here.

**One-day driver's 100-mile Cotswold blitz, including Blenheim:** Use a good map and reshuffle to fit your home base: 9:00–Browse through Chipping Campden; 10:00–Joyride through

Snowshill, Stanway, Stanton, Guiting Power, the Slaughters, and Bourton; 13:00–Lunch and explore Stow-on-the-Wold; 15:00–Drive 30 miles to Blenheim Palace, take the hour-long tour (last tour departs at 16:45); 18:00–Drive home for just the right pub dinner.

## Orientation

The north Cotswolds are best. Two of the region's coziest towns, Chipping Campden and Stow-on-the-Wold, are eight and four miles, respectively, from work-a-day Moreton, the only Cotswold town with a train station. Any of these three towns make a fine home base for your exploration of the thatch-happiest of Cotswold villages and walks.

## Cotswold Appreciation 101

Much history can be read into the names of the area. *Cotswold* could come from the Saxon phrase meaning "hills of sheep's coats." Or it could mean shelter ("cot" like *cottage*) on the open upland ("wold").

In the Cotswolds, a town's main street (called High Street) needed to be wide to accommodate the sheep and cattle being marched to market (and today, to park tour buses). Some of the most picturesque cottages were once humble row houses of weavers' cottages, usually located along a stream for their water wheels (Bibury, Castle Combe). The towns run on slow clocks and yellowed calendars. An entire village might not have a phone booth that accepts a telephone card.

Fields of yellow (rapeseed) and pale blue (linseed) separate pastures dotted with black and white sheep. In just about any B&B, when you open your window in the morning you'll hear sheep baaing. The decorative "toadstool" stones that litter front yards throughout the region are medieval staddle stones. Buildings were set upon these to keep the rodents out.

Cotswold walls and roofs are made of limestone. The limestone roof tiles hang by pegs. To make the weight more bearable, smaller, lighter tiles are higher up. An extremely strict building code keeps towns looking what many locals call "overly quaint."

The area is provincial and gossipy. People are ever so polite but commonly catch themselves saying, "It's all very...ummm... yyya." Rich people open their gardens to support their favorite charities, while—until recently—the less couth enjoyed "badger baiting" (a gambling cousin of cockfighting in which a badger, with his teeth and claws taken out, is mangled by right-wing dogs).

This is walking country. The English love their walks and vigorously defend their age-old right to free passage. Once a year the Rambling Society organizes a "Mass Trespass," when each of the country's 50,000 miles of public footpaths is walked.

## The Cotwolds

By assuring each path is used at least once a year, they stop land-lords from putting up fences. Any paths found blocked are unceremoniously unblocked.

Questions to ask locals: Does badger baiting survive? Do you approve of foxhunting with hounds? Who are the Morris men? What's a kissing gate?

## Getting around the Cotswolds

**By Bus:** Ask about the Cotswold Link X55 bus service that may run twice daily in both directions between Bath and Stratford, making up to 13 stops en route and hitting the highlights of the Cotswolds, including Chipping Campden, Stow-on-the-Wold, and Moreton-in-Marsh. This service was stopped in 2001—a casualty of the foot-and-mouth troubles. If it's resurrected in 2002, take advantage of this handy line. Otherwise, remember the Cotswolds are so well preserved in part because public transport to this area has long been miserable. You can cobble together a trip with buses connecting major towns, but you'll need to be on the ball and flexible (see "Transportation Connections," below). Bus service is very limited on Sundays. Tourist offices have plenty of schedule information.

**By Bike:** In Stow, **Stow Cycle Hire** rents mountain bikes (£12.50/day, £8/half day, includes helmets, friendly, helpful, and easygoing, can deliver, a block off the Market Square at 21 Glebe Close, tel. 01451/870-425, cellular 079-4121-8526). In Moreton-in-Marsh, **Country Lanes Cycle Centre** rents 21-speed bikes for £15 a day and offers bike tours (closed in 2001, likely to reopen in 2002: Easter-Oct daily 9:30–17:30, includes helmets, free route plans, £5 maps, reserve ahead, at train station, tel. 01608/650-065, www.countrylanes.co.uk). In Chipping Campden, try **Cotswold Country Cycles** (£10/day, daily 9:00–dusk, includes helmets, route maps, delivery for a fee, 1.5 miles north of town at Longlands Farm Cottage, tel. 01386/438-706, cellular 077-1500-2972). Despite narrow roads and high hedgerows (blocking some views), bikers enjoy the Cotswolds—free from the constraints of bus schedules.

**By Foot:** Walking guidebooks abound, giving you a world of choices for each of my recommended stops (choose one with clear maps). Villages are generally no more than three miles apart, and most have pubs that would love to feed and water you. For a list of guided walks, ask at any TI for the free AONB (Area of Outstanding Natural Beauty) brochure. The walks are free, range from two to 12 miles, and often involve a stop at a pub or tearoom (April–Sept).

**By Car:** Robinson's car-rental company, near Moreton-in-Marsh, offers one-day rentals from £25 including everything but gas. Figure a delivery charge of £1/mile to just about anywhere in the Cotswolds (Mon–Fri 8:30–17:00, Sat 8:30–12:30, closed Sun, tel. 01608/661-681).

Car hiking is great. Distances are minuscule. In this chapter, I cover the postcard-perfect (but discovered) villages. With a car and the local Ordnance Survey map you can easily ramble about and find your own gems. The problem with having a car is that you are less likely to hike. Try to taxi or bus somewhere so you can hike back to your car and enjoy the scenery.

**By Taxi:** Two or three taxi trips can make more sense than renting a car. While taking a cab cross-country seems extravagant at about £1.50 per mile, the distances are short (Stow-Moreton is 4 miles, Stow-Chipping Campden is 10), and one-way walks are lovely. To scare up a taxi in Morton, call Richard at Four Shires (cellular 077-4780-2555); in Stow, call Cotswold Country Cars (tel. 01451/832-226); in Chipping Campden, try Marnic Cars & Taxis (tel. 01386/840-014, cellular 077-6845-4376).

**By Tour:** From Bath, take a Mad Max tour to Castle Combe, the charming southernmost Cotswold town (book by calling Bath YMCA at tel. 01225/325-900). Another possibility from Bath:

Cotswold Experience, which covers five Cotswold villages in a full-day trip (£21.50, April–Oct Tue, Thu, Sat–Sun, 10:00–18:00, 4-person minimum, 14-seat bus, book at Bath TI or call: daytime tel. 01225/477-101, evening tel. 01453/767-574, www .cotswold-tours.co.uk).

From Stratford, catch the Guide Friday tour (£18, April–Oct daily 13:45–17:15, drive through 15 villages and stop briefly in Stanton, Chipping Campden, and Stow; depart from Civic Hall near Market Square, buy tickets at Guide Friday office in Civic Hall, tel. 01789/294-466).

## Sights—North Cotswolds

▲▲**Chipping Campden**—Ten miles north of Stow-on-the-Wold and nearly as touristy, Chipping Campden (CAM-den) is a working market town, home of some incredibly beautiful thatched roofs and the richest Cotswold wool merchants. Both the great British historian Trevelyan and I call Chipping Campden's High Street the finest in England.

Walk the full length of High Street; its width is characteristic of market towns. Go around the block on both ends. On one end you'll find impressively thatched homes (out Sheep Street, past the public WC and ugly gas station, and right on West-ington Street). Walking north on High Street you'll pass the Market Hall (built in 1627), the wavy roof of the first great wool mansion (the house of William Grevel, from 1380, on left), a fine and free memorial garden (on right), and, finally, the town's famous 15th-century Perpendicular Gothic "wool" church, down Church Street.

Chipping Campden's **TI** wanders around High Street looking for a capable staff and a permanent address (daily 10:00–17:30, 20p town maps, tel. 01386/841-206). For **Internet access**, try the library (High Street, near TI). For accommodations, see "Sleeping," below.

**Stanton, Snowshill, and Guiting Power**—Located between Chipping Campden and Stow, these are my nominations for the cutest Cotswold villages. Like marshmallows in hot chocolate, they nestle side by side, awaiting your arrival.

▲▲**Stanway House**—Stanway is notable for its manor house. Lord Neidpath, whose family tree charts relatives back to 1202, occasionally opens his melancholy home to visitors (£3.50, Aug–Sept Tue and Thu 14:00–17:00, tel. 01386/584-469). The 14th-century Tithe Barn predates the manor and was originally where monks—in the days before money—would accept one-tenth of whatever the peasants produced. Peek inside—this is a great hall for village hoedowns.

While the Tithe Barn is no longer used to greet motley peasants with their feudal "rents," the lord still collects rents from his vast landholdings. The place feels like a time warp even though the lord has recently remarried.

Ask the ticket taker (inside) to demonstrate the spinning rent-collection table. In the great hall marvel at the one-piece oak shuffleboard table and the 1780 Chippendale exercise chair (half an hour of bouncing on this was considered good for the liver).

The manor dogs have their own cutely painted "family tree," but Lord Neidpath admits that his current dog, CJ, is "all character and no breeding." The place has a story to tell. And so do the docents stationed in each room—modern-day peasants who, even without family trees, probably have relatives going back just as far in this village. Really. Talk to these people. Probe. Learn what you can about this side of England.

To get to Stanway, leave the B4077 at a statue of (Christian) George slaying the dragon (of pagan superstition); you'll round the corner and see the manor's fine 17th-century Jacobean gatehouse.

Stanway and Stanton (described below) are separated by a great oak forest and grazing land, with parallel waves echoing the furrows plowed by medieval farmers. Centuries ago, farmers were allotted long strips of land called "furlongs." The idea was to dole out good and bad land equitably. (Two furlongs equals an acre.) Over centuries of plowing these furrows were formed. Let someone else drive so you can hang out the window under a canopy of oaks as you pass stone walls and sheep. Leaving Stanway on the road to Stanton, the first building you'll see (on the left, just outside Stanway) is a thatched cricket pavilion overlooking the village cricket green. Dating only from 1930, it's raised up (as medieval buildings were) on rodent-resistant staddle stones. Stanton's just ahead (follow the signs).

▲▲**Stanton**—Pristine Cotswold charm cheers visitors up this village's main street. Stanton's Church of St. Michael betrays a pagan past. It's safe to assume any church dedicated to St. Michael (the archangel who fought the devil) sits upon a sacred pagan site. Stanton is actually at the intersection of two ley lines (lines of prehistoric sights). You'll see St. Michael's well-worn figure (with a sundial) above the door as you enter. Inside, above the capitals in the nave, find the pagan symbols for the sun and the moon. While the church probably dates back to the ninth century, today's building is mostly 15th century with 13th-century transepts. On the north transept, medieval frescoes weakly show through the 17th-century whitewash. (Once upon a time, medieval frescos were considered too "papist.") Imagine the church interior colorfully decorated throughout. There's original medieval glass behind the altar. The list of rectors (left side wall) goes back to 1269. Finger the grooves in the back pews, worn away by sheepdog leashes. A man's sheepdog accompanied him everywhere.

▲**Snowshill Manor**—Another nearly edible little bundle of

cuteness, Snowshill (SNOWS-hill) has a photogenic triangular square with a fine pub at its base. The Snowshill Manor is a dark and mysterious old palace filled with the lifetime collection of Charles Paget Wade. It's one big, musty celebration of craftsmanship, from finely carved spinning wheels to frightening samurai armor to tiny elaborate figurines carved by prisoners from the bones of meat served at dinner. Taking seriously his family motto, "Let Nothing Perish," Wade dedicated his life and fortune to preserving things finely crafted. The house (whose management made me promise not to promote it as an eccentric collector's pile of curiosities) really shows off Mr. Wade's ability to recognize and acquire fine examples of craftsmanship. It's all very... ummm...yyya. The manor overlooks the town square, but, ridiculously—to stoke business for the overpriced manor shop 300 yards away—has no direct access from the town square (£6, April–Oct Wed–Sun 12:00–17:00, closed Mon–Tue and Nov–March, car park and shop are a pleasant 500-yard walk from the house—golfcar-type shuttle available if desired, live tel. 01386/852-410, recorded info tel. 01684/855-376).

**Broadway**—With the new road allowing traffic to skirt the town, Broadway is cuter than ever. It's one of the postcard-pretty towns filled with inviting shops and fancy teahouses that visitors enjoy browsing through (a couple of miles west of Chipping Campden).

▲**Hidcote Manor**—If you like gardens, the grounds around this manor house are worth a look. Garden designers here pioneered the notion of creating a series of outdoor "rooms," each with a unique theme and separated by a yew-tree hedge. Follow your nose through a clever series of small gardens that lead delightfully from one to the next. Among the best in England, Hidcote gardens are at their fragrant peak in May, June, and July (£5.80, April–Oct 10:30–18:00, always closed Fri, also closed Tue except in June–July, last entrance 17:30, tearoom, 4 miles northeast of Chipping Campden on B4035, tel. 01386/438-333, www.ntrustsevern.org.uk).

**Horseback Riding**—Anyone can enjoy the Cotswolds from the saddle. Jill Carenza's Riding Centre is set just outside Stanton village in the most scenic corner of the region. The facility has 50 horses and takes rank beginners on an hour-long scenic "hack" through the village and into the high country (£17/person for 1 hr, £15/person for groups of 4 or more; also available are lessons, longer rides, rides for experts, and pub tours; well signposted in Stanton, tel. 01386/584-250, www.cotswoldsriding .co.uk). For accommodations, see Jill's recommended Vine B&B in "Sleeping," below.

## Sights—Central Cotswolds

▲▲**Stow-on-the-Wold**—With a name that means "meeting place on the uplands," Stow-on-the-Wold is the highest point of the Cotswolds. Despite its crowds, it retains its charm. Most of the tourists are daytrippers, so even summer nights are peaceful. Stow has no real sights other than itself, some good pubs, antique stores, and cute shops draped seductively around a big town square. Visit the church with its evocative old door guarded by ancient yew trees and the tombs of big shots (who made their money from wool) still boastful in death—find the tombs crowned with the bales of wool. A visit to Stow is not complete until you've locked your partner in the stocks on the green.

At the helpful **TI** on the main square, get the handy little 25p walking-tour brochure called "Town Trail" and the free "Cotswold Events" guide (Mon–Sat 9:30–17:30, Sun 10:30–16:00, Nov–Easter Mon–Sat 9:30–16:30, closed Sun, tel. 01451/831-082). The TI also reserves tickets for events (Stratford plays) and rooms for a £2 fee (save money and book direct). **Internet access** is at Tucan Internet on the main square (2nd floor above the C&G building society, opposite youth hostel, tel. 01451/870-609). You can generally find a parking spot on the main square (free for 2 hrs). For accommodations, see "Sleeping," below.

▲**Moreton-in-Marsh**—This work-a-day town is like Stow or Chipping Campden without the touristic sugar. Rather than gift and antique shops you'll find streets lined with real shops: ironmongers selling cottage nameplates and carpet shops strewn with the remarkable patterns that decorate B&B floors. A traditional market with 260 stalls filling High Street gets the town shin-kicking each Tuesday as it has for the last 400 years (8:00–16:00, handicrafts, farmer produce, clothing, great people watching). There is an economy outside of tourism in the Cotswolds, and you'll feel it here. Moreton has a tiny, sleepy train station two blocks from High Street, lots of bus connections, and a proficient **TI** (Mon–Fri 8:45–17:00, Thu 9:00–19:30, closed Sat afternoon and Sun, free "Town Trail" leaflet for self-guided walk, rail and bus schedules, and racks of flyers, tel. 01608/650-881). For accommodations, see "Sleeping," below.

For **Internet access**, go to Compulight (Mon–Sat 9:00–13:00, 13:30–17:00 but closed Wed afternoon, nearly across from TI, High Street, tel. 01608/652-980). Public WCs are on Corders Lane, next to the co-op on High Street (near bus stop).

▲**Bourton-on-the-Water**—I can't figure out if they call this "the Venice of the Cotswolds" because of its quaint canals or its miserable crowds. If you can avoid the midday and weekend crowds, it's worth a drive-through, a few cynical comments, and maybe a short stop. While mobbed with Japanese tour groups during the day, it's pleasantly empty in the early evening and after dark. Parking is predictably tough. Even during the busy business day, rather than park in the "pay and display" car park far from the center, drive right into town and wait for a

spot on High Street just past the Green (a long row of 2-hr
free spots in front of the Edinburgh Woolen Mills Shop).
Surrounding Bourton's green are sidewalks jammed with disori-
ented tourists with nametags and three sights worth considering:
a Model Railway Exhibition (£2, daily until 17:30, in the back
of a hobby shop, with 3 impressive-only-to-train-buffs set-ups);
the light but fun Miniature World (£2.50, a room full of tiny
models showing off various bits of British life); and the excellent
Motor Museum (described below). Bourton is four miles south
of Stow and a mile from the Slaughters.

▲**Motor Museum**—This fine little museum shows off a lifetime's
accumulation of vintage cars, old lacquered signs, threadbare toys,
and prewar memorabilia. Be sure to peek into the old-time vacation trailers and talk to an elderly Brit touring the place for some
personal memories (£2.25, daily 10:00–18:00, closed Nov–Feb,
in the mill facing the town center, Bourton-on-the-Water, tel.
01451/821-255).

**Upper and Lower Slaughter**—Lower Slaughter is a classic
village, with ducks, a working water mill, and usually an artist
busy at her easel somewhere. Just behind the skippable Old
Mill Museum, two kissing gates lead to the path that goes to
nearby Upper Slaughter. In Upper Slaughter walk between
the yew trees (sacred in pagan days) down a lane between the
raised graveyard (a buildup of centuries of graves) to the peaceful
church. In the back of the fine graveyard, a wistful woman
looks over the tomb of an 18th-century rector (sculpted by
his son). By the way, "Slaughter" has nothing to do with lamb
chops. It comes from the sloe tree (the one used to make sloe
gin). These towns are an easy two-hour round-trip walk from
Bourton. You could also walk from Bourton through the Slaughters to Stow. The small roads from Upper Slaughter to Ford
and Kineton are some of England's most scenic. Roll your
window down and take a slow joyride.

## Sights—South Cotswolds

▲**Cirencester**—Nearly 2,000 years ago, Cirencester (SIGH-
ren-ses-ter) was the ancient Roman city of Corinium. It's 20 miles
from Stow down A429, which was called Foss Way in Roman
times. In Cirencester, stop by the Corinium Museum to find out
why they say, "If you scratch Gloucestershire, you'll find Rome"
(£2.50, Mon–Sat 10:00–17:00, Sun 14:00–17:00, tel. 01285/655-
611). Cirencester's church is the largest of the Cotswolds "wool"
churches. The cutesy Brewery Art crafts center and workshops
entertain visitors with traditional weaving and potting, an interesting gallery, and a good coffee shop. Monday and Friday are gen-
eral-market days, Tuesday is cattle-market day, Friday features
an antique market, and Saturday is a crafts market. The TI is in

the Cornhill Marketplace (Mon–Sat 9:30–17:30, closed Sun, tel. 01285/654-180).

▲**Northleach**—As one of the "untouched and untouristed" Cotswold villages, Northleach is so untouched, it's interesting only for a short stop. Northleach's impressive main square and church attest to its position as a major wool center in the Middle Ages. Park on the square to check out the TI (which has walking brochures), the mechanical music museum (described below), and church. The fine Perpendicular Gothic church of St. Peter and St. Paul has been called the "cathedral of the Cotswolds." It's one of the Cotswolds' top two "wool" churches (along with Chipping Camp-den's)—paid for by 15th-century "woolthy" merchants. Find the oldest tombstone. The brass plaques on the floor memorialize big shots, showing sheep and sacks of wool at their long-dead feet and inscriptions mixing Latin and old English. You're welcome to do some brass rubbing if you get a permit from the post office (£2.50).

▲**Keith Harding's World of Mechanical Music**—This delight-ful little one-room place offers a unique opportunity to listen to 300 years of amazing self-playing musical instruments. It's run by well-respected men who are passionate about the restoration work they do on these instruments. The curators delight in demonstrat-ing each one. You'll hear Victorian music boxes and the earliest polyphones (record players) playing cylinders and then discs. The £5 admission fee includes an essential hour-long tour (tours go constantly, join in progress, daily 10:00–18:00, High Street, Lorthleach, tel. 01451/860-181).

**Cotswold Heritage Center**—Housed in an 18th-century prison, this simple museum features rural life, with re-creations of shops (blacksmith and wheelwright); loads of wagons; a Victorian laundry, dairy, and kitchen; and a prison cell (£2.50, April–Oct Mon–Sat 10:00–17:00, Sun 12:00–17:00, some demonstrations, tearoom, on main A429 road at town of Northleach, south of Stow, tel. 01451/860-715).

▲**Bibury**—Six miles northeast of Cirencester, this is an entertaining but money-grubbing and not-very-friendly village with a trout farm, a Cotswolds museum, a stream teeming with fat fish and proud ducks, a row of very old weavers' cottages, and a church surrounded by rosebushes, each tended by a volunteer of the parish. Don't miss the scenic Coln Valley drive from A429 to Bibury through the enigmatic villages of Coln St. Dennis, Coln Rogers, Coln Powell, and Winson.

▲▲▲**Blenheim Palace**—Too many palaces can send you into a furniture-wax coma. But everyone should see Blenheim. The Duke of Marlborough's home, the largest in England, is still lived in. And that's wonderfully obvious as you prowl through it. (Note: Americans who pronounce the place "blen-HEIM" are the butt of jokes. It's "BLEN-em.")

John Churchill, first duke of Marlborough, beat the French at the Battle of Blenheim in 1704. So the king built him this nice home, perhaps the finest Baroque building in England. Ten dukes of Marlborough later, it's as impressive as ever. The 2,000-acre yard, well designed by "Capability" Brown, is as impressive to some as the palace itself. The view just past the outer gate as you enter is a classic. (The current 11th Duke considers the 12th more of an error than an heir, and what to do about him is quite an issue.)

The well-organized palace tour begins with a fine **Churchill exhibit** centered around the bed in which Sir Winston was born in 1874 (prematurely... while his mother was at a Blenheim Palace party). Take your time in the Churchill exhibit. Then catch the guided tours (5/hr, 1 hr, included with ticket, £9.50, family rates, CC, mid-March–Oct 10:30–17:30, last tour at 16:45, the park is open year-round, live tel. 01993/811-091, recorded info tel. 01993/811-325).

For a more extensive visit, follow up the general tour with a 30-minute guided walk through the actual **private apartments** of the duke. Tours leave at the top and bottom of each hour (£4, 12:00–16:30, tickets are limited, buy from table in library—last room of main tour, enter in corner of courtyard to left of grand palace entry).

Kids enjoy the pleasure **garden** (a tiny train takes you from the palace parking lot to the garden, but, if you're driving, it's more efficient simply to drive there). A lush and humid greenhouse flutters with butterflies. A kid zone (£1) includes a few second-rate games and the "world's largest symbolic hedge maze." The maze is worth a look if you haven't seen one and could use some exercise.

Churchill fans can visit his **tomb**, a short walk away, in the Bladon town churchyard. The train station nearest Blenheim Palace (Hanborough, 1.5 miles away) has no taxi or bus service. Your easiest train connection is to Oxford; then take a bus to Blenheim (from the Oxford train station it's a 5-min walk to Gloucester Green bus station, then catch bus #20a, #20b, or #20c to the palace gate, 2/hr, 30–40 min; Oxford TI: tel. 01865/726-871).

Blenheim Palace sits at the edge of the cute cobbled town of Woodstock. For accommodations, consider the charming **Blenheim Guest House** (Db-from £50, CC, 17 Park Street, in town center, tel. 01993/813-814, fax 01993/813-810, www.theblenheim.com) or the grandmotherly **Wishaw House B&B** (D-£40, 2 Browns Lane, 5-min walk from palace, tel. 01993/811-343, Pat Hillier).

## Sleeping and Eating in the Cotswolds
### (£1 = about $1.50, country code: 44)
Sleep Code: **S** = Single, **D** = Double/Twin, **T** = Triple, **Q** = Quad, **b** = bathroom, **s** = shower only, **CC** = Credit Cards accepted, **no CC** = Credit Cards not accepted.

Chipping Campden is quaint without being overrun. Stow is touristy but offers the widest range of accommodations. Work-a-day

Moreton is the only one of the three with a train station. If you have a car, consider grabbing the opportunity to really be away from it all in one of the smaller villages.

## Sleeping in Chipping Campden (area code: 01386)

**Sandalwood House B&B** is a big, comfy, modern home with a royal lounge and a sprawling back garden. Just a five-minute walk from the center of town, it's in a quiet, woodsy, pastoral setting. Its two cheery pastel rooms are bright and spacious (D-£50, private baths down the hall, cheaper for 3-night stays and families, no CC, no kids under 7, nonsmoking, GL55 6AU, go west on High Street, at church and Volunteer Inn turn right and right again, look for sign in hedge on left, head up long driveway, tel. & fax 01386/840-091, well run by Diana Bendall).

**The Old Bakehouse** rents five pleasant rooms, most with beams, in a 600-year-old home (S-£30, Db or D with private bath down hall-£45, family deals, no CC, fun but dim attic room has beams running through it, small garden, parking, Lower High Street, GL55 6DZ, tel. 01386/840-979, e-mail: oldbakehouse @chippingcampden-cotswolds.co.uk, Sarah Drinkwater).

**Dragon House B&B** rents two tidy two-floor suites—with medieval beams—right on the center of High Street, with parking, laundry machines, and a sumptuous stay-awhile garden (Db-£50, or £45/night if you stay 3 nights, no CC, near market hall, tel. & fax 01386/840-734, e-mail: valatdragonhouse@btinternet.com, Valerie and Graeme, the potter).

**Badgers Hall Tea Room and B&B** hides three cozy, wood-beamed rooms in its medieval attic (Db-£55, no CC, nonsmoking, personal check as deposit, center of High Street, tel. 01386/840-839, e-mail: badgershall@talk21.com, Karen and Paul Pinfold).

**Kettle House B&B** has two comfortable rooms in a 17th-century building. The sitting room and small deck have a lovely view (Db-£65, CC, nonsmoking, near old church, High Street, Leysbourne, GL55 6HN, tel. 01386/840-328, fax 01386/ 841-740, www.kettlehouse.co.uk, e-mail: info@kettlehouse.co.uk, run by gracious Charles and Susie Holdsworth Hunt).

**Noel Arms Hotel** is the characteristic old hotel on the main square, welcoming guests for 600 years. Its lobby is decorated with armor, guns, and heraldry; its medieval air is infused with complex, but not unpleasant, odors; and its 26 rooms are well-furnished with antiques (Sb-£75, standard Db-£115, fancier 4-poster Db-£125–£135, CC, some ground-floor doubles, attached restaurant/bar, High Street, GL55 6AT, tel. 01386/840-317, fax 01386/841-136, www.cotswold-inns-hotels.co.uk).

**Lygon Arms Hotel** has dumpy public areas, but the rooms

## Chipping Campden

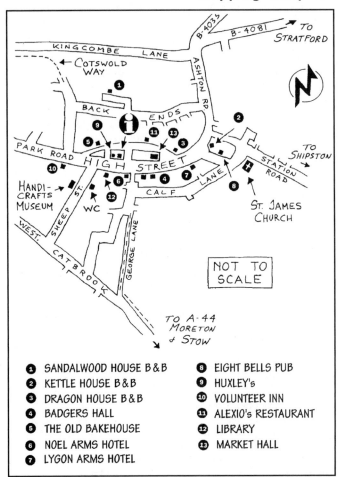

- **1** SANDALWOOD HOUSE B & B
- **2** KETTLE HOUSE B & B
- **3** DRAGON HOUSE B & B
- **4** BADGERS HALL
- **5** THE OLD BAKEHOUSE
- **6** NOEL ARMS HOTEL
- **7** LYGON ARMS HOTEL
- **8** EIGHT BELLS PUB
- **9** HUXLEY's
- **10** VOLUNTEER INN
- **11** ALEXIO's RESTAURANT
- **12** LIBRARY
- **13** MARKET HALL

are decent and likely available when all else fails (D-£45, Db-£55, CC, High Street, tel. 01386/840-318).

### Eating in Chipping Campden

Locals like **Eight Bells** (a charming 14th-century inn on Leysbourne), **Huxley's** (pricey but a good value, closed Mon, in town center on High Street), and **Bantam Tea Rooms** (opposite Town Hall). **Volunteer Inn** serves decent pub grub (grassy courtyard in back, Park Road). In the Cotswolds House Hotel, **Forbes**

**Brasserie** (skip the formal restaurant) has good food, quick service, and vintage Cotswolds photos on its walls (daily 12:00–
20:00). **Lygon Pub** serves good old English grub. **Alexio's**, a fun
Greek restaurant on High Street, breaks plates at closing every
Saturday night (closed Sun to clean up, tel. 01386/840-826). The
small **Your Store**, on High Street, is the town's main grocery
(Mon–Sat 7:00–22:00, Sun 8:00–22:00).

## Sleeping in Stow-on-the-Wold *(area code: 01451)*

The **Old Stocks Hotel**, facing the town square, is a good value,
even though the building itself is classier than its 18 big, simply
furnished rooms. It's friendly and family-run yet professional as
can be. Beware the man-killer beams (Sb-£37.50, Db-£75, Tb-
£112.50, prices promised through 2002 with this book, family
deals, parking, CC, The Square, Stow-on-the-Wold, GL54 1AF,
tel. 01451/830-666, fax 01451/870-014, e-mail: theoldstocks
@btinternet.com, Alan and Julie Rose).

**Stow Lodge Hotel**, on the town square in its own sprawling and peaceful garden, offers 21 large, thoughtfully-appointed
rooms and stately public spaces (Sb-£75–90, Db-£90–100,
CC, closed Jan, nonsmoking, The Square, GL54 1AB, tel.
01451/830-485, fax 01451/831-671, www.stowlodge.com,
Hartley family).

**Crestow House** is a grand manor house dating from the
16th to 19th centuries with four fine rooms run with quiet class by
Jorge, Frank, and their exotic dog. With a gracious spaciousness,
antique furniture, a pool, and exercise equipment, this place mixes
charm and character with modern-day amenities (Db-£68, £64
for 2 nights, £60 for 3 nights, CC, no kids under 15, nonsmoking,
sunny-even-in-the-rain conservatory, 2 blocks from square, intersection of A429 and B4068, GL54 1JX, tel. 01451/830-969, fax
01451/832-129, e-mail: fsimonetti@btinternet.com).

**Chipping House B&B** is a fine old place with three rooms
and a cozy lounge (Db-£52, no CC, nonsmoking, Park Street,
tel. 01451/831-756, Merv and Carolyn Oliver).

**Cross Keys Cottage** offers three attractive, smallish rooms
in a well-maintained 350-year-old cottage (D with private
bath in hall-£48–52, Db-£52–55, no CC, Park Street, GL54
1AQ, tel. & fax 01451/831-128, e-mail: rogxmag@hotmail.com,
Margaret and Roger Welton).

**Number Nine** has three large, well-furnished rooms in a
200-year-old home—with watch-your-head beamed ceilings and
old wooden doors (Db-£50–54, CC, 9 Park Street, GL5 1AQ,
tel. 01451/870-333, e-mail: numbernine@talk21.com, David
and Connie).

**West Deyne B&B**, with two cozy rooms, a peaceful garden,
a fountain, and a small conservatory overlooking the countryside,

## Stow-on-the-Wold

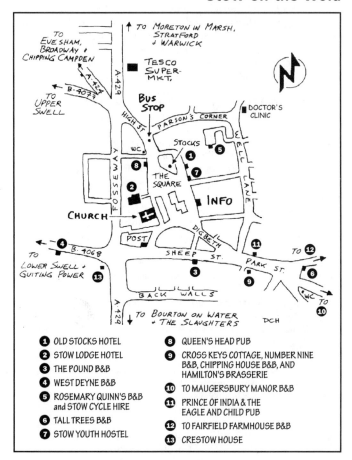

- **1** OLD STOCKS HOTEL
- **2** STOW LODGE HOTEL
- **3** THE POUND B&B
- **4** WEST DEYNE B&B
- **5** ROSEMARY QUINN'S B&B and STOW CYCLE HIRE
- **6** TALL TREES B&B
- **7** STOW YOUTH HOSTEL
- **8** QUEEN'S HEAD PUB
- **9** CROSS KEYS COTTAGE, NUMBER NINE B&B, CHIPPING HOUSE B&B, AND HAMILTON'S BRASSERIE
- **10** TO MAUGERSBURY MANOR B&B
- **11** PRINCE OF INDIA & THE EAGLE AND CHILD PUB
- **12** TO FAIRFIELD FARMHOUSE B&B
- **13** CRESTOW HOUSE

has a comforting grandmotherly charm (D-£36, no CC, evening tea and biscuits, parking, Lower Swell Road, GL54 1LD, tel. 01451/831-011, run by thoughtful Joan Cave).

**The Pound** is the quaint, 500-year-old yet fresh, heavy-beamed home of Patricia Whitehead. She offers two bright, inviting twin-bedded rooms and a classic old fireplace lounge (D-£38, no CC, nonsmoking, downtown on Sheep Street, GL54 1AU, tel. & fax 01451/830-229, e-mail: brent.ford@zoom.co.uk).

**Rosemary Quinn's B&B**, on a peaceful cul-de-sac two blocks off the main square in a tidy modern building, rents two no-nonsense, comfy rooms (S-£18.50, D-£38, no CC, non-smoking, 22 Glebe Close, GL54 1DJ, tel. 01451/830-042, e-mail: ro@quinn39.freeserve.co.uk).

**Tall Trees B&B**, on the Oddington Road at the edge of Stow, rents six modern rooms in an old-style building overlooking a farm (Db-£50, family room, no CC, parking, tel. 01451/831-296, fax 01451/870-049, e-mail: talltreestow@aol.com, Jennifer).

**Fairview Farmhouse B&B** feels more like a countryside mansion than a farmhouse. It's regally situated a mile outside Stow, and its six rooms come with all the thoughtful touches (Db-£48, deluxe Db-£55, no CC, nonsmoking, just down Bledington Road, GL54 1JH, tel. & fax 01451/830-279, e-mail: sdavis0145@aol.com, Susan and Andrew Davis).

In the hamlet of Maugersbury, an easy 10-minute walk from Stow, you'll find the peace Stow once had. The ivy-covered **Maugersbury Manor** rents two huge rooms, one with countryside views. The other is a sprawling ground-floor suite with a kitchen. Although it could use spiffing up, it's grand staying in what could be a haunted house (Db-£45, no CC, family deals, open March–Nov, nonsmoking, GL54 1HP, tel. 01451/830-581, e-mail: karen @manorholidays.co.uk, Mrs. Martin has lived here over 40 years).

**Little Broom B&B**, a few doors down, has five tight rooms, a larger family room, and an open-air pool (S-£30, D-£50, Db-£55, family Db-£60, no CC, nonsmoking, GL54 1HP, tel. 01451/830-510, e-mail: davidandbrenda@talk21.com). To get to either place, drive east on Park Street, taking the right fork to Maugersbury, then turn right on the road marked "No Through Road."

**Holmleigh B&B**, in a working farmhouse in the nearby hamlet of Donnington, rents two rooms, the cheapest around (D-£25, no CC, tel. 01451/830-792, Mrs. Garbett).

**Hostel:** The **Stow-on-the-Wold Youth Hostel**, on Stow's main square, has a friendly atmosphere, good hot meals, and a members' kitchen (dorm bed-£13, includes sheets, nonmembers-£2 extra, 48 beds in 9 rooms, some family rooms with private bathrooms, closed 10:00–17:00, laundry, no lockers, CC, reserve long in advance, tel. 01451/830-497, fax 01451/870-102, e-mail: stow@yha.org.uk).

## Sleeping in Pastoral Villages near Stow-on-the-Wold

**Guiting Guest House** is six miles west of Stow in the tiny village of Guiting Power. Kindly Mrs. Yvonne Sylvester rents five modern, delightful doily rooms in her 400-year-old house. The owners make this place a winner (Sb-£35, Db-£58, CC, Post Office Lane, Guiting Power, Cheltenham, GL54 5TZ, tel. 01451/850-470, fax 01451/ 850-034, www.information-britain.co.uk/bandbs/guiting/, e-mail: guiting@virgin.net). If you're tired of pub grub, Yvonne serves a fine home-cooked dinner with the works for £18. Guiting Power is a great base for walking excursions.

✦ **Vine B&B**, eight miles west of Stow in the postcard-pretty village of Stanton, is another idyllic hideaway. This classic Cotswolds home, run by Jill Carenza, is a block from the Stanton church (Ds/Db-£56, CC, 4 rooms, most rooms with 4-poster beds, WR12 7NE, tel. 01386/584-250, fax 01386/584-385, e-mail: luicarenza@msn.com). Jill's passion is horseback riding. She rents horses by the hour (see "Horseback Riding," above).

**Didbrook Fields Farm** is completely rural with no town in sight. It's an extremely family-friendly place renting four suites in a restored 19th-century barn on a 40-acre environmental farm. The kids' play area comes equipped with dogs, cats, chickens, a pitch-and-putt green, lawn tennis, and loaner bikes (Db-£65–70, Tb-£75, no CC, kitchenettes, 7 miles southwest of Chipping Campden, 400 yards toward Winchecombe from Toddington roundabout, GL54 5PE, tel. & fax 01242/620-950, e-mail: thekettle@aol.com, run by Frank and Jane Kennedy and their pre-teen children Edward and Katie).

## Eating in Stow-on-the-Wold
These places are all within a five-minute walk of each other either on the main square or downhill on Queen and Park Streets. The formal but friendly bar in the **Stow Lodge** serves fine £7 lunches and a popular £18 three-course dinner (daily 12:00–14:00, 19:00–21:00, smoke free, veggie options; they also have a pricier restaurant). Next door, the **Queen's Head**—with a classic pub ambience—is a great place to bring your dog, smoke a cigarette, eat decent, inexpensive grub, and drink the local Cotswold brew, Donnington Ale (Mon–Sat 12:00–14:00, 18:00–21:00). **The Prince of India** serves good Indian food in a delightful atmosphere (nightly 18:00–23:30, CC, Park Street). **The Eagle and Child Pub** serves delicious food at good prices in a stripped-down pub atmosphere (a rare place in town—serving until 22:00, non-smoking section, tel. 01451/830-670). Locals also like **The Unicorn** pub (daily 12:00–14:30, 19:00–21:30, Sheep Street). For fancy and expensive high Brit/Euro cuisine in sleek ambience, consider **Hamilton's Brasserie** (£20 dinners, Mon–Sat, closed Sun, last orders at 14:30 and 21:30, CC, Park Street, tel. 01451/831-700).

## Fine Cuisine in Great Country Pubs near Stow
These three places are known for their great £10 meals and fine settings. All are very popular, so arrive early or call in a reservation. These pubs allow "well-behaved children," and are practical only for those with a car. The first two (in Oddington, 2 miles from Stow) are more trendy and fresh, yet still in a traditional pub setting. The Plough (in Ford, a few miles farther away) is your jolly-old dark pub.

**The Horse and Groom Village Inn** in Upper Oddington

is a smart place with a sea grass–green carpet in a 16th-century inn, serving modern English food with a good wine list (daily 12:00–15:00, 19:00–21:30, nonsmoking section, tel. 01451/830-584).

**The Fox Inn** in Lower Oddington is old but fresh and famous among locals for its quality cooking. It serves lunch until 14:00 and dinner until 22:00 nightly (tel. 01451/870-555).

**The Plough Inn** fills a fascinating old building—once an old coaching inn and later a courthouse. Ask the bar staff for some fun history—like what "you're barred" means. It takes no reservations, so arrive early (4 miles from Stow on the Tewksbury road in the hamlet of Ford, tel. 01386/584-215).

### Sleeping in Moreton-in-Marsh (area code: 01608)

A handy **launderette** is a block in front of the train station on New Road (Laundercentre, daily 7:30–20:00, £3.50 self-service, or drop off Mon–Fri 9:00–10:30 for £1 extra and same-day service, tel. 01608/650-888).

**Treetops B&B** is plush, with six spacious, attractive rooms, a sun lounge, and a three-quarter-acre backyard (large Db-£45, gigantic Db-£50, CC, ground-floor rooms have patios, easy parking, set far back from the busy road, London Road, GL56 0HE, tel. & fax 01608/651-036, e-mail: Treetops1@talk21.com, Liz and Brian Dean). It's an eight-minute walk from town and the railway station (exit station, keep left, go left on bridge over train tracks, look for sign, then long driveway).

**Blue Cedar House** has four comfortable rooms with an airy breakfast room full of plants. It's on a busy road but has double-paned windows and a pleasing setting, surrounded by a bright green half-acre garden (S-£22, D-£42, Db-£44, no CC, smoke-free, easy parking, 5-min walk from center, Stow Road, GL56 0DW, tel. 01608/650-299, e-mail: gandsib@dialstart.net, Sandra and Graham Billinger).

The rest of the listings are within a few blocks of the station.

**Townend Cottage and Coach House** is a 17th-century English-style hacienda with four borderline musty rooms (Db-£50, family deals, no CC, nonsmoking, big garden, attached tearoom, end of High Street, 2 blocks from station; from train station, take footpath on right by green iron fence to High Street, GL56 0AD, tel. 01608/650-846, www.townend-cottage .co.uk, Mark Brown).

**Acacia B&B**, with four small, clean, and cheery rooms on the third floor, is friendly and handy (S-£22, D-£36, Db-£40, less for 3-night stays and off-season, bunky family deals, no CC, non-smoking, across from launderette, when leaving station take right fork about a half block, New Road, GL56 0AS, tel. 01608/650-130, Dot and Mick Ellwood). The **Cottage B&B** nearby on Oxford Street may rent rooms, too (tel. 01608/651-740).

## Moreton-in-Marsh

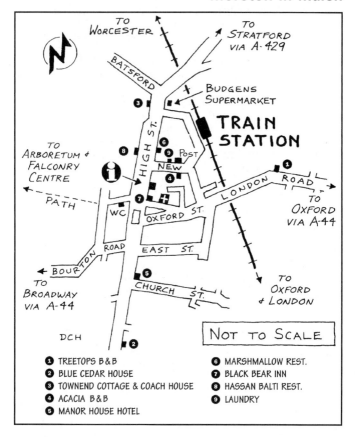

**Manor House Hotel** is Moreton's big old hotel, dating from 1545 but sporting such modern amenities as toilets and electricity (and a swimming pool). Its 39 classy-for-the-Cotswolds rooms and garden invite relaxation (Sb-£90, Db-£115, family suite-£155, CC, elevator, parking, log fire in winter, attached restaurant, on far end of High Street, away from train station, GL56 0LJ, tel. 01608/650-501, fax 01608/651-481, www.cotswold-inns-hotels.co.uk).

### Eating in Moreton-in-Marsh

A stroll up and down High Street lets you survey your small-town options. Consider the upscale but affordable **Marshmallow** (£8–11 entrées, 15 different teas, Wed–Sat 10:00–21:00, closed

Sun–Tue, CC, tel. 01608/651-536) or the **Black Bear Inn**, offering traditional English food (daily 12:00–14:00, 18:30–21:00, after
entering, head to dining room on the left, pub on the right, CC,
tel. 01608/652-992). The friendly **Hassan Balti**, with tasty
Bangladeshi food, is a fine value for sit-down or takeout (daily
12:00–14:00, 18:00–23:30, tel. 01608/650-798). **Mermaid Fish**
is popular for its take-out fish, and the **Budgens** supermarket is
indeed super (Mon–Sat 8:30–22:00, Sun 10:00–16:00, far end of
High Street, near Townend Cottage). There are picnic tables
across the busy street in pleasant Victoria Park. On Oxford Street,
consider **Cotswold Epicure** (Mon–Sat 8:30–16:30, closed Sun,
tel. 01608/652-999) and **Copper Kettle** (Mon–Sat 10:00–16:00)
for a light bite or sandwiches to go.

For a splurge, consider the **Marsh Goose** (posh and pricey
nouveau cuisine, Mon–Sat, closed Sun, High Street, tel. 01608/
653-500) or **Annie's** for fancy French (£30 meals, dinner only,
Mon–Sat, closed Sun, Oxford Street, tel. 01608/651-981).

## Transportation Connections—Cotswolds

Moreton, the only Cotswolds town with a train station, also has
good bus connections.

**Moreton by bus to: Chipping Campden** and **Stratford**
(11/day, same bus connects all 3 towns, Moreton-Chipping
Campden 25 min, Moreton-Stratford 1.25 hrs, First Midland
Red bus company, tel. 01789/292-630), **Circencester** via **Stow**
and **Burton** (13/day, Moreton-Cirencester 1 hr, Moreton-Stow
10 min, Stagecoach buses), **Cheltenham** (8/day, Moreton-
Cheltenham 1 hr, with stops at a few non-touristy towns, Pulham
buses). The Stagecoach Bus Company runs a handy **Oxford-
Blenheim-Moreton-Stratford** route (4/day, tel. 01865/772-
250). Ask for specific schedules at a local TI. Generally, buy
tickets from the driver.

**Moreton by train to: London's Paddington Station**
(£21 one-way, £19 round-trip after 8:00, 10/day, 1.75 hrs; One-
Day Travelcard for £22 includes round-trip and London tube
travel), **Heathrow** (10/day, 2.5 hrs, train to Reading, then
RailAir Link shuttle bus to airport), **Bath** (10/day, 2.5 hrs,
transfers at Oxford or Didcot Parkway), **Oxford** (10/day,
40 min), **Ironbridge Gorge** (1/hr, 3.5 hrs, with transfers at
Worcester Shrub Hill and Birmingham New Street, arrive
Telford, then catch bus or cab 7 miles to Ironbridge Gorge).
Train info: tel. 08457-484-950.

**Drivers' Tips:** Distances are wonderfully short (but only if
you invest in the Ordnance Survey map of the Cotswolds—sold
locally at TIs and newsstands). **Moreton** to: **Broadway** (10 miles),
**Chipping Campden** (8 miles), **Stratford** (17 miles), **Warwick**
(23 miles), **Stow** (4 miles).

# NEAR THE COTSWOLDS: STRATFORD, WARWICK, AND COVENTRY

Stratford is Shakespeare's hometown. To see or not to see? A walking tour with a play is the thing to bring the Bard to life in this touristy town. Explore Warwick, England's finest medieval castle; and stop by Coventry, a work-a-day town with a spirit that Nazi bombs couldn't destroy.

## Planning Your Time

Stratford, Warwick, and Coventry are a made-to-order day for drivers connecting the Cotswolds with Ironbridge Gorge (IBG) or North Wales. While connections from the Cotswolds to IBG are tough, Stratford, Warwick, and Coventry are well served by public transportation.

Stratford is a classic tourist trap. But since you're passing through, it's worth a morning. (Don't spend the night.) Warwick is England's single most spectacular castle. It's very touristy but historic and fun for three hours. Lunch in Warwick town. Coventry, the least-important stop on a quick trip, is most interesting as a chance to see a real, struggling, north-English industrial city (with some decent sightseeing).

The area is worth only a one-day drive-through. If you're speedy, hit all three sights. If you're more relaxed, do Stratford and Warwick and get to your Ironbridge Gorge B&B in time to enjoy the evening ambience of that more interesting stop.

## STRATFORD-UPON-AVON

Stratford is the most overrated tourist magnet in England, but nobody back home would understand if you skipped Shakespeare's house. The old town is compact, with the TI and theater along the riverbank and Shakespeare's birthplace a few blocks off the river; you can walk easily to everything except Anne Hathaway's and Mary Arden's places. The river has an idyllic yet playful feel, with a park along the opposite bank, paddleboats, and an old, one-man, crank-powered ferry just beyond the theater.

**Tourist Information:** Pick up a free Attractions map at the TI (Mon–Sat 9:00–18:00, Sun 11:00–17:00, Nov–March 9:00–17:00 and closed Sun, has American Express office, tel. 01789/293-127).

## Sights—Stratford-upon-Avon

▲**Shakespeare's Birthplace**—This half-timbered Elizabethan building—entirely rebuilt in the 1900s—is furnished as it was when young William was growing up and is filled with bits about his life and work. This is most worthwhile if you get the attendants in each room talking. Ask questions. The attached Shakespeare exhibition gives a fine historical background.

## Cotswolds to North Wales

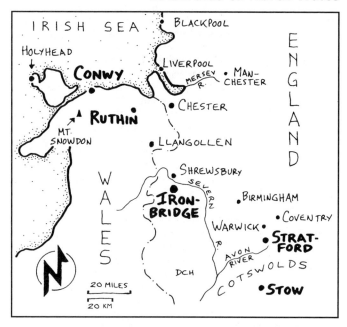

While William Shakespeare (1564–1616) was born in this house, he spent most of his career in London, where he taught his play-going public about human nature with plots that entertained the highest and the lowest minds at the same time. His tool was an unrivaled mastery of the English language. He retired—rich and famous—back in Stratford, spending his last five years at "New Place."

Little is known about Shakespeare the man. The scope of his brilliant work, his humble beginnings, and the fact that no original Shakespeare manuscripts survive raise a few scholarly eyebrows. But while some wonder who penned all these plays, most scholars accept his authorship (£5.50, April–Sept Mon–Sat 9:00–17:00, Sun 9:30–17:00, mid-Oct–late March Mon–Sat 9:30–16:00, Sun 10:00–16:00, last admission 60 min before closing, in town center, tel. 01789/204-016, www.shakespeare.org.uk).

▲**Four Other Shakespeare Properties**—Shakespeare's hometown is blanketed with opportunities for "Bardolatry." There are four other "Shakespearian properties," all run by the Shakespeare Birthplace Trust, in and near Stratford. Each has a garden and helpful docents who love to tell a story. **Anne Hathaway's Cottage**, a mile out of town in Shottery, is a picturesque thatched 12-room farmhouse where the bard's wife grew up. It has little to do with Shakespeare but offers an intimate peek at lifestyles in Shakespeare's day. Guides in each room do their best to lecture to the stampeding hordes. **Mary Arden's House**, the girlhood home of William's mom, is in Wilmcote, about three miles from town. This 16th-century farmhouse sees far fewer tourists, so the guides in each room have a chance to do a little better guiding. A 19th-century farming exhibit and a falconry demonstration are on the grounds. **Hall's Croft**, the home of Shakespeare's daughter, who married a doctor, is in the town. This fine old Tudor house, the richest house of the group, is interesting only if you're into 16th-century medicine. **Nash's House**, where the Bard lived in retirement, is the least impressive of the properties. (Nash was the first husband of Shakespeare's granddaughter.) While Shakespeare's retirement home (New Place) is long gone, Nash's house has survived. It has the town's only general-history exhibit—fascinating if you like chips of Roman pottery. Each property charges £3.50 to £5. Pilgrims save money buying combo tickets: £8.50 for three sights or £12 for all. (Anne Hathaway's Cottage has the same opening hours as Shakespeare's Birthplace; the other sights are open daily mid-March–mid Oct Mon–Sat 9:30–17:00, Sun 10:00–17:00; mid-Oct–mid-March Mon–Sat 10:00–16:00, Sun 10:30–16:00.) **Shakespeare's grave** is in the riverside Holy Trinity Church (a 10-min walk past the theater).

**Avon Riverfront**—The River Avon is a playground with swans and canal boats. These canal boats, which saw their workhorse days during a short window of time between the start of the Industrial Revolution and the establishment of the railways, are now mostly pleasure boats. They are long and narrow, so two can pass in the narrow canals. There are 2,000 miles of canals here in the Midlands. These were built to connect centers of industry with seaports and provided vital transport during the early days of the Industrial Revolution.

▲▲**Guide Friday Bus Tours**—These open-top buses constantly make the rounds, allowing visitors to hop on and hop off at every sight in town. The full circuit takes about an hour and comes with a steady and informative live commentary (£9, buses leave from TI every 15 min 9:30–17:30, every 30 min in winter, buy tickets on bus, tel. 01789/294-466).

Guide Friday offers longer tours of the Cotswolds (£18, 13:45-17:15, drive through 15 villages with brief stops in Stanton—15 min, Chipping Campden—20 min, and Stow—30 min, depart from Civic Hall near Market Square, buy tickets at Guide Friday office in Civic Hall, tel. 01789/294-466).

▲▲**Royal Shakespeare Company**—The RSC, undoubtedly the best Shakespeare company on earth, performs in Stratford year-round and in London in winter and spring (Dec–May). If you're a Shakespeare fan, see if the RSC schedule fits into your itinerary either here or in London. Tickets range from £5 to £50 (Mon–Sat at 19:30, Thu and Sat matinees at 13:30). You'll probably need to buy your tickets in advance, although 50 restricted-view and standing-room places are saved to be sold each morning (from 9:30, £5–15) and returned tickets can sometimes be picked up the evening of an otherwise-sold-out show (box office open Mon–Sat 9:00–20:00, closed Sun, tel. 01789/403-403, www.rsc.org.uk). If you have a car, Stow and Chipping Campden are only 30 minutes from Stratford and an evening of classy entertainment.

Theater tours are given most days (£4, 13:30 and 17:30 if no matinee, sometimes 11:30 on matinee days, tours also given after performances, all tours must be booked in advance, Mon–Sat 9:30–17:30, Sun 11:30–16:00, tel. 01789/403-405). The theater sponsors "Shakespeare's Life in Stratford" walks (£6, Thu and Sat at 10:30 plus July–Sept Sun at 10:30, 2 hrs).

## Transportation Connections—Stratford-upon-Avon

**To: London** (4 trains/day, 2.5 hrs, direct to Paddington Station), **Chipping Campden** (6 buses/day, 1 hr, on Stratford Blue bus, tel. 01789/292-630), **Warwick** (1/hr, 15 min, by bus or train), **Coventry** (1 bus/hr, 1 hr, tel. 01788/535-555). There is a **Stratford-Warwick-Cambridge** bus service (£12, 3/day, 2.5 hrs, tel. 01223/423-900). Train info: tel. 08457-484-950.

**Driving** is easy: Stow to Stratford (20 miles), Warwick (8 miles), and Coventry (10 miles).

## WARWICK AND COVENTRY

▲▲**Warwick Castle**—England's finest medieval castle is almost too groomed and organized, giving its hordes of visitors a decent value for the steep £9.75 entry fee. This cash-poor but enterprising lord hired the folks at Madame Tussaud's to wring maximum tourist dollars out of the castle. The latest marketing strategy is to build up the "kingmaker" reputation of the Earl of Warwick (WAR-ick).

With a lush, green, grassy moat and fairy-tale fornications, Warwick will entertain you from dungeon to lookout. Standing inside the castle gate, you can see the mound where the original Norman castle of 1068 stood. Under this "motte," the wooden stockade, or "bailey," defined the courtyard as the castle walls do today. The castle is a 14th- and 15th-century fortified shell holding an 18th- and 19th-century royal residence surrounded by another dandy "Capability" Brown landscape job.

There's something for every taste—a fine and educational

armory, a terrible torture chamber, a knight in shining armor
on a horse that rotates with a merry band of musical jesters,
a Madame Tussaud re-creation of a royal weekend party with
an 1898 game of statue–maker, a grand garden, and a peacock-
patrolled, picnic-perfect park. The Great Hall and Staterooms
are the sumptuous highlights. The "King Maker" exhibit
(It's 1471 and the town's folk are getting ready for battle…)
is highly promoted but not quite as good as a Disney ride.
Be warned: The tower is a one-way, no-return, 250-step climb
offering a view not worth a heart attack. The £2 CD-ROM
audioguide provides 60 easy-listening minutes of number-
coded descriptions of the individual rooms (rent from kiosk
on lane after turnstile). The £3.25 guidebook gives you nearly
the same script in souvenir-booklet form. Either is worthwhile
if you want to understand the various rooms. If you tour without help, pick the brains of the earnest and talkative docents
(£9.75, daily April–Oct 10:00–18:00, Nov–March 10:00–17:00,
tel. 01926/406-600, 24-hr recorded message).

The Stables self-service restaurant upstairs is much nicer
than the cafeteria near the turnstiles. From the castle, a lane
leads into the old-town center, a block away, where you'll find
the TI (daily 9:30–16:30, tel. 01926/492-212), doll museum,
county museum, and several pubs serving fine lunches.

▲**Coventry's Cathedral**—The Germans bombed Coventry to
smithereens in 1940. From that point on, the German phrase
for "to really blast the heck out of a place" was "to coventrate" it.
But Coventry rose from its ashes, and its message to our world is
one of forgiveness and reconciliation. The symbol of Coventry
is the bombed-out hulk of its old cathedral with the huge new
one adjoining it. The inspirational complex welcomes visitors.
Climb the tower (£1.50, 180 steps). If you're touring the church,
first go downstairs to see the 18-minute audiovisual presentation,
*Spirit of Coventry*, on the cathedral's history (£1.25 for movie, plus
a requested £2 donation at church door, Mon–Sat 10:00–16:00,
closed Sun, tel. 02476/227-597).

Coventry's most famous hometown girl, Lady Godiva, rode
bareback through the town in the 11th century to help lower
taxes. You'll see her bronze statue a block from the cathedral
(near Broadgate). Just beyond that is the Museum of British Road
Transport—the first, fastest, and most famous cars and motorcycles
came from this British "Detroit" (free, daily 10:00–17:00). Other
sights include the Herbert Art Gallery and Museum, which cover
the city's history (free, Mon–Sat 10:00–17:30, Sun 12:00–17:00),
and St. Mary's Guildhall, with 14th-century tapestries, stained
glass, and an ornate ceiling (free, Sun–Thu 10:00–16:00, closed
if event scheduled and sometimes off-season).

Browse through Coventry, the closest thing to normal,

work-a-day, urban England you'll see. Get a map at the TI
(Mon–Fri 9:30–16:30, Sat–Sun 10:00–16:30, Bayley Lane,
tel. 02476/832-303).

## Route Tips for Drivers

**Stratford to Ironbridge Gorge via Warwick and Coventry:**
Entering Stratford from the Cotswolds, you cross a bridge. Veer
right (following "through traffic," "P," and "Wark" signs), go
around the block—turning right and right and right over the
speed humps—then enter the multistory garage (50p/hr, you'll
find no place easier or cheaper). The TI and Guide Friday bus
stop are a block away. Leaving the garage, circle to the right
around the same block but stay on the "Wark" (Warwick, A439)
road. Warwick is eight miles away. The castle is just south of town
on the right. If the free castle lot is full, you'll be directed to a city
lot. You might lurk across the street until someone leaves. After
touring the castle, carry on through the center of Warwick, following signs to Coventry (still A439, then A46). If stopping in
Coventry, follow signs painted on the road into the "city centre"
and then to cathedral parking. Grab a place in the high-rise car
park. Leaving Coventry, follow signs to Nuneaton and M6
North through lots of sprawl, and you're on your way. If you're
skirting Coventry, take the M69 (Leicester) to M6. M6 threads
through giant Birmingham. Try to avoid the 14:00–to–20:00
rush hour (see Ironbridge Gorge chapter for tips). From M6
(northwest), take M54 to the Telford/Ironbridge exit. Follow
the Ironbridge signs and do-si-do through a long series of round-
abouts until you're there.

# IRONBRIDGE GORGE

The Industrial Revolution was born in the Severn River Valley. In its glory days, this valley (blessed with abundant deposits of iron ore and coal and a river for transport) gave the world its first iron wheels, steam-powered locomotive, and cast-iron bridge. The museums in Ironbridge Gorge (IBG) take you back into the days when Britain was racing into the modern age and pulling the rest of the West with her.

## Planning Your Time

Without a car, IBG isn't worth the headache. Drivers can slip it in between the Cotswolds/Stratford/Warwick and North Wales. Speed demons zip in for a midday tour of Blists Hill, look at the bridge, and speed out. For an overnight visit, arrive in the early evening to browse the town and spend the morning and early afternoon touring the sights before driving on to North Wales (10:00–Museum of the Gorge, 11:00–Blists Hill Victorian Town for lunch and sightseeing, 15:30–Drive to Wales).

With a month in Britain I'd spend two nights and a leisurely day: 9:30–Iron Bridge and the town, 10:30–Museum of the Gorge, 11:30–Coalbrookdale Museum of Iron, 14:30–Blists Hill, dinner at Coalbrookdale Inn.

## Orientation (area code: 01952)

The town is just a few blocks gathered around the Iron Bridge, which spans the peaceful, tree-lined Severn River. While the smoke-belching bustle is long gone, knowing that this wooded, sleepy river valley was the Silicon Valley of the 19th century makes wandering its brick streets almost a pilgrimage. The actual museum sites are scattered over three miles. The modern cooling towers (for coal, not nuclear energy) that loom ominously over these red-brick remnants seem strangely appropriate.

**Tourist Information:** The TI is a block downhill from the Iron Bridge (Mon–Fri 9:00–17:00, Sat–Sun 10:00–17:00, room-finding service, tel. 01952/432-166). The TI has lots of booklets for sale; hikers like the home-grown *Walks in the Severn Gorge* (11 walks, £3.60) or the farther-ranging *Ten Walks That Changed the World* (£6).

## Sights—Ironbridge Gorge

▲▲**Iron Bridge**—This first iron bridge was built in 1779, while England was at war with her American colonies, to show off a wonderful new building material. Lacking experience with iron, the builders erred on the side of sturdiness and constructed it as if it was made out of wood. Notice the original construction used traditional timber jointing techniques rather than rivets. (Any rivets are from later repairs.) The valley's centerpiece is free, open all the time, and thought-provoking. Walk across the bridge to the toll booth/gift shop/museum (daily 10:00–17:00, free). Read the fee schedule and notice the subtle slam against royalty (England was not immune to the revolutionary sentiment brewing in the colonies at this time). Pedestrians paid half a penny to cross; poor people crossed cheaper by coracle—a crude tub-like wood-and-canvas shuttle ferry (you'll see old photos of these upstairs). Cross back to the town and enjoy a pleasant walk downstream along the towpath. Where horses once dragged boats laden with Industrial-Age cargo, today locals walk their dogs.

▲▲▲**Ironbridge Gorge Industrial Revolution Museums**— This group of widely-scattered sites has varied admission charges (usually £2–4.50; Blists Hill is £7.50). The £10 Passport ticket (£30 for families) gets you into all the sights, which all have the same hours (April–Oct daily 10:00–17:00; from Nov–March, a few Coalbrookdale sights close, Blists Hill's hours are Sat–Wed 10:00–16:00, closed Thu–Fri; tel. 01952/433-522 or 01952/432-166, www.ironbridge.org.uk). Even though several of the sights may not be worth your time, seeing Blists Hill Victorian Town, Museum of the Gorge, and the Coalbrookdale Museum of Iron costs £14.10 without the £10 Passport ticket.

**Museum of the Gorge:** Orient yourself to the valley here in the Severn Warehouse (£2, daily 10:00–17:00, 500 yards upstream from the bridge, £1-parking). See the eight-minute introductory movie, check out the exhibit and the model of the gorge in its heyday, and buy a Blists Hill guidebook and Passport ticket. From the parking lot, a tiny tour boat sometimes does a 45-minute round-trip Severn River tour (£4, look for sign near WC, slow-moving taped commentary, peaceful photo opportunity for bridge and lazy fishermen along riverbanks, tel. 01952/418-844). Farther

## Ironbridge Gorge

upstream is the fine riverside Dale End Park, with picnic areas and a playground.

**Blists Hill Victorian Town:** Save most of your time and energy for this wonderful town. You'll wander through 50 acres of Victorian industry, factories, and a re-created community from the 1890s, complete with carriage rides, chemists, a candy shop, an ancient dentist's chair, candlemakers, a working pub, a green-grocer's shop, a fascinating squatter's cottage, and a snorty, slippery pigsty. Don't miss the explanation of the winding machine at the Blists Hill Mine (first demonstration occurs at 11:00, confirm time at entry). Walk along the canal to the "inclined plane." Grab lunch in the Victorian Pub or the cafeteria near the squatter's cottage and children's old-time rides. The board by the entry lists which exhibits are staffed and lively (with docents in Victorian dress). The £2 Blists Hill guidebook gives a good step-by-step rundown (£7.50, tel. 01952/583-003).

**Coalbrookdale Museum of Iron:** This does a fine job of explaining the original iron-smelting process (£4.60, opposite

Darby's furnace—see below). The Coalbrookdale neighborhood is the birthplace of the Industrial Revolution. Abraham Darby's blast furnace sits like a shrine inside a big glass pyramid (free), surrounded by the evocative Industrial-Age ruins. It was here that, in 1709, Darby first smelted iron using coke as fuel. If you're like me, "coke" is a drink, and "smelt" is the past tense of smell.... Nevertheless, this event kicked off the modern Industrial Age.

All the ingredients of the recipe for big industry were here in abundance—iron ore, top-grade coal, and water for power and shipping. Wander around Abraham Darby's furnace. Before this furnace was built, iron ore was laboriously melted by charcoal. With a huge waterwheel-powered billows, Darby burned top-grade coal super hot (burning off the impurities to make "coke"). Local iron ore was dumped into the furnace and melted. Impurities floated to the top, while the pure iron sank to the bottom of a clay tub in the bottom of the furnace. Twice a day the plugs were knocked off, allowing the "slag" to drain away on the top and the molten iron to drain out on the bottom. The low-grade slag was used locally on walls and paths. The high-grade iron trickled into molds formed in the sand below the furnace. It cooled into pig iron (named because the molds look like piglets suckling their mother). The pig iron "planks" were broken off by sledgehammers and shipped away. The Severn River became one of Europe's busiest, shipping pig iron to distant foundries, where it was remelted and made into cast iron (for projects such as the Iron Bridge), or to forges, where it was worked like toffee into wrought iron.

**Rosehill House**, just up the hill, is the 18th-century Darby mansion furnished as a Quaker ironmaster's home would have been in 1850 (daily 10:00–17:00). The adjacent Dale House from the 1780s is less interesting.

**Coalport China Museum, Jackfield Tile Museum, and Broseley Pipeworks:** Housed in their original factories, these showcase the region's porcelain, decorated tiles, and clay tobacco pipes. These industries were developed to pick up the slack when the iron industry shifted away from Severn Valley. Each museum features finely decorated pieces, and the china and tile museums offer low-energy workshops.

**Skiing, Swimming, Fishing, and More**—There's a small, brush-covered ski slope with two poma lifts at Telford Ski Centre in Madeley, which is two miles from Ironbridge Gorge; you'll see the signs for it as you drive into IBG (£9/hr including gear, less for kids, Mon–Fri 10:00–22:00, Sat 10:00–18:00, Sun 10:00–20:00, CC, tel. 01952/586-862). A public swimming pool is next door. The Woodlands Farm, on Beech Road, runs a private fishing business where only barbless hooks are used and locals toss their catch back to hook again (kind of a fish hell). In IBG, a steam train runs for fun most Sundays (get schedule at TI).

If you're looking for reasons to linger longer in IBG, these sights are all within a short drive: the medieval town of Shrewsbury, the abbey village of Much Wenlock, the scenic Long Mynd gorge at Church Stretton, the castle at Ludlow, and the steam railway at the river town of Bridgnorth. Shoppers like Chester (en route to North Wales).

## Sleeping in Ironbridge Gorge
**(£1 = about $1.50, country code: 44, area code: 01952)**
Sleep Code: **S** = Single, **D** = Double/Twin, **T** = Triple, **Q** = Quad, **b** = bathroom, **s** = shower only, **CC** = Credit Cards accepted, **no CC** = Credit Cards not accepted.

### Sleeping in the Town Center
**Library House** is "better-homes-and-gardens" elegant. In the town center, a half block downhill from the bridge, it's classy, friendly, and a fine value. Helpful Chris and George Maddocks run this smoke-free place, and their breakfast won a "healthy heartbeat" award. The complimentary drink upon arrival is a welcome touch (Sb-£50, Db-£60, Tb-£75, family room-£70, no CC, video library, free parking, 11 Severn Bank, Ironbridge Gorge, TF8 7AN, tel. 01952/432-299, fax 01952/433-967, www.libraryhouse.com, e-mail: info@libraryhouse.com). George will pick you up from the Telford train station if you request it in advance.

**Severn Lodge B&B** is an elegant, Georgian "captain of industry" house run by a young couple offering three fine rooms (Sb-£45, Db-£59, 10 percent discount with this book, no CC, no kids under 12, no windows on factory side, nonsmoking, 200 yards above river, a block above town center on New Road, tel. 01952/432-148, fax 01952/432-062, www.severnlodge.com, Sarah and Paul).

Three lesser places right in the town center overlook the bridge: **Eley's Bridge View B&B** rents five rooms (Db-£45 with this book through 2002, CC, at bridge find 13 Tontine Hill and climb the metal stairway, tel. 01952/432-541, Rich). The **Post Office House B&B** is literally above the post office. The postmaster's wife, Janet Hunter, rents three rooms (Db-£44, family deals, no CC, 6 The Square, Ironbridge, Shropshire TF8 7AQ, tel. 01952/433-201, fax 01952/433-582, e-mail: hunter @pohouse-ironbridge.fsnet.co.uk). **Tontine Hotel** is the town's big, musty, smoky, Industrial-Age hotel (12 rooms, S-£22, D-£40, Db-£56, 10 percent discount with this book, CC, tel. 01952/432-127, fax 01952/432-094, e-mail: tontine@netscapeonline.co.uk). Check out the historic photos in the bar.

### Sleeping Outside of Town
**In a B&B**: **Coalbrookdale Villa** stands dramatically overlooking a fine yard in Coalbrookdale a mile from Ironbridge town. Once

a mansion, then a brothel, and likely haunted, today it's a cozy and comfortable B&B run by jolly June Ashdown (4 rooms, Db-£54–56, no CC, family rooms, nonsmoking, easy parking, up lane from youth hostel at 17 Paradise, tel. & fax 01952/433-450, e-mail: coalbrookdalevilla@currantbun.com).

**In a Farmhouse**: **Hill View Farm** is a peaceful, thrifty, brave, clean, and reverent B&B run by Rosemarie Hawkins while her husband John raises a "beef suckler herd." If you're looking for calm and country—Auntie Em–style—this is it, in a great rural setting overlooking the ruins of a 12th-century abbey (D–£36 for 1 night, less for longer stays, no CC, nonsmoking, Buildwas, Ironbridge, Shropshire, TF8 7BP, tel. 01952/432-228). It's just outside of Ironbridge on the Much Wenlock road (A4169); pass the huge power plants, take a left over the bridge, and go about a quarter mile (sign on right).

### Hostels

**Coalport Youth Hostel**, plush for a hostel, fills an old factory at the China Museum in Coalport (most beds are in quads, but they have plenty of bunk-bed Ds-£32, Db-£34, no CC). The **Ironbridge Gorge Youth Hostel**, built in 1859 as the grand Coalbrookdale Institute, is another fine hostel (a 20-min walk from the Iron Bridge down A4169 toward Wellington, 4- to 6-bed rooms, no CC). Each hostel charges £11 per bed with sheets, serves meals, has a self-service laundry, closes from 10:00 to 17:00, requires that you have a hostel membership (available for £12.50), and uses the same telephone number (tel. 01952/588-755).

**Wilderhope Manor Youth Hostel**, a beautifully remote and haunted 400-year-old manor house, is one of Europe's best hostels. On Saturdays, tourists actually pay to see what we hostelers sleep in for £11 (dinner served at 19:00, no CC, unreliable hours throughout year, phone first, tel. 01694/771-363). It's six miles from Much Wenlock down B4371 toward Church Stretton.

## Eating in Ironbridge Gorge

**Oliver's** is a smoke-free vegetarian place with prices and meals that make you want to turn—or stay—vegetarian (£8 main course, using CC adds 5 percent, reserved seating Tue–Sat 19:00–21:00, also Sat–Sun 12:00–14:00, reservations essential, not kid-friendly, High Street, tel. 01952/433-086).

**Ironbridge Brasserie & Wine Bar** is an inviting bistro with an imaginative menu, good wine, and real ale (£15 meals, Tue–Sun 18:30– 22:00, also Sat–Sun lunch, closed Mon, CC, plenty of indoor/outdoor seating, smoke-free, veggie options, reservations smart, on High Street half a block uphill from Oliver's, tel. 01952/432-716). Its cool wine bar is a fun place for a drink.

**Da Vinci's** serves good, though pricey, Italian food in a dressy ambience (£12 main course, Tue–Sat 19:00–22:00, Sun 12:00–16:30, closed Mon, CC, 26 High Street, tel. 01952/432-250).

**Aftab** is the place for Indian food—eat in or take out (nightly 17:30–24:00, 25 High Street, tel. 01952/432-055).

**The Malt House**, located in an 18th-century beer house, offers an English menu with a European accent. This is a very popular scene with the local twenty-something gang—and consequently smoky (£12 main course, daily 12:00–14:30, 18:30–21:30, CC, near Museum of the Gorge, 5-min walk from center, The Wharfage, tel. 01952/433-712). The Malt House is *the* vibrant nightspot in town with live music and a fun crowd generally from Wednesday through Sunday.

For a local scene, fine spit-and-sawdust ambience, excellent ales, and surprisingly good food, try the **Coalbrookdale Inn** (dinner from 18:00, last order 20:00, no food Sun, no reservations, folk music on third Sun every month, lively ladies' loo, across street from Coalbrookdale Museum of Iron, 1 mile from IBG, tel. 01952/ 433-953, www.coalbrookdale-inn.com; run by Corrine and Mike, who are on the quest for the perfect pint). This former "best pub in Britain" has a tradition of offering free samples from a lineup of featured beers. Each is listed on a blackboard with its price and alcohol content. Ask a local to explain . . . or ask if he's ever tried a brew called the Prior's Piddle.

Lawrence Welk would prefer eating at the **Meadow Inn**, a local favorite serving prizewinning pub grub (£8 meals, nightly 18:00–21:45, CC, can get crowded, no reservations, a pleasant 15-min walk from the center, head upstream, at Dale End Park take the path along the river, the inn is just after railway bridge, tel. 01952/433-193).

## Transportation Connections— Ironbridge Gorge

IBG is seven miles from Telford, which has the nearest train station. To get between IBG and Telford, take a bus (£1, 1/hr except Sun, 20 min) or taxi (£7.50). Although Telford's train and bus stations are an annoying 15-minute walk apart (or a £2 cab ride), the bus station is part of a large modern mall, an easy place to wait for a bus to IBG. Few buses run Sunday. For **bus information**, call Telford Travelink at 01952/200-005. If you need a **taxi** while in Ironbridge Gorge, call 01952/501-050.

**From Telford by train to: Birmingham** (1/hr, 45 min), **Conwy** in North Wales (4/day, 3 hrs, transfer in Chester), **Blackpool** (1/hr, 4.5 hrs, several transfers), **Keswick**, the Lake District (almost hrly trains, 3.5 hrs to Penrith with 2 changes, then catch a bus to Keswick, 1/hr except Sun 6/day, 40 min), **Edinburgh** (8 hrs, several transfers). Train info: tel. 08457-484-950.

**By Car:** Driving in from the Cotswolds and Stratford, take

M6 through Birmingham then M54 to the Telford/Ironbridge exit. Follow the brown Ironbridge signs through lots of round-abouts to Ironbridge Gorge. The traffic north through Birmingham is miserable from 14:00 to 20:00, especially on Fridays. From Warwick, consider the M40, M42, Kidderminster alternative, coming into IBG on the A442 via Bridgnorth to avoid the Birmingham traffic. Driving from IBG to North Wales takes two hours to Ruthin or 2.5 hours to Conwy.

# NORTH WALES

Wales' top historical, cultural, and natural wonders are found in the north. From towering Mount Snowdon to lush forests to desolate moor country, North Wales is a poem written in landscape. For sightseeing thrills and diversity, North Wales is Britain's most interesting slice of the Celtic crescent. But be careful not to be waylaid by the many gimmicky sights and bogus "best of" lists. The region's economy is poor, and they're wringing every possible pound out of the tourist trade. Sort carefully through your options.

## Welsh

**Language:** The Welsh language, Cymru, has been a written language since about A.D. 600 and was spoken 300 years before French or German. It remains alive and well. Although English imperialism tried to kill it, today the Welsh language and those who speak it are protected by law. In northwest Wales well over half the population is fluent in Welsh. It's either the first or the required second language in the public schools. Tourists hardly notice that the locals chatter away in Welsh and, as they turn to you, switch seamlessly to English. Listen in.

Welsh is a Celtic language (like Irish) and most closely related to the Breton language in western France. The common "ll" is pronounced as if you were ready to make an "l" sound and then blew it out. The language is phonetic but comes with a few tricks: the Welsh "dd" sounds like the English "th," f = v, ff = f, w = oo, and y = i. In a pub, impress your friends (or make some) by toasting the guy who just bought your drink. Say "Yeach-hid dah" ("Good health to you") and "Dee olch" ("Thank you") or "Dee olch un vowr" ("Thanks very much"). If the beer's bad, just make something up.

## North Wales

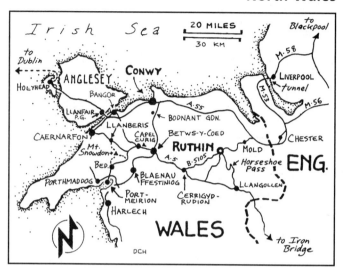

**Choirs:** Every town has a choir (men's or mixed) that practices weekly. Visitors are usually welcome to observe and very often follow the choir down to the pub afterward for a good, old-fashioned, beer-lubricated singsong. Choirs welcome visitors and practice weekly in the towns of **Ruthin** (mixed choir at Tabernacle Church, Thu 19:30–21:30), **Llangollen** (men's choir Fri at 19:30 at Hand Hotel, 21:00 pub singsong afterward, tel. 01978/860-303), **Denbigh** (men's choir Mon at 19:00 except in Aug), **Llandudno** (Sun 19:30–21:00, near Conwy), and **Caernarfon** (Tue 20:00–21:30 at Conservative Club on High Street). Confirm choir schedules with your B&B hostess or a local TI.

## Planning Your Time

Give North Wales two nights and a day (on a 3-week British trip), and it'll give you a medieval banquet, a mighty castle, a giant slate mine, and some of Britain's most beautiful scenery. Many visitors are charmed and find an extra day.

Drivers interested in the medieval banquet should set up in Ruthin and do this loop:

9:00–Drive over Llanberis mountain pass to Caernarfon (with possible short stops in Trefriw Mill, Betws-y-Coed, Pen-y-Gwryd Hotel, and Llanberis), 12:00–Caernarfon Castle. Catch noon tour and 13:00 movie in Eagle Tower. See Prince Charles (of Wales) exhibit. Climb to the top for the view. Browse through Caernarfon town and have lunch. 14:30–Drive the scenic road (A4085) to

Blaenau Ffestiniog, 15:30–Tour Llechwedd Slate Mine,
17:30–Drive home to Ruthin, 19:00–Arrive at home,
19:45–Medieval banquet at castle (if not last night).

With a car and no interest in the banquet, skip Ruthin
and shorten your drive time by spending two nights in Conwy.
Without a car, skip Ruthin. From Conwy you can tour Snowdonia and Caernarfon by bus and train.

With a second day, add the train up Snowdon (or take a hike)
and visit Conwy. With more time and a desire to hike, consider
using the mountain village of Beddgelert as a base.

## Getting around North Wales

North Wales (except Ruthin) is well covered by a combination of
buses and trains. A main train line zips along the north coast from
Chester to Holyhead via Llandudno Junction, Conwy, and Bangor
(1/hr). From Llandudno Junction, the Conwy Valley line goes
scenically south to Betws-y-Coed and Blaenau Ffestiniog (5/day,
1 hr). Without a car you'll manage fine if you use these two train
lines; public buses (get the Gwynedd Public Transport Guide at
any local TI); and Arriva buses, which circle Snowdonia National
Park with the needs of hikers in mind (£5 Explorer day pass available, buy on bus, tel. 01286/870-765).

## RUTHIN

Ruthin (rith-in) is a low-key, work-a-day market town whose
charm is in its ordinary Welshness. The people are the sights.
Admission is free if you start the conversation. The market square,
castle, TI, bus station, and in-town accommodations are all within
five blocks of each other. Ruthin is Welsh as can be, makes a
handy base for drivers doing North Wales, and serves up a great
medieval banquet. You'll find the **TI** in the busy crafts center
(June–Sept daily 10:00–17:30, Oct–May Mon–Sat 10:00–17:00,
Sun 12:00–17:00, tel. 01824/703-992).

## Sights—Ruthin

▲▲**Ruthin Castle Welsh Medieval Banquet**—English, Scottish,
Irish, and Welsh medieval banquets are all variations on the same
touristy theme. This one is fun, more culturally justifiable (if that's
necessary), and less expensive than most. You'll be greeted with
a chunk of bread dipped in salt, which the maiden explains will
"guarantee your safety." Your medieval master of ceremonies then
seats you, and the candlelit evening of food, drink, and music rolls
gaily on. You'll enjoy harp music, angelic singing, and lots of
entertainment, including insults slung at the Irish, Scots, English,
and even us brash colonists. With fanfare (and historic explanation), wenches serve mead, spiced wine, and four hearty traditional
courses. Drink from a pewter goblet, wear a bib, and eat with your

# Ruthin

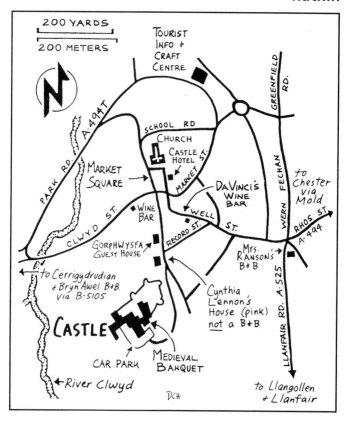

fingers and a dagger. Food and mead are unlimited—just ask for more (£30, CC, starts at 19:45, 2–5 nights per week year-round, depending upon demand; vegetarian options, nonsmoking, call for reservations, easy doorstep parking, down Castle Street from town square, tel. 01824/703-435 or, after hrs, the hotel at 01824/702-664). Ask to be seated with other readers of this book to avoid being stuck in a dreary tour group.

**Walks**—For a scenic and interesting one-hour walk, try the Offa's Dyke Path to Moel Famau (the "Jubilee Tower," a 200-year-old war memorial on a peak overlooking stark moorlands). The trail-head is a 10-minute drive from Ruthin.

▲▲**Welsh Choir**—The mixed choir performs at the Tabernacle Church on Thursday from 19:30 to 21:30 (except Aug, tel. 01824/703-757).

## Sleeping in Ruthin
### (£1 = about $1.50, country code: 44, area code: 01824)
Sleep Code: **S** = Single, **D** = Double/Twin, **T** = Triple, **Q** = Quad, **b** = bathroom, **s** = shower only, **CC** = Credit Cards accepted, **no CC** = Credit Cards not accepted.

**Bryn Awel**, a traditional and charming farmhouse B&B with a paradise garden, is run by Beryl and John Jones in the hamlet of Bontuchel just outside of Ruthin. Beryl, a prizewinning quilter, is helpful with travel tips and key Welsh words (Db-£38 for 2 nights, Db-£42 for 1 night, no CC, nonsmoking, LL15 2DE Bontuchel, tel. 01824/702-481, www.accomodata.co.uk /010797.htm). From Ruthin, take Bala road #494, then B5105/ Cerrigydrudion road. Turn right after the church, at the Bontuchel/Cyffylliog sign. Bryn Awel is on the right, 1.8 fragrant miles down a narrow road. If you get to the Bridge Hotel, backtrack 200 yards.

**Gorphwysfa Guest House**, in a cozy 16th-century Tudor home between the castle and the town square, has a library, a grand piano, and three huge, comfortable rooms (Db-£40, Tb-£54, Qb-£66, no CC, 8a Castle Street, LL15 1DP, tel. & fax 01824/707-529, Margaret O'Riain).

**Margaret Ranson's B&B** is friendly and comfortable with three rooms (Db-£40, no CC, strictly nonsmoking, Rhianfa, Ffordd Llanrhydd, Ruthin, Clwyd, LL15 1PP, a 10-min walk from castle; from Anchor Pub drive 100 yards toward hospital— it's the first big red-brick house on right, Rhianfa sign on stone wall, tel. & fax 01824/702-971). Margaret's husband, John, a natural tour guide, will lend you an excellent North Wales road map. Or you can just play croquet in their sprawling backyard.

**Ruthin Castle**, the ultimate in creaky, faded, old-world elegance for North Wales, is actually not a castle but a hotel near castle ruins (Sb-£80, Db-£106, show this book for 10 percent off room rates or 10 percent off their 2-nights-with-a-banquet-plus-restaurant-dinner deal, CC, tel. 01824/702-664, fax 01824/ 705-978, www.ruthincastle.co.uk). Enjoy lavish public places, armor, antlers, ghosts, and your private snooker table (giant billiards, £1/hr). Explore the fascinating grounds, complete with a drowning pool and 40 peacocks. You'll wake up to their cry thinking it's a loony-tune damsel in distress.

**The Castle Hotel**, not to be confused with the Ruthin Castle hotel, is a 19-room hotel on the town square with imper-sonal staff (Db-£42 with this book through 2002, family suites, CC, front rooms are larger and overlook the town square, some non-smoking rooms, reconfirm reservations, St. Peter's Square, LL15 1AA, tel. 01824/702-479, fax 01824/703-488).

For cheap beds go to the **Llangollen Youth Hostel** (15 miles from Ruthin, see below).

## Eating in Ruthin

These two places serve the best dinners: **Off the Square Wine Bar**, facing the town square and run by the Castle Hotel, serves good modern English cuisine in classy ambience (£8 main courses, daily 12:00–21:30, CC, tel. 01824/707-004). **Da Vinci's Wine Bar**, while pricey with £14 main courses, is a good value (Tue–Sun from 18:00, closed Mon, The Mews, Well Street, tel. 01824/702-200).

For more basic grub, you might try **Wynnstay Arms**, the classier **Manor House Hotel Restaurant** (a tad expensive), or the **Red Lion** pub (a mile out of town in Cyffylliog). For fish and chips, locals paddle over to **Finns** on Clwyd Street (take-away only).

## Transportation Connections—Ruthin

**Ruthin to: Llangollen** (15 miles, 4 buses/day but never on Sun, 1 hr), **Betsw-y-Coed** (30 miles, 3–4 hrs, bus to Rhyl, train to Llandudno Junction, train to Betsw-y-Coed), **Conwy** (3 hrs by bus, with transfer at Llanrwst), **Chester** (6 buses/day, 30 min, or a £20 taxi).

# LLANGOLLEN

Worth a stop if you have a car, Llangollen is famous for its musical **International Eisteddfod** (July 8–14 in 2002, www .international-eisteddfod.co.uk), a very popular and very crowded festival of folk songs and dance. Men's choir practice is held on Friday nights throughout the year (19:30 at the Hand Hotel, 21:00 pub singsong afterward, tel. 01978/860-303).

Walk or ride a horse-drawn boat down the old canal (£3.50, March–Oct, 45 min, 3-mile round-trip, tel. 01978/860-702) toward the lovely 13th-century **Cistercian Vale Crucis Abbey** (£2, daily 10:00–17:00) near the even older cross, **Eliseg's Pillar**. The same outfit offers relaxing and scenic narrow-boat canal trips (£6, 2 hrs).

Llangollen has a handful of other amusements and attractions, including scenic steam-train trips (daily Easter–Dec), the world's largest permanent exhibition of model railways, and the biggest *Doctor Who* exhibition anywhere. (**TI**: daily April–Oct 10:00–18:00, Nov–March 9:30–17:00, tel. 01978/860-828.)

**Sleeping in Llangollen: Glasfryn B&B** rents three rooms (D/Db-£35, no CC, Abbey Road, LL20 8SN, near bridge, tel. 01978/860-757, Eleanor Jones). **Gale's Hotel** is a decent value (Db-£50, CC, Bridge Street 18, LL20 8PF, tel. 01978/860-089, fax 01978/861-313). And the **Llangollen Youth Hostel** is cheap (£12/bed in 2- to 20-bed rooms, £2 less for members, no CC, tel. 01978/860-330).

Llangollen is a 30-minute drive from Ruthin. But if you don't have a car, you can catch a bus (4/day, none on Sun, 60 min, year-round). Llangollen is connected by bus with train stations at Chirk (1/hr), Ruabon (1/hr), and Wrexham (2/hr).

## King Edward's Castles

In the 13th century, the Welsh, under two great princes named Llywelyn, created a united and independent Wales. The English King Edward I fought hard to end this Welsh sovereignty. In 1282 Llywelyn was killed (and went to where everyone speaks Welsh). King Edward spent the next 20 years building or rebuilding 17 great castles to consolidate his English foothold in troublesome North Wales. The greatest of these (such as Conwy Castle) were masterpieces of medieval engineering, with round towers (tough to undermine by tunneling), a castle-within-a-castle defense (giving defenders a place to retreat and wreak havoc on the advancing enemy...or just wait for reinforcements), and sea access (safe to stock from England). These were English islands in the middle of angry Wales. Most were built with a fortified grid-plan town attached and were filled with English settlers. (With this blatant abuse of Wales, you have to wonder, where was Greenpeace 700 years ago?) Edward I was arguably England's best monarch. By establishing and consolidating the UK (adding Wales and Scotland to England), he made his kingdom big enough to compete with the rising European powers.

Castle lovers will want to tour each of Edward's five greatest castles. With a car and two days this makes one of Europe's best castle tours. I'd rate them in this order: **Caernarfon** is most entertaining and best presented (described below). **Conwy** is attached to the cutest medieval town and the best public transport (described below). **Harlech** is the most dramatic (£3, daily early April–late Oct 9:30–17:00 or 18:00, late Oct–early April Mon–Sat 9:30–16:00, Sun 11:00–16:00, tel. 01766/780-552; TI open Easter-Oct, tel. 01766/780-658). **Beaumaris**, surrounded by a swan-filled moat, was the last, largest, and most romantic (£2.50, same hrs as Harlech, tel. 01248/810-361). **Criccieth** (KRICK-ith), built in 1230 by Llywelyn, is also dramatic and remote (£2.50, daily early April–late Sept 10:00–17:00 or 18:00, closed off-season, tel. 01766/522-227; TI open Easter-Oct, tel. 01766/523-633). For photos and more information on the castles, as well as information on Welsh historic monuments in general, check www.cadw.wales.gov.uk.

# CONWY

This garrison town was built with the Conwy castle in the 1280s
to give Edward I an English toehold in Wales (see above). What's
left today are the best medieval walls in Britain surrounding a
humble work-a-day town and crowned by the bleak and barren
hulk of a castle that was awesome in its day. Conwy's charming
High Street leads from Lancester Square (with the bus stop,
unmanned train station, and a column honoring the town's
founder, Welsh prince Llywelyn the Great) down to a fishy
harbor that permitted Edward to safely restock his castle. Since
the highway was tunneled under the town, a strolling ambience
has returned to Conwy. Beyond the castle, the mighty Telford
suspension bridge is a 19th-century slice of English imperialism,
built in 1826 to better connect (and control) the route to Ireland.

**Tourist Information:** The TI is near the castle (April–Oct
daily 9:30–18:00, Nov–March daily 9:30–16:00, tel. 01492/592-
248). Ask about train or bus schedules for your departure (because
Conwy doesn't have a staffed train or bus station—only a lonely
train platform and bus stop). The TI sells books and maps on the
area (such as *Footprints' Walks around Snowdonia*, £3.50, 16 walks
with maps), books rooms for a £1 fee, and does theater bookings.
Don't confuse the TI with the tacky "Conwy Visitors Centre"
near the station with its goofy little 80p video show.

## Helpful Hints

Every Monday night, the gritty Malt Loaf pub hosts the Conwy
Folk Music Club (across from train station) from 20:30 on. Every
Tuesday, a small market hums in the train-station parking lot
(year-round, canceled if rainy).

**Trains**: Train schedules are posted outside the unstaffed
station. Trains do drop off and pick up in Conwy (if your train is
listed with an "x," you'll need to flag it down). The nearest "real"
train station is in Llandudno Junction, a mile away.

**Car Rental:** Several car-rental agencies in the city of
Llandudno (1.5 miles away) offer cars for about £40 per day and
can deliver to you in Conwy (get list of car-rental agencies from
Conwy TI).

**Bike Rental:** Conwy Outdoor rents bikes for £12/day,
including helmets (daily 9:00–18:00, CC, packed lunches available,
9 Castle Street, tel. 01492/593-390).

## Sights—Conwy

▲**Conwy Castle**—Built dramatically on a rock overlooking the
sea with eight linebacker towers, this castle has an interesting
story to tell (£3.60, mid-May–Sept daily 9:30–18:00, April–mid-
May and Oct daily 9:30–17:00, in winter Mon–Sat 9:30–16:00,
Sun 11:00–16:00, tel. 01492/592-358). Guides wait inside to take

# Conwy

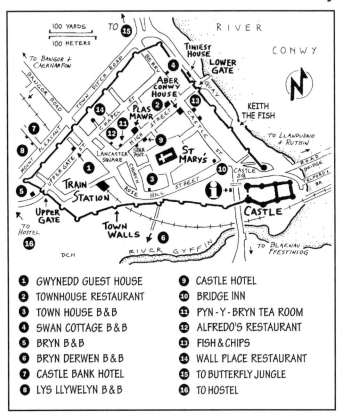

| | |
|---|---|
| ❶ GWYNEDD GUEST HOUSE | ❾ CASTLE HOTEL |
| ❷ TOWNHOUSE RESTAURANT | ❿ BRIDGE INN |
| ❸ TOWN HOUSE B&B | ⓫ PYN-Y-BRYN TEA ROOM |
| ❹ SWAN COTTAGE B&B | ⓬ ALFREDO'S RESTAURANT |
| ❺ BRYN B&B | ⓭ FISH & CHIPS |
| ❻ BRYN DERWEN B&B | ⓮ WALL PLACE RESTAURANT |
| ❼ CASTLE BANK HOTEL | ⓯ TO BUTTERFLY JUNGLE |
| ❽ LYS LLYWELYN B&B | ⓰ TO HOSTEL |

you on a 60-minute, £1 tour. If the booth is empty, look for the group and join it. (These guides also do inexpensive evening city tours; consider enthusiastic Neville Hortop, tel. 01492/878-209.) Built in four years, the castle had a water gate that allowed safe entry for English boats in a land of hostile Welsh.

▲**City Wall**—Much of the wall, with its 22 towers and castle and harbor views, can be walked for free. Start at Upper Gate (the highest point) or Berry Street (the lowest) or do the small section at the castle entrance.

▲**Plas Mawr**—A rare Elizabethan house from 1580, this was built after the reign of Henry VIII. It was the first Welsh home to be built within Conwy's walls. (The Tudor family was Welsh—and therefore relations between Wales and England warmed.) Billed as the oldest house in Wales, Plas Mawr offers a delightful look at domestic life in 16th-century Wales to anyone patient enough to spend an hour following the excellent included audioguide (£4.10, Tue–Sun 9:30–18:00, closed Mon and early off-season).

**St. Mary's Parish Church**—Sitting lonely in the center of town, Conwy's church was the centerpiece of a Cistercian abbey that stood here a hundred years before the town. The Cistercians were French monks who built their abbeys in lonely places—"far from the haunts of man." Popular with the locals because they were French and *not* English—the Cistercians taught locals farming and mussel-gathering techniques. Edward moved the monks 12 miles upstream but kept the church for his town. Notice the tombstone of a victim of the Battle of Trafalgar just left of the north transept. On the other side of the church, a tomb containing seven brothers and sisters is marked "We Are Seven." It inspired Wordsworth to write one of his poems.

**High Street**—Lancester Square marks the top of Conwy's charming High Street. Its centerpiece is a column honoring the town's founder, the Welsh prince Llywelyn the Great. Find the cute pointed arch built into the medieval wall so the train could get through. Side trip up York Place (past Alfredo's restaurant) to a wall of slate memorials from the 1937 coronation of King George (his wife, the Queen Consort Elizabeth, is today's Queen Mum). Notice the Welsh lesson here: the counties (shires), months (only "mai" is recognizable), days, numbers, and alphabet with its different letters.

High Street leads down to the harborfront. Wander downhill enjoying the work-a-day Welsh scene: bakery, butcher, newsstand, old timers, and maybe even suds in the fountain. Plas Mawr (on the left), the first Welsh house built within the town walls, dates from the time of Henry VIII (well worth touring, described above). Opposite the Castle Hotel, a lane leads to the Carmel Church. This is a fine example of stark Methodist "statement architecture"—stern, with no frills, and typical of these churches built in the early 20th century.

Aberconwy House marks the bottom of High Street. One of the oldest houses in town, it's a museum (not worth touring). Imagine this garrison town filled with half-timbered buildings like this. From here Barry Street leads left. Originally "burial street," it was a big ditch for mass burials during a 17th-century plague. Continue downhill, crossing under the wall to the harborfront.

▲**Harborfront**—Still called the King's Quay, the stones date from the 13th century when the harbor served Edward's castle and town. Conwy was once a busy slate port. Slate, barged downstream to here, was loaded onto big three-masters and shipped off to Europe. Back when much of Europe was roofed with Welsh slate, Conwy was a boomtown. In 1900 it had 48 pubs. All the mud is new as the modern bridge caused this part of the river to silt up.

Strolling along the harbor from the castle end you'll find

plenty of interest. The harbormaster house fills the former customs building. The **lifeboat house** welcomes visitors. Each coastal town has a similar house outfitted with a rescue boat suited to the area—in the shallow waters around Conwy, inflatable boats work best. Mussels, historically a big "crop" for Conwy, are processed "in the months with an r" by the **Mussels Center**. And in the other months, it's open for visitors (£1). **Keith the Fish** provides locals with fresh fish and strollers with tasty treats (daily 8:00–18:00). Drop by his shack for a tasty 10p crab stick. Keith, Conwy's honorary secretary of lifeboats, loves to chat. The benches are great for a fish-and-chips meal (two shops are just around the corner, see "Eating," below) or to simply chat with the noisy gulls. The **Queen Victoria tour boat** departs from here (£3, lazy 30-min cruise, nearly 1/hr, pay on boat).

The **Liverpool Arms pub** was built by a captain who ran a ferry service to Liverpool in the 19th century when the North Wales coast was discovered by English holiday-goers. Today it's a fisherman's hangout. It's easy to miss **The Tiniest House in Britain**, but don't. It's red, 72 inches wide, 122 inches high, and worth 50p to pop in and listen to the short audio-tour. (No toilet. But it did have a bedpan.)

From the quay, it's a peaceful half-mile shoreline stroll along the harbor promenade (from smallest house, walk through wall gate and keep going).

**Butterfly Jungle**—Butterflies flutter in a steamy, lush greenhouse with tropical forest sounds. It's sweet, small, and too humid to linger long (£3.50, ticket valid all day—OK to return, 50p identification chart not necessary because charts posted inside, April–Sept daily 10:00–17:30, Oct 10:00–15:30, follow signs from harbor, pleasant 5-min walk north, tel. 01492/593-149). If it's not busy, ask the owner why he started a butterfly house.

**Pony Riding**—Cowpokes mosey on down to Pinewood Riding Stables, a mile from Conwy (£12.50/hr for scenic rides to Conwy Mount, longer rides possible, Sychnant Pass Road, past hostel, tel. 01492/592-256).

▲**Bodnant Garden**—This sumptuous 80-acre display of floral color is six miles south of Conwy. Set in the lush green of Snowdonia, this garden is one of Britain's best. It's famous for its magnolias, rhodies, camellias, and floral arch (£5, mid-March–Oct daily 10:00–17:00, café, best in spring, phone message tells what's blooming, tel. 01492/650-460).

## Sleeping in Conwy
**(£1 = about $1.50, country code: 44, area code: 01492)**
Conwy has decent budget B&Bs, each located within a five-minute walk from the bus and train station. There's no launderette in town.

**Gwynedd Guest House**, spacious, thoughtfully decorated, and charmingly run by Margaret Young, is Conwy's best value (S-£18, D-£32, T/Q-£50, no CC, family deals, Internet access-£1/15 min, laundry-£5, parking, 2 blocks from bus stop and train station, 10 Upper Gate Street, LL32 8RF, tel. & fax 01492/596-537, e-mail: margaret.young1@virgin.net).

**Bryn B&B** offers five large, clutter-free rooms in a big 19th-century house with the city wall right in the backyard (Sb-£23, Db-£40, no CC, 1 ground-floor room, parking, smoke-free, immediately outside upper gate of wall, Sychnant Pass Road, LL32 8NS, tel. 01492/592-449, www.bryn.org.uk, Janet Shaw).

**Town House B&B** rents six tidy, bright rooms—some with views—near the entrance of the castle (S-£16, D-£32, Db-£38 through 2002 with this book, no CC, nonsmoking, parking, Rosehill Street 18, LL32 3LD, tel. 01492/596-454, cellular 0797-465-0609, e-mail: the townhousebb@aol.com, Alan and Elaine Naughton).

**Swan Cottage B&B** is a homey place near the harborfront renting three compact rooms (D/Db-£32 with this book, both D rooms have harbor view, no CC, 18 Berry Street, LL32 8DG, tel. 01492/596-840, Mr. and Mrs. Roberts, e-mail: swancottage @btopenworld.com). Across the street, the **Castle View B&B** rents two basic rooms (D-£32, no CC, 3 Berry Street, tel. 01492/ 596-888, Elaine).

**Castle Bank Hotel** is a small hotel with nine spacious rooms run by the gracious Karen Morton (Sb-£35, Db-£57, 10 percent discount with this book, CC, nonsmoking, easy parking, just out-side town wall at Mount Pleasant, LL32 8NY, tel. 01492/593-888, fax 01492/596-466, e-mail: castlebank@bun.com).

**Llys Llywelyn B&B**, next door and faded in comparison, has nine rooms (Sb-£20, Db-£39, 10 percent discount with this book, CC, easy parking, Mount Pleasant, LL32 8NY, tel. 01492/ 593-257, e-mail: llys-llewelyn@talk21.com, Alan Hughes).

**The Bridge Inn** rents six brightly decorated rooms above its pub. The floor just above the pub is noisy, particularly on weekend nights; the top floor is quieter (Db-£40 weeknights, £50 Fri–Sat, prices promised with this book, CC, some views, nonsmoking, separate entrance from pub, tel. 01492/573-482, www.bridge-conwy.co.uk).

**Bryn Derwen**, an eight-minute walk from town, is in a near-mansion atop a hill, set back from a busy road. Most of its seven rooms are pink and frilly without being sugary (Db-£40, no CC, antlered breakfast room with medieval-type table; exit train station from its farthest and lowest corner, go through gate in city wall to busy road—Woodlands—and turn right, look for sign and climb to hotel, Woodlands, LL32 8LT, tel. 01492/ 596-134, Alan and Wendy). The **Glan Heulog Guest House**, next door in the other half of the mansion, isn't as nice for the same price (tel. 01492/593-845).

The big, old **Castle Hotel** in the town center rents 29 decent but pricey rooms (Sb-£60, Db-£85, 10 percent discount promised with this book, CC, halls musty but rooms OK, nonsmoking rooms, High Street, LL32 8DB, tel. 01492/582-800, fax 01492/582-300, www.castlewales.co.uk, e-mail: mail@castlewales.co.uk).

The **Conwy Hostel**, welcoming travelers of any age, has super views from all its rooms (including 4 bunk-bed doubles). Each room is equipped with either two or four bunk beds and a shower; WCs are down the hall. The airy dining hall and glorious rooftop deck make you feel like you're in the majestic midst of Wales (Db-£30, bed in quad-£13, no CC, book in advance for doubles, Internet access, laundry, lockers, dinners, elevator, parking, 10-min uphill walk from upper gate of Conwy's wall, Larkhill, Sychnant Pass Road, tel. 01492/593-571, fax 01492/593-580, e-mail: conwy@yha.org.uk).

## Eating in Conwy

For dinner, stroll down High Street comparing the cute teahouses and smoky pubs. At the top, on Lancaster Square, is **Alfredo's Restaurant**, a family-friendly place serving good and reasonable Italian food (nightly from 18:00, last orders at 22:00, CC, tel. 01492/592-381, Christine). **Town House Restaurant** is *the* place in town to enjoy modern English cuisine in a romantic candlelit setting (£15 dinners, Tue–Sun 10:00–15:00, 18:00–21:00, closed Mon, CC, High Street, reservations smart, tel. 01492/596-436, Karen). At the bottom of High Street two fish-and-chips joints— **Galleon's** and **Fisherman's**—brag they're the best (Fisherman's probably is). Consider taking your fish and chips down to the harbor and sharing it with the noisy seagulls. Locals like **Anna's Tea Rooms**, located upstairs in the Conwy Outdoor Shop (daily 10:00–17:00, CC, near Fisherman's, 9 Castle Street, tel. 01492/580-908). The quirky little **Wall Place** on Chapel Street is strictly vegetarian; service is sloooow but everything is fresh (£12 3-course dinner, June–Sept daily 12:00–15:00, 19:00–22:00, April–May open weekends and some weekdays, closed Oct–March, tel. 01492/596-326). The smoky **Bridge** pub, at the intersection of Rosehill and Castle Streets, serves decent grub (daily 12:00–14:30, until 19:30 Easter-Sept). The best cheap meal in town is either a picnic from the **Spar grocery** (daily 8:00–22:00, top of High Street) or fish and chips on the harborfront with the locals.

## Transportation Connections—Conwy

Be proactive whether taking the bus or train; let the driver or conductor know you want to stop at Conwy. Consider getting train times and connections for your onward journey at a bigger station before you get to Conwy. For train information in Conwy, ask at the TI or call 08457-484-950. If you want to depart Conwy by train, flag down the train. For a quick pick of more frequent trains, catch a bus—or walk a mile—from Conwy to Llandudno Junction.

**Conwy to: Llandudno Junction** (2 buses/hr, 5 min; 4 trains/day, 5 min), **Caernarfon** (1/hr, 1 hr), **Trefriw-Betws-y-Coed-Penygwryd-Llanberis** (bus #19, 1/hr in summer).

**Llandudno Junction by train to: Chester** (2/hr, 1 hr), **Birmingham** (2/hr, 2.5 hrs), **London's Euston Station** (1/hr, 3.5 hrs).

# CAERNARFON

The small and lively little town of Caernarfon (kah-NAR-von) is famous for its striking castle—the place where the Prince of Wales is "invested." Like Conwy, it was an Edward I garrison town marching out from the castle. It still follows the original medieval grid plan laid within its well-preserved ramparts.

But Caernarfon is mostly a 19th-century town. Then, the most important thing in town wasn't the castle but the area—now a parking lot—that sprawls below the castle. This was once a booming slate port shipping tidy bundles of slate from North Wales mining towns to roofs all over Europe.

The statue of local boy David Lloyd George looks over the town square. A member of parliament from 1890 to 1945, he was the most important politician Wales ever sent to London and ultimately became Britain's prime minister. Boy George began his career as a noisy nonconformist liberal advocating Welsh rights. He ended up an eloquent spokesperson for the notion of Great Britain, convincing his slate-mining constituents that only as part of the Union would their slate industry boom.

A small but lively town, Caernarfon bustles with shops, cafés, and people. Market-day activities fill its main square on Saturdays year-round; a smaller, sleepy market yawns on Monday from late May to September. The charming grid-plan medieval town is worth a wander.

**Tourist Information:** The TI, across from the castle entrance, has a wonderful free town map/guide (with a good self-guided town walk) and train and bus schedules, sells hiking books, and books rooms here and elsewhere for a £1 fee (April–Oct daily 10:00–18:00, Nov–March daily 9:30–16:30 with a 13:00–13:30 lunch break, tel. 01286/672-232). Donna "Caernarfon is more than a castle" Goodman leads historic walks almost nightly through the season (£3, 1.5 hrs, tel. 01286/677-059 for her schedule).

**Arrival in Caernarfon:** If you arrive by bus, walk a few steps to Bridge Street; then go left on Bridge Street until you hit the main square and the castle. The TI faces the castle entrance. Public WCs are off the main square, on the road down to the harbor parking lot. Drivers pay £2.20 to park below the castle.

**Helpful Hints:** Within a couple of blocks of the bus stop, you'll find an **Internet café** (Dimensiwm 4, Mon–Sat 10:00–18:00, closed Sun, Turf Square), the **post office** (main square), and **Pete's Laundromat** (daily 9:00–17:30, £4 same-day full-service, £3 self-service, Skinner Street).

The only **car-rental** agency in town is Caernarfon Rent-a-Car (on the harbor, 2 Slate Quay, tel. 01286/676-171). Two shops rent **bikes**: Cycle Hire (£11/day, on the harbor, tel. 01286/676-804) and Beics Castell (£13/day, includes helmets, closed Thu and Sun, High Street, tel. 01286/677-400).

## Sights—Caernarfon

▲▲**Caernarfon Castle**—Edward I built this impressive castle 700 years ago to establish English rule over North Wales. Modeled after the striped and angular walls of ancient Constantinople, the castle—while impressive—was never finished and never really used. From the inner courtyard you can see the notched walls ready for more walls that were never built. Its fame is due to its physical grandeur and from its association with the Prince of Wales. The English king got the angry Welsh to agree that if he presented them with "a prince, born in Wales who spoke not a word of English," they would submit to the crown. In time, Edward had a son...born in Wales...who spoke not a word of English, Welsh, or any other language. In modern times, as another political maneuver, the Prince of Wales has been "invested" (given his title) here. This "tradition" actually dates only from the 20th century and only 2 of 21 Princes of Wales have taken part.

In spite of its disappointing history, it's a great castle to tour. An essential part of any visit is the guided tour (50-min tours for £1.50 leave on the hr from the courtyard steps just beyond the ticket booth; if you're late, ask to join one in progress). In the huge Eagle Tower (on the seaward side) see the *Chieftains and Princes* history exhibit (ground floor), watch the 20-minute movie (a broad mix of Welsh legend and history, shown on the hour and half hour, upstairs, comfortable theater seats), and climb the tower for a great view. The tower at the opposite end of the castle has an exhibit about the investiture of Prince Charles in 1969 (£4.20, June–Sept daily 9:30–18:00, April–May and Oct daily 9:30–17:00, Nov–March Mon–Sat 9:30–16:00, Sun 11:00–16:00, CC, can store luggage during visit, tel. 01286/677-617). Martin de Lewandowicz gives mind-bending tours of the castle (tel. 01286/674-369).

**Distractions**—A Welsh Highland **steam train** billows through the countryside to Waunfawr and back (£7.60, May–Sept daily, April and Oct weekends only, 4/day, 1.5 hrs, tel. 01766/512-340, www.restrail.co.uk). Narrated **harbor cruises** on the *Queen of the Sea* run daily in summer (June–Sept 11:00–18:00 or 19:00, depending on weather, tides, and demand, 40 min, castle views, tel. 01286/672-772). The **Segontium Roman Fort**, dating from A.D. 77, is the westernmost Roman fort. It was manned for more than 300 years to keep the Welsh and the coast quiet. Little is left but foundations (small museum, 15-min walk from town, tel. 01286/675-625). For **pony riding**, try Snowdonia Riding Stables (£12/1 hr, longer and shorter time available, 3 miles from Caernarfon, off the road to Beddgelert, bus #89 or #95 from Caernarfon, tel. 01286/650-342).

**Men's Choir**—If spending the night, consider dropping by the local men's choir practice (Tue 20:00–21:30, Conservative Club on High Street).

## Sleeping and Eating in Caernarfon
### (£1 = about $1.50, country code: 44, area code: 01286)

**Isfryn B&B** is just down the street from the castle and overlooks the water (6 rooms, S-£20, D-£40, Db-£45, family deals, no CC, 11 Church Street, LL5 51SW, tel. & fax 01286/675-628, e-mail: graham.bailey2@btinternet.co.uk, Graham).

**Caer Menai B&B** is a well-established old place renting six fine rooms (D-£40, Db-£46, no CC, nonsmoking, 15 Church Street, tel. & fax 01286/672-612, e-mail: khlardner@talk21.com).

The **Celtic Royal Hotel** rents 110 comfortable rooms with a gym, pool, Jacuzzi, and sauna. Its grand, old-fashioned look comes with modern-day conveniences—but it's still over-priced (Db-£100, CC, nonsmoking rooms, bar, restaurant; from bus stop, go right on Bridge Street, which turns into Bangor Street; 5-min walk; Bangor Street, LL55 1AY, tel. 01286/674-477, fax 01286/674-139, www.celtic-royal.co.uk).

**Totters Hostel** is a creative little hostel well run by Bob and Henriette (30 beds in 5 dorm rooms, £11/bed with sheets, includes continental breakfast, no CC, couples can have their own room when available, open all day, lockers, welcoming game room/lounge, use of kitchen, a block from the castle at 2 High Street, tel. 01286/672-963, www.applemaps.co.uk/totters).

**Eating in Caernarfon: Ainsworth's**, a fish-and-chips joint, is at 31 Bridge Street, and plenty of cheap and cheery sandwich shops and tearooms line nearby High Street. The nearest **supermarket** is Kwik Save; a larger Safeway is a block beyond (a 5-min walk from city center on Bangor Street).

## Transportation Connections—Caernarfon

**Caernarfon by bus to: Conwy** (2/hr, 1/hr on Sun, 1.25 hrs, buy ticket on bus), **Llanberis** (2/hr, 30 min), **Beddgelert** (1/hr, 30 min), **Blaenau-Ffestiniog** (1 bus/hr, 1.5 hrs), **Beddgelert-Penygwryd-Llanberis** (bus #95, every 2 hrs, 1.5 hrs, June–Sept only). Buy tickets from the driver.

# SNOWDONIA NATIONAL PARK

Snowdonia National Park is Britain's second-largest national park, with Mount Snowdon—the tallest mountain in England and Wales—as its centerpiece. Each year half a million people choose one of seven different paths to the top of 3,560-foot Snowdon (the small book *The Ascent of Snowdon*, by E. G. Bowland, describes the routes, £2, sold by local TIs). Hikes take from five to seven hours. If you're reasonably fit and the weather cooperates, it's an exciting day. Trail info abounds. As you explore the area, notice the slate roofs—they're the local specialty.

## Sights—Snowdonia

**Betws-y-Coed**—The resort center of Snowdonia National Park, Betwys-y-Coed (BET-oos-uh-coyd) bursts with tour buses and souvenir shops. Its good national park, TI, and guided walks are the only reasons to stop here (April–Oct daily 10:00–18:00, Nov–March daily 9:30–13:00, 14:00–16:30, tel. 01690/710-426). Consider a long, guided walk (£3.50, April–early Sept Thu–Sun, depart TI at 10:00, 6- to 8-mile hike, call Robin Hamlett at 0151/488-0052 to book).

If you drive west out of town on A5, after two miles you'll see the car park for scenic Swallow Falls, a pleasant five-minute walk from the road. A half mile past the falls on the right you'll see "The Ugly House," built overnight to take advantage of a 15th-century law that let any quickie building avoid fees and taxes. Buses connect Conwy and Betws-y-Coed (with a connection, 1/hr June–Aug, 50 min). Trains run from Llandudno Junction near Conwy through Betws-y-Coed to Blaenau (6/day).

▲**Trefriw Woolen Mills**—The mill in Trefriw (TREV-roo), five miles north of Betws-y-Coed, is free and surprisingly interesting if the machines are running (April–Oct Mon–Fri 10:00–13:00, 14:00–17:00, same hrs off-season—but only weaving is demonstrated, tel. 01492/640-462). Follow the 11 stages of wool transformation: warping, weaving, carding, hanking, spanking, spinning, and so on. The hand-spinning house (next to the WC) has a charming spinster and a petting cupboard filled with all the various kinds of raw wool that can be spun into cloth (June–Sept only, Mon–Fri 10:00–17:00). Silk worms are also at work (and on display) here. Be sure to enjoy the fine woolen shop, the pleasant town, and the coffee shop. The grade school next door is rambunctious with Welsh-speaking kids—fun to listen to at recess. The woolen mill at Penmachno (also near Betws-y-Coed) is smaller and much less interesting.

▲**Beddgelert**—This is the quintessential Snowdon village, packing a scenic mountain punch without the tourist crowds (17 miles from Betws-y-Coed). Set on a river in the shadow of Snowdon

## Snowdonia Area

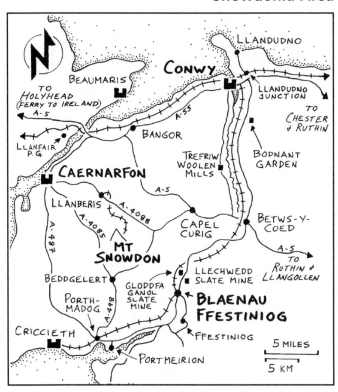

and her sisters, with a fine variety of hikes from its doorstep and pretty good bus service, Beddgelert (BETH-geh-let) makes a good stop for those wanting to experience the peace of Snowdonia. The Glaslyn Homemade Ice Cream shop offers surprising quality and selection for this altitude (TI tel. 01766/890-615).

Locals can recommend walks. You can follow the lane along the river (3 miles round-trip), walk down the river and around the hill (3 hrs, 6 miles, 900-foot gain, via Cwm Bycham), hike along (or around) Llyn Gwynant Lake and four miles back to Beddgelert (ride the bus to the lake), or try the dramatic ridge walks on Moel Hebog (Hawk Hill).

**Sleeping in Beddgelert: Plas Tan Y Graig Guest House**, at the village bridge, is a good value (D-£35, Db-£45, CC, family room, fine lounge, tea garden, LL55 4LT, tel. 01766/890-329, fax 01766/890-629, www.nwi.co.uk/plastanygraig/). Also just over the bridge, Brian Wheatley rents six rooms at **Plas-Gwyn**, a 19th-century townhouse (S-£18, bunk D-£30, Db-£40, no CC, family deals, nonsmoking, tel. 01766/890-215, www.plas-gwyn .com). **Plas Colwyn Guesthouse** is a bigger place just next door (D-£36, Db-£42, bed only-from £12/person, no CC, tel. 01766/ 890-458). The **Royal Goat Hotel** offers well-worn, chandeliered, woody elegance in a grand hotel built for the rugged 19th-century aristocrat (Sb-£45, Db-£79, 10 percent off with this book through 2002, cheaper for 2-night stays, CC, tel. 01766/890-224, fax 01766/890-422, www.royalgoathotel.co.uk).

Mountaineers note that this area was used by Sir Edmund Hillary and his men as they practiced for the first ascent of Mount Everest. The **Pen-y-Gwryd Hotel Pub** (at the top of the pass north of Beddgelert) is strewn with fascinating memorabilia from Hillary's 1953 climb (D-£48, Db-£58, no CC, saggy beds, smoky, old-time-elegant public rooms, those in D rooms get to use museum-piece Victorian tubs and showers, grand 5-course dinners-£17, tel. 01286/870-211). With its crampon ambience, it's ideal for well-bred hikers.

**Llanberis**—A town of 2,000 people with as many tourists on a sunny day, Llanberis is a popular base for Snowdon activities. Along with the station for the Snowdon train, there is a good information center, a few touristy museums, pony trekking, and good bus connections (1 bus/hr to Beddgelert, 45 min).

**Sleeping in Llanberis:** Consider **Dolafon Hotel**, an 1860s Victorian building with seven traditionally-furnished rooms (D with private bath down the hall-£40, Db-£48, large Db-£55, no CC, nonsmoking, garden, High Street, tel. & fax 01286/ 870-993, www.dolafon.com).

▲▲**Mount Snowdon and the Mountain Railway**—The easiest and most popular ascent of Mount Snowdon is by the Snowdon Mountain Railway, a rack-and-pinion railway from 1896 that climbs 3,500 feet over 4.5 miles from Llanberis to the summit (£17 round-trip, 2.5 hrs, includes 30-min stop at summit, CC, tel. 01286/870-223). Discounts are given for the early trains (up to and including 9:30 departure).

The first departure is usually at 9:00. While the schedule flexes with weather and demand, they try to run several trips each day mid-March through October (2/hr in peak season). On sunny summer days, trains fill up (waits are longer in the afternoon; arrive by lunchtime and get a departure appointment time—usually a wait of 1–2 hrs, reservations possible a day in advance). Off-season trains often stop short of the summit (due to snow and high winds).

# BLAENAU FFESTINIOG

This quintessential Welsh slate-mining town is notable for its slate-mine tour and its old steam train. The town—a dark, poor place—seems to struggle on, oblivious to the tourists who nip in and out. Take a walk. The shops are right out of the 1950s. Long rows of humble "two-up and two-down" houses (4 rooms) feel pretty grim. There are some buses from the town to the slate mines; the road isn't pedestrian friendly. (**TI**: daily 10:00–13:00, 14:00–18:00, closed Oct–Easter, tel. 01766/830-360.)

## Sights—Blaenau Ffestiniog

▲▲**Llechwedd Slate-Mine Tour**—Slate mining played a block-buster role in Welsh heritage, and this mine on the northern edge of the bleak town of Blaenau Ffestiniog (BLIGH-nigh FES-tin-yog) does a fine job of explaining the mining culture of Victorian Wales. The Welsh mined and split most of the slate roofs of Europe. For every ton of usable slate found, 10 tons were mined. The exhibit has three parts: a tiny Victorian mining town (with a miners' pub and a view from "The Top of the Tip," free and worthwhile) and two 30-minute tours (which leave 3–4 times/hr). Do the "tramway" tour first—a level train ride with three stops, no walking, and a live guide. It focuses on working life and traditional mining techniques. Then descend into the "deep mine" for a tour featuring an audiovisual dramatization of social life and a half-mile of walking. Both are different and, considering the cheap combo-ticket, worthwhile. Don't miss the slate-splitting demonstration at the end of the tramway tour (£7.25 for 1 tour, £11 for both, March–Sept daily 10:00–18:00, Oct–Feb until 17:00, last tour starts 45 min before closing, tel. 01766/830-306). Dress warmly—I mean it. You'll freeze underground without a sweater. Lines are longer when rain drives in the hikers.

▲**Ffestiniog Railway**—This 13-mile narrow-gauge train line was built in 1836 for small horse-drawn wagons to transport the slate from the Ffestiniog mines to the port of Porthmadog. In the 1860s horses gave way to steam trains. Today hikers and tourists enjoy these tiny titans (£14 round-trip, 1/hr in peak season, 2.5 hrs round-trip; diesel trains are £2 cheaper, first-class observation cars are £5 extra, tel. 01766/512-340). This is a novel steam-train experience, but the full-size Llandudno-Blaenau Ffestiniog train is more scenic and works better for hikers.

**Portmeirion**—Ten miles southwest of Blaenau Ffestiniog, this "Italian Village" was the lifework of a rich local architect who began building it in 1925. Set idyllically on the coast just beyond the poverty of the slate-mine towns, this flower-filled fantasy is extravagant. Surrounded by lush Welsh greenery and a windswept mudflat at low tide, the village is an artistic glob of palazzo arches, fountains, gardens, and promenades filled with cafés, tacky shops, a hotel, and local tourists who always wanted to go to Italy (or who are fans of the cultish British 1960s TV series *The Prisoner*). The architect explains his purpose in a videotaped slide presentation (not worth the £5 admission, daily 9:30–17:30, 2 miles from Porthmadog, tel. 01766/770-000).

## Transportation Connections—North Wales
Two major transfer points out of (or into) North Wales are Chester and Crewe.

**Chester by train to: London** (1/hr, 3 hrs), **Liverpool** (2/hr, 50 min), **Birmingham** (2/hr, 2 hrs), points in **North Wales** (2/hr).

**Crewe by train to: London** (2/hr, 2 hrs), **Bristol**, near Bath (1/hr, 2.5 hrs), **Cardiff** (1/hr, 2.5 hrs), **Holyhead** (nearly 1/hr, 2.25 hrs), **Blackpool** (4/day, 2.5 hrs, more frequent with transfer in Preston), **Keswick**, the Lake District (1 train/hr, 1.75 hrs to Penrith, then catch a bus to Keswick, 1/hr except Sun 6/day, 40 min), **Glasgow** (nearly 1/hr, 3.5 hrs).

## Ferry Connections—North Wales and Ireland
**Holyhead and Dun Laoghaire:** Stena Line sails between Holyhead (North Wales) and Dun Laoghaire near Dublin (4/day, 2 hrs on *HSS Catamaran*, £30 one-way walk-on fare, reserve by phone—they book up long in advance on summer weekends, Dun Laoghaire tel. 01/204-7777, Holyhead tel. 01407/606-666, general reservations number for Stena Lines in Britain: 08705-707-070, can book online at www.stenaline.ie).

**Holyhead and Dublin:** Irish Ferries sail between Holyhead (North Wales) and Dublin (5/day—2 slow, 3 fast; slow boats-3.25 hrs, £22 one-way walk-on fare; fast boats-2 hrs, £28; car fares prohibitively expensive, Holyhead tel. 08705-329-129, Dublin tel. 01/661-0511, www.irishferries.ie).

**Sleeping near Holyhead dock:** The fine **Monravon B&B** has nine smoke-free rooms (Db-£40, CC, family deals, 10-min walk from dock, Porth-Y-Felin Road, LL65 1PL, tel. & fax 01407/762-944, www.monravon.co.uk, e-mail: len@monravon.co.uk).

## Route Tips for Drivers
**Ironbridge Gorge to Ruthin:** Drive for an hour to Wales via A5 through Shrewsbury, crossing into Wales and following the A5 to Llangollen. Cross the bridge in Llangollen, turn left, and follow A542 and A525 past the romantic Valle Crucis abbey, over the scenic Horseshoe Pass, and into Ruthin. Driving to Conwy is faster via Wrexham and then the A55, but more scenic if you stay on the A5 from Llangollen to Betws-y-Coed and then zip north to Conwy from there.

**Ruthin to Caernarfon (56 miles) to Blaenau (34 miles) to Ruthin (35 miles):** This route connects the top sights with the most scenic routes. From Ruthin take B5105 (steepest road off main square) and follow signs to Cerrigydrudion. Then follow

A5 into Betws-y-Coed, with a possible quick detour to the Trefriw Woolen Mill (5 miles north on B5106, well signposted). Climb west on A5 through Capel Curig, then take A4086 over the rugged Pass of Llanberis, under the summit of Mount Snowdon (to the south, behind those clouds), and on to Caernarfon. Park under the castle in the harborside car park (£2.20).

Leaving Caernarfon, take the lovely A4085 southeast through Beddgelert to Penrhyndeudraeth. (Make things even more beautiful by taking the little B4410 road from Garreg through Rhyd.) Then take A487 toward What Maentwrog and A496 to Blaenau Ffestiniog. Go through the dark and depressing mining town of Blaenau Ffestiniog on A470, continue over hills of slate, and turn right into the Llechwedd Slate Mine.

After the mine, continue uphill on A470, snapping photos north through Dolwyddelan (passing a fine old Welsh castle ruin) and back to A5. For a high and desolate detour, return to Ruthin via the curvy A543 road. Go over the stark moors to the Sportsman's Arms Pub (the highest pub in Wales, good food), continue through Denbigh, and then go home.

# BLACKPOOL

This is Britain's fun puddle. It's England's most-visited attraction, the private domain of its working class, a faded and sticky mix of Coney Island, Las Vegas, and Woolworth's. Juveniles of any age love it. My kids declared it better than Disneyland.

Blackpool grew up with the Industrial Revolution. In the mid-1800s entire mill towns would close down and take a two-week break in Blackpool. They came to drink in the fresh air (much needed after a hard year in the mills) and—literally—the seawater. Back then they figured this was healthy.

Blackpool's heydays are past now, as more and more working people can afford the cheap charter flights to sunny Spain. Recently, the resort has become popular for "stag" and "hen" (bachelor and bachelorette) parties—basically a cheap drunk weekend for the twenty-something crowd. Consequently, the late-night ambience suffers. Still, this is an accessible and affordable fun zone for the Anne and Andy Capps of northern England. People come year after year. They stay for a week, and they love it.

Most Americans don't even consider a stop in Blackpool. Many won't like it. It's an ears-pierced-while-you-wait, tipsy-toupee kind of place. Tacky, yes. Lowbrow, OK. But it's as English as can be, and that's what you're here for. An itinerary should feature as many facets of a culture as possible. Blackpool is as English as the queen—and considerably more fun.

Spend the day "muckin' about" the beach promenade of for-tune-tellers, fish-and-chips joints, amusement piers, warped mir-rors, and Englanders wearing hats with built-in ponytails. A million greedy doors try every trick to get you inside. Huge arcade halls advertise free toilets and broadcast bingo numbers into the streets; the wind machine under a wax Marilyn Monroe blows at a steady gale; and the smell of fries, tobacco, and sugar is everywhere. Milk comes in raspberry or banana in this land where people under incredibly bad wigs look normal. If you're bored in Blackpool, you're just too classy.

## Planning Your Time

Ideally, get to Blackpool around lunchtime for a free afternoon and evening of making bubbles in this cultural mud puddle. For full effect, it's best to visit Blackpool during its peak season: June through early November. Blackpool's Illuminations (Aug 30–Nov 3 in 2002), when much of the waterfront is decorated with lights, draws crowds, particularly on weekends. The early evening light is great with the sun setting over the sea. Walk out along the peaceful North Pier at twilight.

Blackpool is easy by car or train. Speed demons with a car can treat it as a midday break (it's just off the M6 on M55) and continue north. If you have kids, they'll want more time here (hey, it's cheaper than Disneyland). If you're into nightlife, this town delivers. If you're before or beyond kids and not into kitsch and greasy spoons, skip it. If the weather's great and you love nature, the lakes are just a few hours north. A visit to Blackpool does sharpen the wonders of Windermere.

## Orientation (area code: 01253)

Everything clusters along the six-mile beachfront promenade, a tacky, glittering goodtime strip mall punctuated by three fun-filled piers reaching out into the sea. The Pleasure Beach rides are near the South Pier. Jutting up near the North Pier is Blackpool's stubby Eiffel-type tower. The most interesting shops, eateries, and theaters are inland from the North Pier. For a break from glitz, you can hike north along the waterfront path for 20 miles or so.

**Tourist Information:** There are two TIs near the tower. The main one is on Clifton Street (April–early Nov Mon–Sat 9:00–17:00, early Nov–March Mon–Sat 9:00–16:30 and closed Sun, tel. 01253/ 478-222, the same number gives recorded entertainment info after hours). The other TI is on the Promenade (June–early Nov daily 9:00–17:00, closed off-season). Get the city map (£1), pick up brochures on the amusement centers, and ask about special shows. The TIs do same-day room bookings for one-night stays for a £2 fee.

For a history fix, get the TI's *Heritage Trail* booklet, which takes you on an hour's walk through downtown Blackpool. Saying much about little, it's endearing (60p).

**Arrival in Blackpool:** The train station is just three blocks from the town center (no maps given but one is posted, no ATM in station but many in town). While the station has no luggage lockers, nearby hotels offer the service. The motorway funnels you down Yeadon Way into a giant parking zone (formerly the central station).

# Blackpool

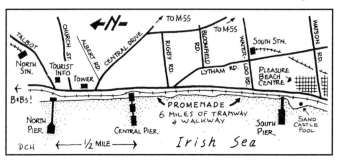

## Helpful Hints

**Internet Access:** Check e-mail or surf the Net at O'Brien's Café on Birley Street or Café Net at Deansgate 16 (between TI and train station).

**Post Office:** The main P.O. is on Abingdon Street, a block inland from the TI (Mon–Sat 9:00–17:30, closed Sun).

**Markets:** At the work-a-day Abingdon Market, vendors sell fruit, bras, jewelry, eggs, and more (Mon–Sat 9:00–17:30, also Sun 10:00–16:00 during season, on Abingdon Street next to P.O.). The Fleetwood Market, eight miles north, is huge, with two buildings full of produce, clothes, and crafts spilling out into the street (May–Oct daily 9:00–17:00 except Wed and Sun, Nov–April Tue, Fri, Sat only; catch trolley marked Fleetwood, 30 min, £1.80 one-way).

**Car Rental:** In case you decide to tour the Lake District by car, you'll find plenty of rental agencies in Blackpool, including Avis (292 Waterloo Road, tel. 01253/408-003), Budget (434 Waterloo Road, tel. 01253/691-632), and Eurocar (181 Clifton Drive, tel. 01232/404-021).

## Getting around Blackpool

Vintage trolley cars run 13 miles up and down the waterfront, connecting all the sights. This first electric tramway in Europe dates from 1885 (90p-£2, depending on length of trip, £4.50 for all-day pass, pay conductor, trolleys come every 5 min or so, Nov–May every 10–20 min, runs 06:00–24:00). Taxis are easy to snare in Blackpool and three to five people travel cheaper by cab than by trolley. Hotels can get a taxi by phone within three minutes (no extra charge).

## Sights—Blackpool

▲▲**The Piers**—Blackpool's famous piers were originally built for Victorian landlubbers who wanted to go to sea but were afraid of getting seasick. Each of the three amusement piers has a personality and is a joy to wander. The sedate North Pier is most traditional and refreshingly uncluttered. Dance down its empty planks at twilight to the early English rock on its speakers. Its Carousel Bar at the end is great for families—with a free kids' DJ nightly from 19:00–23:00 (parents drink good beer while the kids bunny-hop and boogie). The something-for-everyone Central Pier is lots of fun. Ride its great Ferris wheel for the best view in Blackpool (rich photography at twilight, get the operator to spin you as you bottom out). And check out the masochist running the adjacent Waltzer ride—just watch the miserably ecstatic people spinning. The rollicking South Pier is all rides. From the far end of any pier you can see the natural gas drilling platforms lining the horizon.

▲**Blackpool Tower**—This mini–Eiffel Tower is a vertical fun center over 100 years old. You pay £10 to get in; after that, the fun is free. Work your way up from the bottom through layer after layer of noisy entertainment: circus (2–3 acts/day generally at 15:00 and 19:30), Out of This World, Dinosaurland, an aquarium, and a wonderful old ballroom with barely live music and golden oldies dancing to golden oldies all day. Enjoy a break at the dance-floor-level pub or on a balcony perch. Kids love this place. With a little marijuana, adults would, too. Ride the elevator to the tip of the 500-foot-tall symbol of Blackpool for a smashing view, especially at sunset (Easter-May daily 10:00–18:00, June–early Nov daily 10:00–23:00, early Nov–Easter 10:00–18:00 weekends only, top of tower closed when windy, CC, tel. 01253/622-242). If you want to leave and return, request a hand stamp.

▲**Pleasure Beach**—These 42 acres, littered with over 100 rides (including "the best selection of white-knuckle rides in Europe"), ice-skating, circus and illusion shows, and amusements, attract 7 million people a year. The top two rides are The Pepsi Max Big One (one of the world's fastest and highest roller coasters at 235 feet, 85 mph) and Ice Blast (which rockets you straight up before letting you bungee down). Also memorable are the Pasaje del Terror and the Steeple Chase—carousel horses stampeding down a roller-coaster track. The latest ride, Valhalla, zips you on a Viking boat in watery darkness past scary Nordic things like lutefisk. With two 80-foot drops and lots of hype, first you're scared, then you're soaked, and—finally—you're just glad you survived. Most of the rides are variations on the roller-coaster theme. Pleasure Beach medics advise brittle senior travelers to avoid the old wooden-framed rides, which are much jerkier. Only the admission is free. You can pay individually for rides (most are a couple of pounds each), buy a 12-ride £24 package (which can be split among a group but doesn't cover the Pepsi Max Big One), or get unlimited rides with a £25 armband (mid-April–early Nov daily, opens at around 10:30 and closes as early as 17:00 or as late as 24:00, depending on season, weather, and demand, tel. 0870-444-5566).

There are several other major amusement centers, including a popular water park called Sand Castle (across the street from Pleasure Beach, £4, big pool, wave machine, long slides, open until 17:30, tel. 01253/343-602).

▲▲▲**People Watching**—Blackpool's top sight is its people. You'll see England here as nowhere else. Grab someone's hand and a big stick of "rock" (candy) and stroll. Grown men walk around with huge teddies looking for "bowlingo" places. Ponder the thought of actually retiring here and spending your last years, day after day, surrounded by Blackpool and wearing a hat with a built-in ponytail. Blackpool puts people in a talkative mood. Ask someone to explain the difference between tea and supper. Back at your B&B, join in the lounge chat sessions.

▲**Showtime**—Blackpool always has a few razzle-dazzle music, dancing-girl, racy-humor, magic, and tumbling shows. Box offices around town can give you a rundown on what's available (tickets £7–15). Your B&B has the latest. For something more highbrow, try the Opera House for musicals (tel. 01253/292-029) and the Grand Theatre for drama and ballet (tel. 01253/290-190). Both are on Church Street, a couple of blocks behind the tower. For the latest in evening entertainment, see the window display at the tourist office on Clifton Street.

▲▲**Funny Girls**—Blackpool's current hot bar is just a block in from the North Pier. Every night from 20:30 to 23:30 Funny Girls puts on a "glam bam thank you ma'am" burlesque-in-drag show that delights footballers and grannies alike. Cover is only £3 (£4.50 on weekends). Get your drinks at the bar unless the transvestites are dancing on it. The show, while racy, is not raunchy. The music is very loud. The crowd is young, old, straight, gay, very down-to-earth, and fun-loving. Go on a weeknight; Friday and Saturday are too jammed. While the area up front can be a mosh pit, there are more sedate tables in back where service comes with a vampish smile. You can pay £10 for VIP seats to avoid any weekend lines and look down on the show and crowded floor from a mezzanine level (must be 18 to enter, to reserve tel. 01253/624-901).

Blackpool's **clubs and discos** are cheap, with live bands and an interesting crowd (nightly 22:00–02:00). With all the stag and hen parties, the late-night streets are clotted with rude rowdies.

The pubs of Blackpool have a unique tradition of "and your own, luv." Say that here and your barmaid will add 20p to your bill and drop it into her tip jar. (Say it anywhere else and they won't know what you mean.)

▲**Illuminations**—Blackpool was the first town in England to "go electric" in 1879. Now, every fall (Aug 30–Nov 3 in 2002), Blackpool stretches its tourist season by illuminating its six miles of waterfront with countless lights, all blinking and twinkling. The American in me kept saying, "I've seen bigger, and I've seen better," but I filled his mouth with cotton candy and just had some simple fun like everyone else on my specially-decorated tram. Look for the animated tableaux on North Shore.

## Sleeping in Blackpool
**(£1 = about $1.50, country code: 44, area code: 01253)**
Sleep Code: **S** = Single, **D** = Double/Twin, **T** = Triple, **Q** = Quad, **b** = bathroom, **s** = shower only, **CC** = Credit Cards accepted, **no CC** = Credit Cards not accepted.

Blackpool's 140,000 people provide 120,000 beds in 3,500 mostly dumpy, cheap, nondescript hotels and B&Bs. Remember, the town's in the business of accommodating the people who can't afford to go to Spain. Most have the same design—minimal character, maximum number of springy beds—and charge £15 to £20 per person. Empty beds abound except from September through November and summer weekends. It's only really tight on Illumination weekends. I've listed regular high-season prices. With the huge number of hotels in town, prices get really soft in the off-season. And everyone bumps things up during the Illuminations. There's usually a launderette within a five-minute walk of your B&B; ask your host or hostess.

### Sleeping North of the Tower
These listings are on or near the waterfront in the quiet area they call "the posh end," a mile or two north of the tower, with easy parking and easy access to the center by trolley.

**Robin Hood Hotel** is a super place, cheery and family-run, with a big, welcoming living room and 10 tastefully-refurbished, spacious rooms with big beds (Sb-£20.50, Db-£37, family deals, CC, entirely nonsmoking, trolley stop: St. Stevens Avenue and walk 1 block north; 1.5 miles north of tower across from a peaceful stretch of beach, 100 Queens Promenade, North Shore FY2 9NS, tel. 01253/351-599, www.robinhoodhotel.co.uk). Your hosts, Tony and Barbara, enjoy hanging out with their guests in their fine lounge after dinner.

**Prefect Hotel** is all smiles and pink-flamingo pretty. Its 13 rooms are older but clean, with fun touches—ask to see Bill's amazing shoe collection. The double beds are small. Twin rooms are bigger for the same price. You can't miss the painted parking lot (Sb-£18, Db-£36, CC, smoking allowed but not in breakfast room, trolley stop: Bispham, 2 miles north of tower at 204 Queens Promenade, FY2 9JS, tel. 01253/352-699, www.chesbyte.co.uk/hotel, run with warmth by Bill and Pauline Acton).

**Beechcliffe Private Hotel** is clean, smoke-free, and family-run, with more charm than average and cute but tight rooms (S-£15.50, D-£31, no CC, they can pick up from station if arranged in advance; trolley stop: Uncle Tom's, walk a block away from

## Blackpool Center

1. VALENTINE PRIVATE HOTEL
2. TO HOTELS NORTH OF THE TOWER
3. HARRY RAMSDEN'S FISH & CHIPS
4. ROBERT'S OYSTER BAR
5. MITRE BAR
6. IL CORSARO REST.
7. KWIZEEN REST.
8. SEPTEMBER BRASSERIE
9. MARKS & SPENCER SUPERMARKET
10. FUNNY GIRLS

the beach, 16 Shaftesbury Avenue, North Shore FY2 9QQ, tel. 01253/353-075, www.thebeechcliffehotel.co.uk, Harry and Lesley).

I know, staying at the **Hilton Hotel** in Blackpool is like wearing a tux to eat a falafel. But if you need a splurge, this is a grand place with lots of views, a pool, sauna, kids' playground, and comfortable rooms (Db-£106, "club deal Db"—£126 with lots of extras including a nice view of the sea, ask if there are any "special rates" being advertised, request room with view—no extra charge, includes breakfast, CC, nonsmoking rooms, trolley stop: Stakis Hotel, North Promenade, FY1 2JQ, tel. 01253/623-434, fax 01253/627-864, www.hilton.com).

### Sleeping near the Train Station

**Valentine Private Hotel** is a handy and friendly 13-room place. Smoking is allowed, but the breakfast room is smoke-free (Db-£32, CC, bunky family deals, 1 kid sleeps free, 3 blocks from station, with back to tracks, exit station far right, go up Springfield 3 blocks to Dickson, 35 Dickson Road, FY1 2AT, tel. & fax 01253/622-775, Denise and Garry Hinchliffe).

## Eating in Blackpool

Your hotel may serve a cheap, early-evening meal. Generally, food in the tower and along the promenade is terrible. The following places are all between the tower and the North Pier.

**"World Famous" Harry Ramsden's** is *the* place for mushy peas, good fish and chips, and a chance to get goofy with waiters—call the place *Henry* Ramsden's (£4–8, order a side of mushy peas, daily 11:30–22:00, 60 The Promenade, tel. 01253/294-386).

**Robert's Oyster Bar** is a fixture that actually predates the resort—as do some of its employees. Read the plaque on the outside wall. You can take out or eat in—just point to what looks good (daily 9:30–22:00, at the corner of West Street and the Promenade, 1 block south of North Pier, tel. 01253/621-226).

The **Mitre Bar** serves light lunches and beers in a truly rare old-time Blackpool ambience. Drop in anytime to survey the great photos of old Blackpool and for the great people scene (daily 11:00–23:00, around corner from Oyster Bar on West Street).

Clifton Street is lined with decent eateries: Indian, Chinese and Italian. **Il Corsaro** takes its Italian cooking seriously (nightly 18:00–23:00, 36 Clifton Street, tel. 01253/627440).

When pressed to recommend the best places in town, locals like **Kwizeen**, a bistro which serves good Mediterranean and modern English "kwizeen" in a—refreshing for Blackpool—plain atmosphere (£10 main courses, Mon–Sat from 18:00, closed Sun, 47 King Street, tel. 01253/290-045); and **September Brasserie**, which requires reservations and serves traditional and modern English in a dressy second-floor location (£19 3-course dinners, 15 Queen Street, tel. 01253/23282).

**Marks & Spencer** has a big supermarket in its basement (Mon–Sat 9:00–17:30, Sun 10:30–16:30, near recommended eateries, on Coronation Street and Church Street). Picnic at the beach.

## Transportation Connections—Blackpool

If you're heading to (or from) Blackpool by train, you'll usually need to transfer at **Preston** (3/hr, 30 min). Train info: tel. 08457-484-950.

**Preston to: Keswick**, the Lake District (hrly trains, 30 min to Penrith, then catch a bus to Keswick, 1/hr except Sun 6/day, 40 min), **Edinburgh** (8/day, 3 hrs).

**Points south:** To **Moreton-in-Marsh** in the Cotswolds (every 2 hrs, 5 hrs, 2 transfers), **Bath** (1/hr, 5 hrs, 2 transfers), **Conwy** in North Wales (nearly hrly, 3 hrs, 2 transfers). Although you'll usually have transfers, sometimes you'll find fast and frequent trains. Some trains go direct from **Blackpool** to: **London** (1/day, 4 hrs), **Liverpool** (every 2 hrs, 1.5 hrs), **York** (1/hr, 3.25 hrs).

**Drivers entering and leaving Blackpool:** As you approach Blackpool, the motorway dumps you right onto Yeadon Way, which funnels you into a huge city parking lot. Daytrippers need to park here. Leaving, to go anywhere, follow signs to M55, which starts at Blackpool and zips you to the M6 (for points north or south).

# NEAR BLACKPOOL: LIVERPOOL

Liverpool, a gritty but surprisingly enjoyable city, is a fascinating stop for Beatles fans and those who would like to look urban England straight in its eyes.

**Tourist Information:** One of Liverpool's TIs is in the midst of most of the sights—on the huge, tidy Albert Dock (daily 10:00–17:30, tel. 0151/708-8854). Get a free, small map (also available at station for £1). In summer, guided hour-long city walking tours leave from another TI on Queen Square (£3, mid-June–Sept daily at 11:00, also Sun at 14:00 year-round, tel. 0151/652-3692 for schedule; TI tel. 0151/709-8111).

**Arrival in Liverpool:** From the train station to the dock, it's a 20-minute walk or short ride on a bus (#1), taxi (£3), or metro (get off at James Street). When returning to the center from the dock, it's best to walk or take the bus (since the metro makes a long loop before returning to the station). Luggage storage at the station costs £2 (daily 7:00–22:00).

**Market:** On Sunday, Heritage Market transforms Stanley Dock into a commotion of clothes, fruits, veggies, sweets, and furniture (9:30–16:00).

## Planning Your Time

Here's an easy day plan: From the station, take the metro to Albert Dock. At the dock, choose among museums, shops, cafés, and the Beatles' Story. Consider a 50-minute ferry cruise on the river (departs Mersey Ferry dock, a 5-min walk from Albert Dock). Then walk back to the station, stopping at Mathew Street if you're a Beatles fan and browsing the central pedestrian core (Church Street, Williamson Square, and more) on the way. You'll have seen the art and the heart of the city.

## Sights—Liverpool's Albert Dock

Opened in 1852 by Prince Albert and enclosing seven acres of water, Albert Dock is surrounded by five-story brick warehouses. In its day, Liverpool was England's greatest seaport. It prospered as one corner of the triangular commerce of the 18th-century slave trade. As England's economy boomed, so did the port of Liverpool. From 1830 to 1930, 9 million emigrants sailed from Liverpool to find their dreams in the New World. But the port was not deep enough for the big new ships; trade declined after 1890, and by 1972 it was closed entirely. Like Liverpool itself, the docks have enjoyed a renaissance, and today they are the featured attraction of the city. The city's main attractions are lined up here out of the rain and padded by lots of shopping mall–type distractions (daily 10:00–17:30, tel. 0151/708-8838). There's plenty of parking.

▲**Merseyside Maritime Museum**—This museum, which tells the story of this once-prosperous shipping center, gets an A for effort but feels designed for visiting school groups. While the ships section is pretty dull, the slavery, smuggling, customs, and emigration sections are interesting. The associated **Museum of Liverpool Life** offers a good look at the town's story (free, daily 10:00–17:00, check events board upon arrival).

**Tate Gallery Liverpool**—This prestigious gallery of modern art is next to the Maritime Museum. It won't entertain you as well as its London sister, but if you're into modern art, any Tate's great (free, Tue–Sun 10:00–18:00, closed Mon, tel. 0151/702-7400).

▲**The Beatles Story**—It's sad to think the Beatles are stuck in a museum (and Ringo's in reruns of *Shining Time Station*). While overpriced and not very creative, the story's a great one, and even an avid fan will pick up some new information (£8, daily 10:00–18:00, until 17:00 in winter, CC, tel. 0151/709-1963). The shop is an impressive pile of Beatles buyables. For more on the Beatles, see "Beatle Tours," below.

## More Sights—Liverpool

**Ferry Cruise**—Mersey Ferries offer narrated cruises departing from Mersey Dock, an easy five-minute walk from Albert Dock. The cruise makes two brief stops on the other side of the river; you can hop off and catch the next boat back (£3.75, year-round, Mon–Fri 10:00–15:00, Sat–Sun 10:00–18:00, leaves at top of hr, café, WCs on board, tel. 0151/639-0609).

**Beatles Tours**—Die-hard Beatles fans may want to invest a couple of hours taking the Beatles "Magical Mystery" bus tour, which hits the lads' homes, Penny Lane, and so on (£11, 2 hrs, generally departing 12:30 and 15:00). The TI has specifics on the big bus that goes daily.

For something more extensive, fun, and intimate, consider a three-hour minibus Beatles tour from Phil Hughes. It's longer because it includes information on historic Liverpool as well as the Beatles stuff (£11/person, minimum £65/group, includes free beverages and 2-for-1 coupons to Beatles Story, 8-seat minibus, tel. & fax 0151/228-4565, cellular 07961-511-223, www.tourliverpool.co.uk).

The "sights" each tour covers are basically houses where the Fab Four grew up, places they performed, and spots made famous by the lyrics of their hits ("Penny Lane," "Strawberry Fields," the Eleanor Rigby graveyard, etc.). While perfectly boring to anyone not into the Beatles, fans will enjoy the commentary and seeing the shelter on the roundabout, the fire station with the clean machine, and the barber who shaves another customer.

▲**Mathew Street**—Beatles fans will want to explore Mathew

Street (a 15-min walk into the center from Albert Dock), including the famous Cavern Club, the new Cavern Club nearby, a statue of the young John Lennon, and the Beatles Shop at #31.

## Sleeping in Liverpool
**(£1 = about $1.50, country code: 44, area code: 0151)**
You can sleep on Albert Dock at **Holiday Inn Express**, which has 117 comfortable, American-style rooms, with great harbor views and bits of the original brick warehouse arches and walls (Db-£63, £70 Fri–Sat, includes breakfast, CC, best to book at least a week ahead, next to Beatles' Story, Albert Dock, tel. 0151/709-1133, fax 0151/709-1144, e-mail: liverpool@premierhotels.co.uk). **Henry's Premier Lodge**, older and more central, is a budget hotel with 39 decent rooms that could use sprucing up (Db-£46, up to 2 adults and 2 kids OK, breakfast-£4–6, CC, parallel to Mathew Street, 5-min walk from station, 45 Victoria Street, tel. 0870/700-1422, fax 0870/700-1423).

## Transportation Connections—Liverpool
**By train to: Blackpool** (every 2 hrs, 1.5 hrs, more frequent with transfer at Preston), **York** (1/hr, 2.5 hrs), **Edinburgh** (7/day, 4 hrs, can involve transfer), **London** (1/hr, 2.5 hrs), **Crewe** (18/day, 45 min), **Chester** (2/hr, 45 min). Train info: tel. 08457-484-950.

**By ferry to Dublin, Ireland:** Merchant Ferries sails most mornings (Tue–Sat) and every evening year-round (8 hrs, £30 one-way day crossing, £35 one-way overnight, cabins-£30 extra, can carry cars, British tel. 0870/600-4321, Dublin tel. 01/819-2999, www.merchant-ferries.com).

## Route Tips for Drivers
**Ruthin to Blackpool via Liverpool:** From Ruthin, follow signs to Mold, then Queensferry, then Manchester M56, then Liverpool M53, which tunnels under Mersey River (£1). In Liverpool, follow signs to City Center and Albert Dock, where you'll find a huge car park at the dock. Leaving Liverpool, drive north along the waterfront, following signs to M58 (Preston). Once on M58 (and not before), follow signs to M6, and then M55 into Blackpool.

**Ruthin to Blackpool (100 miles):** From Ruthin, take A494 through the town of Mold and follow the blue signs to the motorway. M56 zips you to M6, where you'll turn north toward Preston and Lancaster. Don't miss your turnoff. A few minutes after Preston, take the not-very-clearly signed next exit (#32, M55) into Blackpool and drive as close as you can to the stubby Eiffel-type tower in the town center. Downtown parking is terrible. If you're not spending the day, head for one of the huge £6/day garages. If you're spending the night, drive to the waterfront and head north. My top B&Bs are north on the promenade (easy parking).

# LAKE DISTRICT

In the pristine Lake District, Wordsworth's poems still shiver in trees and ripple on ponds. This is a land where nature rules and man keeps a wide-eyed but low profile. Relax, recharge, take a cruise or a hike, and maybe even write a poem. Renew your poetic license at Wordsworth's famous Dove Cottage.

The Lake District, about 30 miles long and 30 miles wide, is nature's lush, green playground. Explore it by foot, bike, bus, or car. While not impressive in sheer height (Scafell Pike, the tallest peak in England, is only 3,206 feet), there's a walking-stick charm about the way nature and the local culture mix. Walking along a windblown ridge or climbing over a rock fence to look into the eyes of a raga-muffin sheep, even tenderfeet get a chance to feel very outdoorsy.

You'll probably have rain mixed with brilliant bright spells. Drizzly days can be followed by delightful evenings. Pubs offer atmospheric shelter at every turn. As the locals are fond of saying, "There's no such thing as bad weather, only unsuitable clothing."

While the south lakes (Windermere, Bowness, Beatrix Potter's cottage) get the promotion and tour crowds and are closer to London, the north lakes (Ullswater, Derwentwater, Buttermere) are less touristy and at least as scenic.

The town of Keswick, the lake called Derwentwater, and the vast time-passed Newlands Valley will be our focus. The area works great by car or by train or bus. And Wordsworth and Potter fans can easily side trip south to see the authors' homes.

## Planning Your Time
On a three-week trip in Britain, I'd spend two days and two nights in the area. The quickest way in is to leave the motorway or train line at Penrith.

Those without a car will use Keswick as a springboard. Cruise the lake and take one of the many hikes in the Cat Bells area. Nonhikers can take a minibus tour.

Here's the most exciting way for drivers to pack their day of arrival: Get an early start from Blackpool or North Wales, leave the motorway at Kendal by 10:30, drive along Windermere and through Ambleside, 11:30–Tour Dove Cottage, 12:30–Backtrack to Ambleside, where a small road leads up and over the dramatic Kirkstone Pass (far more scenic northbound than southbound, get out and bite the wind) and down to Glenridding on Ullswater. You could catch the 14:55 boat. Hike six miles (15:30–18:45) from Howtown back to Glenridding. Drive to your farmhouse B&B near Keswick, with a stop as the sun sets at Castlerigg Stone Circle.

On your second day, explore Buttermere Lake, drive over Honister Pass, explore Derwentwater, and do the Cat Bells High Ridge walk. Spend the evening at the same B&B.

If great scenery is commonplace in your life, the Lake District can be more soothing (and rainy) than exciting. If you're rushed, you could make this area a one-night stand—or even a quick drive-through.

## Getting around the Lake District

Those based in Keswick without a car can manage fine. Be sure to pick up the excellent *Lakeland Explorer* magazine (free from TIs and some hotels), which explains all the local bus and boat schedules and outlines some great walks for the first-time visitor.

**By Foot:** Piles of hiking information are available everywhere you turn. Consider buying a detailed map (such as the various Ordnance Survey maps, £6–11, sold at Keswick TI). For easy hikes, the fliers at TIs and B&Bs describing particular routes are helpful. The best ridge walk is immediately outside of town (see "Cat Bells High Ridge Hike," below). The Lake District's TIs advise hikers to check the weather before setting out (for an up-to-date weather report, ask at TI or tel. 017687/75757), wear suitable clothing, and bring a map.

**By Boat:** A circular boat service glides you easily around Derwentwater (for a sail/hike option, see "Derwentwater," below).

**By Bus:** Buses take you quickly and easily (if not always frequently) to all nearby points of interest. Stop by the TI for a free, 30-page *Lakeland Explorer* bus brochure for schedules and suggested bus/hike outings. Lakeland Explorer bus passes (4-day £15 passes) are sold at the TI and the Keswick post office (April–Sept Mon–Sat 8:30–17:30, Sun 10:30–16:00, less off-season, just off main square at corner of Main and Bank Streets). Purchase £6.50 one-day passes on the bus.

**By Bus Tour:** Mountain Goat Tours runs an interesting variety of minibus tours from Keswick (£15/half-day, £26 all-day

# Lake District

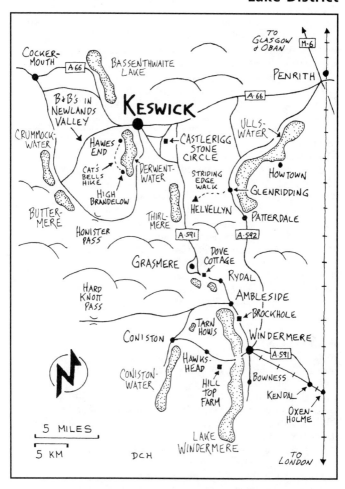

TO GLASGOW & OBAN
M·6
PENRITH
COCKERMOUTH
A·66
BASSENTHWAITE LAKE
A·66
**KESWICK**
B&B's IN NEWLANDS VALLEY
ULLSWATER
CRUMMOCKWATER
HAWES END
CASTLERIGG STONE CIRCLE
CAT'S BELLS HIKE
DERWENTWATER
STRIDING EDGE WALK
HOWTOWN
HIGH BRANDELOW
HELVELLYN
GLENRIDDING
BUTTERMERE
THIRLMERE
PATTERDALE
HONISTER PASS
A·591
A·592
GRASMERE
DOVE COTTAGE
RYDAL
HARD KNOTT PASS
AMBLESIDE
BROCKHOLE
TARN HOWS
CONISTON
WINDERMERE
A·591
HAWKSHEAD
CONISTONWATER
HILL TOP FARM
BOWNESS
KENDAL
OXENHOLME
5 MILES
5 KM
DCH
LAKE WINDERMERE
TO LONDON
N

tour includes admission to either a sight or 30-min lake cruise during tour, daily Easter-Oct). The tours are informative, off the beaten path, led by local guides, and great for people with bucks who'd like to see the area without hiking or messing with public transport (office at Keswick central car park, Mon–Sat 8:30–17:30, Sun 9:00–14:30, phone answered until 20:30, smart to book 1 day ahead, CC, tel. & fax 017687/73962, www.mountain-goat.com). Mountain Goat's head office in Windermere offers similar tours at the same prices (tel. 015394/45161).

The National Trust offers more sedate, less expensive, week-day-only tours with an emphasis on conservation (£11/half day, £21/full day, April–Oct, book at TI or NT office between town theater and Keswick boat dock, Mon–Tue 9:15–17:30, Wed–Fri 9:15–18:30, Sat–Sun 10:15–18:30, CC, tel. 017687/73780, www.nationaltrust.org.uk).

As a super-cheap alternative to tours, take a round-trip on bus #77 from Keswick to Buttermere and back; it loops around Honister Pass (£5.35, May–Oct, 4/day clockwise, 4/day "anti-clockwise," 1.5 hrs, bus info: tel. 0870-608-2608).

**By Bike:** Several shops rent bikes in Keswick; Keswick Mountain Bikes has the largest selection (£13/day, daily 9:00–17:30, Oct–March closed Tue, includes helmet, tandems available, guided bike tours by request, CC, Southey Hill Trading Estate past Pencil Museum, tel. 017687/75202, www.keswickbikes.co.uk). Keswick Mountain Bikes and the TI sell cycling maps (£1–3).

**By Car:** Nothing is very far from Keswick and Derwentwater. Get a good map, get off the big roads, and leave the car, at least occasionally, for some walking. In summer, the Keswick-Ambleside-Windermere-Bowness corridor (A591) suffers from congestion. If you want to rent a car in Keswick, Fiat is your only choice (from £34/day, Mon–Sat 8:30–17:30, closed Sun, CC, only ages 25–70, must have U.S. license and passport, Lake Road in town center, tel. 017687/72064, e-mail: aftersales.keswickmotorcompany .53807@fiatuk.net).

# KESWICK

As far as touristy Lake District centers go, Keswick (KEZZ-ick, pop. 5,000) is far more enjoyable than Windermere, Bowness, or Ambleside. An important mining center (slate, copper, lead) through the Middle Ages, Keswick became a resort in the 19th century. Its fine Victorian buildings recall those romantic days when city slickers first learned about "communing with nature." Today the compact town is lined with tearooms, pubs, gift shops, and hiking-gear shops. The lake is a pleasant five-minute walk from the town center.

Keswick is the ideal home base: plenty of good B&Bs (see "Sleeping," below), an easy bus connection to the nearest train station at Penrith, and a prime location near the best lake in the area, Derwentwater. In Keswick everything is within a five-minute walk of everything else: the pedestrian market square, the TI, recommended B&Bs, a grocery store, the municipal pitch-and-putt golf course, the bus stop, the Mountain Goat minibus tour starting point, a lakeside boat dock, the post office (with Internet access), and a central car park. Saturday is market day, and the town square is packed and lively.

Keswick hosts an annual convention in July that books up a lot of rooms. Reserve well in advance if you plan to visit in July.

**Tourist Information:** The helpful TI is in Moot Hall right in the middle of the main square (daily 9:30–17:30, Nov–Easter 9:30–16:30, tel. 017687/72645, www.lake-district.gov.uk). The staff books rooms (free) and are pros at advising you about hiking routes and helping figure out public transportation to outlying sights. The bookstore has fine books and maps for hikers, cyclists, and drivers. The TI also sells great brochures outlining nearby hikes (60p–£1, including a 50p Keswick Town Trail for history buffs), tickets to the town theater and Mountain Goat and National Trust minibus tours, Lakeland Explorer bus passes (see "Getting around the Lake District," above), and discounted Derwentwater Launch tickets (£4.20; £5.20 at the lake). Check the What's On boards (inside TI's front vestibule and on outside wall at post-office end) for information about walks, talks, and entertainment. Pick up *Right Here, Right Now!*, a monthly events guide for the area. The TI posts a daily weather forecast just outside the front door. Pop upstairs for a series of short videos (free) about the history of Keswick and the Lake District.

**Internet Access:** U-Compute, a computer store above the post office, provides the cheapest Internet access (£2.35/hr, July–Sept Mon–Sat 8:30–20:00, Sun 9:30–16:30; Oct–June until 17:30, CC; head to staircase midway through building on the right, don't wait in P.O. queue, just off main square at corner of Main and Bank Streets, tel. 017687/75127).

## Sights—Keswick

▲▲**Daily Walks**—Walks of varying levels of difficulty led by local guides depart from the Keswick TI daily at 10:15, regardless of the weather (£5, Easter–Oct, bring a lunch; sometimes taxi, bus, or boat fare required; return by 17:00, meet at TI 10 min before departure, tel. 017687/72645). For a list of free daily guided walks offered throughout the Lake District by "Voluntary Wardens," check the *Events 2002* booklet at any local TI. Many of the hikes start at Brockhole National Park Visitors Centre, which is an easy bus ride or a short drive from Keswick, but usually two hikes a week originate in Keswick (on Sun and Wed afternoons, July–Sept).

▲**Pencil Museum**—Graphite was first discovered centuries ago in Keswick. A hunk of the stuff proved great for marking sheep in the 15th century, and the rest is history (which you can learn all about here). While you can't tour the 150-year-old factory where the famous Derwent pencils are made, the charming museum on the edge of Keswick is a good way to pass a rainy hour. Take a look at the "war pencils" made for WWII bomber crews (and filled with tiny maps and compasses) and the 25-foot pencil that took a crew of 15 four weeks to create. The pencil people are waiting to hear back from the Guinness people (£2.50, daily 9:30–16:00, until 17:30 July–Aug, free 20-min film is worthwhile, cheap brass rubbing in the shop, CC, tel. 017687/73626, www.pencils.co.uk).

▲**Plays**—Locals are proud of their Theatre by the Lake, which offers events year-round and plays comedy, drama, music, and dance almost nightly in the summer. This is a fine opportunity to do something completely local (£10–17, discounts for old and young, 20:00 shows in summer, 19:30 in winter, smart to book ahead July–Aug, parking £1.25/2 hrs but free after 19:00, CC, tel. 017687/74411, www.theatrebythelake.com).

▲**Golf**—A lush nine-hole pitch 'n' putt golf course separates the town from the lake and offers a classy, cheap, and convenient chance to golf near the birthplace of the sport (daily 9:30–20:00, £3 for 9 holes, £1.50 for 18 tame holes of "obstacle golf," tel. 017687/73445).

**Swimming**—The Leisure Center has an indoor pool kids love, with a huge water slide and wave machine (pool: £3.50-adults, £2.70-kids ages 3–16, cheaper in winter, Mon–Fri 9:00–21:00, Sat–Sun 10:00–18:00, shorter hrs off-season, no towels or suits for rent, lockers-50p deposit, a 10-min walk from town center, follow Station Road past Fitz Park and veer left, tel. 017687/72760).

**Fitz Park**—A pleasant grassy park stretches alongside Keswick's tree-lined, duck-filled River Greta. There's plenty of room for kids to burn off energy. Consider an after-dinner stroll on the footpath. You may catch men in white playing a game of cricket or lawn bowling.

## Sights—Derwentwater Area

**Derwentwater**—This is one of the region's most photographed and popular lakes. With four islands, good circular boat service, plenty of trails, and the pleasant town of Keswick at its north end, Derwentwater entertains.

The roadside views aren't much, so walk or cruise. You can walk around the lake (fine trail, floods in heavy rains, 9 miles, 3 hrs), cruise it (50 min), or do a hike/sail mix. I suggest the hike/sail combo. From mid-March to October, boats run from Keswick about every 30 minutes—alternating clockwise and "anticlockwise"—from 10:00 to 20:00 (at start and end of season until 15:30; in winter 5/day on weekends), making seven stops on each 50-minute round-trip. The boat trip costs £5.20 per circle (£4.20 if you book through TI), with free stopovers, or 80p per segment. Stand on the pier or the boat may not stop. The Keswick Launch also offers a 60-minute cruise every evening mid-June through September (£5.80, free glass of wine or soft drink, 20:30 May–mid-Aug, 19:30 mid-Aug–mid-Sept) and rents rowboats (£4/30 min; CC, located at town dock at the end of Lake Road, tel. 017687/72263).

# Keswick

① BERKELEY GUEST HOUSE

② PARKFIELD B&B, HOWE KELD LAKELAND HOTEL, & WEST VIEW GUEST HOUSE

③ STRANGER STREET B&Bs

④ MORREL'S RESTAURANT

⑤ MAYSONS RESTAURANT

⑥ THE FOUR IN HAND RESTAURANT

⑦ KITCHINS RESTAURANT & DOG & GUN PUB

⑧ BRYSON'S BAKERY

⑨ COFFEE LOUNGE

⑩ MOUNTAIN GOAT TOURS

⑪ THEATRE BY THE LAKE

⑫ NATIONAL TRUST TOURS

⑬ KESWICK LAUNCH CRUISES

P = PARKING LOTS

¼ MILE
400 METERS

The best hour-long lakeside walk is the 1.5-mile path between the docks at High Brandlehow and Hawse End. You could continue on foot along the lake back into Keswick. Lodore is an easy stop for its Lodore Falls, a 10-minute walk from the dock (falls behind Lodore Hotel, which serves lunch).

▲▲**Cat Bells High Ridge Hike**—For a great (and fairly easy)

"king of the mountain" feeling, sweeping views, and a close-up look at the weather blowing over the ridge, hike about two hours from Hawes End up along the ridge to Cat Bells (1,480 feet) and down to High Brandlehow. From there you can catch the boat or take the easy path along the shore of Derwentwater to your Hawes End starting point. This is probably the most dramatic family walk in the area (but wear sturdy shoes, bring a raincoat, and watch your footing). From Keswick, the lake, or your farmhouse B&B, you can see silhouetted stick figures hiking along this ridge. Drivers can park free at Hawes End or at the Littletown Farm on the Newlands Valley side of Cat Bells (£1.50, tel. 017687-78353). The Keswick TI sells a *Skiddaw & Cat Bells* brochure on the hike (60p).

Cat Bells is just the first of a series of peaks all connected by a fine ridge trail. Hardier hikers continue up to nine miles along this same ridge, enjoying valley and lake views as they arc around the Newlands Valley toward (and even down to) Buttermere. After High Spy you can descend an easy path into Newlands Valley. An ultimate day plan would be to bus to Buttermere, climb Robinson, and follow the ridge around to Cat Bells and back to Keswick.

▲▲**Car Hiking from Keswick**—Distances are short, roads are narrow and have turnouts, and views are rewarding. Ask your B&B host for advice. Particularly scenic drives include Latrigg (from a car park just north of Keswick walk a few minutes to the top of the hill for a commanding view of the town and lake). Two miles south of Keswick on the lakeside B5289 Borrowdale Valley Road, take the small road left (signposted Watendlath) for a half mile to the Ashness packhorse bridge (a quintessential Lake District scene) and, a half mile farther, to a car park and the "surprise view" of Derwentwater. Following the road to its end, you hit the idyllic farm hamlet of Watendlath, where you can ponder the tiny lake and lazy farm animals. (On summer Sundays, free shuttle buses—offered to minimize traffic congestion—run hrly between Keswick and Watendlath. Ride to the end and hike home.) Return down to B5289 and back to Keswick or farther south to scenic Borrowdale and over the dramatic pass to Buttermere.

▲▲**Buttermere**—This ideal little lake with a lovely, encircling four-mile stroll offers nonstop, no-sweat, Lake District beauty. If you're not a hiker but kind of wish you were, take this walk. If you're very short on time, at least stop here and get your shoes dirty. (Parking and pubs are in Buttermere village.) Buttermere is connected with Borrowdale and Derwentwater by a great road over the rugged Honister Pass, strewn with glacial debris and curious shaggy Swaledale sheep (looking more like goats with their curly horns). In the other direction you can explore the cruel Newlands Valley or carry on through gentler scenery along Crummock Water and through the forested Whinlatter Pass (fine Visitors Centre with a café the flying squirrels love) and back to

Keswick. From May through October, bus #77 makes a round-trip loop between Keswick and Buttermere over Honister Pass (£5.35, 4/day in both directions, 1.5 hrs).

▲▲**Castlerigg Stone Circle**—These 38 stones, 90 feet across and 3,000 years old, are mysteriously laid out on a line between the two tallest peaks on the horizon. For maximum goose pimples (as they say here), show up at sunset (free, open all the time, 3 miles east of Keswick, follow brown signs, 3 min off A66, easy parking).

▲▲**More Hikes**—The area is riddled with wonderful hikes. B&Bs all have fine advice. From downtown Keswick you can walk the seven-mile Latrigg trail, which includes the Castlerigg Stone Circle (pick up 50p map/guide from TI). From the car park at Newlands Pass, at the top of Newlands Valley, an easy one-mile walk to Knottrigg probably offers more thrills per calorie burned than any walk in the region.

▲**Lakeland Sheep & Wool Centre**—If you're from farm country this is nothing special. But for a city slicker, the Sheep & Wool Centre offers an interesting and entertaining introduction to the region's most famous residents: its sheep. In the 50-minute show you'll meet 19 different breeds of sheep, watch one get sheared, and see sheepdogs do their impressive thing. Afterward you'll meet the stars of the show. It's a hands-on experience kids enjoy (£3, 4 shows daily: 10:30, 12:00, 14:00, and 15:30, only Wed–Sun in winter, unimpressive exhibition but good sheep-stuff shop, drive west from Keswick 15 min on A-66, at A-5086 roundabout you'll see the 300-seat auditorium on left, tel. 01900/822-673, www.sheepwoolcentre.co.uk).

**Keswick Sheepdog Demonstration**—Every Wednesday afternoon, five sheepdogs at various levels of training (some championship) round up sheep and ducks for this simple, down-home demonstration (£2, May–Sept 16:00–17:00, on Brundholme Road a mile northeast of Keswick off A66, tel. 017687/79603).

## Sights—Windermere Area

▲**Brockhole National Park Visitors Centre**—Check the events board as you enter. The center offers a free 15-minute life-in-the-Lake-District slide show (views from farmers, shopkeepers, and B&B owners, played upon request), an information desk, organized walks, exhibits, a bookshop, a good cafeteria, gardens, nature walks, and a large car park. It's in a stately old lakeside mansion between Ambleside and the town of Windermere on A591 (April–Oct daily 10:00–17:00, free entry but £3 to park, tel. 015394/46601, www.lake-district.gov.uk). The bookshop has an excellent selection of maps and guidebooks. I enjoyed Hunter Davies' refreshingly opinionated (but now a bit dated) *Good Guide to the Lakes* (£6).

▲▲**Dove Cottage**—William Wordsworth, the poet whose

appreciation of nature and back-to-basics lifestyle put this area on the map, spent his most productive years (1799–1808) in this well-preserved old cottage on the edge of Grasmere. Today it's the obligatory sight for any Lake District visit. Even if you're not a fan, Wordsworth's "plain living and high thinking," his appreciation of nature, his romanticism, and the ways his friends unleashed their creative talents are appealing. The 20-minute cottage tour (departures every few min) and adjoining museum are excellent. In dry weather the garden where the poet was much inspired is worth a wander (open weather permitting). Even a speedy, jaded museum-goer will want at least an hour here (£5.50, includes voucher for 15 percent off Rydal Mount, below, and Cockermouth, Wordsworth's birthplace, daily 9:30–17:30, last entry at 17:00, tel. 015394/35544, www.wordsworth.org.uk). The new modern-art gallery next to Dove Cottage has rotating exhibits dedicated to "contemporary meditations on Romantic themes."

**Rydal Mount**—Wordsworth's final, higher-class home with a lovely garden and view lacks the charm of Dove Cottage. He lived here 37 years. Just down the road from Dove Cottage, it's worthwhile only for Wordsworth fans (£4, includes voucher for 15 percent off Dove Cottage and Cockermouth, March–Oct daily 9:30–17:00; Nov–Feb Wed–Mon 10:00–16:00, closed Tue; 1.5 miles north of Ambleside, tel. 015394/33002).

▲**Beatrix Potter's Hill Top Farm and Other Sights**—Many come to the lakes on a Beatrix Potter pilgrimage. Sensing that, entrepreneurial locals have dreamed up a number of BP sights. This can be confusing. Most important (and least advertised) is **Hill Top Farm**, the 17th-century cottage where Potter wrote many of her Peter Rabbit books (£4, April–May and Sept–Oct Sat–Wed 11:00–16:30, June–Aug Sat–Wed 10:00–17:00, closed Thu–Fri and Nov–March, last entry 30 min before closing, in Near Sawrey village, 2 miles south of Hawkshead, tel. 015394/36269, e-mail: rpmht@smtp.ntrust.org.uk). Small, dark, and crowded, it gives a good look at her life and work.

The **Beatrix Potter Gallery** (in the neighboring, likeable town of Hawkshead) shows off BP's original drawings and watercolor illustrations used in her children's books and tells more about her life and work (£3, Sun–Thu 10:30–16:30, closed Fri–Sat and Nov–March, Main Street, tel. 015394/36355, e-mail: rhabpg@smtp.ntrust.org.uk).

The gimmicky **World of Beatrix Potter** tour—a hit with children—features a five-minute video trip into the world of Mrs. Tiggywinkle and company, a series of Lake District tableaus starring the same imaginary gang, and a 15-minute video biography of BP (not worth £3.50, daily 10:00–17:30, Oct–Easter 10:00–16:30, closed Jan, in Bowness near Windermere town, tel. 015394/88444).

**Hard Knott Pass**—Only 1,300 feet above sea level, this pass is a thriller, with a narrow, winding, steeply graded road. Just over the pass are the scant but evocative remains of the Hard Knott Roman fortress. There are great views but miserable rainstorms, and it can be very slow and frustrating when the one-lane road with turnouts is clogged by traffic. Avoid it in summer.

## Sights—Ullswater Area

▲▲**Ullswater Hike and Boat Ride**—Long, narrow Ullswater offers eight miles of diverse and grand Lake District scenery. While you can drive it or cruise it, I'd ride the boat from the south tip halfway up and hike back. Boats leave Glenridding regularly—from four to nine a day, depending on the season (£3.60 one-way, £5.80 round-trip, daily 9:00–16:15, less off-season, 35-min ride to Howtown, cheap and safe parking lot, café, free timetable shows walking route, tel. 017684/82229 for schedule, arrive 20 min before departure in summer, www.ullswater-steamers.co.uk). Ride to the first stop, Howtown, halfway up the lake. Then spend four hours hiking and dawdling along the well-marked path by the lake south to Patterdale and then along the road back to Glenridding. This is a serious seven-mile walk with good views, varied terrain, and a few bridges and farms along the way. Wear good shoes and be prepared for rain. For a shorter hike from Howtown Pier, consider a three-mile loop around Hallin Fell.

Several steamer trips chug daily up and down Ullswater. A good rainy-day plan is to ride the covered boat up and down the lake (to the farthest point—Pooley Bridge, £7 round-trip, 2 hrs) or to Howtown and back (£5.80 round-trip, 1 hr). To reach Glenridding by bus from Keswick, allow two hours with a transfer at Penrith (sometimes direct buses in summer, 5/day, 40 min).

**Helvellyn**—Often considered the best high-mountain hike in the Lake District, this breathtaking, round-trip route from Glenridding includes the spectacular Striding Edge ridge walk. Be careful; do this six-hour hike only in good weather and get advice from the Glenridding TI (tel. 017684/82414). While there are shorter routes, the Glenridding ascent is best. The Keswick TI has a helpful *Helvellyn from Glenridding* leaflet on the hike (50p).

## Sleeping in the Lake District
**(£1 = about $1.50, country code: 44, area code: 017687)**
Sleep Code: **S** = Single, **D** = Double/Twin, **T** = Triple, **Q** = Quad, **b** = bathroom, **s** = shower only, **CC** = Credit Cards accepted, **no CC** = Credit Cards not accepted.

### Sleeping in Keswick
The Lake District abounds with attractive B&Bs, guest houses, and hostels. It needs them all when summer hordes threaten the serenity

of this romantic mecca. Alert: Book well in advance if you plan to
visit during Keswick's annual convention in July.

Outside of summer, if you have a car, you should have no
trouble finding a room. But to get a particular place (especially on
Sat), call ahead. Those using public transportation should stay in
Keswick. With a car, drive into a remote farmhouse experience.
Lakeland hostels are cheaper and filled with an interesting crowd.
The Keswick TI can give you phone numbers of places with
vacancies if you call or book you a room if you drop in.

In Keswick I've featured two streets, each within three blocks
of the bus station and town square. "The Heads" is a classier
street lined with proud Victorian houses, close to the lake and
new theater, overlooking a golf course. Stanger Street, a bit
humbler but also quiet and handy, has smaller homes. All of my
Keswick listings are strictly smoke free.

The **launderette** is around the corner from the bus station on
Main Street (daily 7:30–19:30, £3 wash and dry, change machine and
coin-op flake dispenser, £2 extra for full service by 10:00 or earlier;
if you drop off before 9:00 just leave clothes and a note inside by
the office door closest to the front, tel. 017687/75448).

## Sleeping on The Heads

**Berkeley Guest House**, a big slate mansion enthusiastically run
by Barbara Crompton, has a pleasant lounge, narrow hallways, and
carefully appointed, comfortable rooms. The chirpy, skylight-bright
£38 bathless double in the attic is a fine value if you don't mind the
stairs (D-£36–44, Db-£50, family deals, great family room, no CC,
The Heads, Keswick, Cumbria, CA12 5ER, tel. 017687/74222,
www.berkeley-keswick.com, e-mail: berkeley@tesco.net).

**Parkfield** is thoughtfully run and decorated by John and
Susan Berry. This big Victorian house is bright and pastel, with
a wonderful view lounge and sincere warmth from its hosts (Db-
£50–52 with this book through 2002, discount for longer stays,
8 rooms, 1 on the ground floor, CC, car park, no kids under 16,
vegetarian options, plenty of fruit at breakfast, The Heads, CA12
5ES, tel. 017687/72328, www.kencomp.net/parkfield).

**Howe Keld Lakeland Hotel** offers more of a guest-house feel,
with 15 fine rooms, a wide variety of breakfast selections, and £13
evening meals (Sb-£30, Db-£54, minimum 2 nights, prices with
this book through 2002, 2 ground-floor rooms, CC but prefer cash,
family deals, 5-7 The Heads, CA12 5ES, tel. & fax 017687/72417,
www.howekeld.co.uk, run with care by David and Valerie Fisher).

**West View Guest House**, next door to Parkfield, is run by
friendly Carole and John Fullagar. The tasteful, doily lounge and
seven flowery pink-and-plum rooms are pleasant and a decent
value. John, an avid walker, helps guests map out hiking routes
(Db-£52, no CC, The Heads, CA12 5ES, tel. 017687/73638).

## Sleeping on Stanger Street

**Dunsford Guest House** is an old Victorian slate townhouse run by an energetic couple who get their exercise "fellrunning"—running the mountain trails. The four color-coordinated rooms are a fine value. Stained glass and wooden pews give the blue-and-white breakfast room a country-chapel feel (Db-£40, veggie breakfast options, no CC, no kids under 16, can book theater tickets for you, 16 Stanger Street, CA12 5JU, tel. 017687/75059, www.dunsford.net, run by Pat and Peter Richards).

**Fell House B&B**, with six charming rooms, is run by Barbara Hossack, who sets out cakes each afternoon and is a perennial "healthy heartbeat" award-winner for her cooking (S-£18, D-£36, Db-£44, parking, no CC, 28 Stanger Street, CA12 5JU, tel. & fax 017687/72669, e-mail: info@fellhouse.co.uk).

**Abacourt House**, with a daisy-fresh breakfast room, has five pleasant doubles with firm beds, TVs, and shiny, modern bathrooms (Db-£44, veggie options, parking, no children, no CC, 26 Stanger Street, Keswick, CA12 5JU, tel. 017687/72967, www.abacourt.co.uk, Judith and David Lewis).

**Badgers Wood B&B**, at the top of the street, has six bright, pastel, stocking-feet-comfortable rooms (S-£18, D-£36, Db-£44 with this book, 2 rooms share 1 toilet and shower, no children under 12, no CC, 30 Stanger Street, CA12 5JU, tel. & fax 017687/72621, www.badgers-wood.co.uk, Irene and David).

**Ellergill Guest House** has three spic-and-span rooms, one with a super view (D-£39, Db-£42 with this book, large showers, no CC, can book theater tickets, 22 Stanger Street, CA12 5JU, tel. 017687/73347, www.ellergill.uk.com, run by Keith Taylor, a lively one-man show).

Two former hotels now operate as hostels with £11 dorm beds. **Keswick Youth Hostel**, with 90 beds, has a great riverside balcony lined with church pews (3- to 10-bed rooms, Internet access, laundry machines, 23:00 curfew, 3 meals served/day but cost extra, no CC, center of town just off Station Road before river, tel. 017687/72484, e-mail: keswick@yha.org.uk). The **Derwentwater hostel**, two miles south of Keswick, has 88 beds (4- to 22-bedrooms, Internet access, laundry machines, 23:30 curfew, 3 meals served/day but cost extra, no CC, follow B5289 from Keswick, look for sign 100 yards after Ashness exit, tel. 017687/77246, e-mail: derwentwater@yha.org.uk).

## Sleeping in Newlands Valley

With a car, I'd drive 10 minutes past Keswick down the majestic Newlands Valley. Hiking opportunities are wonderful. If the place had a lake it would be packed with tourists. But it doesn't—and it isn't. The valley is studded with 500-year-old farms that have been in the same family for centuries. Shearing day is reason to rush home from school. Sons get school out of the way ASAP and follow their dads. Neighbor girls marry sons and move in. Grandparents retire to the cottage next door. With the price of wool depressed, most of the wives supplement the family income by running B&Bs. The rooms are much plainer than in town. Traditionally, farmhouses lacked central heating, and, while they are now heated, you can still request a hot-water bottle to warm up your bed.

Newlands Valley is just over the Cat Bells ridge from Derwentwater between Keswick and Buttermere. Leave Keswick heading west on the Cockermouth Road (A66). For Birkrigg, Keskadale, Ellas Crag, and Uzzicar B&Bs, take the second Newlands Valley exit through Braithwaite and follow signs through Newlands Valley (drive toward Buttermere). You'll pass Uzzicar first, then Ellas Crag, then the curious purple house, then Birkrigg Farm B&B, and finally Keskadale Farm (about 4 miles before Buttermere). The road is one lane with passing turnouts. For the Low Skelgill Farm, take the first Newlands Valley exit, head through Portinscale on the Buttermere Road for three miles to Stair, then look for the sign.

**Ellas Crag B&B**, with a glorious view of Cat Bells, is more a comfortable stone house than a farm. This homey place, with a good mix of modern and traditional, is enthusiastically run by Tony, Jean, and Catherine Hartley, who cook up great gourmet-type breakfasts with an emphasis on freshness (S-£22.50, Ds-£45, 6 rooms, 1 with a spectacular valley view, nonsmoking, veggie options, packed lunches, laundry possible, no CC, Stair, Newlands Valley, CA12 5TT, tel. 017687/78217, www.ellascragguesthouse.co.uk, e-mail: ellascrag@talk21.com). Catherine, who hand-squeezes the orange juice and bakes her own bread, runs a small tearoom in the front of the house (farm-fresh scones, cakes, soups, and tea; Thu–Tue 10:00–16:00, tearoom closed Wed).

**Birkrigg Farm** is the ideal farmhouse B&B. Mrs. Margaret Beaty offers visitors a comfy lounge, evening tea (good for socializing with her other guests), a classy breakfast, a territorial view, and perfect peace on this 220-acre working farm. Take your toast and last cup of tea out to the front-yard bench (£17–18 per person in S, D, T, or Q, discounts for kids, 1 shower, 1 tub, and 3 WCs for 6 rooms, no CC, parking, closed Dec–March, Newlands Pass Road, Keswick, Cumbria, CA12 5TS, tel. 017687/78278).

**Keskadale Farm B&B** is another great farmhouse experience, with valley views and ponderosa hospitality. This working farm has lots of curly-horned sheep and three rooms to rent (D/Db-£44–48, closed Dec–Feb, nonsmoking, no CC, 1 min farther down Newlands Pass Road to Buttermere Road on a hairpin turn, Keskadale Farm, Newlands, Keswick CA12 5TS, tel. 017687/78544, fax 017687/78150, e-mail: keskadale.b.b @kencomp.net, Margaret Harryman). One of the valley's oldest, it's made from 500-year-old ship beams.

**Low Skelgill Farm**, with two rooms sharing two bathrooms, is immediately under Cat Bells. This is ideal for hikers, since you can leave your car there for the Cat Bells ridge walk (S-£18, D-£34, no CC, take Buttermere Road to Stair, make a sharp left at intersection in tiny Stair, then follow "narrow-gated" road, look for Low Skelgill, not simply Skelgill, tel. 017687/78453, Ann Grave). She also runs a rustic "camping barn" with mattresses for £3.50 a night on weekdays (no bedding provided).

**Uzzicar** rents two rooms in a 16th-century farmhouse on a working sheep farm (D-£38, 2 rooms share 1 shower and 2 toilets, families welcome, nonsmoking, no CC, Newlands Valley, CA12 5TS, tel. & fax 017687/78367, Christine Simpson).

## Sleeping in Buttermere

The **Bridge Hotel**, just beyond Newlands Valley at Buttermere, offers a classy, musty, old-world, countryside-hotel experience (21 rooms, £65/person with a 5-course dinner, cheaper for 4 nights or more, £50-per-person B&B only upon request, CC, nonsmoking rooms, Buttermere, Cumbria, CA13 9UZ, tel. 017687/70252, fax 017687/70215, www.bridge-hotel.com, e-mail: enquiries @bridge-hotel.com). There are no shops within 10 miles—only peace and quiet a stone's throw from one of the region's most beautiful lakes. Buttermere also has a hostel (see below).

## Lake District Hostels

The Lake District's inexpensive hostels, usually located in great old buildings, are handy sources of information and social fun. Local TIs have lists. The Lake District's free booking service (Easter-Oct daily 9:00–18:00, tel. 015394/31117) will tell you which of the area's 30 hostels have available beds and can even book a place on your credit card (no more than 7 days in advance). Since most hostels don't answer their phones during the day and many are full, this is a helpful service. Hostelers need to be members or buy a £13 membership.

The **Buttermere King George VI Memorial Hostel**, a quarter-mile south of Buttermere village on Honister Pass Road, has good food, family rooms, and a royal setting (£11.25/bed in 4- to 6-bed rooms, 70 beds, CC, 3 meals served/day but cost extra, office open 7:00–10:00, 17:00–23:00, 23:00 curfew, tel. 017687/ 70245, e-mail: buttermere@yha.org.uk).

The well-run **Borrowdale Hostel** is secluded in Borrowdale Valley just south of Rosthwaite (£11/bed, 88 beds, no CC, Internet access, laundry machines, 23:00 curfew, 3 meals served/day but cost extra, tel. 017687/77257, e-mail: borrowdale@yha.org.uk).

# Eating in the Lake District

## *Eating in Keswick*

Most restaurants stop serving by 21:00.

The bus station faces a fine **supermarket** (Mon–Sat 9:00–19:00, Fri until 20:00, Sun 10:00–16:00, The Headlands) and the smoke-free **Tithe Barn Coffee Shop and Restaurant**, which is popular with locals. It features daily regional specialties and a menu that's healthy for your body and your pocketbook (Mon–Sat 9:30–17:00, until 18:00 July–Aug, Sun 10:00–16:00).

A number of appealing restaurants line Lake Road. Starting from the market square, and walking up Lake Road, you'll find the restaurants in this order:

**The Dog and Gun** serves good pub food, but mind your head—low ceilings and wooden beams (£5, daily 12:00–23:00, meals until 21:00, lamb curry and goulash, no chips and proud of it, can get smoky, CC, 2 Lake Road, tel. 017687/73463, warmly run by Ede family). On Thursday nights at 21:30, Papa Ede hosts Quiz Night (£1 entry/table); proceeds go to Keswick's Mountain Rescue team (also the recipients of the coin contributions wedged in the stone fireplace).

**Kitchins Cellar Bar** is a local favorite for its reasonable prices and good food, a cut above pub grub (£7–10, daily 12:00–14:00, 18:00–21:00, same menu for restaurant or cellar bar, but "lite" meals available only in bar, reservations smart Fri–Sat, CC, ivy-walled beer garden in back open fair-weather eves, 18 Lake Road, tel. 017687/72990).

**The Four in Hand** is another good bet, with hefty portions and fine trout. Despite the American colonial interior, the place used to be a stop-over for stagecoach drivers who pulled up with their team of four horses and four (reins) in hand (£7–9, daily 12:00–20:45, CC, Lake Road, tel. 017687/72069).

**Maysons Whole Food Restaurant** is favored for its home cooking: curry, Cajun, vegetarian options, and not a chip in sight. It feels Californian (£6.50 meals, June–Oct daily 10:00–20:45, otherwise 10:30–16:30, family-friendly, 33 Lake Road, tel. 017687/74104). Maysons has a small take-out shop directly across the street.

The town splurge, **Morrel's**, is simple yet elegant, with wood floors and gauzy yellow drapes (£12–18, daily 18:00–21:00, early-bird dinner specials before 19:00, creative menu, reservations recommended, CC, 34 Lake Road, tel. 017687/72666).

The **Pheasant Inn**, on the outskirts of town, is known for its pub-simple country fare. It's decorated with photos and memorabilia from the area's well-known Blencathra foxhunting club (£6, Mon–Sat 12:00–14:00, 17:30–20:00, Sun 19:00–20:00, Crosthwaite Road, tel. 017687/72219). The Inn is a pleasant 10-minute walk from the Stanger Street B&Bs. (At top of Stanger Street turn right at gravel alley, walk 100 yards, and make a sharp left toward river. Across river, turn left along riverside path, turn right at Crosthwaite Road, then continue straight, passing hospital.)

It's easy to find ready-made sandwiches for your hike: Try the supermarket or the popular, aromatic **Bryson's Bakery** on the main square (Mon–Sat 8:30–17:30, Sun 9:30–17:00, Jan–Easter closed Sun, meaty pasties and gooey pastries, 42 Main Street, tel. 017687/72257), or get one fresh at the **Coffee Lounge** (£2, daily 9:00–16:30, less off-season, behind TI, squeeze down narrow alley between Pattison Shoes and the Rock Shop to 5 Lupton Court, tel. 017687/73075).

### Eating in Newlands Valley
Since most farmhouses don't serve dinner to their guests, take the lovely 10-minute drive to Buttermere for your evening meal at the **Fish Hotel** pub (£5, nightly 18:00–21:00, family-friendly, limited menu, good fish, beaucoup chips, no vegetables) or the more expensive but much cozier and tastier **Bridge Hotel** pub (£6 or £7, daily 12:00–21:30, more interesting menu, crunchy veggies). On the Keswick side of Newlands Valley, the **Farmer's Arms** pub in Portinscale also serves good pub grub. **Swinside Inn**, the only pub actually in Newlands Valley, is a little tatty but serves decent meals.

**Ellas Crag**, one of the recommended B&Bs (see "Sleeping in Newlands Valley," above), serves fresh baked goods, homemade preserves, and beverages most of the day. Even if you're not staying in the Newlands Valley, the fine food at Ellas Crag and the pastoral scenery are two powerful incentives for a country drive (Thu–Tue 10:00–16:00, tearoom closed Wed, tel. 017687/78217).

## Transportation Connections—Lake District
The nearest train station to Keswick is in Penrith.

**Keswick by bus to: Penrith** (1/hr 7:00–21:50, only 6 on Sun, 40 min, £3.25, pay driver, Stagecoach X4 and X5 buses), **Buttermere** (4/day via Whinlatter Forestry Centre and Lorton, 40 min), **Borrowdale** (8/day to the scenic valley south of Derwentwater, Grange, and Seatoller, 30 min), **Grasmere/Ambleside/Windermere** (1/hr, 1 hr). The Keswick bus stop is at the supermarket on The Headlands (schedules are posted on poles). Bus info: tel. 0870-608-2608 or 01604/676-060.

**Penrith by bus to: Keswick** (1/hr 7:15–22:30, only 6 on Sun, 40 min, £3.25, pay driver, Stagecoach X4 and X5 buses), **Ullswater** and **Glenridding** (6/day, 1 hr, direction: Patterdale). The Penrith bus stop is in the train station's parking lot (bus schedules posted inside and outside station). Bus info: tel. 0870-608-2608 or 01604/676-060.

**Penrith by train to: Oban** (1/hr to Glasgow, 2 hrs; then to Oban, 3/day, 3 hrs), **Edinburgh** (7/day, 2 hrs), **Blackpool**

(1/hr to Preston, 1 hr; then to Blackpool, 3/hr, 20 min), **Liverpool** (1/day, 2.5 hrs), **Birmingham**'s New Street Station (1/hr, 3 hrs), **London**'s Euston Station (1/hr, 4 hrs). Penrith's small train station has a ticket window (Mon–Sat 05:30–21:00, Sun 11:30–21:00) but no lockers. Train info: tel. 08457-484-950.

## Route Tips for Drivers

**North Wales or Blackpool to the Lake District:** The direct, easy way to Keswick is to leave the M6 at Penrith and take the A66 highway 16 miles to Keswick. For the scenic sightseeing drive through the south lakes to Keswick, exit the M6 on A590/A591 through the towns of Kendal and Windermere to reach Brockhole National Park Visitors Centre. From Brockhole, the A road to Keswick is fastest, but the high road—the tiny road over Kirkstone Pass to Glenridding and lovely Ullswater—is much more dramatic.

For the drive north to **Oban**, see the Oban chapter.

# YORK

Historical York is loaded with world-class sights. Marvel at the York Minster, England's finest Gothic church. Ramble through the Shambles, York's wonderfully preserved medieval quarter. Enjoy a walking tour led by an old Yorker. Hop a train at Europe's greatest Railway Museum, travel to the 1800s in York Castle Museum, and head back a thousand years to Viking York at the Jorvik exhibit.

York has a rich history. In A.D. 71 it was Eboracum, a Roman provincial capital. Constantine was actually proclaimed emperor here in A.D. 306. In the fifth century, as Rome was toppling, a Roman emperor sent a letter telling England it was on its own, and York became Eoforwic, the capital of the Anglo-Saxon kingdom of Northumbria. A church was built here in 627, and the town became an early Christian center of learning. The Vikings later took the town, and from about 860 to 950 it was a Danish trading center called Jorvik. The invading and conquering Normans destroyed then rebuilt the city, giving it a castle and the walls you see today. Medieval York, with 9,000 inhabitants, grew rich on the wool trade and became England's second city. Henry VIII spared the city's fine minster in order to use York as his Anglican church's northern capital. The Archbishop of York is second only to the Archbishop of Canterbury in the Anglican Church. In the Industrial Age, York was the railway hub of North England. When it was built, York's train station was the world's largest. Today, York's leading industry is tourism. Its leading drug? Starbucks and Costa are doing their best to turn high tea into high coffee.

## Planning Your Time
York rivals Edinburgh as the best sightseeing city in Britain after London. On even a 10-day trip through Britain, it deserves two

nights and a day. For the best 36 hours, follow this plan: Catch the 19:00 city walking tour on the evening of your arrival. The next morning, be at the Castle Museum at 9:30 when it opens—it's worth a good two hours. Then browse and sightsee through the day. Train buffs love the National Railway Museum, and scholars give the Yorkshire Museum three stars. Tour the minster at 16:00 before catching the 17:00 evensong service (at 16:00 Sat–Sun). Finish your day with an early evening stroll along the wall and perhaps through the abbey gardens. This schedule assumes you're there in the summer (evening orientation walk) and that there's an evensong on. Confirm your plans with the TI.

## Orientation (area code: 01904)

The sightseer's York is small. Virtually everything is within a few minutes' walk: the sights, train station, TI, and B&Bs. The longest walk a visitor might take (from a B&B across the old town to the Castle Museum) is 15 minutes.

Bootham Bar, a gate in the medieval town wall, is the hub of your York visit. At Bootham Bar (and on Exhibition Square facing it) you'll find the TI, the starting points for most walking tours and bus tours, handy access to the medieval town wall, and Bootham Street, which leads to the recommended B&Bs. (In York, a "bar" is a gate and a "gate" is a street. Go ahead, blame the Vikings.) When finding your way, navigate by sighting the tower of the minster or the strategically-placed green signposts pointing out all places of interest to tourists.

**Tourist Information:** The TI at Bootham Bar sells an 80p *York Map and Guide*. Ask for the free monthly *What's On* guide and the monthly *Gig Guide* for live music (April–Oct Mon–Sat 9:00–18:00, Sun 10:00–16:00, sometimes longer in summer, always shorter in winter but no one really knows, pay WCs next door, tel. 01904/621-756). The TI books rooms for a £4 fee and sells theater tickets. The train-station TI is smaller but provides all the same information and services (April–Sept Mon–Sat 9:00–18:00, Sun 9:30–16:00, shorter hrs off-season).

**Arrival in York:** The train station, which stores luggage for daytrippers (£1.50, Mon–Sat 8:00–20:30, Sun 9:00–20:30, platform 1), is a five-minute walk from town; turn left down Station Road and follow the crowd toward the Gothic towers of the minster. After the bridge, a block before the Minster, signs to the TI send you left on St. Leonard's Place. Recommended B&Bs are a five-minute walk from there. (For a shortcut to B&B area from station, walk 1 block toward the minster, cut through parks to riverside, cross railway bridge/pedestrian walkway, cross parking lot for B&Bs on St. Mary's Street, or duck through pedestrian walkway under tracks to B&Bs on Sycamore and Queen Anne's Road.) **Taxis** zip new arrivals to their B&B for £3.

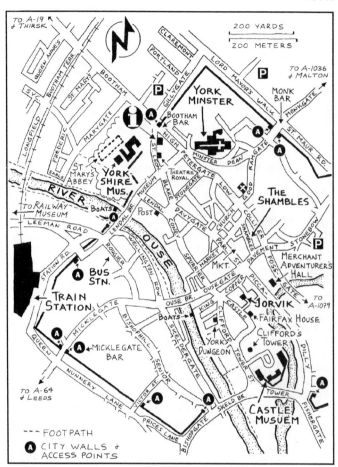

## Helpful Hints

**Study Ahead:** York has a great Web site: www.york.gov.uk.

**Internet Access:** Get online at Internet Exchange (Mon–Sat 8:00–21:00, Sun 10:00–18:00, 13 Stonegate), Gateway (Mon–Wed 10:00–20:00, Thu–Sat 10:00–23:00, Sun 12:00–22:00, 26 Swinegate, tel. 01904/646-446) or Comms.port (near Betty's at Coney Street 2a, first floor, tel. 01904/658-270).

**Festivals:** The Viking Festival in late February is a lot of fun, with lur-blowing, warrior drills, and re-created battles. The Early Music Festival zings its strings in mid-July. The York Festival of

Food and Drink takes a 10-day bite out of the last half of September. Book a room well in advance during festival times and weekends any time of year.

**Bike Rental:** Trotters, just outside Monk Bar, has free cycling maps. The riverside path is fun (£8/day, helmets-£2, Mon–Sat 9:00–17:30, Sun 10:00–16:00, tel. 01904/622-868). Europcar at the train station also rents bikes (£9/day, helmets-£1, platform 1, tel. 01904/656-161).

**Car Rental:** If you're nearing the end of your trip, consider dropping your car upon arrival in York. The money saved by turning it in early nearly pays for the train ticket that whisks you effortlessly to Edinburgh or London. Here are some car-rental agencies in York: Avis (Mon–Sat, closed Sun, 3 Layerthorpe, tel. 01904/610-460), Hertz (April–Sept daily 9:00–13:00, at train station, tel. 01904/612-586), Kenning Car & Van Rental (Mon–Fri, closed Sun, inconveniently 3 miles out of town at Clifton Moor Industrial Estate, tel. 01904/659-328), Budget (daily 9:00–11:00, 1 mile past recommended B&Bs at Clifton 82, tel. 01904/644-919), and Europcar (daily 9:00–13:00, train station platform 1, tel. 1904/656-161). Beware, car-rental agencies close Saturday afternoon and some close all day Sunday—when dropping off is OK but picking up is impossible.

## Tours of York

▲▲▲**Walking Tours**—Charming local volunteer guides give energetic, entertaining, and free two-hour walks through York (daily 10:15 all year, plus 14:15 April–Oct, plus 19:00 June–Aug, from Exhibition Square across from TI). There are many other commercial York walking tours. YorkWalk Tours, for example, has reliable guides and many themes from which to choose, such as Roman York, City Walls, or Snickleways—small alleys (£5, tel. 01904/622-303, TI has schedule). The ghost tours, all offered after nightfall, are more fun than informative. Haunted Walk relies a bit more on storytelling and history rather than masks and surprises (£3, April–Nov nightly at 20:00, 90 min, just show up, depart from Exhibition Square, across street from TI, end in the Shambles, tel. 01904/411-578).

▲**Guide Friday Hop-on Hop-off Bus Tours**—York's Guide Friday offers tour guides who can talk enthusiastically to three sleeping tourists in a gale on a topless double-decker bus for an hour without stopping. Buses make the 60-minute circuit, covering secondary York sights that the city walking tours skip—the work-a-day perimeter of town (£6.50, pay driver cash, can also buy from TI with CC, fliers at TI give £1 off on tickets, departures every 15 min from 9:15 until around 17:00, tel. 01904/640-896). While you can hop on and off all day, the York route is of no value from a transportation-to-the-sights point of view. I'd catch it at the Bootham Bar TI and ride it for an orientation all the way around or get off at the Railway Museum, skipping the last five minutes. Guide Friday's competitors give you a little less for a little less.

**Boat Cruise**—Even though York turns its back on its river, the York Boat does a lazy 60-minute lap along the River Ouse (£5, Feb–Nov daily from 10:30 on, narrated cruise, leaves from Lendal Bridge and King's Staith landing), and also offers themed evening cruises: ghost, dinner, floodlit, and so on (boat rentals possible, tel. 01904/628-324, www.yorkboat.co.uk).

## Sights—York Minster

▲▲▲**Minster**—The pride of York, this largest Gothic church north of the Alps (540 feet long, 200 feet tall) brilliantly shows that the High Middle Ages were far from dark. The word "minster" means a place from which people go out to minister or spread the word of God.

Your first impression might be the spaciousness and brightness of the nave (built 1280–1350). The nave—from the middle period of Gothic, called "Decorated Gothic"—is one of the widest Gothic naves in Europe. Notice the Great West Window (1338) above the entry. The heart in the tracery is called "the heart of Yorkshire."

Look down the nave. The mysterious gold-and-red dragon's head (in the middle of the nave, sticking out of the side) was probably used as a crane to lift a font cover.

The north and south transepts are the oldest parts of today's church (1220–1270). The oldest complete window in the minster is the entire wall of glass in the north transept (1260). Known as the Five Sister's Window, these 50-foot-high panels were made of modern-looking grisaille (gray-silver) glass.

The fanciful choir and the east end (high altar) is from the last stage of Gothic, Perpendicular (1360–1470). The Great East Window (1405), the largest medieval glass window in existence, shows the beginning and the end of the world, with scenes from Genesis and the book of Revelation. A chart (on the right, with a tiny, more helpful chart within) highlights the core Old Testament scenes in this hard-to-read masterpiece. Enjoy the art close up on the chart and then step back and find the real thing.

There are three more extra visits to consider. The **Chapter House**, an elaborately decorated 13th-century Gothic dome—the largest in England without a central supporting pillar—features playful details carved in the stonework (pointed out in the flier that comes with the £1 admission, enter from north transept). You can scale the 275-step **tower** for £3 and enjoy a great view (south transept). The **Undercroft**, also in the south transept, consists of the crypt, treasury, and foundations (£3). The crypt is an actual bit of the Romanesque church, featuring 12th-century Romanesque art, excavated in modern times. The foundations give you a chance to climb down—archaeologically and physically—through the centuries to see the roots of the much smaller—but still huge, Norman church (Romanesque, 1100) that stood on this spot and, below that, the Roman excavations. Constantine was proclaimed Roman emperor here in A.D. 306. Peek also at the modern concrete save-the-church foundations.

**Hours and Tours:** The cathedral opens daily at 7:00. The closing time flexes with the season (roughly 20:30 July–Aug, 19:30 May–June and Sept, 18:00 Oct–April, £2 to use your camera, tel. 01904/557-222). The Chapter House, tower, and Undercroft have shorter hours (usually 9:30–18:30, Oct–April 10:00–16:30). The minster is open for sightseeing from 12:30 on Sundays.

While a donation of £2.50 to visit the church is reasonably requested, I skip that and pay for admission to all the little overpriced extra spots inside—eventually giving more than the £2.50.

When you enter go directly to the welcome desk, pick up the worthwhile "Welcome to the York Minster" flier, and ask when the next free guided tour departs (tours go frequently, even with just 1 or 2 people; you can join one in progress). The helpful blue-armbanded minster guides are happy to answer your questions.

**Evensong and Church Bells:** To experience the cathedral in musical and spiritual action, attend an evensong (Tue–Sat 17:00, Sat–Sun 16:00, 45 min). When the choir is off on school break (mid-July–Aug), visiting choirs usually fill in. Arrive 10 minutes early and wait just outside the choir in the center of the church from where you'll be ushered in and can sit in one of the big wooden stalls. If you're a fan of church bells, Sunday morning (around 10:00) and the Tuesday-evening practice (19:30–21:30) are heavenly.

## Sights—York

▲**City Walls**—The historic walls of York provide a fine two-mile walk. Walk from Bootham Bar (gate) to Monk Bar for outstanding cathedral views. They're free and open from dawn until dusk (barring attacks).

▲**The Shambles**—This is the most colorful old York street in the half-timbered, traffic-free core of town. Ye olde downtown York, while very touristy, is a window-shopping, busker-filled, people-watcher's delight. Don't miss the more frumpy Newgate Market or the old-time Hamilton's candy store just opposite the bottom end of the Shambles. For a cheap lunch, consider the cute, tiny **St. Crux Parish Hall**. This medieval church is now used by a medley of charities selling tea, homemade cakes, and light meals. They each book the church for a day, often a year in advance. Chat up the volunteers (Mon–Sat 10:00–16:00, closed Sun, at bottom end of the Shambles, at intersection with Pavement).

▲▲▲**Castle Museum**—Truly one of Europe's top museums, this is a Victorian home show, the closest thing to a time-tunnel experience England has to offer. It includes the 19th-century Kirkgate (a collection of old shops well stocked exactly as they were 150 years ago); a "From Cradle to Grave" exhibit; and a fine costume collection. The one-way plan allows you to see everything: a working water mill (April–Oct), prison cells, World War II fashions, and old toys. Bring 10p coins to jolt a mechanical Al Jolson into song. The museum's £2.50 guidebook isn't necessary but makes a fine souvenir (£6, April–Oct daily 9:30–17:00, Nov–March until 16:30, gift shop, parking, cafeteria midway through museum, CC, tel. 01904/653-611).

**Clifford's Tower** (across from Castle Museum, not worth the £2, daily 10:00–18:00, until 16:00 Oct–March) is all that's left of York's castle (13th century, site of a 1190 massacre of local Jews—read about this at base of hill). If you do climb inside, there are fine city views from the top of the ramparts.

▲**Jorvik**—Sail the "Pirates of the Caribbean" north and back 800 years and you get Jorvik—more a ride than a museum. Innovative 10 years ago, the commercial success of Jorvik (yor-vik) inspired copycat ride/museums all over England. You'll ride a little Disney-type train car for 13 minutes through the re-created Viking street of Coppergate. It's the year 975, and you're in the village of Jorvik. Next, your little train takes you through the actual excavation site that inspired it. Finally you'll browse through a small gallery of Viking shoes, combs, locks, and other intimate glimpses of that redheaded culture (£7, daily from 9:00 with last entry at 17:30, Nov–March closing varies from 15:30–16:30, tel. 01904/643-211, www.vikingjorvik.com).

Midday lines can be an hour long. Avoid the line by going very early or very late in the day or by pre-booking (call 01904/543-403, you're given a time slot, £1 booking fee, CC). Some love this "ride"; others call it a gimmicky rip-off. If you're looking for a grown-up museum, the Viking exhibit at the Yorkshire Museum is far better. If you're thinking Disneyland with a splash of history, Jorvik's fun. To me, Jorvik is a commercial venture designed for kids with nearly as much square footage devoted to its shop as to the museum.

▲▲**National Railway Museum**—If you like model railways, this is train-car heaven. The thunderous museum shows 150 fascinating years of British railroad history. Fanning out from a grand roundhouse is an array of historic cars and engines, including Queen Victoria's lavish royal car and the very first "stagecoaches on rails." There's much more, including exhibits on dining cars, post cars, sleeping cars, train posters, and videos. At the "Works" section you can see live train switchboards. And don't miss the English Channel Tunnel video (showing the first handshake at breakthrough). Red-shirted "explainers" are everywhere, eager to talk trains. This biggest and best railroad museum anywhere is interesting even to people who think "Pullman" means "don't push" (£7.50, under 17 and over 60 free, daily 10:00–18:00, CC, tel. 01904/621-261). Cute little "street trains" shuttle you between the minster and the Railway Museum (£1.50 each way, leaves Railway Museum every 30 min from 12:00–17:30 at the top and bottom of the hour; leaves minster—from Duncombe Place—every 30 min 15 and 45 min after the hour).

▲▲**Yorkshire Museum**—Located in a lush and lazy park next to the stately ruins of St. Mary's Abbey, Yorkshire Museum is the city's forgotten, serious "archaeology of York" museum. While the hordes line up at Jorvik, the best Viking artifacts are here—with no crowds and a better historical context. A stroll around this museum takes you through Roman (wonderfully described battle-bashed skull in first case), Saxon (great Anglo-Saxon helmet from A.D. 750), Viking, Norman, and Gothic York. Its prize piece is the delicately etched 15th-century pendant called the Middleham Jewel—for which the museum raised $4 million to buy. The 20-minute video about the creation of the abbey is worth a look (£4, various exhibitions can increase price, daily 10:00–17:00, tel. 01904/551-800).

**Theatre Royal**—A full variety of dramas, comedies, and works by Shakespeare is put on to entertain the locals (£10–15, 19:30 or 20:00 almost nightly, tickets easy to get, closes for 6-week period starting in June, CC, on St. Leonard's Place next to TI and a 5-min walk from recommended B&Bs, recorded info tel. 01904/610-041, booking tel. 01904/623-568, www.theatre-royal-york.co.uk).

## Honorable Mention

York has a number of other sights and activities (described in TI material) that, while interesting, pale in comparison to the biggies. **Fairfax House** is perfectly Georgian inside, with docents happy to talk with you (£4, Sat–Thu 11:00–17:00 except Sun 13:30–17:00, Fri by tour only at 11:00 and 14:00, a tour helps bring this well-furnished building to life, on Castlegate, near Jorvik, tel. 01904/655-543). The **Hall of the Merchant Adventurers** claims to be the finest medieval guildhall in Europe (from 1361). It's basically a vast half-timbered building with marvelous exposed beams and 15 minutes worth of interesting displays about life and commerce back in the days when York was England's second city (£2, Mon–Sat 9:00–17:30, Sun 12:00–16:00, early Nov–mid-March until 15:30, below the Shambles off Piccadilly). The **Richard III "Museum"** is interesting only for Richard III enthusiasts (£1.50, daily 9:00–17:00, Nov–Feb until 16:00, Monk Bar). The **York Dungeon** is gimmicky but, if you insist on papier-mâché gore, is better than the London Dungeon (£6.50, daily 10:30–18:00, less off-season, 12 Clifford Street).

Visitors are welcome at the **lawn bowling green** on Sycamore Place (near recommended B&Bs, tell them which B&B you're staying at); you can buy a pint of beer and watch the action (best in evenings). Another green is in front of the Coach House Hotel Pub on Marygate.

York—with its medieval lanes lined with classy as well as tacky little shops—is a hit with shoppers. I find the **antique malls** interesting. Three places within a few blocks of each other are filled with stalls and cases owned by antique dealers from the countryside. The malls sell the dealers' bygones on commission. Serious shoppers do better heading for the countryside, but York's shops are a fun browse: Stonegate Antiques Centre (daily 9:00–18:00, 41 Stonegate, tel. 01904/613-888), the antique mall at 2 Lendal (Mon–Sat 10:00–17:00, closed Sun), and the Red House Antiques Centre (daily 9:30–17:30, as late as 20:00 in the summer, a block from the Minster at Duncombe Place, tel. 01904/637-000).

## Sights—Near York

**Eden Camp**—Once an internment camp for German and Italian POWs during World War II, this is now a theme museum on Britain's war experience. Various barracks detail the rise of Hitler and the fury of the Blitz (with the sound of bombs, the acrid smell of burning, and quotes such as "Hitler will send no warning—so always carry your gas mask.") This award-winning museum energetically conveys the spirit of a country Hitler couldn't conquer. Don't miss hut #10, which details the actual purpose of the camp—as a prison for captured Nazis during World War II. Consider the relative delight of being in the care of the gentlemanly English rather than in a Nazi camp. It's no wonder the Germans settled right in (£4, daily 10:00–17:00, closed late-Dec–mid-Jan, mess-kitchen cafeteria, Malton, 18 miles northeast of York, tel. 01653/697-777, www.edencamp.co.uk). To get to the camp from York, catch the Coastliner bus at the York Railway Station (leaves from front of station, on station side of road). Buses are marked with the destination "Whitby" or "Pickering" and are numbered #840, #842, or #X40, depending on the time of day (£4 round-trip, Mon–Sat 11/day, fewer on Sun, 50 min). From York, drivers take A169 toward Scarborough, then follow signs to the camp.

## Sleeping in York
### (£1 = about $1.50, country code: 44, area code: 01904)
Sleep Code: **S** = Single, **D** = Double/Twin, **T** = Triple, **Q** = Quad, **b** = bathroom, **s** = shower only, **CC** = Credit Cards accepted, **No CC** = Credit Cards not accepted.

I've listed peak-season, book-direct prices. Don't use the TI. Outside of July and August some prices go soft. B&Bs will sometimes turn away one-night bookings, particularly for peak-season

Saturdays. (York is worth 2 nights.) Remember to book ahead during festival times (late Feb, mid-July, latter half of Sept) and weekends year-round.

## Sleeping in B&Bs near Bootham

These recommendations are in the handiest B&B neighborhood, a quiet residential area just outside the old-town wall's Bootham gate, along the road called Bootham. All are within a five-minute walk of the minster and TI and a 10-minute walk or taxi ride (£3) from the station. If driving, head for the cathedral and follow the medieval wall to the gate called Bootham Bar. Bootham "street" leads away from Bootham Bar.

These B&Bs are all small, nonsmoking, and family run. They come with plenty of steep stairs but no traffic noise. For a good selection, call well in advance. B&Bs will generally hold a room with a phone call and work hard to help their guests sightsee and eat smartly. Most have permits for street parking. And most don't take credit cards.

**Laundry**: Regency Dry Cleaning does small loads for £8 (Mon–Fri 8:30–18:00, Sat 9:00–17:00, closed Sun, drop off by 9:30 for same-day service, 75 Bootham, at intersection with Queen Anne's, tel. 01904/613-311). The next-nearest place is a long 15-minute walk away (Washeteria Launderette, 124 Haxby Road, tel. 01904/623-379).

**Airden House**, the most central of my Bootham-area listings, has eight spacious rooms, a grandfather clock–cozy TV lounge, and brightness and warmth throughout. Susan and Keith Burrows, a great source of local travel tips, keep their place tastefully simple, clean, comfortable, and friendly (D-£40–42, Db-£50–52, no CC, 1 St. Mary's, York YO30 7DD, tel. 01904/638-915, www.airdenhouse.co.uk, e-mail: info@airdenhouse.co.uk).

**The Sycamore**, run by Margaret and David Tyce, is a fine value, with seven homey rooms strewn with silk flowers and personal touches. It's at the end of a dead end opposite a fun-to-watch bowling green (S-£20–24, D-£32–34, Db-£42–44, T-£48–50, no CC, 19 Sycamore Place off Bootham Terrace, YO30 7DW, tel. & fax 01904/624-712, e-mail: thesycamore@talk21.com).

**Abbeyfields Guest House** has nine cozy, bright rooms and a quiet lounge. This doily-free place, which lacks the usual clutter, has been designed with care (S-£23, Sb-£33, Db-£52, no CC, 19 Boothham Terrace, YO30 7DH, tel. & fax 01904/636-471, www.abbeyfields.co.uk, Richard and Gwen Martin).

**23 St. Mary's** is extravagantly decorated. Mrs. Hudson has done everything super-correctly and offers nine comfortable rooms, a classy lounge, and all the doily touches (Sb-£34–36, Db-£64–75 depending on season and size, no CC, 23 St. Mary's, YO30 7DD, tel. 01904/622-738, fax 01904/621-168).

# York's Hotels & Restaurants

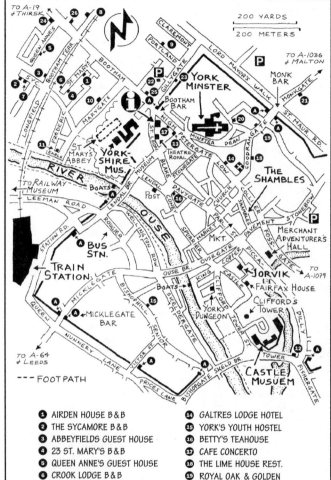

1. AIRDEN HOUSE B & B
2. THE SYCAMORE B & B
3. ABBEYFIELDS GUEST HOUSE
4. 23 ST. MARY'S B & B
5. QUEEN ANNE'S GUEST HOUSE
6. CROOK LODGE B & B
7. ALCUIN LODGE
8. ARNOT HOUSE
9. THE HAZELWOOD B & B
10. THE COACH HOUSE HOTEL & PUB
11. WATER'S EDGE B & B, RIVERSIDE WALK B & B, & ABBEY GUEST HOUSE
12. TRAVELODGE
13. DEAN COURT HOTEL
14. GALTRES LODGE HOTEL
15. YORK'S YOUTH HOSTEL
16. BETTY'S TEAHOUSE
17. CAFE CONCERTO
18. THE LIME HOUSE REST.
19. ROYAL OAK & GOLDEN SLIPPER PUB
20. ST. WILLIAM'S REST.
21. THE VICEROY OF INDIA REST.
22. GILLYGATE FISHERIES REST.
23. WAGGON AND HORSES PUB
24. GRANGE HOTEL BRASSERIE
25. JACKSON'S GROCERY STORE
26. LAUNDRY
Ⓐ CITY WALLS & ACCESS POINTS

**Queen Anne's Guest House** has seven clean, cheery rooms (May–Sept D-£34, Db-£36, Oct–April D-£30, Db-£32, prices good through 2002 with this book, CC, 1 family room, lounge, 24 Queen Anne's Road, Y030 7AA, tel. 01904/629-389, fax 01904/619-529, e-mail: info@queenannes.fsnet.co.uk, Judy and David).

**Crook Lodge B&B**, with seven charming, tight rooms, is a bit more elegant than the rest (Db-£50–56, no CC, parking, quiet, 26 St. Mary's, Y030 7DD, tel. & fax 01904/655-614, www.crooklodge.co.uk, e-mail: crooklodge@hotmail.com, Susan and John Arnott).

**Alcuin Lodge** is a good value, with seven flowery rooms and solid-wood furnishings (Db-£42–50, 1 small top-floor D-£35, no kids, CC, 15 Sycamore Place, Y030 7DW, tel. 01904/632-222, fax 01904/626-630, e-mail: Alcuinlodg@aol.com, Susan Taylor and her husband, General Patton).

**Arnot House**, run by a hard-working daughter-and-mother team, is homey, cluttered, and lushly decorated with early-1900s memorabilia. The four well-furnished rooms have little libraries (Db-£54–58, CC, minimum 2-night stay, 17 Grosvenor Terrace, Y030 7AG, tel. & fax 01904/641-966, www.arnothouseyork.co.uk, e-mail: kim.robbins@virgin.net, Kim and Ann Robbins).

**The Hazelwood**, my most hotelesque listing in this neighborhood, is plush, though it lacks the intimacy of a B&B. This spacious house has 14 beautifully decorated rooms with modern furnishings and lots of thoughtful touches (Db-£75–85–95 depending on room size, CC, 2 ground-floor rooms, classy breakfast, quiet for being so central, laundry service-£5; a fridge, ice, and great travel library in the pleasant basement lounge; 24 Portland Street, Gillygate, YO31 7EH, tel. 01904/626-548, fax 01904/628-032, e-mail: hazwdyork@aol.com.

**The Coach House Hotel** is a labyrinthine, funky old place—a little musty, but well-located facing a bowling green and the abbey walls. It offers 12 comfortable old-time rooms and a crackerjack lounge (Sb-£32, D-£60, Db-£64, CC, free parking, 20 Marygate, Bootham, tel. 01904/652-780, fax 01904/679-943, e-mail: coach_house@btclick.com).

### Sleeping in B&Bs along the Riverside

Three fine smoke-free places front the River Ouse midway between the train station and the minster. Each faces a pedestrian path and comes with a delightful front garden and absolutely no traffic noise. Front rooms overlook the river; back rooms watch a sprawling car park.

**Water's Edge B&B**, a pastel place with five comfy rooms a teddy bear would like, is well-run by Julie Mett (Db-£50, 4-poster river-view Db-£55–60, CC, 5 Earlsborough Terrace, Marygate,

Y030 7BQ, tel. 01904/644-625, fax 01904/731-516, www
.watersedgeyork.co.uk, e-mail: julie@watersedgeyork.co.uk).

**Riverside Walk B&B** has 14 small shipshape rooms, steep
stairs, and narrow hallways (Db-£52–55, CC for 2.5 percent extra,
free parking, 8 Earlsborough Terrace, Marygate, Y030 7BQ,
tel. 01904/620-769, fax 01904/646-249, www.riversidewalkbb
.demon.co.uk, Mr. Summers).

**Abbey Guest House** is similar with seven rooms (S-£25,
Sb-£30, D-£45, Db-£55, Tb-£65, Qb-£70, CC adds a small fee,
free parking, Internet access, 14 Earlsborough Terrace, Marygate,
Y030 7BQ, tel. 01904/627-782, fax 01904/671-743, e-mail:
abbey@rsummers.cix.co.uk, Hilary Summers).

### Sleeping in Hotels in the Center

**Travelodge** offers 90 identical, affordable rooms near the Castle
Museum (Db-£60, Oct–June Db discounted to £50, kids' bed free,
CC, some smoke-free rooms, 90 Piccadilly, central reservations
tel. 0870-085-0950, www.travelodge.co.uk).

**Dean Court Hotel**, facing the minster, is a big, stately Best
Western–style place that has classy lounges and 40 comfortable
rooms (small Db-£105, standard Db-£130, superior Db-£145,
spacious deluxe Db-£160, CC, some nonsmoking rooms, tearoom,
restaurant, elevator to most rooms, Duncombe Place, YO1 7EF, tel.
01904/625-082, fax 01904/620-305, www.deancourt-york.co.uk).

**Galtres Lodge Hotel**, a block from the minster, offers comfy
rooms above a restaurant in the old-town center (S-£28, Sb-£40,
Db-£70, 1 refurbished Db-£75 and worth it, CC, nonsmoking,
54 Low Petergate, Y01 7HZ, tel. 01904/622-478, fax 01904/
627-804, www.yorkshireholidays.com).

**York's Youth Hotel** is well run, with a kitchen, launderette,
bar, game room, and 120 beds (S-£16, bunk bed D-£30, £14 beds
in 4- to 6-bed dorms, £9 beds in larger dorms, CC, less for multinight stays, same-sex or coed possible, no breakfast, 10-min
walk from station at 11 Bishophill Senior Road, YO1 1EF, tel.
01904/625-904, fax 01904/612-494, e-mail: info@yorkyouthhotel
.demon.co.uk).

## Eating in York

### Traditional Tea

York is famous for its elegant teahouses. Drop into one around
16:00 for tea and cakes. Ladies love **Betty's Teahouse** where you
pay £5 for a cream tea (tea and scones) or £9 for a full traditional
English afternoon tea (tea, elegant sandwich, scones, and sweets).
Your table is so full of doily niceties that the food is served on a
little three-tray tower. While Betty's food is nothing special, the
ambience and people watching are hard to beat (daily 9:00–21:00,

piano music nightly 18:00–21:00, CC, mostly nonsmoking, St. Helen's Square; fine view of street scene from a window seat on the main floor, downstairs near WC is a mirror signed by WWII bomber pilots—read the story). If there's a line, it moves quickly. I'd wait for a seat by the windows on ground level rather than sit in the much bigger basement.

### Eating near the Minster

Of these listings, the first faces the minster, the last two are behind the minster, and the rest are on Goodramgate near the minster.

**Café Concerto**, a French-style bistro with a fun menu, has an understandably loyal following. Their food is the best I've had in York (great £8 lunches, £15 dinners, daily 10:00–22:00, serves meals all day, CC, smoke-free, smart to reserve for dinner, facing the minster, Petergate 21, tel. 01904/610-478).

The **Lime House Restaurant** is a small, modern, candlelit place enthusiastically run by chef Adam Fisher. His menu features European dishes revolving with the seasons and always includes a good vegetarian plate. Adam offers a free glass of house wine to anyone with this book (£10 plates, 10 percent off on orders before 19:00, Tue–Sat 12:00–14:00, 18:00–22:00, closed Sun–Mon, lunch specials, CC, 55 Goodramgate, tel. 01904/632-734).

For **Italian**, three popular places compete along Goodramgate. There's a pub serving grub on every block. Eat where you see lots of food. The **Royal Oak** offers £5 pub grub throughout the day, a small nonsmoking room, and hand-pulled ale (daily 11:00–20:00, heavy meat dishes, fat fries, but don't look in their kitchen, CC, Goodramgate, a block from Monk Bar, a block east of the minster, tel. 01904/653-856). The **Golden Slipper**, next door, is also a classic for basic pub grub and darts.

**St. Williams Restaurant**, just behind the great east window of the minster in a wonderful half-timbered, 15th-century building (read the history), serves quick and tasty lunches and elegant candlelit dinners (2 courses-£14, 3 courses-£17, daily 10:00–17:00 plus Tue–Sat 18:00–22:00, traditional and Mediterranean, CC, College Street, tel. 01904/634-830).

The **Viceroy of India**—just outside Monk Bar and therefore outside the tourist zone—serves great Indian food at good prices to mostly locals. If you've yet to eat Indian on your trip, do it here (£8 plates, nightly 18:00–24:00, friendly staff, CC, continue straight through Monk Bar—pass the big old "nightly bile beans keep you healthy, bright-eyed, and slim" sign on your left—to 26 Monkgate, tel. 01904/622-370).

### Eating near Bootham Bar and Your B&B

**Gillygate Fisheries** is a wonderfully traditional little fish-and-chips joint where tattooed people eat in and housebound mothers take out

(Mel serves £4–5 meals, "eat your mushy peas," Mon 17:00–23:30, Tue–Fri 11:30–14:00, 17:00–23:30, Sat 11:30–23:30, closed Sun, smoke-free seating, 2 blocks from the TI at 59 Gillygate).

The **Waggon and Horses** pub has local color and serves cheap "pub food with attitude" in a cozy smoke-free room or with the smoking beer drinkers (Mon–Sat 11:30–21:00, Sun 12:00–15:00, fresh vegetables, across from Wackers at Gillygate 48, tel. 01904/654-103).

The well-worn **Coach House** serves good-quality food with fresh vegetables but can be smoky (£8–11, nightly 18:30–21:30, CC, 20 Marygate, tel. 01904/652-780).

The **Grange Hotel's Brasserie**, a couple of blocks from the B&Bs, is classier than a pub and serves a smattering of traditional European dishes. Go downstairs—avoid the pricey ground-floor restaurant (£9 meals, Mon–Sat 12:00–14:00, 18:00–22:00, Sun 19:00–22:00, CC, 1 Clifton, tel. 01904/644-744).

Jacksons **grocery store** is open every day from 7:00–23:00 (near B&Bs, outside Bootham Bar, on Bootham). For an atmospheric **picnic spot,** try the Museum Gardens (near Bootham Bar) at the evocative 12th-century ruins of St. Mary's Abbey.

## Transportation Connections—York

**By train to: Durham** (4/hr, 45 min), **Edinburgh** (2/hr, 2.5 hrs), **London** (2/hr, 2 hrs), **Bath** (1/hr, 5 hrs, change in Bristol), **Cambridge** (nearly hrly, 2 hrs, change in Peterborough), **Birmingham** (2/hr, 2.5 hrs), **Keswick** (with transfers to Penrith then bus, 4.5 hrs). **Train info**: tel. 08457-484-950.

**Connections with London's Airports: Heathrow** (1/hr, allow 2.5–3 hrs, take Heathrow Express train to London's Paddington station, tube to King's Cross, train to York—2/hr, 2 hrs), **Gatwick** (from Gatwick catch low-profile Thameslink train to King's Cross-Thameslink station in London; from there, walk 100 yards to King's Cross station, train to York—2/hr, 2 hrs).

The **York Bus Information Centre** is at 20 Hudson Street, near the train station (Mon–Fri 8:30–17:00, tel. 01904/551-400, phone answered Mon–Sat 8:00–20:00, Sun 8:00–14:00).

## Route Tips for Drivers

As you near York (and your B&B), you'll hit the A1237 ring road. Follow this to the A19/Thirsk roundabout (next to river on northeast side of town). From roundabout, follow signs for York City, traveling through Clifton into Bootham. All recommended B&Bs are four or five blocks before you hit the medieval city gate (see neighborhood map). If you're approaching York from the south, take M1 until it ends. Then follow A64 for 10 miles until you reach York's ring road (A1237), which allows you to avoid driving through the city center.

# NORTH YORK MOORS

The North York Moors are a vacant lot compared with the Cumbrian Lake District. But that's unfair competition. In the lonesome North York Moors you can wander through the stark beauty of its time-passed villages, bored sheep, and powerful landscapes.

If you're driving, get a map. Without wheels, you have several choices: take a bus/steam-train combination (below); choose one of several guided bus tours from York (focusing on Herriot or Brontë country, moors, Lake District, or Holy Island, different tour every day, offered by various companies for roughly £10/half day or £16/full day); or hire a private guide. John Smith, a licensed guide and driver, can take up to three people on one of his Yorkshire Tours—such as Herriot Country, a Castle Howard/steam train/Whitby combination, or a tour tailored to your interests (£15/hr, admissions extra, tel. 01904/636-653, cellular 07850-260-511).

▲**The Moors**—Car hike across the moors on any small road. You'll come upon tidy villages, old Roman roads, and maybe even a fox hunt. The Moors Visitors Centre provides the best orientation for exploring the moors. It's a grand old lodge offering exhibits, shows, nature walks, an information desk with plenty of books and maps, brass rubbing, a cheery cafeteria, and brochures on several good walks that start right there (free but £1.50 parking fee, April–Oct daily 10:00–17:00, Nov–Dec and March daily 11:00–16:00, Jan–Feb weekends only 11:00–16:00, a half mile from train station, tel. 01287/660-654, www.northyorkmoors-npa.gov.uk).

▲**North Yorkshire Moors Railway**—This 18-mile, one-hour steam-engine ride between Pickering and Grosmont (grow-mont) goes through some of the best parts of the moors almost hourly. Even with the windows small and dirty (wipe off the outside of yours before you roll) and the track mostly in a scenic gully, it's a good ride. You can stop along the way for a moors walk and catch the next train (£10 round-trip, March–Oct, first train departs Pickering about 10:20, last train departs Grosmount about 16:50, allow 3.5 hrs round-trip due to scheduling, CC, tel. 01751/472-508, talking timetable tel. 01751/473-535). It's not possible to leave luggage at any stop on the steam-train line—pack lightly if you decide to hike.

**Pickering**, with its rural-life museum, castle, and Monday market (produce, knickknacks), is worth a stop. You could catch an early York-Pickering bus (Mon–Sat 1/hr, only 1 on Sun, 65 min, leaves from train station), see Pickering, and carry on to Grosmont. Grosmont is on a regular train line with limited connections to Whitby (see below) and points north and south (TI tel. 01751/473-791).

▲**Hutton-le-Hole**—This postcard-pretty town is home of the fine Ryedale Folk Museum, which illustrates "farm life in the moors" through reconstructed and furnished 18th-century local buildings (£3.25, mid-March–Oct daily 10:00–17:30, tel. 01751/417-367).

# North York Moors

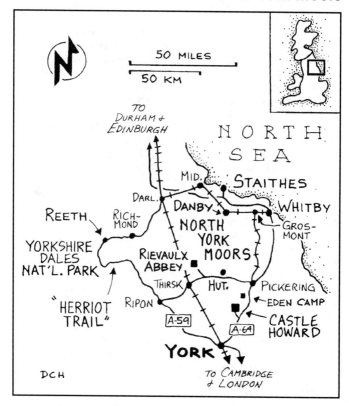

50 MILES

50 KM

TO DURHAM & EDINBURGH

N O R T H
S E A

MID.
STAITHES
DARL.
DANBY
WHITBY
REETH
RICH-MOND
GROS-MONT
YORKSHIRE DALES NAT'L. PARK
NORTH YORK MOORS
RIEVAULX ABBEY
THIRSK
HUT.
PICKERING
"HERRIOT TRAIL"
RIPON
A-59
EDEN CAMP
CASTLE HOWARD
A-64
YORK
DCH
TO CAMBRIDGE & LONDON

**Castle Howard**—Especially popular since the filming of *Brideshead Revisited*, this fine, palatial 300-year-old home is about half as interesting as the Cotswolds' Blenheim Palace (£7.50, daily 11:00–17:00, closed early Nov–mid-March, 2 buses/day from York, 40 min, tel. 01653/648-333).

**Rievaulx Abbey**—Rievaulx (ree-voh) is a highlight of North York Moors and beautifully situated, but if you've seen other fine old abbeys, this is a rerun (£3.60, April–Sept daily 10:00–18:00, Aug 9:30–19:00, Oct 10:00–17:00, Nov–March 10:00–16:00, tel. 01439/798-228).

▲**James Herriot Country**—Herriot fans will be more interested in the Yorkshire Dales than the neighboring moors. Local booklets at the TI lay out the *All Creatures Great and Small* pilgrimage route for drivers, or you could consider a tour from York (see leaflets at TI).

# WHITBY AND STAITHES

These towns are seaside escapes worth a stop for the seagulls, surf, and Captain Cook lore. Whitby is accessible by train, but Staithes makes sense only with a car.

▲**Whitby**—An important port since the 12th century, Whitby is now a fun coastal resort town with a busy harbor and steep and salty old streets. It's a carousel of Coney Island–type amusements overseen by the stately ruins of its seventh-century abbey. The **Captain Cook Memorial Museum** offers an interesting look at the famous hometown sailor and his exotic voyages (£2.80, daily 9:45–17:00, closed Nov–March, down Grape Lane in the old town just over the bridge). Two of Captain Cook's boats (*Resolution* and *Endeavour*) were built in the Whitby shipyards. The **TI** is on the harbor next to the train and bus stations (May–Sept daily 9:30–18:00, Oct–April daily 10:00–12:30, 13:00–16:30, tel. 01947/602-674).

If driving, upon arrival park across from the TI at the pay-and-display supermarket lot near the train and bus station. Wander along the harbor out along Pier Road and Fish Quay past all the Coney Island–type amusements. The Magpie Restaurant is famous for its fish and chips (generally a line of hungry pilgrims waiting to get in). The small Dracula exhibit is a reminder that some of that story was set here. As you return to your car, cross the bridge where you'll find a warren of touristy lanes filled with hard candy, knickknack shops, and the small Captain Cook Memorial Museum.

**Sleeping in Whitby:** Whitby has plenty of rooms. August is the only tight month. The **Crescent House** rents six good rooms just south of the harbor with some sea views (Db-£44, family deals, no CC, nonsmoking, on the bluff at the top of Khyber Pass at 6 East Crescent, YO21 3HD, tel. & fax 01947/600-091, e-mail: janet@whitby.fsbusiness.co.uk, Janet and Mike Paget). **Dolphin Hotel**, in the old-town center at the bridge overlooking the harbor, is a colorful old pub with seven salty rooms upstairs (Db-£50, CC, pub closes at 23:30, 3 blocks from train station, Bridge Street, Y022 4BG, tel. 01947/602-197). The **hostel** is next to the abbey above the town (£11/bed, 58 beds in 8 rooms, no CC, office closed 10:00–17:00, tel. 01947/602-878).

**Connections:** Buses connect Whitby and York (4–6/day depending on season, 2 hrs, tel. 01653/692-556). Trains connect Durham with Middlesbrough (5/day, 50 min, more frequent with transfer in Darlington); the Middlesbrough-Whitby train (4/day, 90 min) stops at Grosmont (where you can catch the Moors steam train) and Danby (a half mile from the Moors info center).

▲**Staithes**—A ragamuffin village where the boy who became Captain James Cook got his first taste of the sea, Staithes (just north of Whitby) is a salty tumble of cottages bunny-hopping down a ravine into a tiny harbor. While tranquil today, in 1816 it was home to 70 boats and the busiest fishing station in north England. Ten years ago the town supported 20 fishing boats—today, only three. But fishermen (who pronounce their town "steers") still outnumber tourists in undiscovered Staithes. The town has changed little since Captain Cook's days. Little is done to woo tourism here. Lots of flies and seagulls seem to have picked the barren cliffs raw. There's nothing to do but drop by the lifeboat house (a big deal in England; page through the history book, read the not-quite-stirring accounts of the boats being called to duty; drop a coin in the box), stroll the beach, and nurse a harborside beer or ice cream. Just an easy drive north of Whitby, Staithes is worthwhile by car—probably not by bus (hrly Whitby-Staithes buses, 30 min; 10-min walk from bus stop into town).

**Sleeping in Staithes:** There are no fancy rooms. It's a cash-only town with no ATMs. Parking is tough—generally you can drive in only to unload. Service trucks clog the windy main (and only) lane much of the day. There's a pay-and-display lot at the top of the town (when paying the night before, time spills over past 9:00 the next morning). Each of these three- or four-bedroom places is cramped, with tangled floor plans that make you feel like a stowaway. **Greystones B&B** provides the best beds in town (D-£40, Db-£48, family deals, no CC, nonsmoking, Internet access, High Street, tel. 01947/841-694, www.staithes-uk.co.uk, e-mail: tonyrd@lineone.net, Tony and Eve). The **Endeavour Restaurant B&B** is a tidy little place and the only one in town offering parking (D/Db-£55—your choice: a loo or a view, no CC, serves great food—see below, 1 High Street, tel. 01947/840-825, Lisa Chapman). **Harborside Guest House** is the roughest place, but the only place actually on the harbor. It provides rumpled old beds, three sea-view rooms, breakfast on linoleum, and the sound of waves to lull you to sleep (D-£40, no CC, tel. 01947/841-296, James and Sue).

**Eating in Staithes**: The oddly classy-for-this-town **Endeavour Restaurant** offers excellent £20 dinners (Tue–Sat 18:45–21:00, closed Sun–Mon, seafood, vegetarian, reservations wise, tel. 01947/840-825). Three pubs serve dinner (generally 19:00–21:00): the **Black Lion**, the **Royal George**, and the **Cod and Lobster**. The Cod and Lobster overlooks the harbor, with outdoor benches and a cozy living room warmed by a coal fire. Drop in to see its old-time Staithes photos. For fish and chips or a coffee on the harbor, try the friendly **Sea Drift Sweet Shop** or **Harborside Guest House**.

# DURHAM AND NORTHEAST ENGLAND

Some of England's best history is harbored in the northeast. Hadrian's Wall reminds us that Britain was an important Roman colony 2,000 years ago. After a Roman ramble, you can make a pilgrimage to Holy Island, where Christianity gained its first toehold in Britain. At Durham, marvel at England's greatest Norman church and enjoy an evensong service. And, at the Beamish Open-Air Folk Museum, you can travel back in time to the year 1913.

## Planning Your Time

Of the sights described in this chapter, train travelers will find Durham the most convenient stop on a three-week British train trip. You can see Hadrian's Wall en route (doable with transfers, easiest late May–late Sept), a worthwhile visit for those inspired by Roman ruins. The Beamish Folk Museum is an easy daytrip from Durham (hrly bus, 20 min).

By car you'll be driving right by Holy Island, Bamburgh Castle, Hadrian's Wall, and the Beamish Folk Museum.

By car, connect Edinburgh and York by this string of sights, spending a night near Hadrian's Wall and a night in Durham on a one-month trip. On a three-week train trip, I'd spend just a night in Durham. For drivers (or train travelers) with 36 hours between Edinburgh and York, leave Edinburgh early, hike a bit of Hadrian's Wall and tour Housesteads Fort, and get to Durham in time to tour the cathedral and enjoy the evensong service (Tue–Sat 17:15, Sun 15:30). Sleep in Durham. Tour Beamish (15 min north of Durham by car or bus) or drive through the North York Moors the next day, arriving in York by late afternoon.

# DURHAM

Without its cathedral it would hardly be noticed. But this magnificently-situated cathedral is hard not to notice (even if you're zooming by on the train). Durham sits, seemingly happy to go nowhere, along its river and below its castle and famous cathedral. It has a work-a-day, medieval, cobbled atmosphere and a scraggly peasant's indoor market just off the main square (closed Sun). While Durham is the home of England's third-oldest university, the town feels working class, surrounded by newly-closed coal mines and filled with tattooed and stapled people in search of job security. Yet Durham has a youthful vibrancy and a small-town warmth that shines especially on sunny days, when most everyone is licking an ice-cream cone or plans to.

## Orientation (area code: 0191)

Tidy little Durham clusters everything safely under its castle within the protective hairpin bend of its river. The longest walk you'd make would be a 15-minute jaunt from the train station to the cathedral.

**Tourist Information:** The TI, located on the town square, books rooms and local theater tickets, provides train times, and, from June through September, offers 90-minute city walks generally on Wednesday, Saturday, and Sunday at 14:00 for £3 (June–Sept Mon–Sat 9:30–17:30, July–Aug also Sun 11:00–16:00; Oct–May Mon–Fri 10:00–17:00, Sat 10:00–13:00; public WC next door in indoor market, tel. 0191/384-3720). The brochure *Guided Walks in County Durham* lists themed walks led by local experts (£1, several times weekly, some hikes start in Durham).

**Arrival in Durham:** From the train station, follow the road downhill and take the second pedestrian turnoff (within sight of railway bridge), which leads almost immediately over a bridge above busy Alexander Crescent road. Then take North Road into town or to the first couple of B&Bs (take Alexander Crescent to the other B&Bs). Daytrippers can store luggage at the station (£1.50, daily 7:00–20:00, ask at ticket window). Drivers simply surrender to the wonderful Prince Bishop's car park (at the roundabout at the base of the old town). It's perfectly safe, inexpensive, and an elevator deposits you right in the heart of Durham (a short block from the town square).

**Internet Access:** Reality-X is hard core, with 18 computers and no food (£3/30 min, daily 10:00–19:00, sometimes until 22:00, at the west end of Framwelgate Bridge, tel. 0191/384-5700).

## Getting Around Durham

While all listed hotels, eateries, and sights are easily walkable in Durham, taxis can zip tired tourists to their B&Bs in a snap (£2, wait on Market Place or on west side of Framwelgate Bridge).

# Durham

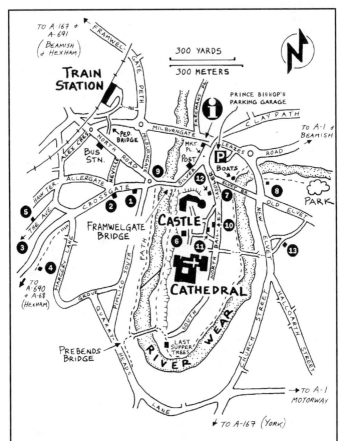

**1** CASTLEVIEW GUEST HOUSE

**2** GEORGIAN TOWN HOUSE

**3** FARNLEY TOWER B&B

**4** CASTLEDENE B&B

**5** #12 B&B

**6** DURHAM CASTLE HOUSING

**7** CHADWICK'S BRASSERIE

**8** WATERSIDE HOTEL & DURHAM MARRIOT

**9** PIZZERIA VENEZIA & INTERNET ACCESS

**10** SHAHEEN'S RESTAURANT

**11** THE ALMSHOUSES REST.

**12** HOGSHEAD ALE HOUSE

**13** COURT INN PUB

## Sights—Durham

▲▲▲**Cathedral**—Built to house the much-venerated bones of St. Cuthbert from Lindisfarne, the cathedral offers the best look at Norman architecture in England. (Norman is British for Romanesque.) The cathedral is free but a £3 donation is requested (open daily 7:30–18:00, early Sept–Easter until 17:00, limited access Sun morning). For various fees, you can also climb the tower, ogle the treasury, and tour the Monk's Dormitory. I'd skip the A-V show on St. Cuthbert. Try to fit in some music (see "Evensong," below). No photos or videos are allowed. A bookshop, cafeteria, and WC are tucked away in the cloisters.

**A Tour Plan:** From the cathedral green, notice how this fortress of God stands boldly across from the Norman keep of Durham's fortress of man. (The castle, now part of the university, is not worth touring.)

At the cathedral door, notice the big, bronze, lion-faced knocker, a replica of the 12th-century original (now in the treasury), which was used by criminals seeking sanctuary (read the explanation).

Immediately inside you'll see the **information desk**. Church attendants happily answer questions. Ideally, follow a church tour (£3 donation, July–early Sept Mon–Sat at 10:30, 11:30, and 14:30; if one's in session you're welcome to join). The *A Walk Round Durham Cathedral* guide pamphlet is informative but dull (60p).

Notice the modern window with the novel depiction of the Last Supper (above and to the left of the entry door). It was given to the church by a local department store in 1984. The shapes of the apostles represent worlds and persons of every kind from the shadowy Judas to the brightness of Jesus. This window is a good reminder that the cathedral remains a living part of the community.

Near the entrance, the black marble strip on the floor was as close to the altar as women were allowed in the days when this was a Benedictine church (until 1540). Sit down (ignoring the black line) and let the fine proportions of England's best Norman (and arguably Europe's best Romanesque) nave stir you. Any frilly woodwork and stonework were added in later centuries.

The architecture of the **nave** is particularly harmonious because it was built in a mere 40 years (1093–1133). Few additions were made, and the bulk of what you see today—especially the round arches and zigzag carved decorations—are textbook Norman. The church was also proto-Gothic, built by well-traveled French masons and architects who knew the latest innovations from Europe. Its stone and ribbed roof, Britain's first pointed arches, and first flying buttresses were revolutionary in this country. Notice the clean lines and simplicity. It's not as cluttered as other churches for several reasons. Out of respect for St. Cuthbert, for centuries no one else was buried here. During Reformation

## Durham Cathedral

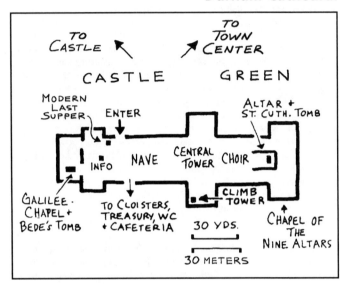

times, sumptuous Catholic decor was cleaned out. And subsequent fires and wars destroyed what Protestants didn't.

Enter the **Galilee Chapel** (late Norman, from 1175) in the back of the nave. The paintings of St. Cuthbert and St. Oswald (7th-century king of Northumbria) on the side walls of the side altar niche are rare examples of Romanesque or Norman paintings. Facing this altar, look above to your right to see more faint paintings on the upper walls above the columns. Near the center of the chapel, the upraised tomb topped with a black slab contains the remains of the Venerable Bede, an eigth-century Christian scholar who wrote the first history of England. The Latin reads: In this tomb are the bones of the Venerable Bede.

Back in the main church, stroll down the nave to the center, under the highest bell tower in Europe (218 feet). Gaze up. The ropes pull hammers that ring the bells. If you're stirred by the cheery ringing of **church bells**, tune into the cathedral on Sunday (9:30–10:00 and 14:30–15:00) or Thursday (19:30 practice) when the resounding notes tumble merrily through the entire town.

Continuing east (all medieval churches faced east), you enter the **choir**. Monks worshiped many times a day, and the choir in the center of the church provided a cozier place to gather in this vast, dark, and cold building. Here in the heart of the cathedral, Mass has been said daily for 900 years. The fancy wooden chairs are from the 17th century. Behind the altar is the delicately carved stone Neville Screen from 1380 (made of Normandy stone in London, shipped to Newcastle by sea, then brought here by wagon); until the Reformation the niches contained statues of 107 saints. Exit the choir from the far right side (south). Look for the stained-glass window (to your right) commemorating the church's 1,000th anniversary in 1995. The colorful scenes depict England's history from coal miners to cows to computers.

Step down into the **apse**, the Gothic east end of the church. Climb a few stairs to the tomb of St. Cuthbert. An inspirational leader of the early Christian church in North England, St. Cuthbert lived in the Lindisfarne monastery on Holy Island (100 miles north of Durham). He died in 687. Eleven years later his body was exhumed and found to be miraculously preserved. This stoked the popularity of his shrine, and pilgrims came in growing numbers. When Vikings raided Lindisfarne in 875, the monks fled with his body (and the famous illuminated *Lindisfarne Gospels*, now in the British Library in London). In 995, after 120 years of roaming, the monks settled in Durham on an easy-to-defend tight bend in the Wear River. The cathedral was built over Cuthbert's tomb. Throughout the Middle Ages a shrine stood here—and was visited by countless pilgrims. In 1539, during the Reformation—whose proponets advocated focusing on God rather than saints—the shrine was destroyed. Cuthbert's tomb is part of the larger 13th-century Gothic Chapel of the Nine Altars—taller, lighter, and relatively more extravagant than the Norman nave.

Consider the cathedral's other sights. The entry to the **tower** is in the south transept; the view from the tower will cost you 325 steps and £2 (April–Oct Mon–Sat 10:00–16:00, Nov–March Mon–Sat 10:00–15:00, closed Sun). The following sights are within the cloisters: The **treasury**, filled with medieval bits and holy pieces (including Cuthbert's coffin, vestments, and cross), fleshes out this otherwise stark building. The actual relics from St. Cuthbert's tomb are at the far end (treasury well worth the £2 admission, Mon–Sat 10:00–16:30, Sun 14:00–16:00). The **Monks' Dormitory**, now a library with an original 14th-century timber roof filled with Anglo-Saxon stones, is worth 80p (Mon–Sat 10:00–15:30, Sun 12:30–15:00). The unexceptional A-V show in the unexceptional undercroft tells about St. Cuthbert (daily 10:00–15:00, not worth 80p). The fine cafeteria (daily 10:00–16:30, lunch 12:00–14:30, nonsmoking), bookshop (in the old kitchen), and WCs are near the treasury.

**Evensong:** For a thousand years this cradle of English Christianity has been praising God. To really experience the cathedral, go for an evensong service. Arrive early and ask to be seated in the choir. It's a spiritual Oz, as 40 boys sing psalms—a red-and-white-robed pillow of praise, raised up by the powerful pipe organ. If you're lucky and the service went well, the organist runs a spiritual musical victory lap as the congregation breaks up (Tue–Sat 17:15, Sun at 15:30, 1 hr, normally not sung on Mon; when choir is off on school break during mid-July–Aug visiting choirs often fill in; tel. 0191/386-2367).

**Riverside Walk**—For a 20-minute woodsy escape, walk Durham's riverside path from busy Framwelgate Bridge to sleepy Prebends Bridge. Just beyond the Prebends Bridge on the old-town side of the river, you'll find the Upper Room, a cluster of trees carved to show the Last Supper when viewed from the tree-trunk throne provided. Where are the apostles? Count the tree trunks.

**Boat Cruise and Rental**—For a relaxing 60-minute narrated cruise of the river, hop on the "Prince Bishop" (£3.50, for schedule call 0191/386-9525, check at TI, or go down to the dock at Brown's Boat House at Elvet Bridge, just east of old town). For some exercise with the same scenery, you can rent a rowboat at the same pier (£2.50/hr per person, £5 deposit, Easter-Sept daily 10:00–18:00, tel. 0191/386-3779).

# Near Durham: Beamish Open-Air Museum

This huge museum, which re-creates the year 1913 in northeast England, takes at least three hours to explore. A vintage tram shuttles visitors to the four stations: Coal Mine Village, Home Farm, The Town, and an 1820s manor house and steam train. This isn't wax. If you touch the exhibits, they may smack you. Attendants at each stop happily explain everything. In fact, the place is only really interesting if you talk to these attendants.

Start with the **Coal Mine Village** (company village around a coal mine), with a school, church, miners' homes, and a fascinating—if claustrophobic—20-minute tour into a real "drift" mine.

**"The Town"** is a bustling street featuring a 1913 candy shop, a dentist's office, a garage, a working pub (fun for a smoky beer), and a modern, smoke-free cafeteria (Dainty Dinah's Tea Room, upstairs). The old train station isn't much.

The Pockerley Manor is an 1820s **manor house** whose attendants have plenty to explain. Adjacent is the re-created first-ever passenger train from 1825, which takes modern-day visitors for a spin on 1825 tracks—a hit with railway buffs. The Home Farm is the least interesting section (£10, daily 10:00–17:00; from Nov–March only "The Town" is open, 10:00–16:00, closed Mon and Fri; check events schedule as you enter, last tickets sold 2 hrs before closing, tel. 0191/370-4000).

The museum is five minutes off the A1/M1 motorway (1 exit north of Durham at Chester-le-Street, well sign-posted). To get to Beamish from Durham, catch a #720 bus (marked "Stanley via Beamish," 1/hr, 20 min, stops 500 yards from museum).

# Sleeping in Durham
**(£1 = about $1.50, country code: 44, area code: 0191)**
Sleep Code: **S** = Single, **D** = Double/Twin, **T** = Triple, **Q** = Quad,
**b** = bathroom, **s** = shower only, **CC** = Credit Cards accepted, **no**
**CC** = Credit Cards not accepted.

The B&Bs are a 5- or 10-minute walk from the station and
the town center. Durham hosts a rowing regatta the second
weekend in June; book ahead.

The only **launderette** in town is at Dunelm House, the
Student Union building—a 10- to 15-minute walk east of the
B&B neighborhood (daily 8:00–21:00 during school term, other-
wise 9:00–15:00, open to public, self-service only, east end of
Kingsgate Bridge, tel. 0191/374-3310).

## *Sleeping in B&Bs*
**Castleview Guest House**, 300 yards off Framwelgate Bridge,
rents six airy, comfortable rooms in a classy well-located house
(Sb-£40, Db-£55, no CC, prices promised with book through
2002, nonsmoking, 4 Crossgate, DH1 4PS, tel. & fax 0191/386-
8852, e-mail: castleview@hotmail.com, Mike and Anne Williams).

**Georgian Town House**, a few doors up the street, has a
cheery bossa nova ambience with a breezy garden, plush sitting
room, and eight bright rooms decorated with care and flair. The
hearty breakfast is served in the conservatory (Db-£65 with this
book, no CC, nonsmoking, tubs lack showers, some rooms with
castle views, 10 Crossgate, DH1 4PS, tel. & fax 0191/386-8070,
e-mail: enquiries@georgian-townhouse.fsnet.co.uk, Charlotte Weil).

**Farnley Tower** is a luxurious B&B. Opened in mid-1999,
it still feels like it just came out of the box. Its eleven spacious
doubles have all the comforts, and some have views. The hotel is
on a quiet dead end at the top of a hill, a 10-minute uphill hike
from the town center (1 Sb-£45, Db-£65, superior Db-£75, CC,
nonsmoking, phones in rooms, pleasant bar, easy parking, inviting
yard, The Avenue, DH1 4DX, tel. 0191/375-0011, fax 0191/383-
9694, www.farnley-tower.co.uk, e-mail: enquiries@farnley-tower
.co.uk, John and Gail Khan).

**Castledene B&B** is tidy, simple, and friendly, with two
twin-bedded rooms and double-glazed windows to keep the house
quiet and warm (D-£40, no CC, at intersection of Crossgate and
Margery Lane, go up stairway to pedestrian-only walkway—running parallel to Crossgate Peth—to last house, 37 Nevilledale
Terrace; drivers go a few yards past Crossgate intersection and
turn right on Summerville, tel. & fax 0191/384-8386, Lorna and
Brian Byrne).

The low-key **Bed & Breakfast** has two simple rooms on a
quiet dead-end street (small S-£20, D-£40 with this book, no
CC, nonsmoking, no sign on door, 12 The Avenue, DH1 4ED,

tel. 0191/384-1020, e-mail: jan.hanim@aol.com, run by kindly Jan Metcalfe).

**Student Housing—Open to Anyone:** Durham Castle, a student residence actually on the castle grounds facing the cathedral, rents 100 singles and 30 doubles during the summer break (July–Sept only, £20.50/person, £30.50 with private facilities, CC, can reserve long in advance, elegant breakfast hall, parking-£5 on the cathedral green, University College, The Castle, Palace Green, DH1 3RW, tel. 0191/374-3863 or 374-3873, fax 0191/374-7470, Julie Marshall). Request a room in the classy old main building or you may get one of the few bomb shelter–style modern dorm rooms.

### Hotels Near the Old Center

**Waterside Private Hotel**, perched on the river and hemmed in by the Marriott Hotel (below), offers 11 pleasant rooms in a world of brick and flowers (Db-£75, CC, nonsmoking, parking, Elvet Waterside, tel. 0191/384-6660, fax 0191/384-6996, e-mail: watersidedurham@breathemail.net).

**Durham Marriott Royal County Hotel**, a four-star hotel, scatters its 151 posh rooms among several buildings sprawling along the river. The Leisure Club has a pool, sauna, Jacuzzi, and fitness equipment (Db-£120, breakfast extra, CC, 2 restaurants, bar, parking, Old Elvet, DH1 3JN, tel. 0191/386-6821, fax 0191/386-0704, www.marriotthotels.co.uk).

## Eating in Durham

Durham is a university town with plenty of lively, inexpensive eateries. Stroll from Framwelgate Bridge through Market Place and up Saddler considering the places listed here (in walking order). **Lau's Buffet King** is a cheap and modern Chinese buffet near the bridge (85 North Road). **Pizzeria Venezia** serves good, affordable Italian food (Mon–Sat 12:00–13:45, 18:00–21:45, early-bird specials 18:00–19:00, west end of Framwelgate Bridge through Millburngate Shopping Centre archway, tel. 0191/384-6777). **Bimbi's** is a stand-by for fish and chips (daily 11:00–22:30, on Market Place).

Saddler Street, leading from Market Place up to the cathedral, is lined with eateries. After the pasta place and the pizza place, consider the **Hogshead Ale House** for pub grub (£4–5, serving food daily 12:00–21:00, more drinking than eating in evening, smoky, tel. 0191/386-9550). Across the street, **Chadwick's Brasserie** serves the best modern Continental cuisine in the old town (Mon–Sat 18:00–21:30, closed Sun, fun, jazz-filled ambience, CC, 39 Saddler Street, tel. 0191/384-1999). In 2002, Chadwick's will keep its address but may change its name. **Shaheen's** is the place for good Indian (Tue–Sun 18:00–23:30, closed Mon, CC, 48 Saddler Street, just past the turnoff to the cathedral, tel. 0191/386-0960). **The Almshouses** on the cathedral green is good for a tasty light meal (daily 9:00–20:00, Oct–Easter until 17:00, CC, tel. 0191/386-1054).

For more traditional pub grub, locals like the **Court Inn** (daily 11:00–22:30, 5-min walk east of old town, take Elvet or Kingsgate Bridge, Court Lane, tel. 0191/384-7350). Drivers looking for a nontouristy splurge can eat modern French/English at **Bistro 21** (£25 meals, Mon–Sat 12:00–14:00, 19:00–22:00, closed Sun, CC, Aykley Heads, 3 miles north of town, tel. 0191/ 384-4354).

**Supermarkets**: Of Durham's two supermarkets, **Safeway** has longer hours and is closer to the recommended B&Bs (Mon–Fri 8:30–20:00, Sat 8:00–18:00, closed Sun, in Millburngate Shopping Center, west end of Framwelgate Bridge). In the old town, try **Marks & Spencers**, just off the main square (Mon–Sat 9:00– 17:30, closed Sun, on Silver Street; across from P.O., which has same hours). You can picnic on the benches and grass outside the cathedral entrance (but not on the Palace Green, unless the park police have gone home).

## Transportation Connections—Durham
**By train to: Edinburgh** (nearly hrly, 2 hrs), **York** (1–3/hr, 1 hr), **London** (1/hr, 3 hrs), **Hadrian's Wall** (take train to Newcastle— 1–4/hr, 15 min; then a train/bus combination to Hadrian's Wall, see "Hadrian's Wall," below), **Bristol** (near Bath, 9/day, 5 hrs). From September to May only about half of the London-Edin-burgh trains stop in little Durham; frequency drops to about six trains daily in winter (for more options, catch train to busier Newcastle—1–4/hr, 15 min—where all the trains stop). Train info: tel. 08457-484-950.

## HADRIAN'S WALL
This is one of England's most thought-provoking sights. Around A.D. 130, during the reign of Emperor Hadrian, the Romans built this great stone wall. Its actual purpose is still debated. While Rome ruled Britain for 400 years, it never quite ruled its people. The wall may have been used to define the northern edge of the empire, protect Roman Britain from invading Scottish tribes (or at least cut down on pesky border raids), monitor the movement of people, or simply give an otherwise bored army something to do. (Nothing's more dangerous than a bored army.) Stretching 74 miles coast to coast across the narrowest stretch of northern England, it was built and defended by nearly 20,000 troops. The wall was flanked by ditches, and a military road lies on the south side. At every mile of the wall a castle guards a gate, and two turrets stand between each castle. The mile castles are numbered.

(Eighty of them cover the 74 miles because a Roman mile was slightly shorter than our mile.) Today, several chunks of the wall, ruined forts, and museums thrill history buffs. About a dozen Roman sites cling along the wall's route; the best are Housesteads Fort and Vindolanda. Housesteads shows you where the Romans lived; Vindolanda's museum shows you how they lived.

Note: The Hadrian's Wall area was hard hit by the 2001 foot-and-mouth crisis. Some locals in the region expect the problem to continue into 2002. As a result, many businesses are either closed down or for sale. In 2001 the actual wall and Housesteads Fort (which is literally on the wall) were closed to hikers and visitors. But other major wall-related sights (such as Vindolanda) remained open.

## Sights—Hadrian's Wall

▲▲**Housesteads Fort**—With its tiny museum, powerful scenery, and the best-preserved segment of the wall, this is your best single stop. All Roman forts were the same rectangular shape and design, containing a commander's headquarters, barracks, and latrines (lower end); this fort even has a hospital. The fort is built right up to the wall, which is on the far side (£3 for site and museum, June–Oct daily 10:00–18:00, Nov–May 10:00–17:00 or dusk, parking-£1, tel. 01434/344-363). At the car park are WCs, a snack bar, and a gift shop. You can leave your baggage at the gift shop, but confirm its closing hours. From the car park, it's a half-mile, mostly uphill walk to the entrance of the minuscule museum and sprawling fort.

▲▲**Hiking the Wall**—From Housesteads, hike west along the wall speaking Latin. For a good, craggy, three-mile walk along the wall, hike between Housesteads and Steel Rigg. You'll pass a castle sitting in a nick in a crag (castle #39, called Castle Nick). There's a car park near Steel Rigg (take the little road up from Twice Brewed Pub). In 2003, it will be possible to walk along the wall's route on a new path stretching from coast to coast.

▲**Vindolanda**—This larger Roman fort (which actually predates the wall by 40 years) and museum are just south of the wall. Although Housesteads has better ruins and the wall, Vindolanda has the better museum, revealing intimate details of Roman life. Eight forts were built on this spot. The Romans, by carefully sealing the foundations from each successive fort, left modern-day archaeologists seven yards of remarkably well-preserved artifacts to excavate: keys, coins, brooches, scales, pottery, glass, tools, leather shoes, bits of cloth, and even a wig. Impressive examples of early Roman writing were recently discovered here. While the actual letters, written on thin pieces of wood, are in London's British Museum, see the interesting video here and read the translations—the first known example of a woman writing to a woman

# Durham and Northeast England

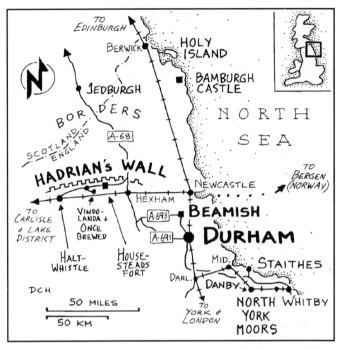

is an invitation to a birthday party. These varied letters, about parties held, money owed, and sympathy shared, bring Romans to life in a way that stones alone can't.

From the car park you'll walk through 500 yards of grassy parkland decorated by the foundation stones of the Roman fort and a full-size replica chunk of the wall. At the far side of the site is the museum, gift shop, and cafeteria (£4, £5.60 combo ticket includes Roman Army Museum, daily 10:00–17:00 or 18:00 depending on the season, closed late-Nov–early-Feb, can leave baggage at entrance, tel. 01434/344-277). The **Roman Army Museum**, a few miles farther west at Greenhead, is redundant if you've seen Vindolanda (£3, or buy combo ticket, see above, same hours).

## Sleeping and Eating near Hadrian's Wall
**(£1 = about $1.50, country code: 44, area code: 01434)**
Note: Because of the economic problems caused by the foot-and-mouth crisis, several of these places may not be in business in 2002.

**Crindledykes Farm** is a classy old farmhouse in an idyllic and peaceful setting a mile south of the wall (small D-£38, spacious twin room with view-£40, enough space for a child's bed, WC down the hall, no CC, nonsmoking, accessible by car only, signposted from B6318 at Housesteads, Bardon Mill, Hexham, NE47 7AF, tel. 01434/344-316, Judy Davidson).

**East Wharmley Farm** rents two spacious rooms in a wonderfully rural setting. The farm is six miles from Housesteads on the A69, midway between Haydon Bridge and Hexham (D-£36, family deals, no CC, nonsmoking, Hexham, NE46 2PL, tel. & fax 01434/674-259, Dorothy and Harold Foster).

**Crow's Nest B&B** offers three rooms in a remodeled farmhouse a quarter mile from the wall (D-£38, no CC, on B6318 road 500 yards from the Once Brewed TI and hostel at East Twice Brewed, Bardon Mill, Hexham, tel. 01434/344-348, Jean Wanless). The nearby **Mile Castle Pub** cooks up all sorts of exotic game and offers the best dinner around, according to hungry national park rangers. Two miles west of Housesteads, the **Twice Brewed Pub and Hotel** serves decent pub grub nightly to a local darts-and-pool crowd (cheap, dreary rooms, rarely full, tel. 01434/344-534). Next door to the Twice Brewed Pub is the comfortable **Once Brewed Youth Hostel** (£11/bed with sheets, 4–7 beds/room, no CC, breakfast-£3.50, cheap lunches and dinners, Military Road, Bardon Mill, tel. 01434/344-360, fax 01434/344-045, e-mail: oncebrewed@yha.org.uk).

In Haltwhistle, consider the **Old Schoolhouse B&B** (3 Db-£40, no CC, quiet, nonsmoking, also serves as writers' retreat, 5-min walk from Haltwhistle train station, Fairhill Road, tel. & fax 01434/322-595, cellular 077-1180-9180, www.oshouse.freeserve.co.uk).

## Transportation Connections—Hadrian's Wall

**By Car:** Take B6318; it parallels the wall and passes several viewpoints, minor sights, and "severe dips." (If there's a certified nerd or bozo in the car, these road signs add a lot to a photo portrait.)

**By Train and Bus:** A train/bus combination (which operates with greatest frequency late May–late Sept) delivers you to the wall. From England's east coast, Newcastle is the gateway to the Newcastle-Carlisle train paralleling the wall (10/day, from Newcastle it's 30 min to Hexham, 20 more min to Haltwhistle). But the train only gets you near the wall. During peak season, take Hadrian's Wall bus #122AD to get to the wall and all the Roman sights. Get off the train at either Hexham or Haltwhistle to catch this bus (10 buses/day in each direction, late May–late Sept; Hexham-Housesteads 30 min, Housesteads-Vindolanda 10 min, Vindolanda-Haltwhistle 20 min).

At Newcastle's train station, pick up a Hadrian's Wall bus schedule at the TI (Mon–Fri 9:30–17:30, Sat 9:30–17:00, Sun 10:00–16:00, call for schedule, tel. 0191/261-0610). Or call

Haltwhistle's helpful TI for schedule information (Mon–Sat 9:30–13:00, 14:00–17:30, until 18:00 late-May–Sept, Sun 13:00–17:00; Nov–Easter Mon–Tue and Thu–Sat 10:00–12:30, 13:00–15:30, closed Wed and Sun, tel. 01434/322-002, www.hadrians-wall.org). If you start from Newcastle by at least 11:00 (earlier is better), you can fit in both Housesteads and Vindolanda. Daytrippers can store luggage at Newcastle's train station (£2–3, daily 8:00–18:00, return by 18:00 or get it next day).

To visit Housesteads off-season (late Sept–late May), take a train to Haltwhistle and catch a taxi (taxi services: Sprouls tel. 01434/321-064, Turnbulls tel. 01434/320-105, £8 one-way; arrange for return pickup or have museum staff call a taxi). If you're staying on the wall, your B&B host can arrange a taxi.

# HOLY ISLAND AND BAMBURGH CASTLE

▲**Holy Island**—Twelve hundred years ago, this "Holy Island" was Christianity's toehold on England. It was the home of St. Cuthbert. We know it today for the *Lindisfarne Gospels*, decorated by monks in the seventh century with some of the finest art from Europe's "Dark Ages" (now in the British Museum). It's a pleasant visit, a quiet town with a striking castle (not worth touring) and an evocative priory. The Priory Exhibit is a tiny but instructive museum (£3) adjacent the ruined abbey. You can wander the abbey grounds and graveyard and pop into the church without paying. Holy Island is reached by a two-mile causeway that's cut off daily by high tides. Tidal charts are posted, warning you when this holy place becomes Holy Island and you become stranded. For TI and tide information, call the **Berwick TI** at tel. 01289/330-733 (Mon–Sat 10:00–17:00, Sun 11:00–16:00, Oct–April Mon–Sat until 16:00, closed Sun). Park at the pay-and-display lot (£2) and walk five minutes into the village. For a peaceful overnight, a few good B&Bs cluster in the town center (**Britannia Guest House**, D-£36, Db-£40, no CC, tel. 01289/389-218, Mrs. Patterson).

▲▲**Bamburgh Castle**—About 10 miles south of Holy Island, this grand castle dominates the Northumbrian countryside and overlooks Britain's loveliest beach. The place was bought and passionately refurbished by Lord Armstrong, a Ted Turner–like industrialist and engineer in the 1890s. Its interior, lined with well-described history, feels lived in because it still is—with Armstrong family portraits and aristocratic-yet-homey knicknacks hanging everywhere. The included Armstrong Museum features the inventions of the industrialist family that has owned the castle through modern times (£4.50, daily 11:00–17:00, closed Nov–March, tel. 01668/214-515, www.bamburghcastle.com). Rolling dunes crisscrossed by walking paths lead to a vast sandy beach and lots of local families on holiday. This area is only worthwhile for those with a car.

# EDINBURGH

Edinburgh, the colorful city of Robert Louis Stevenson, Sir Walter Scott, and Robert Burns, is Scotland's showpiece and one of Europe's most entertaining cities. Historical, monumental, fun, and well organized, it's a tourist's delight.

Promenade down the Royal Mile through Old Town. Historic buildings pack the Royal Mile between the castle (on the top) and Holyrood Palace (on the bottom). Medieval skyscrapers stand shoulder to shoulder, hiding peaceful courtyards connected to High Street by narrow lanes or even tunnels. This colorful jumble is the tourist's Edinburgh.

Edinburgh (ED'n-burah) was once the most crowded city in Europe—famed for its skyscrapers and filth. The rich and poor lived atop one another. In the Age of Enlightenment, a magnificent Georgian city, today's New Town, was laid out to the north giving the town's upper class a respectable place to promenade. Georgian Edinburgh, like the city of Bath, shines with broad boulevards, straight streets, square squares, circular circuses, and elegant mansions decked out in colonnades, pediments, and sphinxes in the proud, neoclassical style of 200 years ago.

While the Georgian city celebrated the union of Scotland and England (with streets and squares named after English kings and emblems), "devolution" is the latest craze. In a 1998 election, the Scots voted for more autonomy and to bring their parliament home. Though Edinburgh has been the historic capital of Scotland for centuries, parliament had not met in Scotland since 1707. In 2000—while London still calls the strategic shots—Edinburgh resumed its position as home to the Scottish Parliament. A strikingly modern new parliament building, opening in 2003, will be one more jewel in Edinburgh's crown.

## Planning Your Time

While the major sights can be seen in a day, on a three-week tour of Britain I'd give Edinburgh two days and three nights.

**Day 1:** Tour the castle. Then consider catching one of the city bus tours (from a block below the castle at Tolbooth church) for a 60-minute loop, returning to the castle. Explore the Royal Mile, going downhill—lunching, museum-going, shopping, taking a walking tour (one leaves at 14:00 from Mercat Cross). If you tour Holyrood Palace, do it near the end of the day and the bottom of the Mile. In the evening, take in live music at a pub, a literary pub crawl, or a haunted walk.

**Day 2:** Tour the Museum of Scotland. After lunch, stroll through the Princes Street Gardens and the Scottish National Gallery. Then tour the good ship *Britannia*.

## Orientation (area code: 0131)

The center of Edinburgh holds the Princes Street Gardens park and Waverley Bridge, where you'll find the TI, Princes Mall, train station, bus info office (starting point for most city bus tours), National Gallery, and a covered dance-and-music pavilion. Weather blows in and out—bring your sweater.

**Tourist Information:** The crowded TI is as central as can be atop the Princes Mall and train station (May–June and Sept Mon–Sat 9:00–19:00, Sun 10:00–19:00; July–Aug daily until 20:00; Nov–March daily until 17:00; ATM outside entrance, tel. 0131/473-3800). Unfortunately, all their information—even which car-rental companies "exist" and their assessment of museums— is skewed by tourism payola. Buy a map (£1 if in stock, or the excellent £3.50 Collins Illustrated Edinburgh map, which comes with opinionated commentary and locates virtually every major shop and sight), and ask for the free monthly entertainment *Gig Guide* if you're interested in late-night music. The *Essential Guide to Edinburgh* (£1), while not essential, lists additional sights and services. Book your room direct without the TI's help (B&Bs charge more for rooms booked through the TI, and you pay the TI a £3 finder's fee). Browse the racks (tucked away in hallway at back of TI) for brochures on the various Scottish folk shows, walking tours, and regional bus tours. Connect@edinburgh, a small Internet café, is beyond the brochure racks (see "Hints," below). The best monthly entertainment listing, *The List*, is sold for £1.95 at newsstands.

**Haggis Backpackers Ltd.** has budget travel information and sells cheap one- to six-day tours around Scotland (Mon–Sat 9:00–18:00, summer Sun 14:00–18:00, 60 High Street, at Blackfriars Street, tel. 0131/557-9393, www.radicaltravel.com).

**Arrival in Edinburgh:** Arriving by train at Waverley Station puts you in the city center and below the TI (go up the many stairs until you surface at street level, TI to your left) and the

# Edinburgh

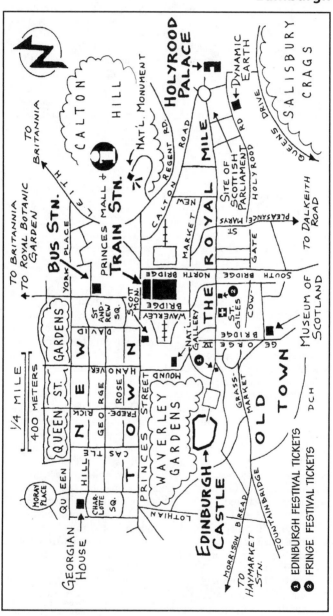

city bus to my recommended B&Bs (see "Sleeping," below, for directions to B&B neighborhood by bus). Both Scottish Citylink and National Express buses use the bus station two blocks north of the train station on St. Andrew Square in New Town.

Edinburgh's slingshot-of-an-**airport** is 10 miles northwest of the center and well-connected by taxi (£14, 30 min) and by shuttle buses with Waverley Bridge (LRT "Airline" bus #100, £3.30 or £4.20 with all-day "Airsaver" city-bus pass, 6/hr, 30 min, roughly 05:00–23:00). Flight info: tel. 0131/333-1000, BMI British Midland tel. 0870-607-0555, British Air tel. 0845-773-3377, Aer Lingus tel. 0845-973-7747.

## Helpful Hints

**Sunday Activities:** Many sights close on Sunday, but there's still a lot to do: Royal Mile walking tour, Edinburgh Castle, St. Giles Cathedral, Holyrood Palace, Royal Botanic Gardens, climb Arthur's Seat, and city bus tour. An open-air market including antiques is held every Sunday from 10:00 to 16:00 at New Street Car Park near the train station. The Georgian House and National Gallery are open Sunday afternoon.

**Internet Access:** It's a cinch to get plugged in. Try Connect@edinburgh at the TI (£1/20 min, Mon–Sat 9:00–18:00, Sun 10:00–18:00, as you enter TI head back to the left down a corridor) or International Telecom Centre on the Royal Mile (£1/15 min, daily 9:00–23:00, also has cheap phones with rare sit-down booths, 52 High Street, half block east of Tron Kirk and South Bridge).

**Late-Night Pharmacy:** Try Boots at 48 Shandwick Place (tel. 0131/225-6757).

**Car Rental:** Consider Avis (5 West Park Place, tel. 0131/337-6363, airport tel. 0131/344-3900); Europcar (24 East London Street, tel. 0131/557-3456, airport tel. 0131/333-2573); Hertz (Pickardy Place, tel. 0131/556-8311, airport tel. 0131/333-1019); or Budget (394 Ferry Road, tel. 0131/551-3322, airport tel. 0131/333-1926).

## Getting around Edinburgh

Nearly all Edinburgh sights are within walking distance of each other. City **buses** are handy and inexpensive (about 80p/ride, buy tickets on bus, LRT transit office at Old Town end of Waverley Bridge has schedules and route maps, tel. 0131/555-6363). Tell the driver where you're going, have change handy (most buses require exact change; you lose any excess), take your ticket as you board, push the stop button as you near your stop (so your stop isn't skipped), and exit from the middle door. Two companies handle the city routes: LRT (or Lothian) does most of it and First does the rest (e.g., to get from the city center to the recommended

B&Bs on Dalkeith Road, you can catch LRT buses #14, #21, and
#33 or First buses #C3 and #86). Day passes sold by each company
are valid only on their buses (£2.20, or £1.50 after 9:30 weekdays
and all day weekends, buy from driver). Buses run from about
06:00 to 23:00. **Taxis** are reasonable (easy to flag down, average
ride between downtown and B&B district-£4).

## Bus Tours of Edinburgh

▲**Hop-on Hop-off City Bus Tours**—Three companies offer
60-minute bus tours that circle the town center stopping at the
biggies—Waverley Bridge, the castle, Royal Mile, Georgian
New Town, and Princes Street—with an informative narration
and pickups about every 10 to 15 minutes. You can hop on and
off with one ticket all day, but not 24 hours. Hop on at any stop
or go to Waverley Bridge to comparison shop between your
bus-tour options.

Guide Friday has a live guide (£8.50, £10 combo ticket
includes round-trip transportation to Britannia—which normally
costs £3.50, ticket gives 10 percent discount off castle admission,
tel. 0131/556-2244). LRT's "Edinburgh Classic Tour," which runs
a little more frequently, uses headphones with a recorded narration (£7.50, tel. 0131/555-6363). Mac Tours' "Edinburgh by Vintage Bus" has a live guide, fewer buses, and a shorter route (£7.50,
3/hr, 50 min, ticket bought after 17:00 also valid the next day).

On sunny days they go topless (the buses), but they also suffer
from traffic noise and congestion. Buses run year-round. First and
last buses leave Waverley Bridge around 9:00 and continue until
19:00 mid-June through early September (last buses leave earlier
off-season).

## Sights—Edinburgh

▲▲▲**Edinburgh Castle**—The fortified birthplace of the city
1,300 years ago, this imposing symbol of Edinburgh sits proudly
on a rock high above the city. While the castle has been both a
fort and a royal residence since the 11th century, most of the
buildings today are from its more recent use as a military garrison.
It's a fascinating and multifaceted sight deserving several hours
(£7.50, daily 9:30–18:00, Oct–March 9:30–17:00, CC, cafeteria,
tel. 0131/225-9846; consider avoiding the long uphill walk from
the nearest city bus stop by taking a cab to the castle gate).

**Entry Gate:** Start with the wonderfully droll 30-minute
guided introduction tour (free with admission, departs 2–4
times/hr from entry, see clock for next departure; few tours run
off-season). The audioguide is excellent, with four hours of quick
digital dial descriptions (free with admission, pick up at entry gate
before meeting the live guide). The clean WC at the entry annually wins "British Loo of the Year" awards (marvel at the plaques

near men's room), but they use a one-way mirror showing the sink area in the women's room (women: pop your head into office near men's room to complain or make sure mirror is curtained).

In the castle there are five essential stops: Crown Jewels, Royal Palace, Scottish National War Memorial, St. Margaret's Chapel with city view, and the excellent National War Museum of Scotland. The first four are at the highest and most secure point—on or near the castle square, where your introductory guided tour ends. The War Museum is 50 yards below by the cafeteria and big shop.

**1. Crown Jewels:** The line of tourists leads from the square directly to the jewels. Skip this line and enter the building around to the left (next to WC) where you'll get to the jewels via a wonderful *Honors of Scotland* exhibition about the crown jewels and how they survived the harrowing centuries.

Scotland's **Crown Jewels** are older than England's. While Cromwell destroyed England's, the Scots hid theirs successfully. Longtime symbols of Scottish nationalism, they were made in Edinburgh—of Scottish gold, diamonds, and gems—in 1540 for a 1543 coronation. They were last used to crown Charles II in 1651. While the Act of Union, which dissolved Scotland's parliament into England's to create the United Kingdom in 1707, was forced upon the Scots, part of the deal was that they could keep their jewels locked up in Edinburgh. They remained hidden for over 100 years. In 1818 Walter Scott and a royal commission rediscovered the jewels intact.

The **Stone of Scone** sits plain and strong next to the jewels. This big gray chunk of rock is the coronation stone of Scotland's ancient kings (9th century). Swiped by the English, it sat under the coronation chair at Westminster Abbey from 1296 until 1996. With major fanfare, Scotland's treasured Stone of Scone returned to Edinburgh on Saint Andrew's Day, November 30, 1996. Talk to the guard for more details.

**2. The Royal Palace** (facing castle square under the flag pole) has two historic yet unimpressive rooms (through door reading 1566) and the Great Hall (separate entrance from the same castle square). Remember, Scottish royalty only lived here when safety or protocol required. They preferred the **Holyrood Palace** at the bottom of the Royal Mile. Enter the **Mary Queen of Scots room**, where in 1566 the queen gave birth to James VI of Scotland, who later became King James I of England. The **Presence Chamber** leads into **Laich Hall** (Lower Hall), the dining room of the royal family.

The **Great Hall** was the castle's ceremonial meeting place in the 16th and 17th centuries. In modern times it was a barracks and a hospital. While most of what you see is Victorian, two medieval elements survive: the fine hammer-beam roof and the big iron-barred peephole (above fireplace on right). This allowed the king to spy on his partying subjects.

**3. The Scottish National War Memorial** commemorates the 149,000 Scottish soldiers lost in World War I, the 58,000 lost in World War II, and the 750 lost in British battles since. Each bay is dedicated to a particular Scottish regiment. The main shrine, featuring a green Italian-marble memorial containing the original WWI rolls of honor, actually sits upon an exposed chunk of the castle rock. Above you, the archangel Michael is busy slaying the dragon. The bronze frieze accurately shows the attire of various wings of Scotland's military. The stained glass starts with Cain and Abel on the left and finishes with a celebration of peace on the right. If the importance of this place is hard to understand, consider that one out of every three adult Scottish men died in World War I.

**4. St. Margaret's Chapel**, the oldest building in Edinburgh, is dedicated to Queen Margaret, who died here in 1093 and was sainted in 1250. Built in 1130 in the Romanesque style of the Norman invaders, it is wonderfully simple, with classic Norman zigzags decorating the round arch that separates the tiny nave from the sacristy. Used as a powder magazine for 400 years, very little survives. You'll see an 11th-century gospel book of St. Margaret's and small windows featuring St. Margaret, St. Columba (who brought Christianity to Scotland via Iona), and William Wallace (the brave defender of Scotland). The place is popular for weddings and, since it seats only 20, particularly popular with brides' fathers.

Mons Meg—a huge and once-upon-a-time frightening 15th-century siege cannon that fired 330-pound stones nearly two miles—stands in front of the church.

Belly up to the bannister (outside the chapel below the cannon) to enjoy the great view. Below you are the guns—which fire the one o'clock salute—and a sweet little line of doggie tombstones, the soldiers' pet cemetery. Beyond stretches the Georgian New Town (read the informative plaque).

**5. The National War Museum of Scotland** thoughtfully covers four centuries of Scottish military history. Instead of the usual musty, dusty displays of endless armor, this museum has an interesting mix of short films, uniforms, weapons, medals, mementos, and eloquent excerpts from soldiers' letters. A pleasant surprise just when you thought your castle visit was about over, this rivals any military museum you'll see in Europe.

When leaving the castle, turn around and look back at the gate. There stand King Robert the Bruce (on the left, 1274–1329) and Sir William Wallace (Braveheart—on the right, 1270–1305). Wallace (newly famous, thanks to Mel Gibson) fought long and hard against English domination before being executed in

London—his body cut to pieces and paraded through the far corners of jolly olde England. Bruce beat the English at Bannockburn in 1314. Bruce and Wallace still defend the spirit of Scotland. The Latin inscription above the gate between them reads (basically) "What you do to us... we will do to you."

## Sights—Along the Royal Mile

These are listed in walking order, from top to bottom. (Bus #35 runs along the Mile, handy for going up after you've hit bottom.)

▲▲▲**Royal Mile**—This is one of Europe's most interesting historic walks. Start at the top and amble down to the palace. The Royal Mile, which consists of a series of four different streets— Castlehill, Lawnmarket, High Street, and Canongate (each with its own set of street numbers)—is actually 200 yards longer than a mile. And every inch is packed with shops, cafés, and lanes leading to tiny squares. As you walk, remember that originally, there were two settlements here, divided by a wall: Edinburgh lined the ridge from the castle at the top. The lower end, Cannongate, was outside the wall until 1856. By poking down the many side alleys, you'll find a few rough edges of a town well on its way to becoming a touristic mall. See it now. In a few years tourists will be slaloming through the postcard racks on bagpipe skateboards.

**Royal Mile Terminology:** A "close" is a tiny alley between two buildings (originally with a door that closed it at night). A close usually leads to a "court" or courtyard. A "land" is a tenement block of apartments. A "pend" is an arched gateway. A "wynd" is a narrow winding lane. And "gate" is from an old Scandinavian word for street.

**Royal Mile Walking Tours:** Mercat Tours offers two-hour guided walks of the Mile—more entertaining than historic (£6, April–Sept daily at 11:00 and 14:00, Oct–March daily 11:15 only, from Mercat Cross on the Royal Mile, tel. 0131/557-6464). The guides, who enjoy making a short story long, ignore the big sights, taking you behind the scenes with piles of barely historic gossip, bully-pulpit Scottish pride, and fun but forgettable trivia. They also offer a variety of other tours. In August only, the Voluntary Guides Association leads free tours of Edinburgh; call for a schedule (tel. 0131/664-7180).

**Castle Esplanade**—At the top of the Royal Mile, the big parking lot leading up to the castle was created as a military parade ground in 1816. It's often cluttered with bleachers under construction for the Military Tattoo—a spectacular massing of the bands that fills the square nightly for most of August (see "Edinburgh Festival," below). At the bottom, on the left (where the square hits the road), a plaque above the tiny witch's fountain memorializes 300 women who were accused of witchcraft and burned here. Scotland burned more witches per capita than any other country—17,000 between

# Royal Mile

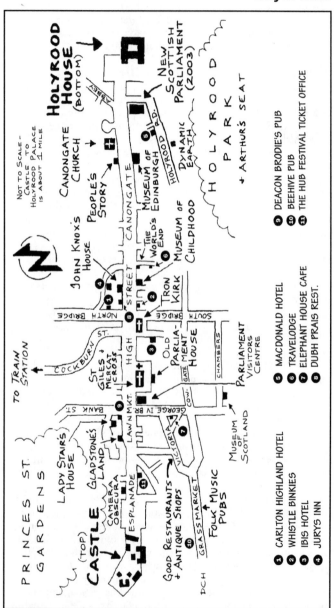

NOT TO SCALE -
CASTLE TO
HOLYROOD PALACE
IS ABOUT 1 MILE

HOLYROOD HOUSE (BOTTOM)

NEW SCOTTISH PARLIAMENT (2003)

HOLYROOD PARK

+ ARTHUR'S SEAT

ABBEY

HOLYROOD RD.

DYNAMIC EARTH

CANONGATE CHURCH

PEOPLE'S STORY

CANONGATE

MUSEUM OF EDINBURGH

JOHN KNOX'S HOUSE

THE WORLD'S END

MUSEUM OF CHILDHOOD

HIGH STREET

TRON KIRK

NORTH BRIDGE

SOUTH BRIDGE

PARLIAMENT VISITORS CENTRE

CHAMBERS

OLD PARLIAMENT HOUSE

COCKBURN ST.

TO TRAIN STATION

ST. GILES + MERCAT CROSS

GATE ST.

GEORGE IV BR.

COW-

MUSEUM OF SCOTLAND

BANK ST.

VICTORIA

LAWN MKT.

LADY STAIR'S HOUSE

GLADSTONE'S LAND

CAMERA OBSCURA

ESPLANADE

GOOD RESTAURANTS + ANTIQUE SHOPS

FOLK MUSIC PUBS

GRASSMARKET

PRINCES ST. GARDENS

CASTLE (TOP)

DCH

## Legend

- ❶ CARLTON HIGHLAND HOTEL
- ❷ WHISTLE BINKIES
- ❸ IBIS HOTEL
- ❹ JURYS INN
- ❺ MACDONALD HOTEL
- ❻ TRAVELODGE
- ❼ ELEPHANT HOUSE CAFE
- ❽ DUBH PRAIS REST.
- ❾ DEACON BRODIE'S PUB
- ❿ BEEHIVE PUB
- ⓫ THE HUB FESTIVAL TICKET OFFICE

1479 and 1722. But in a humanitarian gesture, rather than burning them alive as was the custom in the rest of Europe, Scottish "witches" were strangled to death before they were burned. The plaque shows two witches: one good and one bad. (For 90 minutes of this kind of Royal Mile trivia, take the guided tour described above.)

**Camera Obscura**—A big deal when built in 1853, this observatory topped with a mirror reflected images onto a disc before the wide eyes of people who had never seen a photograph or captured image. Today you can climb 100 steps for an entertaining 15-minute demonstration (3/hr). At the top enjoy the best view anywhere of the Royal Mile. Then work your way down through three floors of illusions, holograms, and early photos. This is a big hit with kids (£4.75, daily 9:30–19:30, less off-season, tel. 0131/2263709).

**Scotch Whiskey Heritage Centre**—This touristy ambush is designed only to distill £6.50 out of your pocket. You get a video history, a short talk, and a little whiskey-keg train-car ride before downing a free sample and finding yourself in the shop 45 minutes later. Those in a hurry are offered the unadvertised quickie—a sample and a whiskey-keg ride for £4.25. People do seem to enjoy it, but that might have something to do with the sample (tel. 0131/220-0441).

**The Hub/Tolbooth Church**—This neo-Gothic church (1844), with the tallest spire in the city, is now The Hub, Edinburgh's Festival Ticket and Information Centre. From here, Johnston Terrace leads down to Grassmarket Street's lively pub scene (see "Nightlife in Edinburgh," below).

**▲▲Gladstone's Land**—Take a good look at this typical 16th- to 17th-century merchant's house, complete with a lived-in furnished interior and guides in each room who love to talk (£3.50, Mon–Sat 10:00–17:00, Sun 14:00–17:00, last entry at 16:30). For a good Royal Mile photo, lean out the upper-floor window (or simply climb the curved stairway outside the museum to the left of the entrance). Notice the snoozing pig outside the front door. Just like every house has a vacuum cleaner today, in the 14th century a snorting rubbish collector was a standard feature of any well-equipped house.

**▲Writers' Museum at Lady Stair's House**—This interesting house, built in 1622, is filled with well-described manuscripts and knickknacks of Scotland's three greatest literary figures: Robert Burns, Sir Walter Scott, and Robert Louis Stevenson. It's worth a few minutes for anyone and is fascinating for fans (free, Mon–Sat 10:00–17:00, closed Sun). Wander around the courtyard here. Edinburgh was a wonder in the 17th and 18th centuries. Tourists came here to see its skyscrapers, which towered 10 stories and higher. No city in Europe was so densely populated as "Auld Reekie."

**Deacon Brodie's Tavern**—This is a decent place for a light meal (see "Eating," below). Read the story of its notorious name-sake on the wall facing Bank Street. Then check out both sides of the hanging signpost.

**Visitors Centre of the Scottish Parliament**—Scotland's Parliament goes back to 1293, was dissolved by England in 1707, and returned in 1999. This new center, kitty-corner to Deacon Brodie's on George IV Bridge, proudly introduces the new Scottish Parliament. Exhibits explain how the parliament works, and models show the building where it will work (currently an expensive hole in the ground near Holyrood Palace, due to open in 2003). At the Visitors Centre (free, Mon–Fri 10:00–17:00, closed Sat–Sun), you can sign up to witness the new Scottish Parliament debating and creating Scottish history in their temporary quarters, a few steps off the Royal Mile, tucked away in Mylnes Court, across from The Hub (debates Wed 14:30–17:30, Thu 9:30–12:30, 14:30–17:30, tel. 0131/348-5411).

**Heart of Midlothian**—Near the street in front of the cathedral, find the outline of a heart in the brickwork. This marks the spot of a gallows and a prison now long gone. Traditionally, locals stand on the rim of the heart and spit into it. Hitting the middle brings good luck. Go ahead . . . do as the locals do.

▲▲**St. Giles Cathedral**—Wander through Scotland's most important church. Stepping inside, find John Knox's statue. Look into his eyes for 10 seconds from 10 inches away. Knox, the great reformer and founder of austere Scottish Presbyterianism, first preached here in 1559. His insistence that every person should be able to read the word of God gave Scotland an educational system 300 years ahead of the rest of Europe. For this reason it was Scottish minds that led the way in math, science, medicine, engineering, and so on. Voltaire called Scotland "the intellectual capital of Europe."

Knox preached Calvinism. Consider that the Dutch and the Scots were about the only nations to embrace this creed of hard work, thrift, and strict ethics. This helps explain why the English and the Scottish are so different (and why the Dutch and the Scots—both famous for their thriftiness and industriousness—are so much alike).

Speaking of intellects, look up at the modern window filling the West Wall celebrating Scotland's favorite poet, Robert Burns. It was made in 1985 by an Icelandic artist (Leifur Breidfjord).

The oldest parts of the cathedral—the four massive central pillars—date from 1120. After the English burnt the cathedral in 1385, it was rebuilt bigger and better than ever, and in 1495 its famous crown spire was completed. During the Reformation—when Knox preached here (1559–1572)—the place was simplified and whitewashed. Before this, with the emphasis on holy services provided by priests, there were lots of little niches. With the new focus on sermons rather than rituals, the floorplan was opened up and the grand pulpit took center stage. The organ (1992, Austrian-built) is one of the best in Europe and comes with a glass panel in the back for peeking into the mechanism.

The neo-Gothic **Chapel of the Knights of the Thistle** (in the far right corner, from 1911), with its intricate wood carving, was built in two years entirely with Scottish material and labor. Find the angel tooting the bagpipes (from inside chapel, above the door to the right). The Scottish crown steeple from 1495 is a proud part of Edinburgh's skyline (Mon–Sat 9:00–17:00, open later and on Sun in summer; ask about concerts—some are free, usually Thu at 13:00; café and WC downstairs; see "Eating," below).

John Knox is buried out back—austerely, under the parking lot, at spot 44. The statue among the cars shows King Charles II riding to a toga party back in 1685.

**Parliament House**—Stop in to see the grand hall with its fine 1639 hammer-beam ceiling and stained glass. This hall housed the Scottish Parliament until the Act of Union in 1707 (explained in history exhibition under the big stained-glass depiction of the initiation of the first Scottish High Court in 1532). It now holds the law courts and is busy with wigged and robed lawyers hard at work in the old library (peek through the door) or pacing the hall deep in discussion. The friendly doorman is helpful (free, public welcome Mon–Fri 9:00–16:30, best action midmornings Tue–Fri, open-to-the-public trials 10:00–16:00—doorman has day's docket, entry behind St. Giles Cathedral near parking spot 21).

**Mercat Cross**—This chunky pedestal, on the downhill side of St. Giles, holds a slender column topped with a white unicorn. Royal proclamations have been read from here since the 14th century. The tradition survives. In 1952, three days (traditionally the time it took for a horse to speed here from London) after the actual event, a town cryer heralded the news that England had a new queen. Today Mercat Cross is the meeting point of various walking tours—both historic and ghostly. Pop into the police information center, a few doors downhill, for a little local law-and-order history (free, May–Aug daily 10:00–22:00, less off-season).

**Tron Kirk**—This fine old building, used as a sales base for a local walking-tour company, sits over an old excavation site and houses a free Old Town history display.

**Cockburn Street**—Across from Tron Kirk, this street was cut through High Street's dense wall of medieval skyscrapers in the 1860s to give easy access to the new Georgian town and the train station. Notice how the sliced buildings were thoughtfully capped with facades in a faux 16th-century Scottish Baronial style. In medieval times, only tiny lanes (like the Fleshmarket Lane just uphill from Cockburn Street) interrupted the long line of Royal Mile buildings. Continue downhill to the old half-timbered building jutting out (John Knox House). Across the street is the . . .

## Scottish Words

| | | | |
|---|---|---|---|
| **aye** | yes | **inch, innis** | island |
| **ben** | mountain | **inver** | river, mouth |
| **bonnie** | beautiful | **kyle** | strait |
| **carn** | heap of stones | **loch** | lake |
| **creag** | rock, cliff | **neeps** | turnips |
| **tattie** | potato | **cello tape** | scotch tape |

**haggis**   rich assortment of oats and sheep organs stuffed into a chunk of sheep intestine, liberally seasoned, boiled, and eaten mostly by tourists. Usually served with "neeps and tatties." Tastier than it sounds.

▲**Museum of Childhood**—This five-story playground of historical toys and games—called the noisiest museum in the world because of its delighted tiny visitors—is rich in nostalgia and history (free, Mon–Sat 10:00–17:00, closed Sun). Just downhill is a fragrant fudge shop offering free samples.

▲**John Knox House**—Fascinating for Reformation buffs, this fine 16th-century house offers a well-explained look at the life of the great reformer (£2.25, Mon–Sat 10:00–17:00, closed Sun, 43 High Street). While Knox never actually lived here, it was called "his house" to save it from the wrecking ball in 1850.

**The World's End**—For centuries, a wall halfway down the Royal Mile marked the end of Edinburgh and the beginning of Cannongate, a community associated with the Holyrood Abbey. Today, where the mile hits St. Mary's and Jeffrey Streets, High Street becomes Cannongate. Just below John Knox House (at #43) notice the hanging sign showing the old gate. At the intersection, find the brass bricks tracing the gate (demolished in 1764). Look down St. Mary's Street to see a surviving bit of that old wall. Then, entering Cannongate, you leave what was Edinburgh . . .

▲**People's Story**—This interesting exhibition traces the lot of the working class through the 18th, 19th, and 20th centuries (free, Mon–Sat 10:00–17:00, closed Sun). Curiously, while this museum is dedicated to the proletariat, immediately around the back is the tomb of Adam Smith—the author of *Wealth of Nations* and the father of modern capitalism (1723–1790).

▲**Museum of Edinburgh**—Another old house full of old stuff, this one is worth a look for its early Edinburgh history and handy ground-floor WC. Don't miss the original copy of the National Covenant (written in 1638 on an animal skin), sketches of pre-Georgian Edinburgh (which show a lake, later filled in to become

Princes Street Gardens when New Town was built), and early golf balls (free, Mon–Sat 10:00–17:00, closed Sun).

**White Horse Close**—Step into this 17th-century courtyard (bottom of Canongate, on the left, a block before Holyrood Palace). It was from here that the Edinburgh stagecoach left for London. Eight days later, the horse-drawn carriage pulled into its destination: Scotland Yard. Across the street is the extravagant new Scottish Parliament building (described below).

▲**Holyrood Palace**—A palace since the 14th century, this marks the end of the Royal Mile. The queen spends a week in Scotland each summer, during which this is her official residence and office. The abbey—part of a 12th-century Augustinian monastery—stood here first. It was named for a piece of the cross brought here as a relic by queen-then-saint Margaret. Scotland's royalty preferred living here to the blustery castle on the rock, and, gradually, the palace grew. The building is rich in history and decor. But without information or a guided tour ("there's none of either," snickered the guy who sells the boring £3.70 museum guidebooks), you're just another peasant in the dark. Docents in each room are happy to give you the answer if you know the question. After wandering through the elegantly furnished rooms and a few dark older rooms filled with glass cases of historic bits and Scottish pieces that must be fascinating, you're free to wander through the ruined abbey and the queen's gardens (£6.50, daily 9:30–18:00, Nov–April until 16:30, while no tours are offered during peak season guided tours are mandatory off-season—2/hr, last admission 45 min before closing, CC; closed last 2 weeks in May, 10 days in early July, when the queen's home, and whenever a prince drops in, tel. 0131/556-7371).

▲**New Scottish Parliament Building**—Slated to open in 2003, the parliament building is being constructed at the base of the Royal Mile next to Holyrood Palace. England forced the union in 1707 and only in 1999 did Scotland win back its parliament and autonomy (at least for domestic concerns). The Visitor Centre (free, daily 10:00–16:00, between Holyrood Palace and big white Dynamic Earth tent) makes a valiant effort to sell this extravagant and therefore controversial building to the Scotch public (don't miss the 10-min video in a room filled with interior/exterior photos of Europe's other great parliament buildings). As a conversation starter, ask a local what he/she thinks about the building's architect, expense, design, and so on.

**Dynamic Earth**—This immense exhibit, filling several underground floors under a vast Gortex tent appropriately pitched at the base of the Salisbury Crags, tells the story of our planet. It's designed for younger kids and does the same thing an American science exhibit would do—but with a charming Scottish accent. Standing in a time tunnel, you watch time rewind from Churchill to dinosaurs to that first big poof. After several short films on stars, tectonic plates, and ice caps, you're free to wander past salty pools, a re-created rain forest, and various TV screens, ending your visit with a 12-minute video finale (£8, family deals, April–Oct daily 10:00–18:00, Nov–March Wed–Sun 10:00–17:00, last ticket sold 70 min before closing, on Holyrood Road, between the palace and mountain, tel. 0131/550-7800).

▲▲▲**Museum of Scotland**—This huge new museum has amassed more historic artifacts than everything I've seen in Scotland combined. It's all wonderfully displayed with fine descriptions offering a best-anywhere hike through the history of Scotland: prehistoric, Roman, Viking, the "birth of Scotland," all the way to life in the 20th century. Audioguides (£2, worthwhile if planning to spend a couple of hours) offer a pleasant (if slow) description of various rooms and exhibits and even provide mood music for your wanderings (free, Mon–Sat 10:00–17:00, Tue until 20:00, Sun 12:00–17:00, free 1-hr orientation tours daily at 14:00, 2 long blocks south of Royal Mile from St. Giles Church, Chambers Street, off George IV Bridge, tel. 0131/247-4422, www.nms.ac.uk).

The **Royal Museum**, next door, fills a fine iron-and-glass Industrial-Age building (built to house the museum in 1851) with all the natural sciences as it "presents the world to Scotland." It's great for school kids, but of no special interest to foreign visitors (free, same hrs as Museum of Scotland). The famous statue of Greyfriars Bobby (Edinburgh's favorite dog—a terrier immortalized by Disney—who stood by his master's grave for 14 years) is across the street. Every business nearby is named for the pooch that put the fidelity into Fido.

## More Bonnie Wee Sights

▲**Georgian New Town**—Cross Waverley Bridge and walk through Georgian Edinburgh. According to the 1776 plan, it was three streets (Princes, George, and Queen) flanked by two squares (St. Andrew and Charlotte), woven together by alleys (Thistle and Rose). George Street—20 feet wider than the others (so a 4-horse carriage could make a U-turn)—was the main drag. And, while Princes Street has gone down market, George Street still maintains its old elegance. The entire elegantly-planned New Town—laid out when George was king—celebrated the hard-to-sell notion that Scotland was an integral part of the United Kingdom. The streets and squares are named after the British royalty (Hanover was the royal family surname). Even Thistle and Rose Streets are emblems of the two happily paired nations. Rose Street, mostly pedestrian-only, is famous for its rowdy pubs. Where it hits St. Andrew's Square, Rose Street is flanked by the venerable Jenners department store and a Sainsbury supermarket. Sprinkled with popular restaurants and bars, stately New Town is turning trendy.

▲▲**Georgian House**—This refurbished Georgian house, set on

Edinburgh's finest Georgian square, is a trip back to 1796. A volunteer guide in each of the five rooms is trained in the force-feeding of stories and trivia. Start your visit with two interesting videos (£5, Mon–Sat 10:00–17:00, Sun 14:00–17:00, videos total 30 min and cover architecture and Georgian lifestyles, shown in the basement, 7 Charlotte Square, tel. 0131/225-2160). A walk down George Street after your visit here can be fun for the imagination.

▲▲**National Gallery**—This elegant neoclassical building has a delightfully small but impressive collection of European master-pieces, from Raphael, Titian, and Rubens to Gainsborough, Monet, and van Gogh. And it offers the best look you'll get at Scottish paintings. The gallery's free, but investing £2 in the fine audioguide makes the museum's highlights yours as well (Mon–Sat 10:00–17:00, Sun 12:00–17:00, tel. 0131/624-6200). After your visit, if the sun's out, enjoy a wander through Princes Street Gardens.

**Princes Street Gardens**—This grassy park, a former lake bed, separates Edinburgh's New and Old Towns and offers a wonderful escape from the city. Once the private domain of the local wealthy, it was opened to the public in about 1870, not as a democratic ges-ture, but because it was thought that allowing the public into the park would increase sales for the Princes Street department stores. There are plenty of free concerts and country dances in the summer and the oldest floral clock in the world. Join the local office workers for a picnic lunch break.

▲**Walter Scott Monument**—Built in 1840, this elaborate, neo-Gothic monument honors the great author, one of Edinburgh's many illustrious sons. Scott, who died in 1832, is considered the father of the romantic historical novel. The 200-foot monument shelters a marble statue of Scott and his dog Maida, surrounded by busts of 16 great Scottish poets and 64 characters from his books. Scott was a great dog lover. Of the 30 dogs he had in his lifetime, his favorite was a deerhound named Maida. Climb 287 steps for a fine view of the city (£2.50, March–Oct Mon–Sat 9:00–18:00, Nov–Feb until 16:00, closed Sun).

**Royal Botanic Garden**—Britain's second-oldest botanical garden, established in 1670 for medicinal herbs, is now one of Europe's best (free, March and Sept 9:30–18:00, April–Aug 9:30–19:00, Nov–Jan 9:30–16:00, Feb and Oct 9:30–17:00, 90-min "rain forest to desert" tours April–Sept daily at 11:00 and 14:00 for £2, 1 mile north of center at Inverleith Row, tel. 0131/552-7171).

## Sights—Near Edinburgh

▲*Britannia*—This much-revered vessel, which carted around Britain's royal family for over 40 years and 900 voyages, is retired, permanently moored at Edinburgh's Port of Leith. It's open to the public and worth the 15-minute bus or taxi ride from the center. After watching a video about the ship, wander through the museum filled with fascinating royal-family-afloat history. Then, armed with your included audioguide, hike the stairs to the ship's top deck and begin working your way down. You'll tour the bridge, dining room, and living quarters, following in the historic footsteps of such notables as Churchill, Gandhi, and Reagan. It's easy to see how the royals must have loved the privacy this floating retreat offered (£8, April–Oct daily 9:30–18:00, Oct–March daily 10:00–17:00, last ticket sold 1.5 hrs before closing; to get to ship from Edinburgh, catch city bus X50 at Waverley Bridge—£3 round-trip, or take the Guide Friday bus—£3.50 round-trip—covered by Guide Friday's £10 combo city-tour ticket; cheap café on site, tel. 0131/555-5566, www.royalyachtbritannia.co.uk).

**Edinburgh Crystal**—Blowing, molding, cutting, polishing, and engraving, the Edinburgh Crystal Company glassworks tour smashes anything you'll see in Venice (£3, daily 10:00–16:30, kids under 8 not admitted). There is a shop full of "bargain" second-quality pieces, a video show, and a cafeteria. A free minibus shuttle departs from Waverley Bridge at the top of the hour (summer daily 10:00–15:00), or you can drive 10 miles south of town on A701 to Penicuik. You can schedule a more expensive VIP tour (£5) where you actually blow and cut glass (tel. 01968/675-128).

## Activities in Edinburgh

▲▲**Arthur's Seat Hike**—A 45-minute hike up the 822-foot volcanic mountain (surrounded by a fine park overlooking Edinburgh), starting from the Holyrood Palace, rewards you with a commanding view. You can drive up most of the way from behind (follow the one-way street from the palace, park by the little lake) or run up like they did in *Chariots of Fire*. From the parking lot (immediately south of Holyrood Palace), you'll see two trails going up. For an easier grade, take the wide path to the left and skip the steeper path that begins with steps and skirts the base of the cliffs. You can also hike up to the Seat from the Dalkeith B&B neighborhood. Take the road (Holyrood Park Road) that borders the Commonwealth pool, turn right (on Queen's Drive), and continue to a small car park. From here, it's a 20-minute hike.

**Brush Skiing**—If you'd rather be skiing, the Midlothian Ski Centre in Hillend has a hill on the edge of town with a chair-lift, two slopes, a jump slope, and rentable skis, boots, and poles. While you're actually skiing over what seems like a million toothbrushes, it feels like snow skiing on a slushy day. Beware: Local doctors are used to treating an ailment called "Hillend Thumb"—thumbs dislocated when people fall here and get tangled in the brush (£6.60/first hr, then £2.70/hr, includes gear, Mon–Fri 9:30–21:00, Sat–Sun 9:30–17:00, closed last 2 weeks of June, probably closed if it snows, LRT bus #4 from Princes Street—garden side, tel. 0131/445-4433).

▲**Royal Commonwealth Games Swimming Pool**—This immense pool is open to the public, with a well-equipped fitness center (£5.80, includes swim), sauna (£6.50 extra, BYO suit), and a cafeteria overlooking the pool (£3 for pool admission only, Mon–Fri 06:00–21:30, Sat–Sun 10:00–16:30, closed 9:00–10:00 every Wed, no towels or suit rentals, tel. 0131/667-7211).

**More Hikes**—You can hike along the river (called Water of Leith) through Edinburgh. Locals favor the stretch between Roseburn and Dean Village, but the 1.5-mile walk from Dean Village to the Royal Botanic Garden is also good. This and other hikes are described in the TI's *Walks in and around Edinburgh* (ask for the free 1-page flyer, not their £2 guide to walks).

**Shopping**—For shopping consider: Princes Street (the elegant old Jenners department store is nearby on Rose Street, at St. Andrew's Square), Victoria Street (antiques galore), Nicolson Street (south of the Royal Mile for a line of interesting second-hand stores), and the Royal Mile (touristy but competitively-priced, shops usually open 9:00–17:30, later on Thu, some closed Sun).

**Bus Tours to Countryside**—Many companies offer daytrips to regional sights (such as Loch Ness). Comparison-shop at the TI's brochure rack. Haggis Backpackers (see "Orientation," above) runs very cheap daytrips (£21, choose between distillery visit and northern Highlands or Loch Lomond and southern Highlands) and overnight trips for young backpackers (but welcoming travelers of all ages) wanting a quick look at the bonnie countryside. Three-daytrips (£80, overnights in hostels on Isle of Skye and Loch Ness) and six-daytrips (£140, overnights in hostels in Oban, Isle of Skye, and Loch Ness) include a tour guide and transport on a 22-seat bus, but hostels cost extra.

## Edinburgh Festival

One of Europe's great cultural events, Edinburgh's annual festival turns the city into a carnival of culture. There are enough music, dance, art, drama, and multicultural events to make even the most jaded traveler drool with excitement. Every day is jammed with formal and spontaneous fun. A number of festivals—official, fringe, book, film, and jazz and blues—rage simultaneously for about three weeks each August, with the Military Tattoo starting a week earlier (the best overall Web site is www.edinburghfestivals.co.uk). Many city sights run on extended hours, and those that normally close on Sunday (Writers' Museum, Museum of Edinburgh, People's Story, and Museum of Childhood) open in the afternoon. It's a glorious time to be in Edinburgh.

The official festival (August 11–31 in 2002) is the original, more formal, and likely to get booked up first. Major events sell out well in advance. The ticket office is at The Hub, located in a former church (with café, ATM, and WC) near the top of the

Royal Mile (tickets-£4-55, CC, booking from mid-April on, office open Mon–Sat 10:00–17:00 or longer, in Aug until 20:00 plus Sun 10:00–17:00, tel. 0131/473-2000, fax 0131/473-2003). Or book online at www.eif.co.uk.

The less-formal **Fringe Festival** features "on the edge" comedy and theater (CC, Aug 4–26 in 2002, ticket/info office just below St. Giles Cathedral on the Royal Mile, 180 High Street, tel. 0131/226-0001, bookings tel. 0131/226-0000, can book online from mid-June on, www.edfringe.com). Tickets are usually available at the door, but popular shows can sell out.

Other festivals in August: jazz and blues (tel. 0131/467-5200, www.jazzmusic.co.uk), film (tel. 0131/229-2550, www.edfilmfest .org.uk), and book (tel. 0131/228-5444, www.edbookfest.co.uk).

The **Military Tattoo** is a massing of the bands, drums, and bagpipes with groups from all over what was the British Empire. Displaying military finesse with a stirring lone-piper finale, this grand spectacle fills the castle esplanade nightly except Sunday, normally from a week before the festival starts until a week before it finishes (Aug 2–24 in 2002). Shows occur Monday through Friday at 21:00 and on Saturdays at 19:30 and 22:30 (£10–28, CC, booking starts in Dec, Fri–Sat shows sell out first; office open Mon–Fri 10:00–16:30, during Tattoo open until showtime and Sat 10:00–19:30 and Sun 12:00–17:00; 33 Market Street, behind—and south of—Waverley train station, tel. 0131/225-1188, www.edintattoo.co.uk). If nothing else, it is a really big show.

If you do manage to hit Edinburgh during the festival, book a room far in advance and extend your stay by a day or two. While Fringe tickets and most Tattoo tickets are available the day of the show, you may want to book a couple of official events in advance. Do it directly by telephone, leaving your credit-card number. Pick up your ticket at the office the day of the show. Several publications—including the festival's official schedule, the *Edinburgh Festivals Guide Daily*, *The List*, the *Fringe Program*, and the *Daily Diary*—list and evaluate festival events.

## Nightlife in Edinburgh

▲**Ghost Walks**—These walks are an entertaining and cheap night out (offered nightly, usually 19:00 and 21:00, easy socializing for solo travelers). The theatrical and creatively staged **Witchery Tours**, the most established of the ghost tours, offer two different walks: "Ghosts and Gore" and "Murder and Mystery" (£7, 90 min, reservations required, leave from the top of the Royal Mile near Castle esplanade, tel. 0131/225-6745).

▲▲**Literary Pub Tour**—This two-hour walk is interesting even if you think Walter Scott was an arctic explorer. You'll follow the witty dialogue of two actors as they debate whether the great literature of Scotland was the creative re-creation of fun-loving louts fueled by a love of whiskey or high art. You'll wander from the Grassmarket, over Old Town to New Town, with stops in three pubs as your guides share their takes on Scotland's literary greats. The tour meets at the Beehive Pub on Grassmarket (£7, nightly in summer at 19:30, with earlier and later tours according to demand, most nights off-season; call 0131/226-6665 to confirm).

▲**Scottish Folk Evenings**—These £35 to £40 dinner shows, generally for tour groups and Japanese travelers intent on photographing old cultural clichés, are held in huge halls of expensive hotels. (Prices are bloated to include 20 percent commissions.) Your "traditional" meal is followed by a full slate of swirling kilts, blaring bagpipes, and Scottish folk dancing with an "old-time music hall"–type emcee. You can often see the show without dinner for about half the price. The TI has fliers on all the latest venues. **Carlton Highland Hotel** offers its Scottish folk evening with or without dinner, nearly nightly (£15 for show only at 20:45–22:30, £39.50 includes super-traditional dinner at 19:30, CC, at High Street and North Bridge, tel. 0131/556-7277).

▲▲**Folk Music in Pubs**—Edinburgh used to be a good place for folk music, but in the last few years, pub-owners—out of economic necessity—are catering to twenty-somethings more interested in beer drinking than traditional music. Pubs that were regular venues for folk music have gone popular. Especially on weekends, you're unlikely to find much live folk music. The monthly *Gig Guide* (free at TI and various pubs, www.gigguide.co.uk) lists most of the live-music action. **Whistle Binkies** still offers nightly ad-lib traditional music, which can start as early as 19:30 or as late as 22:30 and goes until the wee hours (just off the Royal Mile on South Bridge, another entrance on Niddry Street, tel. 0131/557-5114).

**Grassmarket Street** (below the castle) is sloppy with live music and rowdy people spilling out of the pubs and into what was once upon a time a busy market square. It's fun to just wander through Grassmarket late at night. **Finnigan's Wake** has live music—often Irish rock—nightly (starts at 22:00, a block off Grassmarket at 9 Victoria Street, tel. 0131/226-3816). The **Fiddlers Arms**, **Biddy Mulligan**, and **White Hart Inn**, among others, all feature live music. By the noise and crowds you'll know where to go and where not to. Have a beer and follow your ear.

**Theater**—Even outside of festival time, Edinburgh is a fine place for lively and affordable theater. Pick up *The List* for a complete rundown of what's on (£1.95 at newsstands).

## Sleeping in Edinburgh
**(£1 = about $1.50, country code: 44, area code: 0131)**
Sleep Code: **S** = Single, **D** = Double/Twin, **T** = Triple, **Q** = Quad, **b** = bathroom, **s** = shower only, **CC** = Credit Cards accepted, **no CC** = Credit Cards not accepted.

The advent of big, cheap hotels has made life tough for B&Bs. Still, book ahead, especially in August when the annual festival fills Edinburgh. Conventions, school holidays, and weekends can make finding a room tough at almost any time of year. For the best prices, book directly rather than through the TI, which charges a higher room fee and levies a £3 booking fee. "Standard" rooms, with toilets and showers a tissue-toss away, save you £10 a night.

Room prices in this section are usually listed as a range, from low season (winter) to high season (July–Sept). I have not listed the higher "festival prices"—which are limited to August. Prices get soft off-season, for longer visits, and sometimes for midweek stays outside of summer.

## Sleeping off Dalkeith Road

These recommendations are south of town near the Royal Commonwealth Pool, just off Dalkeith Road. This comfortable and safe neighborhood is a 20-minute walk or 10-minute bus ride from the Royal Mile. All listings are nonsmoking, on quiet streets, a two-minute walk from a bus stop, and well-served by city buses. B&Bs are unlikely to accept bookings for one-night stays in August.

Near the B&Bs you'll find plenty of eateries (see "Eating," below), easy free parking, and **Laundromats**—one at 208 Dalkeith Road (Mon–Sat 8:30–17:00, closed Sun, £4-self-service, £5.50-full-service, drop off by 11:00 for same-day service, June–Sept they'll deliver your clean clothes to your B&B for free, tel. 0131/667-0825) and another at 13 South Clerk Street (Mon–Fri 8:00–20:00, Sat 9:00–17:00, Sun 10:00–16:00, opposite Queens Hall).

To reach the hotel neighborhood from the train station, TI, or Scott Monument, cross Princes Street and wait at the **bus stop** under the small C&A sign on the department store (80p; LRT buses #14, #21, and #33, or First buses #86 and #C3; tell driver your destination is "Dalkeith Road;" red bus: exact change or pay more; green bus: makes change; ride 10 min to first or second stop—depending on B&B—after the pool, push the button, exit middle door). These buses also stop at the corner of North Bridge and High Street on the Royal Mile. Buses run from 06:00 to 23:00, and after 9:00 on Sunday morning. **Taxi** fare between the station or Royal Mile and the B&Bs is about £4.

## B&Bs off Dalkeith Road

**Dunedin Guest House** (dun-EE-din)—bright, plush, and elegantly Scottish, with seven huge rooms—is a fine value (S-£20–35, Db-£40–70, no CC, family rooms for up to 5, strong showers, 8 Priestfield Road, EH16 5HH, tel. 0131/668-1949, fax 0131/668-3636, e-mail: dunedin-guesthouse@edinburgh-EH16.freeserve.co.uk, Marsella Bowen).

**Turret Guest House** is teddy-on-the-beddy cozy, with a great

## Edinburgh, Our Neighborhood

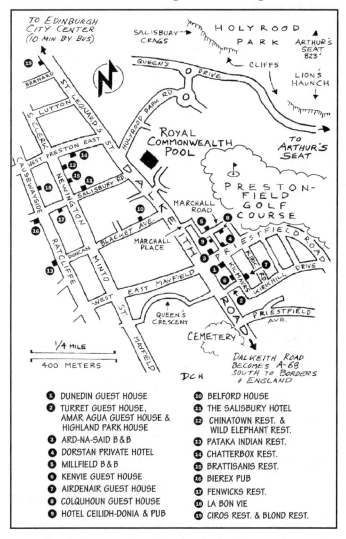

● ① DUNEDIN GUEST HOUSE
● ② TURRET GUEST HOUSE,
   AMAR AGUA GUEST HOUSE &
   HIGHLAND PARK HOUSE
● ③ ARD-NA-SAID B & B
● ④ DORSTAN PRIVATE HOTEL
● ⑤ MILLFIELD B & B
● ⑥ KENVIE GUEST HOUSE
● ⑦ AIRDENAIR GUEST HOUSE
● ⑧ COLQUHOUN GUEST HOUSE
● ⑨ HOTEL CEILIDH-DONIA & PUB

● ⑩ BELFORD HOUSE
● ⑪ THE SALISBURY HOTEL
● ⑫ CHINATOWN REST. &
   WILD ELEPHANT REST.
● ⑬ PATAKA INDIAN REST.
● ⑭ CHATTERBOX REST.
● ⑮ BRATTISANIS REST.
● ⑯ BIEREX PUB
● ⑰ FENWICKS REST.
● ⑱ LA BON VIE
● ⑲ CIROS REST. & BLOND REST.

bay-windowed family room and a vast breakfast menu that includes haggis and vegetarian options (7 rooms, S-£20–23, Sb-£23–28, D-£42–48, Db-£44–58, £2/person discount with this book and cash, no CC, 8 Kilmaurs Terrace, EH16 5DR, tel. 0131/667-6704, fax 0131/668-1368, www.turret.clara.net, Mrs. Jackie Cameron).

**Amar Agua Guest House**, next door to Turret, is an inviting Victorian home away from home (7 rooms, S-£18–27, Db-£36–58, £2/person discount with this book, no CC, 10 Kilmaurs Terrace, EH16 5DR, tel. 0131/667-6775, fax 0131/6677687, e-mail: amaragua @cableinet.co.uk, run by energetic young couple Dawn-Ann and Tony Costa).

**Ard-Na-Said B&B** is an elegant 1875 Victorian house with a comfy lounge and five classy rooms (1 S-£22–28, Db-£44–56, family deals, no CC, 5 Priestfield Road, EH16 5HH, tel. 0131/6 67-8754, fax 0131/271-0960, www.ardnasaid.freeserve.co.uk, enthusiastically run by Jim and Olive Lyons).

**Dorstan Private Hotel** is more formal, professional, and hotelesque, with all the comforts. Several of its 14 thoughtfully-decorated rooms are on the ground floor (2 Ds-£60, Db-£66, family rooms, CC, no clothes washing except for "smalls," 7 Priest-field Road, EH16 5HJ, tel. 0131/667-6721, fax 0131/668-4644, e-mail: reservations@dorstan-hotel.demon.co.uk, Mairae Campbell).

**Millfield B&B**, run graciously by Liz Broomfield, is thought-fully furnished with antique class, a rare sit-and-chat ambience, and a comfy TV lounge. Since the showers are down the hall, you'll get spacious rooms and great prices (S-£21–23, D-£38–40, T-£48–52, no CC, reconfirm reservation by phone, 12 Marchhall Road, EH16 5HR, tel. & fax 0131/667-4428). Decipher the break-fast prayer by Robert Burns. Then try the "Taste of Scotland" breakfast option. See how many stone (14 pounds) you weigh in the elegant throne room.

**Kenvie Guest House**, well run by Dorothy Vidler, comes with six pleasant rooms and lots of personal touches (1 small twin-£40, D-£42, Db-£50, family deals, 3 percent more with CC, 16 Kilmaurs Road, EH16 5DA, tel. 0131/668-1964, fax 0131/ 668-1926, www.kenvie.co.uk, e-mail: dorothy@kenvie.co.uk).

**Airdenair Guest House**, offering views and homemade scones (made by the owner's mom), has five attractive rooms with a lofty above-it-all feeling (Sb-£25–35, Db-£40–50, CC, 29 Kilmaurs Road, EH16 5DB, tel. 0131/668-2336, http://airdenair .edinburghnet.co.uk/, Jill McLennan).

**Highland Park House** has bright, basic rooms (S-£20–25, D-£40–44, Db-£44–52 with this book, family deals, no CC, 16 Kilmaurs Terrace, EH16 5DR, tel. & fax 0131/667-9204, e-mail: highlandparkhouse@hotmail.com, Margaret and Brian Love).

**Colquhoun Guest House**, in an elegant building, has seven fine rooms, several on the ground floor (S-£22–25, D-£40, Db-£50, family room, no CC, 5 Marchhall Road, EH16 5HR, tel. 0131-667-8481, run by amazing Grace McAinsh).

**Hotel Ceilidh-Donia** is a work in progress with 14 basic rooms and a fun pub (Db-£45–60, CC, 14 Marchhall Crescent, tel. 0131/667-2743, run by Max, a creative man with a big vision).

**Belford House** is a tidy, homey place offering seven good rooms and a warm welcome (D-£40–44, Db-£50–54, family deals, CC, 5 percent off with cash, 13 Blacket Avenue, tel. 0131/667-2422, fax 0131/667-7508, e-mail: mailbox@belfordguesthouse .com, Isa and Tom Borthwick).

**The Salisbury**, more like a hotel than its neighbors, fills a classy old Georgian building with 12 rooms, a large lounge, tired carpeting, and even a dumbwaiter in the breakfast room (D-£44–52, Db-£50–56, 5 percent off with cash and this book, CC, free parking, 45 Salisbury Road, EH16 5AA, tel. & fax 0131/667-1264, http://members.edinburgh.org/salisbury/, Brenda Wright).

## Big, Modern Hotels

Four of these listings are cheap as hotels go and offer more comfort than character. One's a splurge. In each case I'd skip the institutional breakfast and eat out.

**Sleeping cheap near the Royal Mile: Travelodge**, the cheapest hotel in the center, has 193 no-nonsense, central rooms all decorated in dark blue. All rooms are the same and suitable for two adults with two kids or three adults. While sleepable, it has a cheap feel with a quickly-revolving staff (Sb, Db, Tb all £50 except £70 Fri–Sun in Aug, breakfast-£8, CC, 33 St. Mary's Street, a block off the Royal Mile, tel. 08700-850-950, www.travelodge.co.uk).

**Ibis Hotel**, mid–Royal Mile behind Tron Church, is well-run and perfectly located. It has 98 soulless but clean and comfy rooms drenched in pre-fab American charm (Sb-£54–70, Db-£60–70, top price July–Aug, discounted in off-season, lousy continental breakfast-£4, CC, nonsmoking rooms, elevator, 6 Hunter Square, EH1 1QW, tel. 0131/240-7000, fax 0131/240-7007, e-mail: H2039@accor-hotels.com).

**Jurys Inn**, another cookie-cutter place with 186 dependably comfortable rooms, is well-located a short walk from the station and capably run (Sb, Db, Tb all £90 Fri–Sat, £70 Sun–Thu, much cheaper in off-season, CC, breakfast-£8, 2 kids sleep free, nonsmoking rooms, some views, pub/restaurant, on quiet street just off Royal Mile, 43 Jeffrey Street, EH1 1DG, tel. 0131/200-3300, fax 0131/200-0400, www.jurys.com).

**Splurge near the Royal Mile: MacDonald Hotel**, my only fancy listing, is an opulent five-star splurge across the street from the new parliament. With its classy marble-and-wood decor, fitness center, and pool, it's hard to leave. On a gray winter day in Edinburgh, this could be worth it. Prices vary wildly (50 rooms, Db-£170, breakfast-£13, CC, near bottom of Mile, across from Dynamic Earth, Holyrood Road, EH8 6AE, tel. 0131/550-4500, fax 0131/550-4545, www.macdonaldhotels.co.uk). Beg for free breakfast before reserving and you'll likely get it.

**Away from the center: Travel Inn**, the biggest hotel in Edinburgh, has even less character—with a clientele to match—but a great price and a mediocre location about a mile west of the Mile. Each of its 280 rooms is modern and comfortable, with a sofa that folds out for two kids if necessary (Db-£52 for 2 adults and up to 2 kids under 15, breakfast is extra, CC, elevators, non-smoking rooms, weekends booked long in advance, near Haymarket station west of the castle at 1 Morrison Link, EH3 8DN, tel. 0131/228-9819, fax 0131/228-9836, www.travelinn.co.uk).

## Hostels
Although Edinburgh's hostels are well-run and open to all—providing Internet access, laundry facilities, and £12 bunk beds in 8- to 16-bed single-sex dorms (about a £9–12 savings over B&Bs)—they are scruffy and don't include breakfast.

**Castle Rock Hostel** is hip and easygoing, offering cheap beds, plenty of friends, and a great central location just below the castle and above the pubs with all the folk music (15 Johnston Terrace, tel. 0131/225-9666). Their sister hostels are nearly across the street from each other: **High Street Hostel** (laundry-£2.50, kitchen, 8 Blackfriars Street, just off High Street/Royal Mile, tel. 0131/557-3984) and **Royal Mile Backpackers** (105 High Street, tel. 0131/557-6120).

For more regulations and less color, try the IYH hostels: **Bruntsfield Hostel** (6–12 beds/room, near golf course, 7 Bruntsfield Crescent, buses #11, #15, #16, and #17 from Princes Street, tel. 0131/447-2994) and **Edinburgh Hostel** (4–10 beds/room, 5-min walk from Haymarket station, 18 Eglinton Crescent, tel. 0131/337-1120).

# Eating in Edinburgh
## Eating along the Royal Mile
Historic pubs and doily cafés with reasonable, unremarkable meals abound. Here are some handy, affordable places for a good bite to eat (listed in downhill order). **Deacon Brodie's Pub** serves soup, sandwiches, and snacks on the ground floor and good £8 meals upstairs in the restaurant. As in all Edinburgh pubs, kids are allowed only in the restaurant section (daily 12:00–22:00, CC, tel. 0131/225-6531). Or munch prayerfully in the **Lower Aisle** restaurant under St. Giles Cathedral (Mon–Fri 8:30–16:30, Sun 10:00–14:00, closed Sat except in Aug). The **Filling Station**, a big noisy bar decorated with car parts, has an American-type menu, serves good burgers, and rocks at night (daily 12:00–22:30, 235 High Street, near North Bridge, tel. 0131/226-2488). **Bann UK**, a vegetarian café, serves healthy cuisine that goes way beyond tofu and granola (daily 11:00–23:00, CC, just off South Bridge behind Tron Church

at 5 Hunter Square, tel. 0131/226-1112). **Dubh Prais Scottish Restaurant**—the only serious restaurant on this list—is a dressy little place filling a cellar 10 steps and a world away from the High Street bustle. The owner/chef promises to serve Scottish fayre at its very best. The only thing not Scottish here is the wine list and some of the guests (£10 lunches Tue–Fri 12:00–14:00, £25 dinners Tue–Sat 18:30–22:30, closed Sun–Mon, CC, reservations smart at night, opposite Crowne Plaza at 123b High Street, tel. 0131/557-5732). **Food Plantation** has good, inexpensive, fresh sandwiches to eat in or take out (Mon–Fri 10:00–15:30, closed Sat–Sun, 274 Canongate). **The Tea Room** serves light lunches, scones, and fine tea in yellow elegance (Mon–Sat 10:30–16:45, Sun 11:00–16:45, next to Museum of Edinburgh at 158 Canongate). **Clarinda's Tea Room**, near the bottom of the Royal Mile, is a charming and tasty place to relax after touring the Mile or palace (daily 9:00–16:45, 69 Cannongate, tel. 0131/557-1888).

For a break from the touristic grind just off the top end of the Royal Mile, consider the **Elephant House**, where locals browse newspapers in the stay-awhile back room, listen to classic rock, and sip coffee or munch a light meal (Mon–Fri 8:00–23:00, Sat–Sun 9:00–23:00, 2 blocks south of Royal Mile near Museum of Scotland at 21 George IV Bridge, tel. 0131/220-5355).

**Grassmarket Street**, below the castle, is lined with lots of eateries and noisy pubs. This is the place for live music and absorbent food.

### Eating in the New Town

**Princes Mall Food Court**, below the TI and above the station, is a circus of sticky fast-food joints littered with paper plates and shoppers (Mon–Sat 8:30–18:00, Thu until 19:00, Sun 11:00–17:00). If you'd prefer pubs, browse the nearby Rose Street.

**The Dome Restaurant** serves decent meals around a classy bar under the elegant 19th-century skylight dome of what was a fancy bank. With soft jazz and dressy, white-tablecloth ambience, it feels a world apart (£10 lunches until 17:00, £16 dinners until 24:00, daily 12:00–24:00, modern cuisine, borderline smoky, open for a drink anytime under the dome or in the adjacent art deco bar, 14 George Street, tel. 0131/624-8624). Notice the façade of this former bank building—the various ways to make money fill the pediment with all the nobility of classical gods.

The **Undercroft**, in the basement of St. Andrew's church, is the cheapest place in town for lunch (£1 sandwich or soup and roll, Mon–Fri 12:00–14:00, closed Sat–Sun, on George Street, just off St. Andrew's Square).

**Café Royal** is a movie producer's dream pub—the perfect *fin de siècle* setting for a coffee, beer, or light meal (parts of *Chariots of Fire* were filmed in here). Drop in, if only to admire the 1880

## Edinburgh's New Town

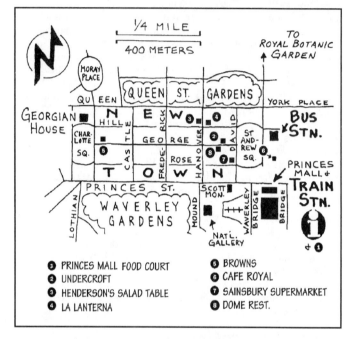

- ❶ PRINCES MALL FOOD COURT
- ❷ UNDERCROFT
- ❸ HENDERSON'S SALAD TABLE
- ❹ LA LANTERNA
- ❺ BROWNS
- ❻ CAFE ROYAL
- ❼ SAINSBURY SUPERMARKET
- ❽ DOME REST.

tiles featuring famous inventors (2 blocks from Princes Mall on West Register Street).

A generation of New Town vegetarians have munched hearty cuisine and salads at **Henderson's Salad Table and Wine Bar** (£5–6, Mon–Sat 8:00–22:45, closed Sun, CC, nonsmoking section, strictly vegetarian, pleasant live jazz nightly in Wine Bar, between Queen and George Streets at 94 Hanover Street, tel. 0131/225-2131). Henderson's has two different seating areas, but both use the same self-serve cafeteria line. They also run Henderson's Bistro upstairs with table service.

Local office workers pile into the friendly and family-run **La Lanterna** for good Italian food (Mon–Sat 12:00–14:00, 17:15–22:00, closed Sun, CC, dinner reservations wise, 2 blocks off Princes Street, 83 Hanover Street, tel. 0131/226-3090).

**Supermarket**: The glorious **Sainsbury** supermarket, with a tasty assortment of take-away food and specialty coffee, is just one block from the Walter Scott Monument and the lovely picnic-perfect Princes Street Gardens (Mon–Sat 7:00–22:00, Sun 10:00–19:00, CC, on corner of Rose Street, on St. Andrew's Square, across the street from Jenners, the classy department store).

## Eating in Dalkeith Road Area, near Your B&B

All these places are within a 10-minute walk of the recommended B&Bs. Most are on or near the intersection of Newington and East Preston Streets. For location, see map on page 279.

**Ethnic Restaurants: Chinatown**—an oasis of Asian calm—is a delightful Chinese restaurant with sharp service and loyal local clientele (£7–10, Tue–Fri 12:00–14:00, 17:30–23:30, Sat–Sun 17:30–23:00, closed Mon, CC, reservations smart on weekend nights, take-away food is 25 percent off, Newington Road, tel. 0131/662-0555).

**Pataka Indian and Bengali Restaurant**, a 10-table "Indian bistro" with attentive service and great food, is understandably popular with locals. Portions are big, but not overly spicy, and prices are small. This tight little restaurant can be a bit smoky (£7 dishes, nightly 17:30–23:30, CC, also offers take-away, 190 Causewayside, tel. 0131/668-1167).

**Wild Elephant**, a few doors down from recommended Chinatown restaurant, is a plain, cheap place serving decent Thai food to locals who dress like grunge is the new craze (£4–7, Wed–Mon 16:30–22:00, closed Tue, they don't serve wine but you can BYO wine for £1 corkage fee, CC, also does take-away, 21 Newington Road, tel. 0131/662-8822).

**Scottish/French Restaurants:** Several classy little eight-table places feature "Auld Alliance" cuisine—Scottish cooking with a French flair (seasoned with a joint, historic disdain for England). They offer small menus with three or four items per course for two- or three-course meals (about £10 for a 2-course lunch, £20 for a 3-course dinner). These popular places take credit cards, and reservations are smart on weekends evenings. Many offer less-expensive meals outside of weekends.

**Fenwicks** is cozy and reliable, with tasty food and no French fries (daily 12:00–14:00, dinner 18:00–late, open all day Sun, CC, 15 Salisbury Place, tel. 0131/667-4265).

**Ciros Restaurant** is a hard-working, well-established family affair (£10 2-course lunches, £24 3-course dinners, £15 dinner Tue–Thu; open Tue–Sat 12:00–14:00, 18:30–21:45, closed Sun–Mon; 93 St. Leonards Street, tel. 0131/668-4207, run by Christine, Jean, and Stuart Stevenson).

**La Bon Vie Restaurant** is perhaps the liveliest with the most enticing menu (Mon–Sat 18:00–22:00, closed Sun, 49 Causewayside, tel. 0131/667-1110).

**Blond Restaurant**, with a more eclectic and European menu, is less expensive and bigger than the others with no set-price dinners (about £12 for 2 courses, Tue–Sun 12:00–14:00, 18:00–22:00, closed Mon, 75 St. Leonard's Street, tel. 0131/668-2917).

**Pubs: Hotel Ceilidh-Donia's pub** serves good grub with live folk music most nights and offers free Internet access to diners (£6–7, Mon–Fri eves plus Sun lunch 12:00–14:30, CC, within a block of most recommended B&Bs at 14 Marchhall Crescent, tel. 0131/667-2743, Max).

**Bierex**, a modern and youthful pub, is the neighborhood favorite for edible grub and a social atmosphere (132 Causeway-side, tel. 0131/667-2335).

**Cheaper Choices**: **Chatterbox**, a grandmotherly little place, is fine for a light meal with tea (£4 meals, Thu–Mon, open only until 18:00, closed Wed, around corner from Chinatown on East Preston Street).

**Brattisanis** is your basic fish-and-chips joint serving lousy milkshakes and great haggis. Add a cheap touch of class by bringing in a beer or half bottle of wine from next door (daily 11:30–23:00, 87 Newington Road).

On Dalkeith Road, the huge Commonwealth Pool's noisy **cafeteria** is for hungry swimmers and budget travelers alike (Mon–Fri 10:00–20:00, Sat–Sun 10:00–17:00, pass the entry without paying).

**Supermarket**: The nearest supermarket, **Tesco**, is located between the Royal Mile and the Dalkeith B&B neighborhood (Mon–Sat 8:00–21:00, Sun 9:00–19:00, 5 long blocks south of the Royal Mile, on Nicolson, just south of intersection with West Richmond Street).

## Transportation Connections—Edinburgh

**By train to: Inverness** (7/day, 4 hrs), **Oban** (3/day, change in Glasgow, 4.5 hrs), **York** (1/hr, 2.5 hrs), **London** (1/hr, 5 hrs), **Durham** (1/hr, 2 hrs, less frequent in winter), **Newcastle** (1/hr, 1.5 hrs), **Keswick**, the Lake District (south past Carlisle to Penrith, then catch bus to Keswick, 1/hr except Sun 6/day, 40 min), **Birmingham** (6/day, 4.5 hrs), **Crewe** (6/day, 3.5 hrs), **Bristol**, near Bath (1/hr, 6–7 hrs). Train info: tel. 08457-484-950.

**By bus to: Oban** (1/day, 9:15 departure, 4 hrs, not on Sun), **Fort William** (1/day, 4 hrs), **Inverness** (1/hr, 4 hrs), **Blackpool** (requires change in Glasgow, 5 hrs), **York** (1/day at 9:45, 5 hrs). For bus info, call Scottish Citylink (tel. 08705-505-050, www.citylink.co.uk) or National Express (tel. 08705-808-080). You can get info and tickets at the bus desk inside the Princes Mall TI.

## Route Tips for Drivers

**Arriving in Edinburgh from the north:** Rather than drive through downtown Edinburgh to the recommended B&Bs, circle the city on the A720 City Bypass road. Approaching Edinburgh on the M-9, take the M-8 (direction: Glasgow) and quickly get onto the A720 City Bypass (direction: Edinburgh South). After four miles you'll hit a roundabout. Ignore signs directing you into Edinburgh North and stay on A720 for 10 more miles to the next and last roundabout, named Sheriffhall. Exit the round-about on the first left (A7 Edinburgh). From here it's four miles to the B&B neighborhood (see "Arriving from the south," below, and B&B neighborhood map).

**Arriving from the south:** Coming into town on A68 from the south, take the "A7 Edinburgh" exit off the roundabout. A7 becomes Dalkeith Road. If you see the huge swimming pool, you've gone a couple of blocks too far (avoid this by referring to B&B neighborhood map above).

**Leaving Edinburgh, heading south:** It's 100 miles from Edinburgh to Hadrian's Wall; to Durham it's another 50 miles. From Edinburgh, Dalkeith Road leads south and eventually becomes A68 (handy Cameron Toll supermarket with cheap gas is on the left as you leave Dalkeith Town, 10 min south of Edinburgh; gas and parking behind store). A68 takes you to Hadrian's Wall in two hours. You'll pass Jedburgh and its abbey after one hour. (For one last shot of shop-Scotland, there's a coach tour's delight just before Jedburgh, with kilt makers, woolens, and a sheepskin shop.) Across from Jedburgh's lovely abbey is a free parking lot, a good visitors center, and public toilets (20p to pee). The England/Scotland border is a fun, quick stop (great view, ice cream, and tea caravan). Before Hexham, roller-coaster two miles down A6079 to B6318, following the Roman wall westward. (See "Hadrian's Wall" in the Durham chapter for more driving instructions.)

# OBAN, ISLANDS, AND HIGHLANDS

Filled with more natural and historical mystique than people, the Highlands are where Scottish dreams are set. Legends of Bonnie Prince Charlie swirl around crumbling castles as pipers and kilts swirl around tourists. The harbor of Oban is a fruit crate of Scottish traditions, and the wind-bitten Hebrides are just an island hop, skip, and jump away.

The Highlands are cut in two by the impressive Caledonian Canal, with Oban at one end and Inverness at the other. The major sights cluster along the scenic 120-mile stretch between these two towns. Oban is a fine home base for western Scotland, and Inverness makes a good overnight stop on your way through eastern Scotland.

## Planning Your Time

While Ireland has more charm and Wales has better sights, this area provides your best look at rural Scottish culture. There are a lot of miles, but they're scenic, the roads are good, and the traffic's light. In two days you can get a feel for the area with the car hike described below. To do the islands, you'll need more time. Iona is worthwhile but adds a day to your trip. Generally, the region is hungry for the tourist dollar, and everything overtly Scottish is designed to woo the tourist. You'll need more than this quick visit to get away from that.

The charm of the Highlands deserves more time and a trip farther north (ideally to the Isle of Skye). But with a car and two days to connect the Lake District and Edinburgh, this blitz tour is more interesting than two more days in England.

**Day 1:** 9:00–Leave Lake District (see Castlerigg Stone Circle if you haven't yet), 12:00–Rest stop on Loch Lomond, then joyride on, 13:00–Lunch in Inveraray, 16:00–Arrive in Oban, tour whiskey distillery, and drop by the TI, 20:00–Have dinner with music at McTavish's Kitchens or dinner with class at The Studio.

**Day 2:** 9:00–Leave Oban, 10:00–Visit Glencoe museum and the valley's Visitors Centre, 12:00–Drive to Fort William and follow Caledonian Canal to Inverness, stopping at Fort Augustus for a wander around the locks and at Loch Ness to take care of any monster business, 16:00–Visit the evocative Culloden Battlefield near Inverness, 17:00–Drive south, 20:00–Set up in Edinburgh.

With more time, spend a second night in Oban and tour Iona, get to know Arthur Smith at Glencoe, or sleep in Inverness or Pitlochry, both fun and entertaining towns.

# OBAN

Oban, called the "gateway to the isles," is a busy little ferry-and-train terminal with no important "sights" but a charming shiver-and-bustle vitality that gives you a feel for small-town Scotland. Wind, boats, gulls, layers of islands, and the promise of a wide-open Atlantic beyond give it a rugged and salty charm.

## Orientation (area code: 01631)

Oban's business action, just a couple of streets deep, stretches along the harbor and its promenade. Everything's close together, and the town seems eager to please its many visitors. There's live, touristy music nightly in several bars and restaurants; woolen and tweed are perpetually on sale (tourist shops open until 20:00 and on Sun); and posters announce a variety of day tours to Scotland's wild and rabbit-strewn western islands.

**Tourist Information:** The TI has brochures on everything from bike rental to golf courses to horseback riding to rainy-day activities as well as a fine bookshop (Mon–Sat 9:00–20:00, Sun 9:00–19:00, less Sept–June, Internet access-£5/hr, £1 room reservation fee, no WC, on Argyll Square, just off the harbor a block from the train station, tel. 01631/563-122, www.visitscottishheartlands .org). Wander through their exhibit on the area and pick up a few phones to hear hardy locals talk about their life on the wild, west edge of Scotland. Check the TI's "What's On" board for the latest on Oban's small-town evening scene (free live entertainment nightly at the Great Western Hotel, with a Scottish Night every Wed, tel. 01631/563-101).

## Helpful Hints

Hazelbank Motors rents **bikes** (£8/half day, £14/day) and mopeds (£15/half day, £25/day, over 18 only, must have U.S. license) behind Tesco supermarket on Lynn Road (Mon–Sat 8:30–17:30, closed Sun, at intersection with Mill Lane, tel. 01631/566-476). The New Age Café na Lusan at 9 Craigard Road provides the

# Oban Town

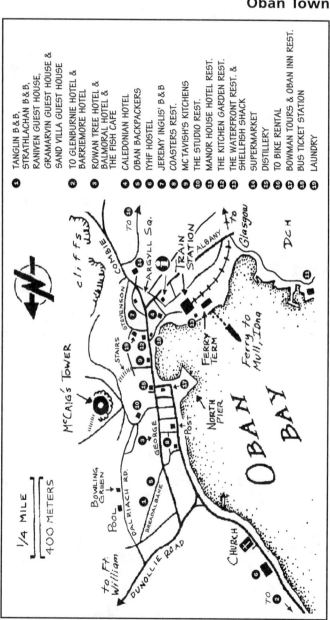

- **1** TANGLIN B & B,
  STRATHLACHAN B & B,
  RANIVEN GUEST HOUSE,
  GRAMARVIN GUEST HOUSE &
  SAND VILLA GUEST HOUSE
- **2** TO GLENBURNIE HOTEL &
  BARRIEMORE HOTEL
- **3** ROWAN TREE HOTEL &
  BALMORAL HOTEL &
  THE FISH CAFE
- **4** CALEDONIAN HOTEL
- **5** OBAN BACKPACKERS
- **6** IYHF HOSTEL
- **7** JEREMY INGLIS' B & B
- **8** COASTERS REST.
- **9** MC TAVISH'S KITCHENS
- **10** THE STUDIO REST.
- **11** MANOR HOUSE HOTEL REST.
- **12** THE KITCHEN GARDEN REST.
- **13** THE WATERFRONT REST. &
  SHELLFISH SHACK
- **14** SUPERMARKET
- **15** DISTILLERY
- **16** TO BIKE RENTAL
- **17** BOWMAN TOURS & OBAN INN REST.
- **18** BUS TICKET STATION
- **19** LAUNDRY

cheapest **Internet access** (£3.50/hr, Sun–Mon 11:30–15:30,
Tue–Sat 11:30–21:30, less off-season, tel. 01631/567-268).
Internet access is also available at the TI (see above) and Oban
Backpackers hostel (daily 10:00–19:00, £3/30 min, near B&Bs
on Breadalbane Street, tel. 01631/562-107).

## Sights—Oban
▲**West Highland Malt Scotch Whiskey Distillery Tours**—
The 200-year-old Oban Whiskey Distillery produces over 14,500
liters a week. They offer serious and fragrant 40-minute, £3.50
tours explaining the process from start to finish, with a free,
smooth sample and a discount coupon for the shop. The exhibition preceding the tour gives a quick, whiskey-centric history of
Scotland. This is the handiest whiskey tour you'll see, just a block
off the harbor and better than anything in Edinburgh (July–Sept
Mon–Fri 9:30–20:30, Sat until 17:00, Sun 12:00–17:00, off-season
until 17:00, last tour 1 hr before closing, to avoid a wait, call to
reserve a place, tel. 01631/572-004).

**McCaig's Tower**—The unfinished "colosseum" on the hill
overlooking the town was an "employ-the-workers-and-build-
me-a-fine-memorial" project undertaken by an early Oban tycoon
in 1900. While the structure itself is nothing to see close-up, a
10-minute hike through a Victorian residential neighborhood
gets you to a peaceful garden and a mediocre view.

**Activities**—The Atlantis Sports and Leisure Center has an indoor
**swimming pool** (with big water slide) and a rock-climbing wall
(Mon–Fri 7:00–22:00, Sat–Sun 8:30–21:00, pool: £2.50-adults,
£1.50-kids ages 3–15, no towels or suits for rent, lockers-20p,
2 blocks above recommended B&Bs on Dalriach Road, tel. 01631/
566-8000). The center's outdoor playground is free and open
all the time.

The **Oban Lawn Bowling Club** has welcomed visitors since
1869. This elegant green is the scene of a wonderfully British
spectacle of old men tiptoeing wishfully after their balls. It's fun
to watch, and—if there's no match and the weather's dry—for £2
each you can rent shoes and balls and actually play (next to sports
center on Dalriach Road).

## Sights—Near Oban
▲▲**Daytrip to the Islands of Iona and Mull**—See below.

**Kerrera**—This stark but very green island, nearly opposite Oban,
offers a quick, easy opportunity to get that romantic island experience (ferry-£3 round-trip, 50p for bikes, 2 ferries/hr 10:30–12:00,
14:00–18:00, less off-season, at Gallanach's dock 2 miles south of
Oban, tel. 01631/563-665, if no answer contact TI for info).

**Isle of Seil**—Enjoy a drive, a walk, some solitude, and the sea.
Drive 12 miles south of Oban on A816 to B844 to the Isle of Seil,

connected to the mainland by a bridge. Just over the bridge on the Isle of Seil is a pub called Tigh-an-Truish ("House of Trousers"). After a 1745 English law forbade the wearing of kilts on the mainland, Highlanders used this pub to change from kilts to trousers before crossing the bridge. The pub serves great meals to those in kilts or pants (daily 12:00–14:00, 18:00–20:30, darts anytime, good seafood dish, crispy vegetables, tel. 01852/300-242). Five miles across the island, on a tiny second island, is Easdale, a historic, touristy, windy, little slate-mining town—with a slate-town museum and incredibly tacky egomaniac's "Highland Arts" shop—facing the open Atlantic (shuttle ferry goes the 300 yards).

## Sleeping in Oban
**(£1 = about $1.50, country code: 44, area code: 01631)**
Sleep Code: **S** = Single, **D** = Double/Twin, **T** = Triple, **Q** = Quad, **b** = bathroom, **s** = shower only, **CC** = Credit Cards accepted, **no CC** = Credit Cards not accepted.

The first five places are well located on a quiet street two blocks off the harbor, three blocks from the center, and a 12-minute walk from the train station. By car, as you enter town, turn left after King's Knoll Hotel and take your first right onto Breadalbane. Each has parking from an alley behind the buildings.

Oban Backpackers hostel provides same-day **laundry service** for £2.50 (drop off by 15:00 to pick up by 19:00, 2-min walk from B&Bs, on Breadalbane Street, tel. 01631/562-107). There's also a **launderette** downtown on Tweeddale Street (Mon–Sat 10:00–18:00, closed Sun, £4 self-service, £6 full-service, tel. 01631/565-866).

**Tanglin B&B** is a winner. Liz and Jim Montgomery offer a bright, nonsmoking, and homey place with an easygoing atmosphere (S-£15, D-£29, Db-£36, 5 rooms, flexible rates and family deals, no CC, 3 Strathaven Terrace, Breadalbane Street, tel. 01631/563-247, e-mail: jimtanglin@aol.com).

**Strathlachlan Guest House**, next door, is another fine value. Each of the four rooms has a private adjacent bathroom, and they share a TV lounge. Depending on your standards, you might be more cheered by Mrs. Rena Anderson's warm Scottish hospitality than turned off by the tired carpet in need of an occasional vacuuming (S-£15, D-£30, family deals, entirely smoke free, no CC, 2 Breadalbane Street, Oban, Argyll, tel. 01631/563-861).

**Raniven Guest House**, with six tastefully decorated rooms, is friendly and a great value (Db-£35–40, no CC, 1 Strathlachlan Terrace, tel. 01631/562-713, Jessie Turnbull).

**Gramarvin Guest House**, decorated in cool green tones, is also comfy and quiet (S-£18.50, Db-£37–40, 5 rooms, nonsmoking, no CC, Breadalbane Street, tel. 01631/564-622, www.gramarvin.co.uk, e-mail: gramarvin@freeuk.com, Mrs. Hill).

**Sand Villa Guest House** rents five cheery rooms, but is a lesser value (D-£30–35, Db-£35–40, Tb-£45–52, no CC, 4 Breadalbane Street, tel. 01631/562-803, e-mail: sandvilla@freeuk.com, Joyce).

**Glenburnie Hotel**, a stately Victorian home on Oban's waterfront, has an elegant breakfast room overlooking the bay. Its spacious and comfortable rooms are furnished like plush living rooms (Sb-£26–35, Db-£52–60, CC, good breakfast, good views, nonsmoking, parking, closed mid-Nov–mid-March, The Esplanade, PA34 5AQ, tel. & fax 01631/562-089, e-mail: graeme.strachan@btinternet.com, Graeme and Allyson).

**Barriemore Hotel** is the last place on Oban's grand waterfront esplanade. It has a dark, woody, equestrian feel and 13 large, well-appointed rooms (Sb-£30, Db-£46–60, CC, fine views, nonsmoking, The Esplanade, PA34 5AQ, tel. & fax 01631/566-356, www.barriemore-hotel.co.uk, Ina and Hamish Dawson).

## Sleeping in Hotels

I found only tired and smoky hotels in Oban. You'll get better value and quality at B&Bs. The first listing is acceptable, but the last two are last resorts. **Rowan Tree Hotel** is a group-friendly place with 24 basic, cleanser-clean rooms and a central but quiet locale (Sb-£38–50, Db-£62–70, CC, easy parking, George Street, tel. 01631/562-954, fax 01631/565-071). The weary old **Caledonian Hotel** dominates the center of town (Db-£91 with specials as low as £61, CC, nonsmoking rooms, elevator, tel. 01631/563-133, www.miltonhotels.com). **Balmoral Hotel** is smaller but also central, with street noise and 12 depressing rooms (Db-£50–66, CC, 4 Craigard Road, tel. 01631/562-731, fax 01631/ 566-810, e-mail: balmoral@oban.org.uk).

## Sleeping in Hostels and Dorms

Oban offers plenty of cheap dorm beds. Your choice: fun, orderly, or spacey. **Oban Backpackers** is central, laid-back, and fun, with 6 to 12 bunks per room and a wonderful sprawling public living room (£11/bed, less off-season, no CC, 48 beds, Internet access for non-guests as well, £2.50 laundry service, 10-min walk from the station, on Breadalbane Street, tel. 01631/ 562-107). The orderly **IYHF hostel**, on the waterfront esplanade, is in a grand building with 142 beds and smashing views of the harbor and islands (£13.25/bed, 4- to 12-bed rooms, 11 Db-£14.75, cheaper for youths under 18 and anyone off-season, no CC, great facilities and public rooms, Internet access, laundry machines, tel. 01631/562-025, e-mail: oban@syha .org.uk). **Jeremy Inglis'** spacey B&B, a block from the TI and train station, is least expensive and feels more like a commune than a youth hostel (£6.50/bed, no CC, 12 beds, 21 Airds Crescent, tel. 01631/565-065).

## Eating in Oban

Oban has plenty of fun options. The downtown is full of cheap eateries and pubs serving decent grub: consider the harborfront **Oban Inn**, the oldest building in town (£5, Mon–Sat 12:00–22:00, Sun from 12:30, CC, stained glass coats-of-arms and comfy booth seating, 1 Stafford Street, tel. 01631/562-484) or **Coasters** (£5, Sun–Fri 12:00–23:00, Sat until 24:00, closed 15:00–17:00 off-season, good views but smoky, on Corran Esplanade, 1 block past William Street heading away from station, tel. 01631/566-881).

To mix a sappy folk show inexpensively with dinner, gum haggis at **McTavish's Kitchens**. This huge eating hall is an Oban institution featuring live but tired folk music and dancing. This is your basic tourist trap filled with English vacationers. The food is inexpensive and edible (£7.50 for haggis, neeps, and tatties; £15 for a super Scottish multicourse menu). The piping, dancing, and singing happen nightly May through September (20:00–22:00, mostly a fiddle and 2 accordions, with precious little dancing and bagpiping, tel. 01631/563-064). The show costs £4 without a meal, £2 with dinner, or is free with dinner with a coupon from your B&B. No reservations are required. Nonsmokers get the best harbor views. Smokers sit closest to the stage.

Everyone's favorite "nice dinner out" is at **The Studio,** a small, tightly-packed restaurant with 70s décor featuring serious, first-class Scottish cooking (£12 for a full Scottish meal until 18:30, £13.25 for 3-course meal after 18:30, or a pricey à la carte menu, April–Oct nightly 17:00–22:00, closed Nov–March, CC, always make a reservation, intersection of Craigard Road and Albert Road, tel. 01631/562-030). It has great steaks, trout, and a prawn-and-clam chowder that hits the spot on a stormy day.

For a genteel dining experience—pricey but worthwhile for a waterfront splurge—eat at the well-polished **Manor House Hotel** (£28 set meal, nouveau cuisine, March–Oct nightly 18:45–21:00, Nov–Feb closed Sun–Mon, CC, reservations in summer are wise, a short drive or taxi ride south of town on the waterfront, Gallanach Road, tel. 01631/562-087).

For soup, salad, or sandwiches, consider **The Kitchen Garden**, a deli and gourmet-foods store with a charming café upstairs (£2.50–4.50, Mon–Sat 9:00–17:30, Sun 11:00–16:00, closed Sun off-season, CC, 14 George Street, tel. 01631/566-332).

**The Fish Café**, an artsy, family-run place, has tall tables, blonde wood, and blue cushions, and serves fine fish (£8–15, daily 12:00–14:30, 18:00–21:30, CC, 104 George Street, tel. 01631/565-666). You'll eat decent seafood at **The Waterfront Restaurant** (£7–9 early-bird dinner special, £15–20, daily 10:30–14:15, 17:30–21:30, closed Jan–Feb, CC, views of water and McCaig's Tower, #1 The Pier, tel. 01631/563-110).

For a seafood appetizer drop by the green **Local Shellfish** shack at the ferry dock (often free salmon samples, inexpensive coffee, meal-sized salmon sandwiches, open until the 18:00 boat unloads from Mull—a pleasant way to cap off your day-trip to the islands).

**Supermarket**: Tesco is a five-minute walk from the TI (Mon–Sat 8:00–20:00, Fri until 21:00, Sun 9:00–18:00, WC in front by registers, Lochside Road).

## Transportation Connections—Oban

**Trains** link Oban to the nearest transportation hub in **Glasgow** (3/day, 3 hrs, see below). Oban's small train station lacks lockers and even a WC (ticket window open Mon–Sat 7:00–18:10, Sun 11:00–18:00). Train info: tel. 08457-484-950.

**Ferries** fan out from Oban to the **southern Hebrides** (see "The Islands of Iona and Mull," below). Caledonian MacBrayne Ferry info: tel. 01631/566-688.

**Buses**, operated by Scottish Citylink, run between Oban, Glencoe, and Inverness. **From Oban by bus to**: **Glencoe** (3/day, 2.5 hrs, sometimes longer due to transfer in Fort William, no buses run Sun, one-way: £10.30, kids' discount), **Inverness** (3/day July–Aug, 2/day Sept–June, 4 hrs, transfer in Fort William, no buses on Sun, one-way: £11.50, kids' discount). Pay the driver cash or buy tickets in advance by calling Citylink at 08705-505-050; or, even easier, drop by the Oban bus ticket office (Mon–Fri 9:30–16:00, closed Sat–Sun, CC; luggage storage-£1/bag but can't store overnight—must pick up bag by 16:00; bus agency shares office with Bowman & MacDougall Tours sub-agency, at intersection of George Street and 1 Queens Park Place, tel. 01631/562-856). Buses arrive and depart in front of the Caledonian Hotel, across from the train station.

## Transportation Connections—Glasgow

Glasgow, one of the region's major transportation hubs, has a bus station and two train stations, a seven minutes' walk apart. Train info: tel. 08457-484-950.

A handy shuttle bus connects all three stations (50p, pay driver, or free if connecting between train stations, show train ticket to driver, Mon–Sat 7:00–22:00, Sun 12:00–22:00, every 10 min). All stations have pay WCs (20p).

**Glasgow's Central Station by train to**: **Keswick**/Lake District (1 train/hr, 1.5 hrs to Penrith, then catch a bus to Keswick, 1/hr except Sun 6/day, 40 min), **Stranraer**/ferry to Belfast (8/day, 2.5 hrs, change in Ayr), **Troon**/ferry to Belfast (2/hr, 40 min), **Preston** (1/hr, 3 hrs, easy 30-min connection to Blackpool), **York** (12/day, 4 hrs, some changes), **London** (1/hr, 6 hrs, some direct trains). The station is on Gordon Street, at the intersection with Renfield-Union Street. Lockers are at track 9 (£3/day).

**Glasgow's Queen Street Station by train to: Oban** (3/day, 3 hrs), **Inverness** (3/day, 3.5 hrs, more frequent with change in Perth), **Edinburgh** (4/hr, 1 hr).

**Glasgow by bus to: Oban** (3/day, 3 hrs), **Inverness** (1/hr, 4 hrs, some transfer in Perth), **Edinburgh** (6/hr, 1.25 hrs). Buses depart from Buchanan Bus Station on Killermont Street, two blocks behind Queen Street Station. You can store luggage at the bus station (£2/2 hrs, £3/3–24 hrs, daily 06:30–22:30). Bus info: tel. 0870-608-2608.

# THE ISLANDS OF IONA AND MULL

▲▲**Daytrip to the Islands of Iona and Mull**—For the best one-day look at the dramatic and historic Hebrides island scenery around Oban, take the Iona/Mull tour from Oban (£23, Sun–Fri 10:00–17:40, Sat 10:30–19:00—but always confirm schedule). Bowman & MacDougall is the dominant and most established outfit. They offer a £2 discount on tours for anyone with this book (buy your ticket at the "Iona & Mull Tours" office, daily 8:00–17:30, no tours Nov–April, book 1 day ahead July–Sept, CC, 3 Stafford Street facing harbor next to Oban Inn, tel. 01631/563-221, e-mail: bowmanstours@supanet.com).

Each morning travelers gather on the Oban pier and pile onto the huge Oban-Mull ferry (40 min). On board, if it's a clear day, ask a local to point out Ben Nevis, the tallest mountain in Great Britain. The ferry has a fine cafeteria and a bookshop (though guidebooks are cheaper in Oban). Five minutes before landing on Mull, you'll see the striking Duart castle on the left.

Upon arrival in Mull, you'll find your tour company's bus for the entertaining and informative 35-mile bus ride across the Isle of Mull (75 min, single-lane road). All drivers spend the entire ride chattering away about life on Mull. They are hardworking local boys who know how to spin a yarn, making historical trivia fascinating—or at least fun.

The Isle of Mull, the third-largest in Scotland, has 300 scenic miles of coastline and castles and a 3,169-foot-high mountain. Called Ben More ("big hill" in Gaelic), it was once much bigger. The last active volcano in northern Europe, it was 10,000 feet tall—the entire island of Mull—before it blew. Calmer now, Mull has a notably laid-back population. My bus driver reported there are no deaths from stress and only a few from boredom.

On the far side of Mull the caravan of tour buses unloads at a tiny ferry town. The ferry takes about 200 walk-ons. (Confirm clearly with bus driver when to catch the boat off Iona for your return. Hustle quickly off the bus and to the dock to avoid the 30-min delay if you don't make the first trip over.) After the 10-minute ride, you wash ashore on sleepy Iona.

Tiny Iona, just three miles by 1.5 miles, is famous as the

birthplace of Christianity in Scotland. You'll have about two
hours here on your own before you retrace your steps, docking
back in Oban by about 17:40. While the day is spectacular when
it's sunny, it's worthwhile in any weather.

**Iona's history:** St. Columba, an Irish scholar, soldier, priest,
and founder of monasteries, got into a small war over the posses-
sion of an illegally copied psalm book. Victorious but sickened
by the bloodshed, Columba left Ireland, vowing never to return.
According to legend, the first bit of land out of sight of his home-
land was Iona. He stopped here in 563 and established the abbey.

Columba's monastic community flourished, and Iona became
the center of Celtic Christianity. Iona missionaries spread the gospel
through Scotland and North England, while scholarly monks established Iona as a center of art and learning. The *Book of Kells*—
perhaps the finest piece of art from "Dark Age" Europe—was probably made on Iona in the eighth century. The island was so important that it was the legendary burial place for ancient Scottish and
even Scandinavian kings (including Shakespeare's Macbeth).

Slowly the importance of Iona ebbed. Vikings massacred
68 monks in 806. Fearing more raids, the monks evacuated most
of Iona's treasures (including the *Book of Kells*, which is now in
Dublin) to Ireland. Much later, with the Reformation, the abbey
was abandoned, and most of its finely carved crosses were
destroyed. In the 17th century locals used the abbey only as a
handy quarry for other building projects.

Iona's population peaked at about 500 in the 1830s. In the
1840s a potato famine hit. In the 1850s a third of the islanders
emigrated to Canada or Australia. By 1900 the population was
down to 210, and today it's only around 100.

But in our generation a new religious community has given
the abbey new life. The Iona community is an ecumenical gathering of men and women seeking new ways of living the Gospel in
today's world, with a focus on worship, peace and justice issues,
and reconciliation (£3 entry, tel. 01681/700-512).

A pristine light and a thoughtful peace pervade the stark,
car-free island and its tiny community. While the present abbey,
nunnery, and graveyard go back to the 13th century, much of what
you'll see was rebuilt in the 19th century. But with buoyant clouds
bouncing playfully off of distant bluffs, sparkling white sand crescents, and lone tourists camped thoughtfully atop huge rocks just
looking out to sea, it's a place perfect for meditation. Climb a
peak—nothing's higher than 300 feet above the sea.

The village, Baile Mor, has shops, a restaurant/pub, enough
beds, and a meager heritage center. The Finlay Ross Shop rents
bikes (near ferry dock, £4.50/half day, £8/day, tel. 01681/700-357).

**Sleeping in Iona:** Enjoy the serenity of Iona by spending the
night. When the daytrippers leave, you'll find that special peace.

**Argyll Hotel**, built in 1867, sits proud and classy overlooking the waterfront, with basic rooms above a fine grassy yard and public spaces (15 rooms, Db-£60–116, no CC, dinner deals, Internet access, closed mid-Oct–April, CC, tel. 01681/700-334, fax 01681/700-510, www.argyllhoteliona.co.uk, e-mail: reception @argyllhoteliona.co.uk, helpful Judith). **Finlay B&B** rents 11 no-charm rooms in front of the ferry dock (D-£44, Db-£48, no CC, reception at Finlay Ross Shop, tel. 01681/700-357, fax 01681/700-562, e-mail: finlayross@ukgateway.net).

**Other Island Tours**—The Oban tour companies offer an array of tours. You can spend an entire day on Mull. Those more interested in nature than church history will enjoy trips to the wildly scenic Isle of Staffa with Fingal's Cave. Trips to Treshnish Island brim with puffins, seals, and other sea critters.

# THE HIGHLANDS: OBAN TO INVERNESS

Discover Glencoe's dark secrets in the Weeping Glen, where Britain's highest peak, Ben Nevis, keeps its head in the clouds. Explore the locks and lochs of the Caledonian Canal while the Loch Ness monster plays hide-and-seek. Hear the music of the Highlands in Inverness and the echo of muskets in Culloden, where the English put down Bonnie Prince Charlie and conquered the clans of the Highlands.

## Getting around the Highlands

The trains are scenic, but if schedules frustrate, take the bus. Two buses a day (3 in summer) connect the towns from Oban to Inverness (4 hrs). Ask at the station to see how schedules work for sight hopping or rent a car (rental info at Oban and Inverness TIs). One great option is to ride with the mail carrier on the post bus. While locals do this to get somewhere, tourists do it to chat with the mail carrier—great gossip on the entire neighborhood! This costs only a few pounds and works well in remote spots like Glencoe. Ask at the post office (Fort William) or bus station for post bus schedules and routes.

## GLENCOE

This valley is the essence of the wild, powerful, and stark beauty of the Highlands (and, I think, excuses the hurried tourist from needing to go north of Inverness). Along with its scenery, Glencoe offers a good dose of bloody clan history.

Glencoe town is just a line of houses. One is a tiny thatched building jammed with local history. The huggable Glencoe and North Lorn Folk Museum, purely a homegrown effort, is filled with humble exhibits gleaned from the town's old closets and attics (which come to life when explained by a local). When one house was being rethatched, its owner found a cache of old rifles

## Oban, Islands, and Highlands

hidden there from the British Redcoats after the disastrous battle of Culloden (£2, Mon–Sat 10:00–17:30, closed Sun, tel. 01855/811-314). The museum is run by the colorful Arthur Smith who also owns the Cala Sona B&B (see "Sleeping," below).

A couple of miles into the dramatic valley you'll find the **Visitors Centre**. While little more than a café, WC, and bookshop, it does show a 14-minute video about the 1692 massacre when the Redcoats killed the sleeping MacDonalds and the valley got its nickname, "The Weeping Glen" (50p, daily, May–Aug 9:30–17:30, March–April and Sept–Oct 10:00–17:00, closed Nov–Feb, last entry 30 min before closing, just east of town on A82, tel. 01855/811-307). The nearest **TI** is in Ballachulish (bus timetables, room-booking service for a fee, tel. 01855/811-296).

**Walks:** For a steep one-mile hike, climb the Devil's Staircase (trail leaves from A82, 8 miles east of Glencoe). For a three-hour hike, ask at the Visitors Centre about the Lost Valley of the MacDonalds (trail leaves from A82, 3 miles east of Glencoe). For an easy walk from Glencoe, head to the mansion on the hill (over the bridge, turn left, fine loch views). Above Glencoe is a mansion built by a local big shot for his love—a Canadian Indian. She was homesick, so he actually replicated a Canadian garden/forest. It didn't work, and they eventually returned to British Columbia.

**Glencoe's Burial Island and Island of Discussion:** In the loch just outside Glencoe notice the burial island—where the souls of those who "take the low road" are piped home. (Ask a local about "You take the high road, and I'll take the low road.") The next island was the Island of Discussion—where those with disputes were put until they came to an agreement.

## Sleeping and Eating in Glencoe
**(£1 = about $1.50, country code: 44, area code: 01855)**
Many find Glencoe more interesting than Oban for an over-night stop. In Glencoe village, Arthur Smith runs the **Cala Sona B&B**, aptly named "haven of happiness" in Gaelic. He entertains his guests with a peat fire, ghost stories, and tales of the Glencoe massacre (S-£15, D-£30, no CC, on the main street, tel. 01855/811-314, e-mail: calasona@talk21.com). If Arthur's place is full, try the **Mack-Leven House B&B** (D-£30, Db-£32 with this book, family deals, smoke-free rooms, homey lounge, conservatory, no CC, Lorn Drive, Glencoe, tel. 01855/811-215, Mackintosh family) or **Tulachgorm B&B** (D-£32, no CC, flexible on price in off-season, nonsmoking, just before Cala Sona B&B, tel. 01855/811-391, Ann Blake speaks English and Gaelic).

While nearby hotels and pubs serve food, **Mrs. Matheson's Tea Room Restaurant** (right in the village) is your best bet for good home-cooked meals (£10 meals, daily 11:00–21:00, tel. 01855/ 811-590, www.mrsmathesons-glencoe.com). For evening fun, take a walk or ask your B&B host where to find music and dancing.

## More Sights—Scottish Highlands
**Ben Nevis**—From Fort William, take a peek at Britain's highest peak, Ben Nevis (over 4,400 feet). Thousands walk to its summit each year. On a clear day you can admire it from a distance. Scot-land's only mountain cable cars can take you to a not-very-lofty 2,150-foot perch for a closer look (£7, daily 10:00–17:00, later in summer, 15-min ride, signposted on A82, tel. 01397/705-825).
▲**Caledonian Canal**—Three lochs and a series of canals cut Scot-land in two. Oich, Lochy, and Ness were connected in the early 1800s by the great British engineer Thomas Telford. Traveling between Fort William and Inverness (60 miles), you'll follow Telford's work—20 miles of canals and locks between 40 miles

of lakes, raising ships from sea level to 51 feet (Ness), to 93 feet (Lochy), and to 106 feet (Oich).

While "Neptune's Staircase," a series of locks near Fort William, is cleverly named, the best lock stop is Fort Augustus, where the canal hits Loch Ness. In Fort Augustus, the Caledonian Canal Heritage Centre, three locks above the main road, gives a good rundown on Telford's work (free). Stroll to the top of the locks past several shops and eateries for a fine view.

**Loch Ness**—I'll admit it. I had my zoom lens out and my eyes on the water. The local tourist industry thrives on the legend of the Loch Ness Monster. It's a thrilling thought, and there have been several seemingly reliable "sightings" (monks, police officers, and sonar images). The loch, 24 miles long, less than a mile wide, and the third deepest in Europe, is deepest near the Urquhart Castle. Most monster sightings are in this area.

The Nessie commercialization is so tacky that there are two "official" Loch Ness Exhibition Centres within 100 yards of each other. Each has a tour-bus parking lot and more square footage devoted to their kitschy shop than to the exhibit. The exhibits, while fascinating, are overpriced. The exhibition in the big stone mansion (closest to Inverness) is the better one, headed by a marine biologist who's spent over 15 years researching lake ecology and scientific phenomenon. With a 40-minute series of video bits and special effects, this exhibit explains the geological and historical environment that bred the monster story and the various searches (£5.95, daily 9:00–18:00, until 20:00 in summer, less off-season, tel. 01456/450-573, www.loch-ness-scotland.com). The other (closest to Oban) is a high school–quality photo report followed by the 30-minute *We Believe in the Loch Ness Monster* movie, featuring credible-sounding locals explaining what they saw and a review of modern Nessie searches (£3.50, daily 9:00–19:30, until 21:00 in summer, tel. 01456/450-342).

The nearby **Urquhart Castle** ruins are gloriously situated with a view of virtually the entire lake. Although its new Visitors Centre has a museum with castle artifacts, the castle itself is an overpriced empty shell swarming with tourists (£5, daily 9:30–18:30, July–Aug until 20:30, last entry 45 min before closing, tel. 01456/450-551).

▲**Culloden Battlefield**—Scottish troops under Bonnie Prince Charlie were defeated here by the English in 1746. This last land battle fought on British soil spelled the end of Jacobite resistance and the fall of the clans. Wandering the battlefield, you feel that something terrible occurred here. Locals still bring flowers and speak of "46" as if it just happened.

The excellent Visitors Centre shows a stirring 16-minute audiovisual (3/hr). Wander through a furnished old cottage and the battlegrounds (£4, April–Oct daily 9:00–18:00, otherwise daily

10:00–16:00, closed Jan, look for period actors June–Sept, good tearoom, tel. 01463/790-607). Members of the Guide Friday tour from Inverness receive a discount on the Visitors Centre entry (Guide Friday tel. 01463/224-000).

## INVERNESS

The only sizable town in the north of Scotland, with 42,000 people, Inverness is pleasantly located on the River Ness at the base of a castle (not worth a look) and has a free little museum (worth a look, Mon–Sat 9:00–17:00, closed Sun, cheap café). Check out the bustling pedestrian downtown or stroll the picnic-friendly riverside paths (several footbridges). At the central **TI**, pick up activity brochures and *What's On* for the latest showing in theater, music, and film (Mon–Sat 9:00–18:00, Sun 9:30–16:00, less off-season, Internet access, free WCs behind TI, Castle Wynd, tel. 01463/234-353, www.highlandfreedom.com).

**Mailboxes Etc.**, next door to the station, will mail your packages home and has Internet access (Mon–Fri 8:30–18:00, Sat 10:00–16:00, tel. 01463/234-700). **The Launderette** is just across the Ness Bridge (£5-self-service, £8-same-day full-service, drop off by 12:00, Mon–Sat 8:00–18:00, closed Sun, 17 Young Street, tel. 01463/242-507).

While short on blockbuster sights, Inverness is great for **daytrips**. The biggest attraction is Loch Ness, a 20-minute drive southwest. Consider taking a three-hour Guide Friday bus tour to the lake for a monster hunt. The tour includes a scenic 30-minute boat cruise, a glimpse of Urquhart Castle (entry not included), admission to a "Loch Ness Exhibition Centre," insight-ful commentary from live guides, and plenty of opportunity to search for "Nessie" (£14.50, kids ages 5–14-£6.50, May–Sept daily at 10:30 and 14:30, book at TI or Guide Friday office at station, tour departs from bus stop outside TI, tel. 01463/224-000, www.guidefriday.com). Several companies host daily excursions to Culloden battlefield, whiskey distilleries, 14th-century Cawdor Castle, and the nearby bay for dolphin watching (information and booking for all at TI).

The **Scottish Showtime** evening is a fun-loving, hardwork-ing, Lawrence Welk-ish show giving you all the clichés in a clap-along two-hour package. I prefer it to the big hotel spectacles in Edinburgh (usually June–Sept Mon–Fri at 20:30, no meals, £12.50 but £2.50 off with this book, Spectrum Centre, Margaret Street, adjacent to bus station, tel. 0800-015-8001).

## Sleeping in Inverness
**(£1 = about $1.50, country code: 44, area code: 01463)**
These rooms are all a 10-to-12 minute walk from the train station and town center. To get to the B&Bs from the station,

either catch a taxi (£4) or walk: From the station, go left on Academy Street. At the first stoplight veer right onto Inglis Street in the pedestrian zone. Go up the Market Brae steps. At the top, turn right onto Ardconnel Street toward the B&Bs and hostels (except Ryeford).

**Craigside Lodge B&B** is a treat. Its five spacious, cheery rooms share a cozy lounge with a great city view (Db-£40–42, CC, nonsmoking, some street noise, just above Castle Street at 4 Gordon Terrace, IV2 3HD, tel. 01463/231-576, fax 01463/713-409, e-mail: craigsidelodge@amserve.net, Janette and Wilf Skinner).

**Ardconnel House**, with six rooms, is tasteful, spacious, and comfy with lots of extra touches (Sb-£25–28, D-£42–46, Db-£44–50, CC, family deals, flexible off-season, nonsmoking, 21 Ardconnel Street, IV2 3EU, tel. & fax 01463/240-455, www .scotland-info.co.uk/ardconnel, friendly Isabel and Richard Cowe).

**Crown Guest House**, run by a hard-working, enthusiastic couple, has six clean, simple rooms and a cheery blue-and-yellow breakfast room (S-£20, Sb-£24, D-£40, Db-£44, family room-£52–58, CC, 19 Ardconnel Street, tel. 01463/231-135, e-mail: denise@crownhotel-inverness.co.uk, Denise and Bob Dalgarno).

**Melness Guest House** has three fine rooms and a comfy lounge (D-£42, Db-£52, less off-season, CC, completely smoke free, at 8 Old Edinburgh Road, tel. 01463/220-963, www .melnessie.co.uk, Mrs. Joyce).

**Ryeford B&B** has six flowery rooms with plush carpeting (S-£21, D-Db-£44, family deals, CC, back room has fine garden view, above Market Brae steps, go left on Ardconnel Terrace to #21, tel. & fax 01463/242-871, e-mail: ryeford@btinternet.com, Catriona and Simon Forsyth).

For inexpensive dorm beds near the center and a 12-minute walk from the train station, consider the friendly, side-by-side hostels on Culduthel Road. **Bazpackers Backpackers Hotel**, a stone's throw from the castle, has 24 beds (beds-£9, D-£12, no CC, Internet access, laundry service, 4 Culduthel Road, tel. 01463/717-663). The **Inverness Student Hotel**'s 57 beds are often filled with groups doing the hop-on hop-off bus circuit (£11 beds in 6-bed rooms, breakfast-£1.60, no CC, Internet access, laundry service, 8 Culduthel Road, tel. 01463/236-556).

## Eating in Inverness

You'll find a lot of traditional Highland fare—game, fish, lamb, and beef. Reservations are smart at most of these places, especially on summer weekends.

Several inviting eateries line Castle Street near the recommended B&Bs. The casual **Number 27**, a local favorite, is the Scottish version of TGI Friday's with something for everyone— salads, burgers, seafood, and more (£5–12, £8 2-course special

on Sun night only, daily 12:00–15:00, 17:00–22:00, shorter
hours off-season, generous portions, noisy adjacent bar, CC,
27 Castle Street, tel. 01463/241-999). A few doors up the same
street, the trendy, lively **Café 1** serves up local meaty dishes
with a bistro flair (£8–12, lunch and early-bird dinner specials,
Mon–Sat 12:00–14:00, 18:00–22:00, closed Sun, CC, 75 Castle
Street, tel. 01463/226-200). The nearby **Woodwards**, a soothing
buttery yellow place, is a fine splurge serving Scottish-style
fish and game with a contemporary twist (£18–25, daily 17:30–
22:00, shorter hours off-season, CC, 99 Castle Street, tel.
01463/709-809).

For good seafood, consider **Nico's**, a buttoned-down,
wood-beamed, candlelit restaurant a few minutes' walk beyond
Castle Street (£13–20, Sun–Thu 17:00–21:30, Fri–Sat until
22:30, CC, reservations required, next to Glen Mhor Hotel on
Haugh Road, tel. 01463/234-308). The **Redcliff Hotel** restaurant is convenient (on B&B street) for decent dinners in a bright,
leafy sunroom (daily 18:00–21:30, Fri–Sat until 22:00, dinner
£8–12, CC, 1 Gordon Terrace, tel. 01463/232-767). The adjacent bar serves £4 pub grub daily from 12:00–21:30 (Fri–Sat
until 22:00). For sandwiches and tempting pastries, stop in the
easygoing **Girvans** at the end of the pedestrian zone nearest
the station (£4, Mon–Sat 9:00–22:00, Sun 10:00–21:00, shorter
hours off-season, CC, 2 Stephens Brae, tel. 01463/711-900).

**Rajah Indian Restaurant** provides a tasty break from meat
and potatoes with vegetarian options served in a classy red-
velvet and white-linen atmosphere (£10 meals, Mon–Sat 12:00–
23:00, Sun 15:00–23:00, CC, just off Church Street at 2 Post
Office Avenue, tel. 01463/237-190).

## Transportation Connections—Inverness

**Trains** link Inverness with **Pitlochry** (9/day, 1.5 hrs) and **Edinburgh** (8/day, 3.5 hrs). ScotRail does a great 20:40-to-8:00
sleeper service to **London** (£115 first class or £80 standard class
for a private compartment with breakfast, not available Sat night,
www.scotrail.co.uk). Consider dropping your car in Inverness
and riding to London by train. Train info: tel. 08457-484-950.

Scottish Citylink **buses** link Inverness with **Oban** (3/day
July–Aug, 2/day Sept–June, 4 hrs, Mon–Sat only, one-way:
£11.50, kids' discount, transfer in Fort William) and **Glencoe**
(2/day, 2.5 hrs, Mon–Sat only, one-way: £10.80, kids' discount,
transfer in Fort William). Pay the driver cash or buy tickets in
advance by calling Citylink at 08705-505-050 or stopping by
the Inverness bus station (Mon–Sat 8:30–18:30, Sun 10:00–
18:30, CC; luggage storage-£1/bag, but can't store overnight—
must pick up bag by 18:30; 2 blocks from train station on
Margaret Street, tel. 01463/233-371).

# PITLOCHRY

This likable tourist town, famous for its whiskey, makes an enjoyable overnight stop. Navigate easily by following the black directional signs to Pitlochry's handful of sights.

The staff at Pitlochry's tiny train **station** posts its hours outside the building, but sometimes forgets to show up (Mon–Sat 8:00–18:00, Sun 10:30–13:00, Sun until 18:00 June–Aug only, WC, no lockers). The **TI** is most helpful, providing train schedules and selling good maps for walks and scenic drives (May–Sept daily 9:00–19:00, less off-season, free luggage storage behind counter for daytrippers; exit left from station, turn right on Atholl Road and walk 8 min to TI on left, tel. 01796/472-215).

Pitlochry's cute **Edradour Scotch Distillery**—the smallest in Scotland—offers a free one-hour guided tour, a 10-minute audiovisual show, and, of course, a sample (3/hr, Mon–Sat 9:30–17:00 plus March–Oct Sun 12:00–17:00, less off-season, no tours Jan–Feb but shop is open, a lovely 40-min walk through the forest from downtown, tel. 01796/472-095). The big, ivy-covered **Bell's Blair Athol Distillery** gives £3 hour-long tours with a wee taste at the end (2/hr, Mon–Sat 9:30–16:00, Sun 12:00–16:00, less off-season, last tour starts at 16:00, half mile from town, tel. 01796/482-003). Pitlochry also has plenty of forest walks (brochures at TI) and a salmon ladder that climbs alongside its lazy river (free viewing area—best in May, 10-min walk from town). Adjacent to the salmon ladder, the **Pitlochry Power Station** offers a mildly entertaining exhibit about hydroelectric power in the region (£2, March–Oct daily 10:00–17:30, closed off-season). From May through October, the town **theater** presents a different play every night and concerts on some Sundays (both £18, purchase tickets at theater, tel. 01796/484-626, or at box office off main street on Bonnethill Road). For a unique look at jewelry made of pressed heather stems, tour **Heather-gems** (free, Mon–Sat 9:00–17:00, plus April–Oct Sun 9:30–17:00, behind TI).

**Trains** regularly connect Pitlochry with **Inverness** (9/day, 1.5 hrs) and **Edinburgh** (6/day, 2 hrs). Train info: tel. 08457-484-950.

## Sleeping in Pitlochry
### (£1 = about $1.50, country code: 44, area code: 01796)

Try **Craigroyston House**, a big Victorian country house with eight smoke-free, Laura Ashley–style rooms run by charming Gretta Maxwell (Db-£40–56, family room, no CC, behind TI and next to church at 2 Lower Oakfield, PH16 5HQ, tel. & fax 01796/472-053, www.craigroyston.co.uk, e-mail: reservations @craigroyston.co.uk). Gretta can find you another B&B if her place is full. For a simpler, more rural option, drive two miles south of town on the old A9 to **Donavourd Farmhouse B&B** (Db-£34–44, no CC, dinner extra, nonsmoking, 10-min walk to

Edradour Distillery, tel. 01796/472-254, e-mail: donavourd
@compuserve.com, Somersal Shepley). Pitlochry's fine **hostel** is
on Knockard Road (£9.25 bunks, no CC, Internet access, above
main street, tel. 01796/472-308, fax 01796/473-729, e-mail:
pitlochry@syha.org.uk).

## Route Tips for Drivers

**Lake District to Oban (220 miles):** From Keswick, take A66
for 18 miles to M6 and speed nonstop north (via Penrith and
Carlisle), crossing Hadrian's Wall into Scotland. The road
becomes the M74 south of Glasgow. To slip quickly through
Glasgow, leave M74 at Junction 4 onto M73, following signs to
M8/Glasgow. Leave M73 at Junction 2, exiting onto M8. Stay on
M8 west through Glasgow, exit on Junction 30, cross Erskine
Bridge (60p), and turn left on A82, following signs to Crianlarich
and Loch Lomond. (For a scenic drive through Glasgow, take exit
17 off M8 and stay on A82 toward Dumbarton.) You'll soon be
driving along scenic Loch Lomond. The first picnic turnout has
the best lake views, benches, a park, and a playground. Halfway up
the loch, at Tarbet, take the "tourist route" left onto A83, drive
along Loch Long toward Inveraray via Rest-and-Be-Thankful
Pass. (This colorful name comes from the 1880s, when second-
and third-class coach passengers got out and pushed the coach and
first-class passengers up the hill.) Stop in Inveraray, a lovely castle
town on Loch Fyne. Park near the pier. (TI open July–Aug
9:00–18:00, Sept–June Mon–Sat 9:00–16:00, Sun 11:00–16:00,
tel. 01499/302-063.) The town jail, now a museum, is a "19th-
century living prison" (£4.75, daily 9:30–18:00, tel. 01499/
302-381). Leaving Inveraray, drive through a gate (at the
Woolen Mill) to A819, through Glen Aray, and along Loch
Awe. A85 takes you into Oban.

**Oban to Glencoe (45 miles) to Loch Ness (75 miles) to
Inverness (20 miles) to Edinburgh (150 miles):** Barring traffic,
you'll make great time on good, mostly two-lane roads. Be careful,
but if you're timid about passing, diesel fumes and large trucks
might be your memory of this drive. From Oban, follow the
coastal A828 toward Fort William. After about 20 miles you'll see
the photogenic Castle Staulker marooned on a lonely island. At
Loch Leven and Ballachulish Village, leave A828, taking A82 into
Glencoe. Drive through the village up the valley (Glencoe) for
10 minutes for a grand view and a chance to hear a bagpiper in
the wind—Highland buskers. If you play the recorder (and no
other tourists are there), ask to finger a tune while the piper
does the hard work.

At the top of the valley you hit the vast Rannoch Moor—
500 square and desolate miles with barely enough decent land
to graze a sheep. Then make a U-turn and return through

Glencoe. Continue north on A82, over the bridge, past Fort
William toward Loch Ness. Follow the Caledonian Canal on
A82 for 60 miles, stop at Loch Ness, and then continue on A82
to Inverness.

Leaving Inverness, follow signs to A9 (south toward Perth).
Just as you leave Inverness, detour four miles east off A9 on B9006
to the Culloden Battlefield Visitors Centre. Back on A9 it's a
wonderfully speedy, scenic highway (A9, M90, A90) all the way
to Edinburgh (Inverness–Edinburgh, minimum 3 hrs).

For a scenic shortcut, head north only as far as Glencoe
and then cut to Edinburgh via Rannoch Moor and Tyndrum.
For directions to B&Bs, see the Edinburgh chapter.

# APPENDIX

Britain was created by force and held together by force. It's really a nation of the 19th century. Its traditional industry, buildings, and the popularity of the notion of "Great" Britain are a product of the wealth derived from the empire that was at its peak through the Victorian era...he 19th century. Generally, the nice and bad stories are not true and the boring ones are. To best understand the many fascinating guides you'll encounter in your travels, have a basic handle on the sweeping story of this land.

## What's So Great about Britain?
Regardless of the revolution we had 200 years ago, many American travelers feel that they "go home" to Britain. This most popular tourist destination has a strange influence and power over us.

Britain is small (about the size of Uganda or Idaho)—600 miles long and 300 miles at its widest point. Its highest mountain is 4,400 feet, a foothill by our standards. The population is a quarter that of the United States. Politically and economically, Great Britain starts the 21st century only a weak shadow of the days when it boasted that "the sun never sets on the British Empire."

At one time Britain owned one-fifth of the world and accounted for more than half the planet's industrial output. Today the empire is down to token and troublesome scraps, such as the Falklands and Northern Ireland. Great Britain's industrial production is about 5 percent of the world's total, and—for the first time in history—Ireland has a higher per-capita income.

Still, Britain is a world leader. Her heritage, her culture, and her people cannot be measured in traditional units of power. The United Kingdom is a union of four countries—England, Wales, Scotland, and Northern Ireland. Cynics call it an English empire ruled by London, and there is some tension between the dominant Anglo-Saxon English (46 million) and their Celtic brothers and sisters (10 million).

In the Dark Ages the Angles moved into this region from Europe, pushing the Celtic inhabitants to the undesirable fringe of the islands. The Angles settled in Angle-land (England), while the Celts made do in Wales, Scotland, and Ireland.

Today Wales, with 2 million inhabitants, struggles with a terrible economy, dragged down by the depressed mining industry. A great deal of Welsh pride is apparent in the local music and the bilingual signs—some with the English spray-painted out. The Welsh language is alive and well.

Scotland is big, accounting for one-third of Great Britain's land area, but sparsely inhabited, with only 5 million people. Only about 80,000 speak Gaelic, but the Scots enjoy a large measure of autonomy with their separate Church of Scotland, their own legal system, and Scottish currency (interchangeable with the British). In a 1998 vote, Scotland decided to "devolve" further. In 2000 it pulled its members of Parliament from Westminster and, for the first time in nearly 300 years, reestablished its own parliament. International affairs will still be decided in London, but Edinburgh will call most of the local shots.

Ireland is divided. Most of it is the completely independent Catholic Republic of Ireland. The top quarter is Northern Ireland, ruled from London. Long ago the Protestant English and Scots moved into the north—the Catholic, industrial heartland of Ireland—and told the Catholic Irish to "go to hell or go to Connaught." The Irish moved to the bleak and less productive parts of the island, like Connaught, and the seeds of today's "Troubles" were planted. There's no easy answer or easy blame, but the island has struggled—its population (3 million) is only one-third of what it used to be—and the battle continues. Recently the moderate center (which, in spite of what the headlines imply, is the vast majority) has voted major concessions to each side. Protestants acknowledged Catholics have equal rights in the North, and Catholics removed the lines from the Republic's constitution refusing to recognize British rule in Ulster.

Just as the United States Congress is dominated by Democrats and Republicans, two parties dominate Britain's Parliament: Labor and Conservatives. (Ronald Reagan would fit the Conservative Party and Bill Clinton the Labor Party like political gloves.) Today Britain's Labor Party, currently in charge, is shoring up a social service system undercut by years of Conservative rule (Thatcher, Major). While in charge, the Conservatives (who consider themselves proponents of Victorian values—community, family, hard work, thrift, and trickle-down economics) took a Reaganesque approach to Britain's serious problems.

This eventually led to a huge Labor victory and the prime ministership of Tony Blair. He's the most popular PM in memory, and his party rules Parliament with a vast majority. Blair's Labor Party is "New Labor"—akin to Clinton's "New" Democrats. It's fiscally conservative but with a keen sense for the needs of the people. Conservative Party fears of old-fashioned, big-spending, bleeding-heart, Union-style liberalism have proven unfounded. The Liberal Parliament is more open to integration with Europe. The economy is booming, and inflation, unemployment, and interest rates are all low. Social programs such as health, education, and the minimum wage are being bolstered but in ways more measured than Conservatives predicted. After the Labor landslide victory in June of 2001, it looks like Britain is in for a long period of Labor rule.

## Basic British History for the Traveler

When Julius Caesar landed on the misty and mysterious isle of Britain in 55 B.C., England entered the history books. The primitive

Celtic tribes he conquered were themselves invaders who had earlier conquered the even more mysterious people who built Stonehenge. The Romans built towns and roads and established their capital at "Londinium." The Celtic natives in Scotland and Wales, consisting of Gaels, Picts, and Scots, were not subdued so easily. The Romans built Hadrian's Wall near the Scottish border to consolidate their rule in the troublesome north. Even today, the Celtic language and influence are strongest in these far reaches of Britain.

As Rome fell, so fell Roman Britain, a victim of invaders and internal troubles. Barbarian tribes from Germany and Denmark, called Angles and Saxons, swept through the southern part of the island, establishing Angle-land. These were the days of the real King Arthur, possibly a Christianized Roman general fighting valiantly, but in vain, against invading barbarians. The island was plunged into 500 years of Dark Ages—wars, plagues, and poverty—lit only by the dim candle of a few learned Christian monks and missionaries trying to convert the barbarians. The sightseer sees little from this Saxon period.

Modern England began with yet another invasion. William the Conqueror and his Norman troops crossed the English Channel from France in 1066. William crowned himself king in Westminster Abbey (where all subsequent coronations would take place) and began building the Tower of London. French-speaking Norman kings ruled the country for two centuries. Then followed two centuries of civil wars, with various noble families vying for the crown. In one of the most bitter feuds, the York and Lancaster families fought the War of the Roses, so-called because of the white and red flowers the combatants chose as their symbols. Battles, intrigues, kings, nobles, and ladies were imprisoned and executed in the tower—it's a wonder the country survived its rulers.

England was finally united by the "third-party" Tudor family. Henry VIII, a Tudor, was England's Renaissance king. He was handsome, athletic, highly sexed, a poet, a scholar, and a musician. He was also arrogant, cruel, gluttonous, and paranoid. He went through six wives in 40 years, divorcing, imprisoning, or beheading them when they no longer suited his needs.

Henry also "divorced" England from the Catholic Church, establishing the Protestant Church of England (the Anglican Church) and setting in motion years of religious squabbles. He also "dissolved" the monasteries (around 1540), leaving just the shells of many formerly glorious abbeys dotting the countryside and pocketing their land and wealth for the crown.

Henry's daughter, Queen Elizabeth I, who reigned for 45 years, made England a great trading and naval power (defeating the Spanish Armada) and presided over the Elizabethan era of great writers (such as Shakespeare) and scientists (Francis Bacon).

The long-standing quarrel between England's "divine right"

kings and nobles in Parliament finally erupted into a civil war (1643). Parliament forces under the Protestant Puritan farmer Oliver Cromwell defeated—and beheaded—King Charles I. This civil war left its mark on much of what you'll see in England. Eventually, Parliament invited Charles' son to take the throne. This "restoration of the monarchy" was accompanied by a great colonial expansion and the rebuilding of London (including Christopher Wren's St. Paul's Cathedral), which had been devastated by the Great Fire of 1666.

Britain grew as a naval superpower, colonizing and trading with all parts of the globe. Her naval superiority ("Britannia rules the waves") was secured by Admiral Horatio Nelson's victory over Napoleon's fleet at the Battle of Trafalgar, while the Duke of Wellington stomped Napoleon on land at Waterloo. Nelson and Wellington—both buried in London's St. Paul's— are memorialized by many arches, columns, and squares throughout England.

Economically, Britain led the world into the industrial age with her mills, factories, coal mines, and trains. By the time of Queen Victoria's reign (1837–1901), Britain was at the zenith of power, with a colonial empire that covered one-fifth of the world.

The 20th century was not kind to Britain. Two world wars devastated the population. The Nazi blitzkrieg reduced much of London to rubble. The colonial empire has dwindled to almost nothing, and Britain is no longer an economic superpower. The "Irish Troubles" are constant, as the Catholic inhabitants of British-ruled Northern Ireland fight for the independence their southern neighbors won decades ago. The war over the Falkland Islands in 1982 showed how little of the British Empire is left but also how determined the British are to hang on to what remains.

But the tradition (if not the substance) of greatness continues, presided over by Queen Elizabeth II, her husband Prince Philip, and Prince Charles. With economic problems, the turmoil of Charles and the late Princess Diana, the Fergie fiasco, and a relentless popular press, the royal family is having a tough time. But the queen has stayed above it all, and most British people still jump at an opportunity to see royalty. With the death of Princess Diana and the historic outpouring of grief, it's clear that the concept of royalty is alive and well as Britain enters the third millennium.

The year 2002 will mark Queen Elizabeth's 50th year on the throne complete with an exciting calendar of Golden Jubilee events. While many wonder who will succeed her, the case is fairly straight-forward: the queen sees her job as a life-long position and, legally, Charles (who wants to be king) cannot be skipped over for his son William. Given the longevity in the family (the Queen's mother, born in August of 1900, is still investing in race horses), Charles is in for a long wait.

## Britain's Royal Families

| 802–1066 | Saxon and Danish kings |
|---|---|
| 1066–1154 | Norman invasion (William the Conqueror), Norman kings |
| 1154–1399 | Plantagenet |
| 1399–1461 | Lancaster |
| 1462–1485 | York |
| 1485–1603 | Tudor (Henry VIII, Elizabeth I) |
| 1603–1649 | Stuart (civil war and beheading of Charles I) |
| 1649–1659 | Commonwealth, Cromwell, no royal head of state |
| 1660–1714 | Stuart restoration of monarchy |
| 1714–1901 | Hanover (four Georges, Victoria) |
| 1901–1910 | Edward VII |
| 1910–present | Windsor (George V, Edward VII, George VI, Elizabeth II) |

## Architecture in Britain

From Stonehenge to Big Ben, travelers are storming castle walls, climbing spiral staircases, and snapping the pictures of 5,000 years of architecture. Let's sort it out.

The oldest ruins—mysterious and prehistoric—date from before Roman times back to 3000 B.C. The earliest sites, such as Stonehenge and Avebury, were built during the Stone and Bronze Ages. The remains from these periods are made of huge stones or mounds of earth, even man-made hills, and were created as celestial calendars and for worship or burial. Britain is crisscrossed with lines of these mysterious sights (ley lines). Iron Age people (600 B.C.–A.D. 50) left desolate stone forts. The Romans thrived in Britain from A.D. 50 to 400, building cities, walls, and roads. Evidence of Roman greatness can be seen in lavish villas with ornate mosaic floors, temples uncovered beneath great English churches, and Roman stones in medieval city walls. Roman roads sliced across the island in straight lines. Today, unusually straight rural roads are very likely laid directly on ancient Roman roads.

As Rome crumbled in the fifth century, so did Roman Britain. Little architecture survives from Dark Ages England, the Saxon period from 500 to 1000. Architecturally, the light was switched on with the Norman Conquest in 1066. As William earned his title "the Conqueror," his French architects built churches and castles in the European Romanesque style.

English Romanesque is called Norman (1066–1200). Norman churches had round arches, thick walls, and small windows; Durham Cathedral and the Chapel of St. John in the Tower of London are typical examples. The Tower of London, with its square keep, small windows, and spiral stone stairways, is a typical Norman castle. You'll see plenty of Norman castles—all built to secure the conquest of these invaders from Normandy.

Gothic architecture (1200–1600) replaced the heavy Norman style with light, vertical buildings, pointed arches, soaring spires, and bigger windows. English Gothic is divided into three stages. Early English (1200–1300) features tall, simple spires; beautifully carved capitals; and elaborate chapter houses (such as the Wells Cathedral). Decorated Gothic (1300–1400) gets fancier, with more elaborate tracery, bigger windows, and ornately carved pinnacles, as you'll see at Westminster Abbey. Finally, the Perpendicular style (1400–1600, also called "rectilinear") returns to square towers and emphasizes straight, uninterrupted vertical lines from ceiling to floor, with vast windows and exuberant decoration, including fan-vaulted ceilings (King's College Chapel at Cambridge). Through this evolution, the structural ribs (arches meeting at the top of the ceilings) became more and more decorative and fanciful (the most fancy being the star vaulting and fan vaulting of the Perpendicular style).

As you tour the great medieval churches of England, remember that nearly everything is symbolic. For instance, on the tombs, if the figure has crossed legs, he was a Crusader. If his feet rest on a dog, he died at home, but if the legs rest on a lion, he died in battle. Local guides and books help us modern pilgrims understand at least a little of what we see.

Wales is particularly rich in English castles, which were needed to subdue the stubborn Welsh. Edward I built a ring of powerful castles in Wales, including Conwy and Caernarfon.

Gothic houses were a simple mix of woven strips of thin wood, rubble, and plaster called wattle and daub. The famous black-and-white Tudor, or half-timbered, look came simply from filling in heavy oak frames with wattle and daub.

The Tudor period (1485–1560) was a time of relative peace (the War of the Roses was finally over), prosperity, and renaissance. Henry VIII broke with the Catholic Church and "dissolved" (destroyed) the monasteries, leaving scores of England's greatest churches gutted shells. These hauntingly beautiful abbey ruins (Glastonbury, Whitby, and Tintern) surrounded by lush lawns are now pleasant city parks.

Although few churches were built during the Tudor period, this was a time of house and mansion construction. Heating a home was becoming popular and affordable, and Tudor buildings featured small square windows and many chimneys. In towns where land was scarce, many Tudor houses grew up and out, getting wider with each overhanging floor.

The Elizabethan and Jacobean periods (1560–1620) were followed by the English Renaissance style (1620–1720). English architects mixed Gothic and classical styles, then Baroque and classical styles. Although the ornate Baroque never really grabbed England, the classical style of the Italian architect Andrea Palladio did. Inigo Jones (1573–1652), Christopher Wren (1632–1723), and those they inspired plastered England with enough columns, domes, and symmetry to please a caesar. The Great Fire of London (1666) cleared the way for an ambitious young Wren to put his mark on London forever with a grand rebuilding scheme, including the great St. Paul's and more than 50 other churches.

The celebrants of the Boston Tea Party remember England's Georgian period (1720–1840) for its lousy German kings. Georgian architecture was rich and showed off by being very classical. Grand ornamental doorways, fine cast-ironwork on balconies and railings, Chippendale furniture, and white-on-blue Wedgwood ceramics graced rich homes everywhere. John Wood Jr. and Sr. led the way, giving the trend-setting city of Bath its crescents and circles of aristocratic Georgian row houses. "Georgian" is English for "neoclassical."

The Industrial Revolution shaped the Victorian period (1840–1890) with glass, steel, and iron. England had a huge new erector set (so did France's Mr. Eiffel). This was also a Romantic period, reviving the "more Christian" Gothic style. London's Houses of Parliament are neo-Gothic—just 100 years old but looking 700, except for the telltale modern precision and craftsmanship. Whereas Gothic was stone or concrete, neo-Gothic was often red brick. These were England's glory days, and there was more building in this period than in all previous ages combined.

The architecture of modern times obeys the formula "form follows function"—it worries more about your needs than your eyes. England treasures its heritage and takes great pains to build tastefully in historic districts and to preserve its many "listed" buildings. With a booming tourist trade, these quaint reminders of its—and our— past are becoming a valuable part of the British economy.

## British TV

British television is so good—and so British—that it deserves a mention as a sightseeing treat. After a hard day of castle climbing, watch the telly over tea in the living room of your village B&B.

England has five channels. BBC-1 and BBC-2 are government regulated, commercial free, and traditionally highbrow. Channels 3, 4, and 5 are private, are a little more Yankee, and have commercials—but those commercials are clever and sophisticated and provide a fun look at England. Broadcasting is funded by a £100-per-year-per-household tax. Hmmm, 40 cents per day to escape commercials and public television pledge drives.

Britain is about to leap into the digital age ahead of the rest of the TV-watching world. Ultimately every house will enjoy literally hundreds of high-definition channels with no need for cable or satellites. Right now it's high subscription rates that are slowing the transition.

Whereas California "accents" fill our airwaves 24 hours a day, homogenizing the way our country speaks, England protects and promotes its regional accents by its choice of TV and radio announcers. Commercial-free British TV, while looser than it used to be, is still careful about what it airs and when.

American programs (such as *Friends*, *Oprah*, and trash-talk shows) are very popular. The visiting viewer should be sure to tune the TV to a few typical English shows, including a dose of English situation- and political-comedy fun and the top-notch BBC evening news. Quiz shows are taken very seriously here (where *Who Wants to be a Millionaire* originated). Michael Parkinson is the Johnny Carson of Britain for late-night talk. For a tear-filled, slice-of-life taste of British soap dealing in all the controversial issues, see the popular *Brookside*, *Coronation Street*, or *Eastenders*.

## Let's Talk Telephones

Here's a primer on making direct phone calls. For information specific to Britain, see "Telephones" in the Introduction.

**Making Calls within a European Country:** About half of all European countries—including Britain—use area codes; the other half uses a direct-dial system without area codes.

In countries that use area codes (such as Austria, Britain, Czech Republic, Finland, Germany, Ireland, Netherlands, and Sweden), you dial the local number when calling within a city, and you add the area code if calling long-distance within the country.

To make calls within a country that uses a direct-dial system (Belgium, Denmark, France, Italy, Portugal, Norway, Spain, and Switzerland), you dial the same number whether you're calling across the country or across the street.

**Making International Calls:** You always start with the international access code (011 if you're calling from America or Canada, or 00 from virtually anywhere in Europe), then dial the country code of the country you're calling (see chart below).

What you dial next depends on the phone system of the country you're calling. If the country uses area codes, drop the initial zero of the area code, then dial the rest of the number.

Countries that use direct-dial systems (no area codes) vary in how they're accessed internationally by phone. For instance, if you're making an international call to Denmark, Italy, Norway, Portugal, or Spain, simply dial the international access code, country code, and phone number. But if you're calling Belgium, France, or Switzerland, drop the initial zero of the phone number. Example: To call a Paris hotel (tel. 01 47 05 49 15) from London, dial 00, 33 (France's country code), then 1 47 05 49 15 (phone number without the initial zero).

### International Access Codes

When dialing direct, first dial the international access code of the country you're calling from. For the United States and Canada, it's 011. Virtually all European countries use "00" as their international access code; the only exceptions are Finland (990) and Lithuania (810).

## Country Codes
After you've dialed the international access code, dial the code of the country you're calling.

| | |
|---|---|
| Austria—43 | Greece—30 |
| Belgium—32 | Ireland—353 |
| Britain—44 | Italy—39 |
| Canada—1 | Morocco—212 |
| Czech Republic—420 | Netherlands—31 |
| Denmark—45 | Norway—47 |
| Estonia—372 | Portugal—351 |
| Finland—358 | Spain—34 |
| France—33 | Sweden—46 |
| Germany—49 | Switzerland—41 |
| Gibraltar—350 | United States—1 |

## Calling-Card Operators
You can call direct much more cheaply by using a British phone card from any phone booth, but if you'd prefer to use your American calling card, here are the numbers you'd use: AT&T—0800-89-0011, MCI—0800-89-0222, and Sprint—0800-89-0877.

## Useful Numbers in Britain
**Emergency (police and ambulance):** 999
**Operator Assistance:** 100
**Directory Assistance:** 192 (20p from phone booth, otherwise expensive)
**International Info:** 153 (20p from phone booth, £1.50 otherwise)
**International Assistance:** 155
**United States Embassy:** 55 Upper Brook Street, London, tel. 020/7499-9000, www.usembassy.org.uk
**Eurostar (Chunnel Info):** 08705-186-186 (www.eurostar.com)
**Trains to all points in Europe:** 08705-848-848 (www.raileurope.com)

## Telephone Directory
Note: Understand the various prefixes: 09 numbers are telephone sex–type expensive. Prefixes 0845 (4p/min, 2p evenings and week-ends) and 0870 (8p/min, 4p evenings and weekends) are local calls nationwide. And 0800 numbers are toll free. If you have questions about a prefix, call 100 for free help.

# London's Airports and Airlines

## *Airports*
For online information on the first three airports, check
www.airwise.com/airports/europe.
**Heathrow** (switchboard): 0870-000-0123
**Gatwick** (general info): 0870-0000-2468 for all airlines,
except British Airways—0870-551-1155 (flights) or
0845-773-3377 (booking)
**Stansted** (general info): 0870-0000-303
**Luton** (general info): 01582/405-100 (www.london-luton.com)

## *Airlines*
**Aer Lingus:** 0845-307-7777, 020/8899-4747 (www.aerlingus.ie)
**Air Canada:** 0870-524-7226, 020/8751-1331(www.aircanada.ca)
**Alitalia:** reservations 0870-544-8259, Heathrow 020/8745-5812,
Gatwick 01293/569-926 (www.alitalia.it)
**American:** 0345-789-789, 020/8750-1048 (www.aa.com)
**British Airways:** reservations 0845-773-3377,
flight info 0870-551-1155 (www.britishairways.com)
**BMI British Midland:** reservations 0870-607-0555, info
020/8745-7321 (www.flybmi.com)
**Canadian Airlines:** 0845-761-6767, 0181/577-7722
(www.cdnair.ca)
**Continental Airlines:** 0800-776-464, 01293/511-581
(www.continental.com)
**EasyJet:** 0870-600-0000, Luton 01582/445-354
(www.easyjet.com)
**KLM Royal Dutch Airlines:** 0870-507-4074
(www.klm.com)
**Lufthansa:** 0345-737-747, 020/8750-3300
(www.lufthansa.co.uk)
**Ryanair (cheap fares):** 0870-333-1231
(www.ryanair.com)
**Scandinavian Airlines System (SAS):** 0845-602-1165,
020/8990-7122 (www.scandinavian.net)
**United Airlines:** 0845-844-4777, 07626/915-500
(www.ual.com)
**Virgin Express:** 020/7744-0004
(www.virgin-express.com)

## *London Heathrow Car Rental Agencies*
**Avis**: 0870-606-0100, 020/8899-1000
**Budget**: 0800-181-181, 020/8750-2520
**Europcar**: 0870-607-5000, 020/8897-0811
**Hertz**: 0870-599-6699, 020/8897-2072
**National**: 0870-600-6666, 020/87502-800

## Numbers and Stumblers

- Europeans write a few of their numbers differently than we do: 1 = 1 , 4 = 4 , 7= 7. Learn the difference or miss your train.
- Europeans write dates as day/month/year (Christmas is 25/12/02).
- Commas are decimal points, and decimals are commas. A dollar and a half is 1,50. There are 5.280 feet in a mile.
- When pointing, use your whole hand, palm downward.
- When counting with fingers, start with your thumb. If you hold up your first finger to request one item, you'll probably get two.
- What we Americans call the second floor of a building is the first floor in Europe.
- Europeans keep the left "lane" open for passing on escalators and moving sidewalks. Keep to the right.

## Weights and Measures

1 British pint = 1.2 U.S. pints
1 imperial gallon = 1.2 U.S. gallons or about 4.5 liters
1 stone = 14 pounds (a 168-pound person weighs 12 stone)
28 degrees Centigrade = 82 degrees Fahrenheit
Shoe sizes = about .5 to 1.5 sizes smaller than in the United States

## Metric Conversion (approximate)

1 inch = 25 millimeters
1 foot = 0.3 meter
1 yard = 0.9 meter
1 mile = 1.6 kilometers
1 centimeter = 0.4 inch
1 meter = 39.4 inches
1 kilometer = 0.62 mile

32 degrees F = 0 degrees C
82 degrees F = about 28 degrees C
1 ounce = 28 grams
1 kilogram = 2.2 pounds
1 quart = 0.95 liter
1 square yard = 0.8 square meter
1 acre = 0.4 hectare

## Climate

The first line is the average low temperature, the second line is the
average high, and the third line is the number of days with no rain.

| J | F | M | A | M | J | J | A | S | O | N | D |
|---|---|---|---|---|---|---|---|---|---|---|---|

**LONDON**

| J | F | M | A | M | J | J | A | S | O | N | D |
|---|---|---|---|---|---|---|---|---|---|---|---|
| 36° | 36° | 38° | 42° | 47° | 53° | 56° | 56° | 52° | 46° | 42° | 38° |
| 43° | 44° | 50° | 56° | 62° | 69° | 71° | 71° | 65° | 58° | 50° | 45° |
| 16 | 15 | 20 | 18 | 19 | 19 | 19 | 20 | 17 | 18 | 15 | 16 |

**CARDIFF (South Wales)**

| J | F | M | A | M | J | J | A | S | O | N | D |
|---|---|---|---|---|---|---|---|---|---|---|---|
| 35° | 35° | 38° | 41° | 46° | 51° | 54° | 55° | 51° | 46° | 41° | 37° |
| 45° | 45° | 50° | 56° | 61° | 68° | 69° | 69° | 64° | 58° | 51° | 46° |
| 13 | 14 | 18 | 17 | 18 | 17 | 17 | 16 | 14 | 15 | 13 | 13 |

**YORK**

| J | F | M | A | M | J | J | A | S | O | N | D |
|---|---|---|---|---|---|---|---|---|---|---|---|
| 33° | 34° | 36° | 40° | 44° | 50° | 54° | 53° | 50° | 44° | 39° | 36° |
| 43° | 44° | 49° | 55° | 61° | 67° | 70° | 69° | 64° | 57° | 49° | 45° |
| 14 | 13 | 18 | 17 | 18 | 16 | 16 | 17 | 16 | 16 | 13 | 14 |

**EDINBURGH**

| J | F | M | A | M | J | J | A | S | O | N | D |
|---|---|---|---|---|---|---|---|---|---|---|---|
| 34° | 34° | 36° | 39° | 43° | 49° | 52° | 52° | 49° | 44° | 39° | 36° |
| 42° | 43° | 46° | 51° | 56° | 62° | 65° | 64° | 60° | 54° | 48° | 44° |
| 14 | 13 | 16 | 16 | 17 | 15 | 14 | 15 | 14 | 14 | 13 | 13 |

# British-Yankee Vocabulary

**advert** advertisement
**afters** dessert
**anticlockwise** counter clockwise
**aubergine** eggplant
**Balloons** Belgians
**banger** sausage
**bangers and mash** sausage and mashed potatoes
**bank holiday** legal holiday
**bap** hamburger-type bun
**billion** a thousand of our billions (a million million)
**biro** ballpoint pen
**biscuit** cookie
**black pudding** sausage made from dried blood
**bloody** damn
**bobby** policeman ("copper" is more common)
**Bob's your uncle** there you go (with a shrug), naturally
**bomb** success
**bonnet** car hood
**boot** car trunk
**braces** suspenders
**bridle way** path for walkers, bikers, and horse riders
**brilliant** cool
**bubble and squeak** cold meat fried with cabbage and potatoes
**bum** bottom or "backside"
**candy floss** cotton candy
**car boot sale** temporary flea market with car trunk displays (a good place to buy back your stolen goods)
**caravan** trailer
**cat's eyes** road reflectors
**ceilidh** (kay-lee) informal evening of song and folk fun
**cheap and nasty** cheap and bad quality
**cheerio** good-bye

**chemist** pharmacist
**chicory** endive
**chips** french fries
**chock-a-block** jam-packed
**cider** alcoholic apple cider
**clearway** road where you can't stop
**coach** long-distance bus
**concession** discounted admission
**cotton buds** Q-tips
**courgette** zucchini
**cos** romaine lettuce
**craic** (crack) good conversation (Irish and spreading to England)
**crisps** potato chips
**cuppa** cup of tea
**dear** expensive
**dicey** iffy, risky
**digestives** round graham crackers
**dinner** lunch or dinner
**diversion** detour
**donkey's years** until the cows come home
**draughts** checkers
**draw** marijuana
**dual carriageway** divided highway (four lanes)
**elvers** baby eels
**face flannel** washcloth
**fag** cigarette
**fagged** exhausted
**faggot** meatball
**fanny** vagina
**fell** hill or high plain
**first floor** second floor
**football** soccer
**force** waterfall (Lake District)
**fortnight** two weeks
**Frogs** French people
**Full Monty** The whole she-bang. Everything.
**gallery** balcony

**gammon** ham
**gangway** aisle
**gaol** jail (same pronunciation)
**give way** yield
**glen** Scot. narrow valley
**goods wagon** freight truck
**grammar school** high school
**half eight** 8:30 (not 7:30)
**heath** open treeless land
**holiday** vacation
**homely** likable or cozy
**hoover** vacuum cleaner
**ice lolly** Popsicle
**interval** intermission
**ironmonger** hardware store
**jacket potato** baked potato
**jelly** Jell-O
**Joe Bloggs** John Doe
**jumble** sale, rummage sale
**jumper** sweater
**just a tick** just a second
**keep your pecker up** be brave
**kipper** smoked herring
**knackered** exhausted
   (Cockney: cream crackered)
**knickers** ladies' panties
**knocking shop** brothel
**knock up** wake up or visit
**ladybird** ladybug
**lady fingers** okra
**left luggage** baggage check
**lemon squash** lemonade
**let** rent
**loo** toilet or bathroom
**lorry** truck
**mac** mackintosh coat
**mate** buddy (boy or girl)
**mean** stingy
**mews** courtyard stables,
   often used as cottages
**minced meat** hamburger
**mobile** (MOH-bile) cell phone
**nappy** diaper
**natter** talk and talk
**neep** Scottish for turnip
**nought** zero
**noughts & crosses** tic-tac-toe

**off license** store selling take-
   away liquor
**pasty** crusted savory (usually
   meat) pie
**pavement** sidewalk
**petrol** gas
**pissed (rude), paralytic,
   bevvied, wellied, popped
   up, ratted, pissed as a
   newt** drunk
**pillar box** postbox
**pitch** playing field
**plaster** Band-Aid
**poppers** snaps
**publican** pub manager
**public convenience** toilets
**public school** private
   "prep" school (Eton)
**punter** partygoer
**put a sock in it** shut up
**queue** line
**queue up** line up
**quid** pound (money, worth
   about $1.60)
**randy** horny
**redundant, made** fired
**Remembrance Day**
   Veterans' Day
**return ticket** round-trip
**ring up** call (telephone)
**roundabout** traffic circle
**rubber** eraser
**sanitary towel** sanitary pad
**sausage roll** sausage wrapped
   in a flaky pastry
**Scotch egg** hard-boiled egg
   wrapped in sausage meat
**self-catering** apartment
   with kitchen
**sellotape** Scotch tape
**serviette** napkin
**single ticket** one-way ticket
**sleeping policeman** speed
   bumps
**smalls** underwear
**snogging** kissing, cuddling
**solicitor** lawyer

**starkers**  buck naked
**starters**  appetizers
**stone**  14 pounds (weight)
**subway**  underground
   pedestrian passageway
**sultanas**  golden raisins
**surgical spirit**  rubbing alcohol
**suss out**  figure out
**swede**  rutabaga
**ta**  thank you
**taxi rank**  taxi stand
**telly**  TV
**theater**  live stage
**tick**  a check mark
**tight as a fish's bum**
   cheapskate (water-tight)
**tights**  panty hose
**tipper lorry**  dump truck
**tin**  can
**to let**  for rent
**top hole**  first rate

**topping**  excellent
**top up**  refill a drink
**torch**  flashlight
**towpath**  path along a river
**tube**  subway
**twee**  quaint, cute
**underground**  subway
**vegetable marrow**
   summer squash
**verge**  grassy edge of road
**verger**  church official
**way out**  exit
**Wellingtons, wellies**
   rubber boots
**wee**  urinate
**whacked**  exhausted
**witter on**  gab and gab
**yob**  hooligan
**zebra crossing**  crosswalk
**zed**  the letter "z"

# Road Scholar Feedback for Great Britain 2002

*We're all in the same travelers' school of hard knocks. Your feedback helps us improve this guidebook for future travelers. Please fill this out (or use the online version at www.ricksteves.com/feedback), attach more info or any tips/favorite discoveries if you like, and send it to us. As thanks for your help, we'll send you our quarterly travel newsletter free for one year. Thanks!* **Rick**

**Of the recommended accommodations/restaurants used, which was:**

Best _____

      Why? _____

Worst _____

      Why? _____

**Of the sights/experiences/destinations recommended by this book, which was:**

Most overrated _____

      Why? _____

Most underrated _____

      Why? _____

**Best ways to improve this book:**

_____

_____

**I'd like a free newsletter subscription:**

_____ Yes     _____ No     _____ Already on list

_____
Name

_____
Address

_____
City, State, Zip

_____
E-mail Address

*Please send to: ETBD, Box 2009, Edmonds, WA 98020*

# Faxing Your Hotel Reservation

Use this handy form for your fax (or find it online at
www.ricksteves.com/reservation). Photocopy and fax away.

## One-Page Fax

To: _____ @ _____
                    *hotel*                              *fax*

From: _____ @ _____
                    *name*                              *fax*

Today's date: ____ / ____ / ____
                *day*  *month*  *year*

Dear Hotel _____,

Please make this reservation for me:

Name: _____

Total # of people: _____   # of rooms: _____   # of nights: _____

Arriving: ____ / ____ / ____   My time of arrival (24-hr clock): _____
            *day*  *month*  *year*   (I will telephone if I will be late)

Departing: ____ / ____ / ____
             *day*  *month*  *year*

Room(s):  Single___  Double___  Twin___  Triple___  Quad___

With:  Toilet___  Shower___  Bath___  Sink only___

Special needs:  View___   Quiet___   Cheap___   Ground Floor___

Credit card:  Visa___  MasterCard___  American Express___

Card #: _____

Expiration date:_____

Name on card: _____

You may charge me for the first night as a deposit. Please fax, e-mail, or
mail me confirmation of my reservation, along with the type of room
reserved, the price, and whether the price includes breakfast. Please also
inform me of your cancellation policy. Thank you.

_____
*Signature*

_____
*Name*

_____
*Address*

_____
*City*                          *State*           *Zip Code*      *Country*

_____
*E-mail Address*

# INDEX

# FREE-SPIRITED TOURS FROM

## *Rick Steves*

*Great Guides*

*Big Buses*

*Small Groups*

*No Grumps*

**Best of Europe** ■ **Village Europe** ■ **Eastern Europe** ■ **Turkey** ■ **Italy** ■ **Britain**
**Spain/Portugal** ■ **Ireland** ■ **Heart of France** ■ **South of France** ■ **Village France**
**Scandinavia** ■ **Germany/Austria/Switzerland** ■ **London** ■ **Paris** ■ **Rome**

Looking for a one, two, or three-week tour that's run in the Rick Steves style? Check out Rick Steves' educational, experiential tours of Europe.

Rick's tours include much more in the "sticker price" than mainstream tours. Here's what you'll get with a Europe or regional Rick Steves tour...

- **Group size:** Your tour group will be no larger than 26.

- **Guides:** You'll have two guides traveling and dining with you on your fully guided Rick Steves tour.

- **Bus:** You'll travel in a full-size 48-to-52-seat bus, with plenty of empty seats for you to spread out and read, snooze, enjoy the passing scenery, get away from your spouse, or whatever.

- **Sightseeing:** Your tour price includes all group sightseeing. There are no hidden extra charges.

- **Hotels:** You'll stay in Rick's favorite small, characteristic, locally-run hotels in the center of each city, within walking distance of the sights you came to see.

- **Price and insurance:** Your tour price is guaranteed for 2002. Single travelers do *not* pay an extra supplement (we have them room with other singles). ETBD includes prorated tour cancellation/interruption protection coverage at no extra cost.

- **Tips and kickbacks:** All guide and driver tips are included in your tour price. Because your driver and guides are paid salaries by ETBD, they can focus on giving you the best European travel experience possible.

**Interested?** Call (425) 771-8303 or visit www.ricksteves.com for a free copy of Rick Steves' 2002 Tours booklet!

## Rick Steves' Europe Through the Back Door

130 Fourth Avenue North, PO Box 2009, Edmonds, WA 98020 USA
Phone: (425) 771-8303 ■ Fax: (425) 771-0833 ■ www.ricksteves.com

# FREE TRAVEL GOODIES FROM

*Rick Steves*

## EUROPEAN TRAVEL NEWSLETTER

My *Europe Through the Back Door* travel company will help you travel better *because* you're on a budget—not in spite of it. To see how, ask for my 64-page *travel newsletter* packed full of savvy travel tips, readers' discoveries, and your best bets for railpasses, guidebooks, videos, travel accessories and free-spirited tours.

## 2002 GUIDE TO EUROPEAN RAILPASSES

With hundreds of railpasses to choose from in 2002, finding the right pass for your trip has never been more confusing. To cut through the complexity, ask for my 64-page *2002 Guide to European Railpasses.* Once you've narrowed down your choices, we give you unbeatable prices, including important extras with every Eurailpass, **free:** my 90-minute *Travel Skills Special* video or DVD; your choice of one of my 16 country guidebooks and phrasebooks; and answers to your "top five" travel questions.

## RICK STEVES' 2002 TOURS

We offer 18 different one, two, and three-week tours (180 departures in 2002) for those who want to experience Europe in Rick Steves' Back Door style, but without the transportation and hotel hassles. If a tour with a small group, modest family-run hotels, lots of exercise, great guides, and no tips or hidden charges sounds like your idea of fun, ask for my 48-page 2002 Tours booklet.

## YEAR-ROUND GUIDEBOOK UPDATES

Even though the information in my guidebooks is the freshest around, things do change in Europe between book printings. I've set aside a special section at my website (www.ricksteves.com/update) listing *up-to-the-minute changes* for every Rick Steves guidebook.

*Call, fax, or visit **www.ricksteves.com** to get your...*

- ☑ **FREE EUROPEAN TRAVEL NEWSLETTER**
- ☑ **FREE 2002 GUIDE TO EUROPEAN RAILPASSES**
- ☑ **FREE RICK STEVES' 2002 TOURS BOOKLET**

## Rick Steves' Europe Through the Back Door
130 Fourth Avenue North, PO Box 2009, Edmonds, WA 98020 USA
Phone: (425) 771-8303 ■ Fax: (425) 771-0833 ■ www.ricksteves.com

## AVALON
## TRAVEL
publishing

How far will our travel guides take you? As far as you want.

Discover a rhumba-fueled nightspot in Old Havana, explore prehistoric tombs in Ireland, hike beneath California's centuries-old redwoods, or embark on a classic road trip along Route 66. Our guidebooks deliver solidly researched, trip-tested information—minus any generic froth—to help globetrotters or weekend warriors create an adventure uniquely their own.

And we're not just about the printed page. Public television viewers are tuning in to Rick Steves' new travel series, *Rick Steves' Europe*. On the Web, readers can cruise the virtual black top with *Road Trip USA* author Jamie Jensen and learn travel industry secrets from Edward Hasbrouck of The *Practical Nomad*.

In print. On TV. On the Internet.

We supply the information. The rest is up to you.

Avalon Travel Publishing

Something for everyone

# www.travelmatters.com

Avalon Travel Publishing guides are available at your favorite book or travel store.

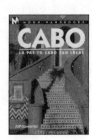

# **M**OON HANDBOOKS

provide comprehensive coverage of a region's arts, history, land, people, and social issues in addition to detailed practical listings for accommodations, food, outdoor recreation, and entertainment. Moon Handbooks allow complete immersion in a region's culture—ideal for travelers who want to combine sight-seeing with insight for an extraordinary travel experience in destinations throughout North America, Hawaii, Latin America, the Caribbean, Asia, and the Pacific.

## **WWW.MOON.COM**

*Rick Steves* shows you where to travel and how to travel—all while getting the most value for your dollar. His Back Door travel philosophy is about making friends, having fun, and avoiding tourist rip-offs.

*Rick* has been traveling to Europe for more than 25 years and is the author of 22 guidebooks, which have sold more than a million copies. He also hosts the award-winning public television series *Rick Steves' Europe*.

## **WWW.RICKSTEVES.COM**

# **ROAD TRIP USA**

Getting there is half the fun, and Road Trip USA guides are your ticket to driving adventure. Taking you off the interstates and onto less-traveled, two-lane highways, each guide is filled with fascinating trivia, historical information, photographs, facts about regional writers, and details on where to sleep and eat—all contributing to your exploration of the American road.

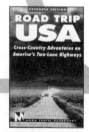

*"[Books] so full of the pleasures of the American road, you can smell the upholstery."*
~**BBC radio**

## **WWW.ROADTRIPUSA.COM**

**FOGHORN OUTDOORS** guides are for campers, hikers, boaters, anglers, bikers, and golfers of all levels of daring and skill. Each guide focuses on a specific U.S. region and contains site descriptions and ratings, driving directions, facilities and fees information, and easy-to-read maps that leave only the task of deciding where to go.

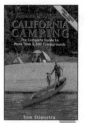

*"Foghorn Outdoors has established an ecological conservation standard unmatched by any other publisher."* **~Sierra Club**

## WWW.FOGHORN.COM

**TRAVEL SMART** guidebooks are accessible, route-based driving guides focusing on regions throughout the United States and Canada. Special interest tours provide the most practical routes for family fun, outdoor activities, or regional history for a trip of anywhere from two to 22 days. Travel Smarts take the guesswork out of planning a trip by recommending only the most interesting places to eat, stay, and visit.

*"One of the few travel series that rates sightseeing attractions. That's a handy feature. It helps to have some guidance so that every minute counts."* **~San Diego Union-Tribune**

**CiTY·SMaRT™** guides are written by local authors with hometown perspectives who have personally selected the best places to eat, shop, sightsee, and simply hang out. The honest, lively, and opinionated advice is perfect for business travelers looking to relax with the locals or for longtime residents looking for something new to do Saturday night.

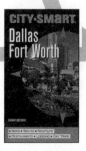